NT INTRO.

THE EARLIEST RECORDS OF JESUS

BY THE SAME AUTHOR

The First Epistle of Peter

The Earliest Records of Jesus

A Commentary on the Epistle to the Philippians

St. Paul and his Letters

The Interpreter's Bible — The Epistles to the Ephesians and to the Colossians
(Introduction and Exegesis)

THE EARLIEST RECORDS OF JESUS

By FRANCIS WRIGHT BEARE, Ph.D.
Professor of New Testament Studies
Trinity College, Toronto

A Companion to the

SYNOPSIS
OF THE FIRST THREE
GOSPELS

By ALBERT HUCK

ABINGDON PRESS

new york · nashville

FIRST PRINTED 1962

REPRINTED 1964

PRINTED IN GREAT BRITAIN

DEDICATION

TO MY COLLEAGUES OF THE

FACULTY OF DIVINITY OF TRINITY COLLEGE, TORONTO

AND TO ALL WHO FROM TIME TO TIME

HAVE PARTICIPATED IN MY SEMINAR ON

THE FIRST THREE GOSPELS

CONTENTS

ACKNOWLEDGMENTS

The author desires to express his thanks to the publishers for their care and co-operation in the preparation of this book.

I would take occasion also to thank the Reverend C. R. Feilding, my colleague for these last sixteen years at Trinity College, for the notes on the sayings concerning Divorce (pp. 191-3) which he prepared for me to use in this book. I can never thank him sufficiently for the way in which he has always relieved me of the burden of administrative tasks in the College to set me free for the writing of books and articles.

F. W. Beare

FOREWORD

This book is intended in the first instance for the use of students in theological colleges and kindred institutions who have in their hands the well-known edition of the Synoptic Gospels arranged in parallel columns, first prepared by Albert Huck. This *Synopsis of the First Three Gospels* is now available in an English edition prepared by Professor F. L. Cross, which is based upon the ninth German edition of Huck, revised by Hans Lietzmann, with the same Greek text, but with prolegomena, section-headings and sub-titles given in English. Students also have at their disposal the same text in the English of the American Revised Standard Version, edited by Burton H. Throckmorton, Jr. (2nd edition, 1957).

As Greek is no longer required in many theological institutions, these notes have been prepared on the assumption that the students who use them will have before them an English text; but the writer himself has worked entirely with the Greek text, and has felt free to make his own renderings on occasion, or to quote from the Authorized Version, as seemed best.

These notes are intended to serve as a companion to the Huck Synopsis. They are not meant to offer anything like a commentary on the first three Gospels. Their purpose is rather to lead the student into an understanding of the nature of the materials with which he has to deal, and of the motives and methods of the Evangelists. Exegesis and exposition are therefore subordinated to the discussion of the problems raised by criticism. It is assumed that the student will have at his disposal a good Introduction, a selection of scientific commentaries on each of the three Gospels with which we are concerned, and some competent works on the life and teaching of Jesus. The following books may be suggested as generally useful:

J. M. Creed, *The Gospel according to St. Luke.* London: Macmillan & Co., 1930.

B. H. Easton, *The Gospel according to St. Luke.* New York: Scribner's, 1926.

F. C. Grant, *The Gospels: their Origin and Growth.* New York: Harpers, 1957.

T. W. Manson, *The Teaching of Jesus.* Cambridge: C.U.P., 1931; *The Sayings of Jesus.* London: S.C.M., 1949. (First published as Book II of *The Mission and Message of Jesus*, by H. D. A. Major, T. W. Manson and C. J. Wright, 1937.)

A. H. McNeile, *The Gospel according to St. Matthew.* London: Macmillan & Co., 1915.

Vincent Taylor, *The Gospel according to St. Mark.* London: Macmillan & Co., 1955; *The Life and Ministry of Jesus.* London: Macmillan & Co., 1955.

General Articles and Commentaries (Introduction and Exegesis) in *The Interpreter's Bible*, vols. VII and VIII. New York and Nashville: Abingdon-Cokesbury, 1951-52.

A much more comprehensive bibliography will be found in Dr. Taylor's recent commentary on St. Mark, pp. xiii-xix.

INTRODUCTION

I. The Making of the Synoptic Gospels and their Relationship to One Another

No attempt will be made here to offer a general discussion of the manifold and complex problems which are involved in the relationships between the Gospels of Matthew, Mark and Luke. For this, the reader is referred to the general text-books of Introduction to the New Testament and to the Introductions to the major commentaries. The paragraphs which follow represent nothing more than a summary statement of the writer's own views on the main questions.

1. All the Gospels are anonymous documents, and nothing is known of the authors. The traditional names attached to them are second-century guesses. If we continue to speak of them by the names of Matthew, Mark, Luke and John, it is simply for the sake of convenience.

2. The Gospels are in a large degree products of the Christian community, and the materials which they employ took shape in the usage of the communities over a period of from thirty to a hundred years before being committed to writing. Short collections of stories and sayings may have been in circulation during the first generation of the Church, but there was no connected account of the ministry of Jesus. The writers of our Gospels constructed them out of materials which had been handed down in fragmentary fashion. Nevertheless, their work was not one of mere compilation. By the selection and arrangement of their inherited materials, and by the exercise of a limited liberty of interpretation, they have made personal contributions of no small importance to the portrait of Jesus which they have transmitted to us.

3. The Gospel according to St. Mark does not stand in any particularly close relationship to St. Peter, and there are no solid grounds for holding to the account of Papias that Mark was the interpreter of Peter, and that we have in this Gospel essentially the reminiscences of the Prince of the Apostles as transmitted by his closest associate, almost his private secretary. On the contrary, it has been made abundantly evident that the materials employed in this Gospel have passed through a complicated process of transmission in the Gentile churches of the first Christian generation. They may best be regarded as the deposit of the tradition concerning Jesus as it was held in the Roman church about A.D. 70. The ultimate sources of this tradition were many and varied, and its diverse elements came to Rome through many channels. St. Peter certainly contributed something to the body of tradition available to Mark. Not only was he one of the principal bearers of the tradition from the very beginning, but he almost certainly laboured in Rome before his death, and suffered martyrdom there in the time of Nero. But the Gospel as a whole is not

a transcript of his reminiscences; it reflects a long transmission of its materials through Gentile narrators.

4. It is probable that Mark, whoever he may have been, was the first to make the attempt to bring the traditional materials together in the form of a connected narrative of the public ministry of Jesus. Before him, the traditions about Jesus were transmitted as brief self-contained anecdotes or sayings or groups of sayings; or at most were gathered in short sequences grouped around a key word or a common theme; and when they came into his hands, there was no sure indication of the order of events or even of the duration of the ministry, which may have lasted one year or may have extended over three years or even longer.

5. The Gospel according to St. Matthew is almost wholly dependent upon Mark for the narrative; such additions as it makes by way of anecdote are legendary. They consist chiefly of the cycle of nativity-stories and some romantic heightening of the Passion-story (the Dream of Pilate's Wife, Pilate's Washing of his Hands, the Placing of the Guard at the Tomb, the Dead in the Streets of Jerusalem, etc.).

6. Matthew employs almost all the narrative material found in Mark, and incorporates in it a large amount of discourse-material — sayings attributed to Jesus. Much of this non-Marcan material he shares with Luke. It is commonly taken to be derived from a second source which is designated by the symbol 'Q' (for the German 'Quelle' — 'source'), which was employed independently by Matthew and Luke and may have been before them in two different recensions. Such a source (if it ever existed) was in the main a collection of sayings of Jesus, with an introductory section concerning Jesus and John the Baptist, but with no account of the Passion. It may well have been put together quite early — even earlier than Mark; indeed, Mark himself may have made occasional use of it. Some good scholars have identified it with the five books of 'Logia' which, according to Papias, were prepared in the 'Hebrew' (Aramaic?) language by the Apostle Matthew (e.g. T. W. Manson, *The Sayings of Jesus*, pp. 15-20). But a number of scholars reject the entire theory of a 'second source' and hold that the material so designated derives from more than one source, written or oral, or else that Luke has taken the materials which he shares with Matthew directly from the Gospel according to St. Matthew itself. The question has been reopened — if it can be said ever to have been closed. Nevertheless, it will be found that most critics and commentators assume the validity of the 'Q' hypothesis, even though they differ widely in the details of its application. The present writer must say that he has been more and more impressed, as he went on with the making of this book, with the strength of the evidence that Luke and Matthew have indeed used a second source in common, and that the phenomena of the non-Marcan parallels are far more plausibly explained on this theory than by any other hypothesis that has been put forward.

7. Matthew has also made use of a source or group of sources, or of a body of oral tradition which shows clear marks of a Jewish-Christian interest and emphasis, and probably represents a Palestinian or Syrian background of transmission. There are good reasons for holding that this Gospel was put

together in Antioch on the Orontes, with some kind of official sponsorship, towards the end of the first century or the beginning of the second. It very soon displaced Mark in the general usage of the Church.

8. The Gospel according to St. Luke is not, like Mark and Matthew, a self-contained work. It was published as the first volume of a two-volume work, to be completed by the book of Acts, dedicated to 'the most excellent Theophilus'. It sets the story of Jesus in the context of the origins of the Church and the history of its expansion from an obscure Jewish sect to a universal society which has erected its victorious standards in the world-capital, Rome.

In the matter of narrative, Luke is almost as dependent as Matthew upon the Marcan material. He adds nothing of importance to the knowledge of the external events of the Ministry which we are able to derive from Mark, though it is possible that he had at his disposal an independent version of the Passion-story. About half of Mark's material is reproduced in Luke; and a large part of his discourse-material is paralleled in Matthew ('Q' – see section 6, above). The remainder, rather more than a third of his Gospel, is found nowhere else. It includes stories of the Annunciation and the Nativity, accompanied by a cycle of Annunciation and Nativity narratives about John the Baptist – all legendary or fictional, like those of Matthew. But some of this 'L' material is priceless, especially its rich collection of parables (including some that have always exercised the greatest appeal – the Prodigal Son, the Good Samaritan, the Pharisee and the Publican), and its cycle of Resurrection-narratives.

The date of this Gospel is difficult to determine; it is wrapped up with the question of the date of the book of Acts, its companion volume. In its present form it seems to bear marks of the second century, and may even be as late as the middle of the century. On the other hand, much of its independently preserved material obviously belongs to an early stage of transmission.

9. It is held by some scholars, following an hypothesis first advanced by Canon B. H. Streeter, that Luke had written the first draft of his Gospel before Mark came into his hands. This first draft (called 'Proto-Luke') will have been made by an interweaving of his 'Q' materials (shared with Matthew), and materials drawn from his own sources ('L'). According to this theory, he will have inserted blocks of Marcan material subsequently into his first draft. It cannot be said that this hypothesis has found any wide following; indeed, as it was put forward shortly before the interest of scholars began to shift from source-criticism to form-criticism, it awakened less interest than it deserved. The present writer is not inclined to accept it.

10. These Gospels were undoubtedly composed in Greek, the language in which they have come down to us, and for the use of Greek-speaking communities. There is no sound basis for the hypothesis that they are translations of Aramaic originals.

11. None of the Gospels was written with the thought that it would require to be supplemented by others, nor does Mark presuppose that his readers have in their hands a collection of sayings of Jesus. Each of the Evangelists intended to provide in his own book a sufficient account of the words and works of Jesus, and each Gospel was used by itself for some decades in the locality or

region for which it was first composed. The formation of the four-gospel Canon is an historical and theological development of the second century which was neither intended nor foreseen by any of the Evangelists.

12. The numerous apocryphal Gospels add no reliable information about Jesus to that which is provided by the Synoptics. Very great interest attaches to some of them, most of all to the recently discovered *Gospel according to Thomas*, which contains more than a hundred sayings attributed to Jesus, with occasional bits of dialogue but no narrative of events. This compilation, put together in Greek towards the middle of the second century, is of interest to the student of the Gospels chiefly for the sake of the variant forms which it gives to parables and other sayings found in the Synoptics. These are probably taken from our canonical Gospels and re-framed by the (Gnostic) editor of Thomas; but it can be argued that in some cases they have been derived from an independent strain of oral tradition.

13. The Qumran documents, the so-called 'Dead Sea Scrolls', contribute very little to the understanding of the Synoptic Gospels. In spite of the extravagant claims that have been made for them, evidence of any significance in relation to the Synoptics is 'as two grains of wheat hid in a bushel of chaff; you shall seek all day ere you find them, and when you have found them, they are not worth the search'.

II. Factors in the Transmission of the Tradition Concerning Jesus

In any serious study of the Gospels, we have always to keep in mind that Jesus himself left nothing in writing, and that the earliest records of his career which have come down to us were not put into writing until about forty years after his death. All our knowledge of him is drawn from the deposit of a tradition which was transmitted for several decades by word of mouth. We are therefore obliged to raise the question of the relationship between the documents as we have them and the events and sayings which they report. For it must be realized that in a generation or more of oral transmission, sayings and stories do not remain unchanged. Once they have been committed to writing, they are to some degree stabilized, as it were; though even at this stage, we have to observe that Luke and Matthew do not shrink from altering the Marcan record which they are both using. Thus the Parable of the Sower takes 19 lines in the Greek text of Mark (Nestle edition), but is reduced to 16 lines in Matthew and to less than 12 lines in Luke. If this freedom is exercised by an Evangelist with a written text in front of him, we must allow for a much greater freedom on the part of innumerable teachers and preachers who transmitted the tradition as they remembered it, as they had heard it from another, not as it lay written in fixed form in a book. Let us take note also that there was never any effort to rehearse the sayings of Jesus, let alone the stories, in a stereotyped way. Where they have been preserved for us through two channels of transmission, they are never – or almost never – verbally identical. Even the Lord's Prayer shows differences that are more than merely verbal, between the version found in Matthew and that found in Luke.

Again, we must keep always in mind the fact that mere reminiscence was never the major factor in the preservation of the tradition concerning Jesus. Obviously enough, the tradition begins with the reminiscences of those who had known him during the days of his flesh. The Apostles, the Mother of the Lord, the faithful followers who accompanied him in Galilee — these and others would speak of the things that they had seen and heard. Such personal reminiscences are the first foundation of our Gospels. Yet it is of the utmost importance that we should grasp the fact that these first Christians were not in a situation comparable to that of the members of the Socratic circle after the death of Socrates. Crito and Phaedo and their friends cherished their recollections of a beloved master who had died; Peter and John and Mary were not living on memories of a dead friend whom they had loved dearly, but were conscious of his continued presence among them as the living Lord. For the guidance and direction of their lives, they were not dependent on their recollections of words which he had once spoken, for they knew that he still spoke to them and in them by his Spirit. They were not looking back wistfully to a bygone friendship. Their fellowship with Jesus remained unbroken, and they were looking forward to seeing him again in the glories of his coming in power. The stories and sayings of Jesus were cherished by them not as memories of past events, but as weapons for the winning and instruction of others, for the building of his Church.

The reminiscences of eye-witnesses, then, provided the initial elements of the tradition, but they were not at any time preserved as recollections of a vanished friend. And as the years went on, an unconscious process of selection set in. The communities did not preserve all the stories and sayings of Jesus that were passed on to them by the apostolic company. Broadly speaking, they preserved and transmitted those elements which they found to be of continuing significance in their corporate life — in their worship of Jesus as the Risen Lord, in their instruction of converts, in their work of evangelism, in their controversies with opponents. With the editors of the Gospels, the selection becomes conscious, and is explicitly affirmed by St. John: 'Jesus did many other signs in the presence of his disciples, which are not written in this book; but these are written that you may believe that Jesus is the Christ, the Son of God, and that you may, in so believing, have life, in his Name' (John xx. 30-31); and his editors, with pardonable hyperbole, tell us that 'if they were to be written down one by one, it would seem that the world itself would not have room for the books written' (John xxi. 25). Here we have the clearest recognition that the gospel record in its written form is selective, making no pretence to be complete or anything like complete; and we have at the same time a definite statement of the central motive that has governed the selection — not the human interest of the story, but the desire to promote faith in Jesus as the Son of God, and to bring to men the life that Jesus imparts to all who believe. A similar motive determined the selection and arrangement of materials made by the other Evangelists. Not one of them is governed in any substantial degree by the biographical interest, or is attempting to write a 'life of Jesus' or to give enduring form to the memories of his days on earth before it might be too late. But we must emphasize that the same purpose — the promotion of faith in Jesus as the living Lord — controls the transmission of the tradition from the very first and determines the selection of that which was to maintain its place in the worship, the teaching and the preaching of the primitive Church until the men of the second and third generations should commit it to writing.

Very little of that which has been preserved for us owes its preservation to sheer human interest. It is significant that we know nothing whatever about the personal appearance of Jesus — whether he was tall or short, thin or stout, dark or fair; whether he was physically robust or delicate; whether his eyes were blue or brown or hazel. Everyone is free to imagine what most pleases him. Such matters were of no concern to the Evangelists, or to the Christian circles which kept the stories and sayings of Jesus in circulation before they were committed to writing. They preserved the things that most struck home to their hearts — the materials that seemed to them to be relevant to the gospel of salvation, to their worship, to the sharp conflicts in which they were engaged. We are wholly dependent, for our knowledge of Jesus, upon the mediation of the early Church — not the gospel writers alone, but the communities which provided them with the stocks of tradition upon which they drew, a store already limited to that which had proved significant to the first generation.

We cannot too lightly assume that what the earliest Christians thought worth preserving would be identical with what we ourselves would regard as most important, or even that it would reflect essentially what Jesus himself regarded as central in his message. It must be regarded as possible that 'Jesus was over the heads of his reporters', and we shall indeed find indications in the Gospels themselves that he from time to time manifested keen disappointment and even a certain impatience with the lack of understanding shown by his immediate disciples. He was not surrounded, like Socrates, by the brilliant young men of a great intellectual circle, but by groups of fishermen, peasants and tax-collectors. This is not to say that the Socratic circle would have provided him with hearers capable of responding more sympathetically to his message; on the contrary, they would probably have proved as unreceptive as the 'wise and prudent' of his own countrymen, who proved blind to the spiritual realities which were revealed to the 'babes' of his company (Matt. xi. 25-26; Luke x. 21). But it is not at all unlikely that the men of the people who followed him may not have been capable of taking in all the range of his thought, and communicating it clearly to others.

Before we allow such considerations, legitimate as they are, to lead us into an unnecessary scepticism concerning the validity of our records, we must recall that the movement which we are studying does not profess to rest upon the limited and fallible minds of men. According to our Christian belief, it is guided by the continual working of the Holy Spirit of God. In this faith we shall hold that the Church has preserved and transmitted to us whatever was needed for the instruction and edification of other generations. And we may well feel that such faith is amply vindicated by the historical experience of the Church, in the manner in which the reflection of Jesus in the gospels, however distorted may be the medium, has proved from generation to generation to have the power to move hearts and to win men to God. The weakness of God is stronger than men, and no scientific investigator has succeeded in giving an account of Jesus which remotely compares with the 'unscientific' portraits of the Evangelists. But such considerations must not lead us to attribute to the Gospels characteristics which they do not possess; their value is not increased, but lessened, by our failure to accept them for what they are. We must be prepared to acknowledge that it will always be impossible for us to remove the pigments in which the early Church has depicted Jesus — to discover a 'Jesus of history' underneath the Christ of the Church's faith. If that faith is not justified, the picture is of no great use. For everything that has been recorded of the Jesus of history was recorded for us by men to whom he was Christ the Lord; and we cannot expunge their faith from the records without making the records themselves virtually worthless. There is no Jesus known to history except him who is depicted by his followers as the Christ, the Son of God, the Saviour of the world.

Our whole approach to the Gospels, therefore, must be governed by the realization that they are not at all 'Memoirs of the Apostles', as Justin Martyr terms them, endeavouring to find a term that would be intelligible to his pagan contemporaries. They are documents of the Christian cult, written from faith to faith; written not to supply information about an interesting historical personage, but to show men the way of salvation and to awaken faith in Jesus as the Son of God, the Saviour. That selection from the tradition which they preserve was determined partly by its relevance to the controversies in which the early Church was engaged, partly by its usefulness as teaching material for the instruction of converts, and partly by its use in the regular worship of Christians. We may characterize these writings as theological, catechetical, liturgical and apologetic documents — not as biographical or historical compositions. This is not at all to say that they have little or no biographical or historical value; on the contrary, they are of priceless significance in these areas also. But we must recognize that the purpose of the writers was not biographical in any primary sense, and that they have not provided us with the materials for a life of Jesus or even for a history of his public ministry.

The fact of selection is undisputed, and there is little room for argument about the motives which governed it, so far as the communal aspect of the transmission is concerned. There is a greater difficulty in ascertaining the factors which entered into the selection and arrangement which the several Evangelists made, in dealing with the materials transmitted to them by the multiple oral tradition of the churches. The two stages in the making of the Gospels must be clearly distinguished. In the stage of oral transmission, the process of selection was largely unconscious, reflecting the instinctive feeling of the believing community for what spoke to its condition, struck roots in its life, and promoted its mission. In the task of authorship undertaken by the Evangelists, it was necessary to make a second selection out of the mass of materials, already sifted in ecclesiastical usage, which remained alive in the communal memory. Each of these writers was set in his own way to proclaim the Gospel message by telling the story of Jesus; but each has his own approach, and brings the choice and the arrangement of his materials into the service of his general conception of the Gospel and the Christian religion as a whole. Each Gospel deserves to be read by and for itself, with some appreciation of its particular character and interest. Mark, composed in the shadow of the Neronian persecution, gains immensely in vividness and power if it is seen to be a document of martyrdom. The Lord who goes to his death, falsely accused of revolutionary agitation, betrayed by one of his closest followers, forsaken by all in his hour of trial, crying out in agony on the eve of his execution and again on his cross, yet vindicated by God in the finding of the empty tomb, is the profoundly moving pattern of those who have been called to take up the cross and follow him along the same journey of suffering in the confidence that he will bring them into the ensuing glory. Matthew, composed in Jewish-Christian circles in the generation that followed the fall of Jerusalem and the destruction of the Temple, sees Jesus as the new Moses who ensures the fulfilling of the Law and the Prophets despite – indeed, even through – the disaster which has befallen the Chosen People because of their rejection of him; and who sends out his disciples to make disciples of all nations. Luke in his turn sets Jesus and his Gospel in the environment of the Roman Empire and of world history, and foreshadows the victory of the cross over the eagles. The narrative of Mark is direct, vigorous and swift; his Jesus is a man of action, and we are given an astonishingly meagre account of the substance of his teaching. In Matthew, the sayings of Jesus are gathered into five main discourses, which constitute the main pattern of his Gospel, being superimposed upon the underlying narrative which he has derived from Mark. His work has a sombre tone, with a recurrent emphasis on Judgment. Luke is 'the scribe of the gentleness of Christ' (Dante), and in many ways his Gospel deserves Renan's tribute to it as 'the most beautiful book ever written'. It is full of a quiet joy and the full assurance of faith. It reflects marked proletarian sympathies, and shows a remarkable tenderness in its sketches of the women who appear in the Gospel story. These differences among the Gospels are caused partly by the choice which each Evangelist made from among the materials available to him, but even more by adaptation and arrangement, often involving a significant measure of reinterpretation – a new assessment of the central significance of sayings or incidents.

Here again we must observe that some element of modification, by way of interpretation and application to changing circumstances, was involved in the transmission of the tradition from the beginning. Sayings of Jesus were remembered when the context was forgotten, and they would be repeated in a new context which would give them an altered significance. An ironical saying: 'It is better that heaven and earth should pass away than that one dot of the Law should fall' (Luke xvi. 17), probably intended as a *reductio ad absurdum* of the excesses of Pharisaic legalism, is taken in Matthew (v. 18) as a formal pronouncement of the attitude of Jesus himself, as if he would out-Pharisee the Pharisees. In a more general way, the transference of the tradition from Jewish to Gentile soil, especially from Semitic to Grecian circles, imposed an inescapable task of interpretation, inseparable from the necessity of translation from Aramaic into Greek. The earliest Christian communities spoke Aramaic, and at one stage — relatively brief — the whole tradition was carried in Aramaic. As the Gospel was brought to Gentiles, it was necessary to translate the sayings of Jesus into Greek, and to compose Greek versions of the stories which were being told; first of all, of the Passion-story, then of the various incidents of the Ministry. Since the words of one language, apart from technical terms, seldom have exact equivalents in another, translation always involves a considerable element of interpretation; something is always lost, and something is always added. The whole of our tradition was of necessity put through this process of interpretation and modification from the moment that the mission ventured into a Greek environment. The interpretations and adaptations made by the Evangelists were but a later stage in a development which was commenced in very early days.

We have now to raise the question whether, in addition to the factors of selection and interpretation, the oral tradition admitted new materials — sayings or stories or both — which became wrongly attached to Jesus. It is necessary to consider the possibility that sayings of John the Baptist or other Jewish teachers came to be attributed to Jesus; or that folk-tales of uncertain origin were woven into the fabric of story concerning him. Some recent scholars have held that a substantial part of the materials included in our Gospels are the creation of the Christian communities, more than authentic survivals of the primitive tradition preserved by eye-witnesses of the Ministry. Radical scepticism seems quite unwarranted — after all, our earliest Gospel was composed during the lifetime of men who had seen and heard Jesus; but we shall find ourselves obliged to admit not merely the abstract possibility but the fact that our Gospels as they stand do incorporate, alongside materials of unmistakable authenticity, elements of legend and folk-tale, and probably also sayings transferred from other teachers, and utterances made by Christian prophets as 'the Word of the Lord'. It may be remarked that the saying: 'Behold, I stand at the door and knock. If anyone hear my voice and open the door, I will go in to him and will sup with him, and he with me' (Rev. iii. 20) is commonly treated by Christian readers today as a saying of Jesus quite as authoritative as any verse in the Gospels; yet no one would claim that it was ever uttered by Jesus in the days of his flesh. Accordingly there is no reason to suppose that anything would have prevented the acceptance of a number of such oracular sayings into the tradition and their attribution to the Jesus of the Galilean highway or of the streets of Jerusalem. For the Church, there was no distinction between the Jesus who had spoken to his disciples on earth, and the Lord who still spoke to his people from heaven through his inspired prophets.

From all this it follows that in studying the Gospels we are studying (i) the record of the earthly ministry of Jesus, (ii) the mind of the early Church — the motives and interests which affected the growth of the tradition; and (iii) the personal contributions of the several Evangelists and the particular interests of the communities in which each worked and wrote. The question of the authenticity of a saying, of the factual in a story, will of course be always before us; but equally important will be the question why the story or the saying —

authentic or not — has found a place in the written record that has come down to us; and this is a matter of determining what it meant to the Church which transmitted it, or to the Evangelist who gave it its place in his Gospel.

III. The Arrangement of the Text

The general outline of the public ministry of Jesus is apparently the creation of St. Mark, the author of our earliest Gospel. He arranged the materials of his story in two main parts: a ministry in Galilee, and in regions adjacent to Galilee to the north and north-east; and a brief ministry in Jerusalem, culminating in the Passion-story. These two parts are linked by a relatively brief section, laid in the journey from the north to Jerusalem, which is mainly given to the theme of the Preparation for the Passion. There can be no doubt that the heart of his Gospel is the Passion-story, and that all the rest is prelude. As truly as St. Paul, he is determined to know nothing except Christ *and him crucified.* But it is evident that for the Crucifixion to have significance, there must be some comprehension of the nature of the one crucified; after all, the Romans crucified thousands of criminals, and the story of Christ's Passion must show why this was not an ordinary crucifixion, but an act of redemption, a sacrifice for sins, a victory over the evil powers that hold mankind enthralled, and not merely another instance of a good man unjustly done to death. The pattern created by St. Mark is followed, as we shall see, by his two fellow Evangelists; each of them distributed his materials among the same three periods of ministry: Galilee and the north; the journey to Jerusalem; and the last days in Jerusalem — except that St. Luke greatly increases the weight of the intermediate section by allotting most of his own new matter to the period of the journey.

In the Huck Synopsis, the divisions reflect this Marcan arrangement. Division I, covering the first nine chapters of Mark, with the parallel sections of Matthew and Luke together with the additional material that these two Evangelists have worked in with this part of the Marcan story, is headed *The Galilean Period.* The central section of Luke, which consists almost entirely of material peculiar to this Evangelist, is given the second division to itself, under the title *The Lucan Travel Narrative.* Division III, covering Mark x to xv, with the parallel sections of Matthew and Luke, is entitled *The Judaean Period*; to it is attached the story of the finding of the empty tomb (Mark xvi. 1-8 and parallels), under the title (in the English editions) *The Resurrection.* The opening and the endings of Matthew and Luke, which have no parallels in Mark, stand apart from the three main divisions of the text, as *The Infancy Narratives* and *The Post-Resurrection Narratives*; in these, the sections are not numbered, but are given sub-titles.

In these notes, the section headings and the sub-titles are taken from Professor Cross's edition of the Huck-Lietzmann Synopsis. It will be found that they do not often differ from those given in Professor Throckmorton's *Gospel Parallels.*

OUTLINE OF THE ARRANGEMENT OF THE MATERIALS

Abbreviations used for Works Frequently Cited

(*see* Foreword, p. 11)

Creed, *St. Luke*
Easton, *St. Luke*
Grant, *Gospels*
Manson, *Teaching*
Manson, *Sayings*
McNeile, *St. Matthew*
Taylor, *St. Mark*
Taylor, *Life and Ministry*
IB – The Interpreter's Bible

Bibliography

Allen, W. C., *The Gospel according to St. Mark* London: Rivingtons, 1915

Bacon, B. W., *Studies in Matthew* New York: Holt, 1930

Beasley-Murray, G. R., *A Commentary on Mark xiii* London: Macmillan, 1957

Beasley-Murray, G. R., *Jesus and the Future* London: Macmillan, 1954

Black, *Aramaic Approach*: M. BLACK, *An Aramaic Approach to the Gospels ana Acts* Oxford: Clarendon Press, 1946 second edition, 1954

Bornkamm, G., *Jesus of Nazareth*, E.T. by Irene and Fraser McLusky, with J. M. Robinson, London: Hodder & Stoughton, 1960

Bornkamm, G., G. Barth and H. J. Held, *Überlieferung und Auslegung im Matthäus-Evangelium*, Neukirchen Kreis Moers: Neukirchener Verlag, 1960. E.T. under the title *Tradition and Interpretation in Matthew*, by Percy Scott, London: SCM, 1963

Bultmann, *History*; R. BULTMANN, *Die Geschichte der synoptischen Tradition* Göttingen: Vandenhoeck & Ruprecht, third edition, 1958. E.T. under the title *The History of the Synoptic Tradition*, by John Marsh, Oxford: Basil Blackwell, 1963

Burkill, T. C., *Mysterious Revelation: An Examination of the Philosophy of St. Mark's Gospel* Ithaca: Cornell U.P., 1963

Cadbury, H. J., *Jesus: What Manner of Man* New York: Macmillan, 1948 (The Schaffer Lectures, Yale University Divinity School, 1946)

Conzelmann, H., *Die Mitte der Zeit: Studien zur Theologie des Lukas* Tübingen: Mohr (Siebeck), third edition, 1960. E.T. under the title *The Theology of St. Luke*, by G. Buswell, London: Faber, 1960

Cullmann, O., *Petrus: Jünger—Apostel—Märtyrer. Das historische und das theologische Problem* Zürich: Zwingli-Verlag, 1952. E.T. under the title *Peter: Disciple—Apostle—Martyr: A Historical and Theological Study* by F. V. Filson, London: SCM and Philadelphia: Westminster Press, 1953. Second edition revised, 1960 (German) and 1962 (E.T.).

Cumont, Franz, *Lux Perpetua* Paris: 1949

Danby, H., *The Mishnah* Oxford University Press, 1933

Daube, David, *The New Testament and Rabbinic Judaism* London: University of London Press, 1946

Dibelius, M., *Die Formgeschichte des Evangeliums* edited by G. Bornkamm, Tübingen: Mohr (Siebeck), third edition 1959. E.T. of second edition, under the title *From Tradition to Gospel*, by B. L. Woolf, London: Ivor Nicholson & Watson, 1934

Dix, Gregory, *Jew and Greek: a Study in the Primitive Church* New York: Harper Bros., 1953

Dodd, C. H., *The Parables of the Kingdom* London: Nisbet & Co., 1935; 2nd ed. rev., 1961, with changed paging

Dodd, C. H., *The Interpretation of the Fourth Gospel* Cambridge: University Press, 1953

Doresse, Jean, *The Secret Books of the Egyptian Gnostics: an Introduction to the Gnostic Manuscripts discovered at Chenoboskion*, E.T. by P. Mairet (with an annotated translation of the *Gospel according to Thomas*) London: Hollis & Carter, 1960

Duncan, G. S., *Jesus, Son of Man: Studies Contributory to a Modern Portrait* London: Nisbet, 1948

Farrer, A. M., *St Matthew and St Mark* London: Dacre (A. & C. Black), 1954

Grant, F. C., *The Earliest Gospel: Studies in the Evangelic Tradition at the Point of its Crystallization in Writing* New York: Abingdon, 1943 (The Cole Lectures at Vanderbilt University)

Grobel, Kendrick, *The Gospel of Truth: a Valentinian meditation on the Gospel* New York: Abingdon, 1960

Guillaumont, A., H.-Ch. Puech, G. Quispel, W. Till and Yassah 'Abd Al Masīḥ, *The Gospel according to Thomas: Coptic Text established and translated* Leiden: Brill, 1959
The numbering of the Logia in this edition is followed in the notes.

Higgins, A. J. B. (Editor), *New Testament Essays: A Memorial Volume to T. W. Manson* Manchester: University Press, 1959

Hooker, M. D. *Jesus and the Servant* London: S.P.C.K., 1959

Jeremias, J., *Die Gleichnisse Jesu* Zurich: Zwingli-Verlag, third edition, 1954. E.T. under the title *The Parables of Jesus*, by S. H. Hooke, London: SCM, 1954

Jeremias, J. *Unknown Sayings of Jesus*, E.T. by R. H. Fuller, London: S.P.C.K., 1958

Jeremias, J., *The Eucharistic Words of Jesus*. E.T. by A. Ehrhardt, Oxford: Blackwell, 1955

Johnson, Sherman E., *The Gospel according to St Mark* London: A. & C. Black, 1960 (Black's N.T. Commentaries)

Johnson, Sherman E. (Editor), *The Joy of Study: Papers in New Testament and Related Subjects Presented to honor Frederick Clifton Grant* New York: Macmillan, 1951

Jülicher, Adolf, *Die Gleichnisreden Jesu* Tübingen: Mohr, 1899. Second Edition, 1910

Kenyon, F. G., *Books and Readers in Ancient Greece and Rome* Oxford: Clarendon Press, second edition 1951

Kilpatrick, *Origins*: G. D. Kilpatrick, *The Origins of the Gospel according to St. Matthew* Oxford: Clarendon Press, 1946

Kirk, K. E. (Editor), *The Apostolic Ministry: Essays on the History and the Doctrine of Episcopacy* London: Hodder & Stoughton, 1947

Klausner, J., *Jesus of Nazareth: his life, times, and teaching*, E.T. by H. Danby, New York: Macmillan, 1925

Klostermann, E., *Das Markusevangelium* Tübingen: Mohr (Siebeck), fourth edition 1950. H. Lietzmann's *Handbuch zum N. T.* 3

Knox, *Sources* I, II: W. L. Knox, *The Sources of the Synoptic Gospels*, 2 vols., ed. H. Chadwick. Cambridge: C.U.P., 1953-55

Knox, W. L., *Some Hellenistic Elements in Primitive Christianity* London: British Academy, 1944 (The Schweich Lectures for 1942)

Kümmel, W. G., *Promise and Fulfilment*, E.T. by D. M. Barton, London: SCM, 1957 (*Studies in Theology*, No. 23)

Lagrange, M.-J., *L'Evangile selon saint Luc* Paris: Gabalda, 1921

Lightfoot, R. H., *History and Interpretation in the Gospels* London: Hodder & Stoughton, 1935 (The Bampton Lectures for 1934)

Lohmeyer, *Markus*: E. Lohmeyer, *Das Evangelium des Markus* (Meyer-Kommentar, Göttingen: Vandenhoeck & Ruprecht, twelfth edition, 1953

Loisy, Alfred, *L'Evangile selon Luc* Paris: Nourry, 1924

Lowe, John, *Saint Peter* Oxford: University Press, 1956

Manson, T. W., *The Servant-Messiah: a Study of the Public Ministry of Jesus* Cambridge: University Press, 1953

Manson, T. W., *Ethics and the Gospel* (published posthumously) London: SCM, 1960

Manson, *Luke*: William Manson, *The Gospel of Luke* (Moffatt N.T. Commentary). London: Hodder & Stoughton, 1930

Manson, William, *Jesus the Messiah* London: Hodder & Stoughton, 1943

Meyer, Eduard, *Ursprung und Anfänge des Christentums* 3 vols. Berlin: Töpelmann, 1921

Nineham, D. E. (Editor), *Studies in the Gospels: Essays in Memory of R. H. Lightfoot* Oxford: Blackwell, 1955

Noack, B., *Das Gottesreich bei Lukas* Uppsala: 1948 (*Symbolae Biblicae Uppsalenses* 10)

Norden, E., *Agnostos Theos: Untersuchungen zur Formgeschichte religioser Rede* Leipzig: Teubner, 1913 (Fourth Edition, 1956)

Otto, R., *The Kingdom of God and the Son of Man*, E. T. by F. V. Filson and B. L. Woolf, London: Lutterworth, 1938

Ramsey, A. M., *The Glory of God and the Transfiguration of Christ* London: Longmans Green, 1949

Rawlinson, A. J. B., *St Mark, with Introduction, Commentary, and Additional Notes* (Westminster Commentaries), London: Methuen, seventh edition, 1949

Rengstorf, K. H., *Apostleship*. Schmidt, K. L., *The Church*. These two articles, translated and edited by J. R. Coates, are included in the series, 'Bible Key Words from G. Kittel's Worterbuch', London: A. & C. Black, 1952

Schweitzer, A., *The Quest of the Historical Jesus* London: A. & C. Black, 1906 (Numerous reprints)

Smith, B. T. D., *The Parables of the Synoptic Gospels* Cambridge: University Press, 1937

Smith, Morton, *Tannaitic Parallels to the Gospels* Philadelphia: Jewish Publication Society, 1951 (*JBL* Monograph Series, No. VI)

Strack, H. L. and P. Billerbeck, *Kommentar zum Neuen Testament aus Talmud und Midrasch* 6 vols Munich: Beck, 1922-56

Streeter, B. H., *The Four Gospels: A Study of Origins* London: Macmillan, 1924

Taylor, Vincent, *Behind the Third Gospel* Oxford: University Press, 1926

Taylor, Vincent, *The Names of Jesus* London: Macmillan, 1953

Torrey, C. C., *The Four Gospels: A New Translation* New York: Harper Bros., second edition, 1947

Torrey, C. C., *Our Translated Gospels* New York: Harper Bros., 1936

Wellhausen, Julius, *Das Evangelium Marci* second edition, Berlin: Reimer, 1909

Wellhausen, Julius, *Einleitung in die drei ersten Evangelien* second edition, Berlin: Reimer, 1911

Wellhausen, Julius, *Das Evangelium Matthaei* Berlin: Reimer, 1904

Wellhausen, Julius, *Das Evangelium Lucae* Berlin: Reimer, 1904

Winter, Paul, *On the Trial of Jesus*, Berlin: De Gruyter, 1961 (Studia Judaica I) This brilliant critical study appeared too late for me to use in this book, apart from mention in a single footnote.

Zahn, Theodor, *Das Evangelium des Lukas* Leipzig: Deichert, 1913

THE INFANCY NARRATIVES

Our earliest Gospel, which bears the name of St. Mark, begins with a brief note on the public ministry of John the Baptist, and the story of the baptism of Jesus by John. Both Matthew and Luke take up the Marcan narrative from that point; but both of them are moved to put before it a prefatory section, consisting of a cycle of legends concerning the birth of the Saviour.

Comparison of the two Infancy Narratives

The two cycles are wholly independent, and have only the following points of agreement:

(*a*) They date the birth of Jesus in the reign of Herod the Great (died 4 B.C.).
(*b*) They tell us that Jesus was born at Bethlehem, but was brought up at Nazareth in Galilee.
(*c*) They tell us that the mother of Jesus was called Mary; that she was a virgin at the time of his birth; and that his conception was a creative action of the Holy Spirit of God.
(*d*) They tell us that Mary's husband Joseph, of the lineage of King David, was thought to be the father of Jesus; and the two genealogies, though differing in other respects, trace the descent of Jesus through Joseph.
(*e*) In both, the name 'Jesus' is given in obedience to the command of the Angel of the Annunciation.

The two cycles differ in the following respects:

(*a*) In Matthew, the Annunciation is made to Joseph, in a dream. In Luke, the Annunciation is made to Mary, in a waking state; the Angel of the Annunciation reveals his name — Gabriel; and Mary freely consents to be the instrument of the divine purpose.
(*b*) In Matthew, Joseph finds his affianced bride pregnant and is minded to cancel the tie with Mary until the Angel of the Annunciation, in a dream, tells him that the Holy Spirit is the agent of the conception. In Luke, the reaction of Joseph to his wife's pregnancy is not mentioned, and indeed his name occurs only as it were incidentally (i. 27; ii. 4, 16). We are told of his presence on the scene, and that is all.
(*c*) Matthew alone tells the story of the Magi; Luke alone tells of the Shepherds.
(*d*) Matthew's cycle assumes that Bethlehem was the home of Mary and Joseph. They leave Bethlehem after his birth, not because their home is elsewhere, but because they receive a warning in a dream; they flee into Egypt,

and at the death of Herod would return to their home in Bethlehem, were it not for their fear of Archelaus the son of Herod, now ruling in Judaea; and it requires another revelation, given in a dream, to direct them to Nazareth. It is implied that some months, perhaps some years have passed, between the birth at Bethlehem and the settlement in Nazareth – long enough for the journey to Egypt, some period of residence there, and the return across the desert to Palestine.

In Luke, Nazareth is the home of Joseph and Mary. They go to Bethlehem only because the Roman census requires them to register in the native city of Joseph's ancestor David. They remain only long enough for the circumcision of Jesus and the completion of the days of Mary's purification (Lev. xii. 2ff.), Then they go to Jerusalem (evidently apprehending no menace from Herod), to present Jesus in the Temple and to offer the prescribed sacrifice for the redemption of the firstborn (Lev. xii. 8). That accomplished, they go home to Nazareth, never thinking of a journey to Egypt.

(*e*) Matthew alone explains the significance of the name Jesus, and links it with the 'Emmanuel' oracle of Isaiah vii.

Besides all this, we find in Luke a parallel cycle of birth-stories bearing upon John the Baptist interwoven with the legends of the birth of Jesus; and the two men are represented as cousins.

The Matthaean genealogy traces the descent of Jesus to David and to Abraham, emphasizing his relation to the People of the covenants. The Lucan genealogy carries his descent back to Adam, reflecting St. Paul's theology of the Second Adam, and emphasizing the relation of Jesus to the whole of mankind. Naturally, these genealogies do not rest on records of any kind, but are artificial constructions, probably modelled on the genealogies of the book of Genesis. Both of them purport to give the genealogy of Joseph, which is wholly irrelevant in association with the story of the Virgin Birth; it follows that they were originally constructed in circles which knew nothing of the belief in the virginity of Mary.

THE MATTHAEAN INFANCY NARRATIVE

Matthew i, ii

(*a*) *The Genealogy of Christ* i $^{1–11}$

Verse 1 may be regarded as the title of the book; it is the Christian 'Book of Genesis', the beginning of the New Creation.

Among the ancestors of Jesus (strictly speaking, of Joseph), Matthew attaches particular importance to David and Abraham. This is the initial indication of the weight that he will give throughout his Gospel to the thought that in Jesus the promises of God to Israel have been fulfilled. The specific mention of irregular unions in the line of descent (Tamar, *v.* 3; Rahab, *v.* 5 and again Ruth, *v.* 5; the wife of Uriah, *v.* 6) is probably a kind of defensive response to calumnies concerning the circumstances of the birth of Jesus.

(*b*) [*The Annunciation of St. Joseph, and*] *The Birth of Christ* i 18–25

Revelation through dreams is often mentioned in the Old Testament (Jacob at Bethel, and Solomon at Gibeah, for instance), and is more frequently found in Greek and Roman literature and legend. A modern reader is apt to feel that a suspicious husband would not be reassured by something which he saw and heard in a dream; but no ancient reader would question the authority of such a dream-experience. The story is of course legendary, but it is the kind of legend that would grow naturally in the climate of the first century.

The name Jesus is the Greek rendering of the Hebrew Joshua, which means 'Yahweh saves' or 'Yahweh is salvation'.

The formula of *v.* 22: 'All this took place that the word of the Lord, given through the prophet, might be fulfilled' is characteristic of Matthew. He is always eager to point out the correspondence of prophecy and fulfilment in the life of Jesus. Often enough, as here, he cites the text of the Septuagint, heedless of the context and indifferent to the meaning of the underlying Hebrew. It is clear to anyone reading Isaiah vii that the prophet, in offering a 'sign' to King Ahaz in 734 B.C., is speaking of something that will occur within a few months, not pointing to events more than seven hundred years distant. Further, the Hebrew text does not suggest that the birth in question is miraculous; it is only the Greek version that introduces the notion that the mother will be a virgin. Again, the name Emmanuel does not, in the oracle itself, suggest that the child to be born will be a divine being; he will be given this name because by the time of his birth it will be clear that the danger (of the Syro-Ephraimitic invasion) has passed away; his name will be a testimony that God is among his people to deliver them. The oracle of Isaiah vii which is here cited was not, in its original context, a Messianic prophecy and certainly not a prophecy of birth from a virgin.

(*c*) *The Visit of the Magi* ii 1–12

'Magi from the East' are Chaldaean astrologers; we have here, at the beginning of the Gospel story, a curious reflection (not by any means unique in the New Testament) of the dominion which was exercised over men's minds by this pseudo-science of antiquity. The story says nothing of the number of Magi, or of their names. That they were three is probably an unconscious inference from the mention of three kinds of gifts (*v.* 11); the names are later elaborations of the legend.

It is folly to search for some conjunction of planets, or for some appearance of a comet or of a nova in the heavens at this time. It was a commonplace of astrological lore that the birth of a great man would be accompanied by a correspondingly great sign in the sky. This story does not move in the field of scientific observation, but in that of the poetic imagination. In the thought of the Evangelist, the 'star' is probably connected with the oracle of Balaam (Num. xxiv. 17 — 'a star shall arise out of Jacob', etc.) — an oracle which was certainly applied Messianically to Bar-Cochba, 'son of the star', the leader of the Jewish revolt against Rome in the time of Hadrian.

(*d*) *The Flight into Egypt* ii $^{13-15}$

(Note: in Huck, our sections (*d*), (*e*) and (*f*) are grouped under a single heading.)

This story, which has been depicted so beautifully in Christian art through the centuries, is probably an outgrowth of the verse from Hosea which is cited at its conclusion: 'Out of Egypt, I called my son.' In the original context this is not a prophecy of the future, but a reference to the past — to the Exodus. But two considerations must be kept in mind. First, Matthew (and the Church of his time) was quite capable of taking an oracle of an Old Testament prophet, which he interpreted rightly or wrongly as a Messianic prophecy, as evidence for an historical event. If an oracle of the Old Testament said that the Messiah was to be called out of Egypt, then it followed that the Messiah must have gone into Egypt. No other evidence was needed. Secondly, there was a general doctrine, widely accepted in rabbinical circles, that the events of the beginning of Israel's history would be duplicated in the end: the Exodus under Moses would be a pattern of the greater Exodus, which was the symbol of the eschatological deliverance of the people of God and the final triumph. The experience of Israel was therefore regarded as a figure of the experience through which the Messianic King, who embodied Israel in his own person, was to pass. Israel, as the son of God who was called out of Egypt, prefigured the true Son of God; and what was said of Israel must therefore apply in an ultimate sense to the eschatological King of Israel.

(*e*) *The Massacre of the Innocents* ii $^{16-18}$

Even more clearly, this legend owes its origin to the prophecy which it cites. The words of Jeremiah are directed to the women of Israel who see their men marching off into captivity in Babylon, and have no bearing at all upon a massacre of infants. The story accords well with the character and conduct of Herod, who killed most of his own children; so notorious was his cruelty that Augustus Caesar, hearing of the murder of one of Herod's sons, is said to have made the grim pun: 'It is better to be Herod's swine than his son (Greek *hus* — 'pig'; *huios* — 'son'). Even though the story of the massacre is not unjust to Herod, it must none the less be regarded as without foundation in fact.

(*f*) *The Return* (*The Settlement in Nazareth*) ii $^{19-23}$

We have already observed that the story implies that Nazareth was not the original home of Joseph and Mary; they settle there only because of supernatural direction. The oracle cited: 'He shall be called a Nazarene' cannot be identified with certainty; perhaps the best conjecture is that it is a distortion of the description of the Messiah as the 'Branch' (*neẓer*), in Jeremiah.

None of the stories of this cycle can reasonably be regarded as historical; they are products of the Christian imagination, weaving pictures of an infancy for which tradition provided no materials. In their own way, they bear testimony to the faith that the son of Mary was also the Son of God; that his coming into the world was no ordinary birth, but a miraculous divine intervention; and that the providence of God safeguarded him from every threat of danger until the time of his sacrifice of himself should come.

The Lucan Infancy Narrative

Luke i, ii

Luke offers us a twofold cycle of nativity-stories, interweaving legends of the birth of John the Baptist with those of Jesus, and representing the two as physically as well as spiritually akin. The Johannine cycle will hardly have been created or preserved in Christian circles; almost certainly it will have taken shape among the followers of John, who seem for a time to have constituted a rival movement, venerating John as the Messiah and not merely as his Forerunner. The history of developments is obscure, but these Johannine groups must have been gradually absorbed into the Christian Church and have learnt to see in the Baptist the herald of the Christ, the Elijah whose coming was to prepare the way for the manifestation of the Lord himself. In this Lucan version the Johannine legends have been given a Christian colouring and have been made to emphasize both the greatness of John as the divinely prepared messenger of good things to come from God, and his subordination to Jesus, acknowledged even in the womb (i. 41-44).

(*a*) *The Prologue* i [1–4]

This paragraph, which dedicates the work to the 'most excellent Theophilus', is cast in a style and diction not to be found again in the Lucan writings; it has the careful balance and one might almost say the elevation of a classical construction. The writer notes that he is undertaking a literary task which many have already attempted; he makes it clear that he and they are working with materials delivered by a tradition which goes back to the beginning of the Gospel; and he claims to be qualified for the task by the care with which he has investigated the matter. The designation of Theophilus suggests the type of reader to whom the author means to appeal — the high Roman official who may be called upon to deal with Christians on trial for their faith.

(*b*) *The Promise of the Baptist's Birth* [*The Annunciation of Zacharias*] i [5–25]

The classical style of the opening paragraph is now abruptly abandoned, and the story is cast in language modelled upon that of the Septuagint. The Semitic flavour is so pronounced as to give grounds for the hypothesis that this whole Infancy Narrative has been translated from an Aramaic original. There are clear reminiscences of the story of the birth of Samuel (1 Sam. i). Luke generally avoids the identification of John with the Elijah of eschatological expectation (cf. § 125), but here the Angel of the Annunciation foretells that John will carry out his mission 'in the spirit and power of Elijah', as depicted in the oracle of Malachi (Mal. iii. 1, iv. 5f).

(*c*) *The Annunciation of the Blessed Virgin* i [26–38]

The scene is laid in Nazareth, which in turn is taken to be the home of Mary and Joseph. Joseph plays no part in the Lucan story, apart from the mention of his name as the man to whom Mary is betrothed, and his descent from

David, which is the only ground given for claiming Davidic descent for Jesus. The story marks an early stage in the development of the cult of the Blessed Virgin.

(*d*) *The Visitation* [*with the Magnificat*] i 39–56

This beautiful little story is told partly to affirm again the subordination of John to Jesus; even before his birth, John leaps with joy at the approach of Jesus, and John's mother hails Mary as 'the mother of my Lord'. Note that there is some textual evidence, by no means negligible, for the ascription of the *Magnificat* to Elizabeth. The Song is one of our earliest specimens of Christian hymnody, but there is no need to suppose that it was composed on the spur of the moment by the Blessed Virgin (or by Elizabeth); the attribution is simply a literary device for introducing the hymn. The *Magnificat* echoes Old Testament phrases in almost every line and is wholly Jewish in tone and spirit; it may have been used in Jewish circles before being adopted into Christian worship. Its theme is one of those congenial to Luke: the fulfilment of God's purpose of redemption will bring sharp reversals of fortune – the exaltation of the lowly and the fall of the rich and powerful.

(*e*) *The Birth of the Baptist* [*with the Benedictus*] i 57–80

This story again has all the marks of belonging to the legend of John as developed in Johannine circles, independently of Christian influence. The *Benedictus* is akin in style and spirit to the *Magnificat* and may well have come into Christian usage from Jewish circles which cherished Messianic expectations, not necessarily connected with John the Baptist. Whatever its origin, it represents for its author, as for us, a lasting testimony of Christian faith and thankfulness to God for the fulfilment of his promises. Note the emergence once again of the Davidic theme (*v*. 69), and of the expectation of a new Elijah (*v*. 76).

(*f*) *The Nativity of Christ* ii 1–20

(i) The Birth of the Child ii 1–7

The census which the writer has in mind is probably that which was made some years later than this, when Archelaus was deposed and Judaea was put under the rule of a Roman procurator in subordination to the governor of Syria; at least we have no evidence for an earlier census. In any case it is inconceivable that everyone who claimed descent from the great King David, now dead for nearly a thousand years, should be required to enrol in the little village of Bethlehem. We are bound to feel that the census is brought into the story for two reasons: (i) to account for the presence of the family at Bethlehem at such a time, when their home was at Nazareth; and (ii) to establish a link between the Christian society and the Roman Empire. Even the decrees of Augustus Caesar unwittingly serve the purposes of God and contribute to the fulfilment of prophecy.

'Her first-born son' – there is nothing in the Gospels to suggest that Mary had no other children; the doctrine of perpetual virginity, like that of the immaculate conception, belongs to a much later stage of theologically motivated legend. The story of the Rejection at Nazareth (§ 108) mentions brothers and sisters of Jesus and there is no hint that they are not, like him, the children of Mary; the notion that they were children of Joseph by a previous marriage is an inference from the doctrine of perpetual virginity.

'The first-born' has undertones of the title of Jesus as 'the first-born of all creation' (Col. i. 17, etc.).

(ii) The Coming of the Shepherds ii 8–20

It is in keeping with Luke's consistent interest in the appeal of the Gospel to the poor and lowly that he brings no people of distinction to the birthplace of the divine Infant, but only a band of shepherds. This story includes another fragment of early Christian hymnody, in the *Gloria in Excelsis*. The story itself perhaps originates in some sense from the impulse to make the life of David a pattern of the life of David's son: Loisy suggests an influence of the saying: 'I took thee from the sheepfold and from following the sheep, and made thee ruler of my people Israel' (addressed to David, in 2 Sam. vii. 8). The ox and ass of the Nativity iconography are not mentioned in the Lucan story, but have been drawn from the opening words of the book of Isaiah: 'The ox knoweth his owner, and the ass his master's crib.'

(*g*) *The Circumcision of Christ and the Presentation in the Temple* ii 21–40

The emphasis is not on the Circumcision in itself, but on the naming of the Child in accordance with the direction given by the Angel of the Annunciation. It should be kept in mind that the name, in the ancient world, was not a mere appellation, but a significant indication of character and function. Luke assumes that his readers will know that the name Jesus indicates the function of salvation (cf. Matt. i. 21); or at least that they will know that it is the equivalent of Joshua, the name of the leader who brought Israel into the Promised Land, consummating the task of redemption begun by Moses. The Presentation story is concerned to mark the due fulfilment of all the requirements of the Law in the person of Jesus. It also affords the occasion to introduce another early Christian hymn, the *Nunc Dimittis*; and to intimate the greatness of the Child, hardly realized as yet even by Joseph and Mary, but predicted by the inspired seer and perceived by the devout old widow Anna.

According to this cycle, the family returns to Nazareth as soon as the rites of the Law have been fulfilled; there is no room here for an intervening journey to Egypt.

(*h*) *Christ at Twelve Years* ii 41–52

This story represents the only attempt in the canonical Gospels to bridge the long gap between the Infancy Narratives and the beginning of the public ministry of Jesus. There is no reason to suppose that it rests on any foundation of reminiscence; it is a legend, reflecting the feeling that the essential greatness of Jesus must have been manifested even in his childhood. The general picture of a Galilean pilgrimage to Jerusalem for the great festival, and of the child missing but not missed until nightfall, is of course true to life; there is perhaps less probability in the picture of the patience of the learned men of the Temple still conversing with a twelve-year-old on the third day.

There is an idyllic charm about this Lucan prelude which can never lose its appeal; but it must be realized that we do not come upon solid historical ground until the Evangelist picks up the thread of the Marcan narrative at the beginning of the public ministry of Jesus — or more precisely, at his baptism by John. There is no indication that any sound tradition was preserved of the life of Jesus before the opening of his ministry, apart from the bare fact that he was reared in the home of a carpenter in the Galilean village of Nazareth.

I. THE GALILEAN PERIOD

§§ 1-136

MATTHEW iii-xviii MARK i-ix LUKE iii. 1-ix. 50

The Ministry of John the Baptist

§§ 1-5

§§ 1 to 5 give a brief general account of John the Baptist, and indicate summarily the substance of his teaching. Only two of them contain Marcan material — viz. §§ 1 and 4. § 2 consists of 'Q' material, used in common, in this case with very little variation even in word-order, by Matthew and Luke. § 4 includes further 'Q' material, much of it preserved in identical wording by Matthew and Luke. § 3 is peculiar to Luke; and § 5, not paralleled at this point in either Mark or Matthew, appears to be a Lucan résumé of the account of John's imprisonment, which will not be mentioned by Mark and Matthew until much later (§ 111). It is clear that Matthew and Luke have had before them the narrative of Mark concerning John and have used it in its entirety, with some changes of wording and some redistribution of material. They have also used in common a second account of the *preaching* of John, much fuller than that which is given in Mark; and they have conflated their sources in different ways.

1. *John the Baptist*

MATTHEW iii. 1-6 MARK i. 1-6 LUKE iii. 1-6

Note that Mark i. 1 is the title of the book. His phrase is the first step in the transition in the Christian use of the word 'gospel' from the message of salvation itself to the book containing the story of Jesus. In Mark it still means 'the joyful proclamation', and has indeed something of the sense of Paul's definition: 'It is God's power put forth to bring salvation to every one who has faith' (Rom. i. 16). The genitive ('of Jesus Christ') may mean either 'proclaimed by Jesus Christ' – and in fact Christ does himself preach 'the gospel of God' (i. 14) – or 'concerning Jesus Christ'. For Mark, the latter meaning is more likely to convey his thought. The words 'Son of God', though not represented in the text of Huck, are rightly restored by the American translators. The textual evidence is so divided as to make the decision uncertain; but the phrase itself is indicative of the basic theology of Mark.

In the Marcan account of John, the following elements should be noted:

(*a*) The link with O.T. prophecy: the Elijah prophecy from Malachi, and the 'voice in the wilderness' prophecy from Isaiah xl. In Mark both are attributed to Isaiah; this error is silently corrected by Matthew and Luke, who cut out the Malachi fragment at this point. In the oracle itself, the phrase 'in the wilderness' is attached to the following verb, not to 'the voice'. The cry of the herald is not raised in the wilderness, but in the streets of Jerusalem; it cries 'Prepare in the wilderness the way of the Lord; make straight in the desert a highway for our God'. It was not difficult for a reader of the Greek version to mistake the grouping of the phrases, and so to find in the oracle a picture of a wilderness preacher, which would seem to point to John.

(*b*) Two aspects of John's ministry are suggested. For the Christian writer, the primary emphasis is clearly on the idea of *preparation*: he thinks of John first as the herald of the coming Christ. Second to this is the idea of the call to repentance, and the promise of remission of sins, of which baptism is the sign. Such a baptism – of Israelites, not of proselytes from paganism, as was customary – involves the doctrine that mere membership in the community of Israel is not sufficient title to a place in the kingdom of God. John's message is of judgment that begins in the house of God itself – that those who claim to be his people must themselves be purified and bring forth in their lives the fruits of righteousness.

(*c*) The influence of John is widely felt: it extends to 'all the Judaean country and all the people of Jerusalem'.

(*d*) The account of his food and clothing, probably accurate in itself, suggests again the figure of Elijah, the great solitary of early times. We must recall that no comparable information is preserved concerning Jesus.

The Matthaean version

(*a*) Note the vague 'in those days' – not a serious indication of time, but a loose introductory phrase. The last events mentioned – the return from Egypt and the settlement in Nazareth – would have to be conceived as taking place some twenty-five years before.

(*b*) John's call to repentance is grounded in the proclamation that 'the kingdom of heaven is at hand'; in Mark, this proclamation is not introduced until Jesus begins to preach. Matthew's phrase 'the kingdom of heaven' (literally 'of the Heavens') is not different in meaning from 'the kingdom of God'; it is simply an indication of Matthew's ingrained reluctance, as a Jew, to mention the Name of God, which led to the use of a variety of surrogates ('the Blessed One;

the Holy One; the Majesty in the Heavens', etc.; and sometimes 'Heaven' or 'the Heavens' as here).

(*c*) The circle of interest aroused by John is widened to include 'all the region of the Jordan'.

The Lucan version

(*a*) Luke dates the beginning of his story by multiple chronological indications, such as are often found in official documents of the time. First comes the regnal year of the Emperor, and this is the only date given with precision. The 15th year of the principate of Tiberius would be A.D. 26-27. Luke thus marks at the outset his conviction that there is a significant relationship between world history and the Christian faith, and especially between the world-empire of Rome and the Christian community. Christianity is not alone the heir of Judaism, but of Greece and the hellenized East and the grandeur of Rome.

(*b*) Luke omits Mark's phrase 'all the Judaean country and all the people of Jerusalem', keeps Matthew's addition 'all the region of the Jordan', but represents John as going through this region instead of waiting for the inhabitants to come to him. These observations point to the possibility that Luke has here followed more closely the 'Q' source which he shares with Matthew, while Matthew has made a conflation of this source with Mark. That is to say: if we suppose that the 'Q' source spoke of the word of the Lord coming to John in the wilderness, and of John then going into all the region of the Jordan with his call to repent, this would give us a sufficient explanation for the variations in the Lucan story, and at the same time account for the much less substantial Matthaean differences — Matthew will have done no more than modify the Marcan story by (*a*) putting the message of John in direct narration; (*b*) correcting the citation; and (*c*) adding the phrase 'all the region of the Jordan'. It is more difficult to explain the variations on the hypothesis that Luke has had the text of Matthew itself before him.

(*c*) Luke extends the Isaiah citation, perhaps because he found it thus in his source, perhaps because he himself wished to bring before his readers the promise of a *universal* extension of the Gospel through the words of the last line: 'all flesh shall see the salvation of God'.

2. *John's Preaching of Repentance*

MATTHEW iii. 7-10 LUKE iii. 7-9

(*a*) In their use of 'Q' material, Matthew and Luke seldom reproduce the words with so little variation as here. In the discourse of John, the 63 words of Matthew and the 64 words of Luke (the extra word is *kai*, 'and'), there is not a single variation in order, and only two changes of word, neither of them affecting the sense. The introductions differ, and may well be framed by the Evangelists themselves. In Matthew the words are addressed to 'many of the scribes and Pharisees'; in Luke to 'the multitudes'. The former makes them a rebuke to the religious leaders, and may perhaps be taken as an indication of Matthew's hostility to the Pharisees; the latter makes them a sweeping denunciation of the whole nation — Luke does not regard the scribes and Pharisees alone as unfaithful. It may also be said that Luke, writing for Gentile readers who will know little and care less about the Jewish sects, does not think it worth while to specify the objects of John's rebuke.

(*b*) The following elements in the report of John's preaching may be noted:

(i) 'The wrath to come' — the phrase is taken up into the preaching of Paul: Jesus is the one 'who rescues us from the wrath to come' (1 Thess. i. 10); 'we shall be saved from the wrath through him' (Rom. v. 9). John's preaching is eschatologically orientated: the imminent terrors of the Last Judgment are made the ground of the appeal to repentance.

(ii) The rejection of descent from Abraham as giving immunity from the approaching Judgment. John insists that the relationship to men of God does not depend upon their ancestry, their membership of the holy community of Israel, but on their personal uprightness. There is an implicit universalism here.

(iii) John speaks of a Judgment that will mean no mere purging, but destruction: 'the axe is laid to the root of the trees', and the fruitless tree is doomed to the fire.

3. *John's Sociological Teaching*

LUKE iii. 10-14

This section, found only in Luke, gives brief indications of the concrete injunctions concerning conduct with which John followed up his call to repentance. They throw interesting sidelights on conditions in Palestine: the dire need of people who lack food and clothing; the rapacity of the tax-collectors, who demand more than is due; the notorious conduct of the soldiery.

4. *John's Messianic Preaching*

MATTHEW iii. 11-12 MARK i. 7-8 LUKE iii. 15-18

(*a*) John's prophecy of a greater to come is of course taken in Christian circles as an unmistakable reference to Christ, and his conception of the mission of his greater successor could not fail to be interpreted by Christians in the light of what they knew of the mission which Christ actually exercised.

(*b*) The contrast of the two baptisms, especially when we examine it in the light of the larger context of John's preaching as given by Matthew and Luke, affords evidence of a Christian reinterpretation of this kind. In Mark, the contrast is put as that of 'baptism with water' — 'baptism with holy spirit'; and Mark, like the modern reader, will have in mind the spiritual gifts of enlightenment, of power, of love — much, if not all, of what the reception of the Holy Spirit in baptism had come to mean in the experience of the Church and in the interpretation of Paul. But when we look again at the words in the context of John's warnings of the wrath to come, and take into account the double phrase of Matthew and Luke 'with holy spirit and fire', we are bound to ask ourselves if the contrast was not actually expressed by John as a contrast between a baptism with water, and a baptism with *wind* and fire. In Greek, as in Hebrew, the same word (Gk. *pneuma*; Heb. *ruach*) means either 'wind' or 'spirit'; here the context seems to impose the meaning 'wind'. John has been speaking of a devastating Judgment. He has spoken of fire as the agent of destruction: 'every tree that does not bear good fruit is hewn down and cast into the fire'; and he goes on at once to speak of the minister of the new baptism as one who comes with his winnowing-fan in his hand, to separate the chaff from the wheat, 'and the chaff he will burn with fire unquenchable'. The symbolism of wind and fire, it would appear, is used by John to indicate the all-consuming thoroughness of the imminent Judgment — the 'baptism with wind and fire' is nothing else than 'the wrath to come'. It is the figure of a dreadful ordeal, not of a blessing. For John, both the baptisms of which he spoke — that which he himself was administering, and that which the Coming One was to administer — will have been conceived as figures of judgment; the willing acceptance of the lesser purging by water, signifying repentance and amendment of life, through his baptism, would deliver men from the devastating judgment by wind and fire which the Coming One would bring upon the world. This was the manner in which John envisaged the mission of the Messiah; and it is not surprising that he was disillusioned by what he heard in his prison of the actual activities of Jesus, and sent to ask: 'Art thou He that should come, or do we look for another?' For Jesus came not to condemn, but to save.

It is not hard to see how, in Christian tradition, the words of John could be altered to convey what Christians had come to regard as the fundamental distinction between the baptism of John and Christian baptism. The transposition was facilitated not only by the accident of language — the fact that the word *pneuma* had the double sense, and could be taken to mean either 'wind' or 'spirit' — but also by the fact that in Christian usage both wind and fire were symbols of the Holy Spirit. John's prediction of a devastating baptism by wind and fire could therefore easily become transformed in the handling of the Church into a foretelling of the regenerative baptism with the Holy Spirit which was actually experienced in every conversion.

5. *John's Imprisonment*

LUKE iii. 19-20

Luke does not tell the story of John's execution, which Mark and Matthew have introduced at a later stage of the narrative. In place of that, he rounds off his account of John by noting here the fact of his imprisonment by Herod.

Jesus Begins His Ministry

§§ 6-17

6. *The Baptism of Christ*

MATTHEW iii. 13-17 MARK i. 9-11 LUKE iii. 21-22

At this point we take up again the Marcan narrative, which is the basis of the narratives of Matthew and Luke, each using it in his own way. As Mark's story stands, it moves naively on from the description of John's baptism as a 'baptism of repentance for the remission of sins', to the statement that 'Jesus came from Nazareth of Galilee and was baptized in the Jordan by John'. It cannot be supposed that Mark himself was capable of thinking that this baptism was for Jesus a baptism of repentance for the remission of sins; he stands too firmly within the frame of the Christian belief that Jesus was without sin. It never occurred to him that any problem was involved for Christian readers in Jesus' acceptance of such a baptism. But Matthew is acutely aware of the difficulty, and represents John himself as protesting that Jesus has no need of his baptism. The reply of Jesus to John's remonstrance indicates that in his case the action is not a purging of sin, but a fulfilment of righteousness. This Matthaean insertion can hardly be regarded as anything but a fragment of Christian apologetic, devised to explain how the Sinless One could have come to John's baptism. At the same time it bears upon a second aspect of apologetic: the matter of how the greater could receive baptism at the hands of the lesser; as elsewhere, John himself is made to acknowledge his subordination to Christ. In Luke there is no such obvious recognition of the difficulty which the scene involves, but it is subtly eased by the phrasing of verse 21 — Jesus participates in a rite which is being administered to all the people; and still more by the (grammatical) subordination of everything else in the narrative to the unique experience of Jesus himself, which is undoubtedly the focal point of all three versions — the opening of the heavens, the descent of the Dove, and the Voice from heaven which reveals that Jesus is the Son of God.

In Mark this experience is represented as given to Jesus alone: it is he alone who sees the opening of the heavens and the descending Dove, and hears the Voice; and the words of revelation are addressed to him. In Matthew it is he alone who sees the Dove descending; but the remainder of the phrasing is so changed as to suggest that what took place was seen and heard by all: the words become a proclamation to all, not an assurance to Jesus. In Luke the impression of objectivity is still more pronounced; it is even said that the Spirit descends *in bodily form* as a Dove; yet the words of the Voice are again addressed to Jesus alone.

We must notice the striking textual variant in the Lucan version of the pronouncement from heaven. The better text appears to be that which cites the second Psalm: 'Thou art my Son; this day have I begotten thee.' But we may observe here one of very many instances of a tendency to *assimilation* in the text of the Gospels: here most of our best manuscripts and versions give the corresponding text of Mark: 'Thou art my beloved Son; in thee I am well pleased.' It should be said that the assimilation of readings in Luke or Matthew to the text of Mark occurs relatively seldom.

The story of the Baptism raises in our minds tantalizing questions, especially in relation to the 'Messianic' consciousness of Jesus. Did he at this time become conscious — or become conscious in a new way — of a unique relationship to God? Was the experience which accompanied the baptism of a mystical nature? Did he interpret it as a call from God to enter upon a public ministry of preaching? These and the many other questions that arise for us are more easily asked than answered. We have not the means of penetrating to the inner personality of Jesus, and we discern only dimly — if, indeed, we can discern at all — the manner in which he apprehended his relationship to the Father. Of *development* in his personality, or in his understanding of his mission, or in his apprehension of his relationship to God, we cannot speak at all; and we should be reluctant to give free play to our imaginations.

7. *The Genealogy of Christ*

LUKE iii. 23-38

This is the point at which Luke has chosen to introduce his genealogy. The details of this artificial *schema* need not concern us. The note that Jesus was about thirty years of age when he began his ministry agrees with the indications that he was born during the last years of Herod the Great (d. 4 B.C.), and that we have now come to the fifteenth year of the Emperor Tiberius (A.D. 26-27). The carrying of the genealogy right back to Adam is a token of Luke's conviction that the mission of Jesus embraces the entire human race; it is related to Paul's doctrine of Christ as the Second Man.

8. *The Temptation*

MATTHEW iv. 1-11 MARK i. 12-13 LUKE iv. 1-13

In Mark and Matthew, the Temptation follows directly upon the Baptism, and thus leaves the impression that the two experiences are closely connected — the Temptation is related to Jesus' understanding of what the Baptism means for him, or perhaps to his decision to respond to the call to ministry which it involves. By inserting his genealogy at this point, Luke has effectively broken the association between the two stories, perhaps of set purpose.

Here Matthew and Luke again exhibit a remarkably close agreement, though it falls far short of the verbal exactitude of § 2, and the order of the second and third temptations is transposed. They show little dependence on the brief Marcan narrative — perhaps none at all, apart from Matthew's use of the phrase: 'angels ministered to him.'

Mark offers no indication of the nature of the temptation, except to say that Jesus was being tempted by Satan. He alone mentions the 'wild beasts', and it is not clear what significance he attaches to them. Are they tamed by the presence of Jesus, in token of the restoration of peace which he is to accomplish in the whole realm of nature (cf. e.g. Isa. xi. 6f.)? Or are they embodied spirits of evil, as in the legends of the desert saints? Mark seems to picture the ministry of the angels and the assaults of Satan as continuing together throughout the period; in Luke, Jesus is undergoing temptation continuously; in Matthew, the devil makes his approach only at the end of the forty days, when Jesus is suffering the pangs of hunger. In Luke, the angels are not introduced at all; in Matthew, they appear when the temptations have been victoriously surmounted.

It is held by many commentators that in the account of the temptations which appears in Matthew and Luke, we have a fragment of spiritual autobiography — that Jesus himself has told the story of his conflict with the

Enemy of God in these terms. Others think of it rather as the imaginative creation of a gifted teacher, who thus supplied the lack of any tradition. In either case, the story is cast in the form of myth, with elements of allegory; as Origen pointed out more than seventeen hundred years ago, no one in his senses would suppose that he should take literally the statement that the devil showed Jesus all the kingdoms of the world in a moment of time, when it would not be possible to see even the whole of Palestine from the highest peak. The significance of the temptations appears to be twofold: (i) Jesus is tempted to doubt that he is in fact the Son of God, and to ask for outward signs or assurances; and (ii) he is tempted to fulfil the mission to which God has called him by means which God has not appointed — as by acknowledging the authority of the devil over the kingdoms of the world and agreeing to rule them as vicegerent for him.

There is no reason to doubt that the presuppositions of the story were accepted by Jesus as by his Jewish contemporaries and by the early Church in general. Satan and the kingdom of demons over which he ruled were a grim reality to them, and they believed that these evil powers stood behind the earthly rulers of the nations. The work of Jesus was seen as the decisive victory over these powers, and the story of the Temptation in all its forms is told not as a sidelight on the inner experience of Jesus, but as a symbol and an anticipation of the victory which was to be consummated on the Cross. If the Matthaean-Lucan story be indeed in any sense autobiographical, it may be taken to throw some light on the workings of Jesus' mind as he entered upon his ministry; but no such psychological interest entered into its use by the Church or gave it its place in the Gospel story; and we must feel that it is precarious to read in it an answer to modern questions which never entered the minds of the narrators.

The responses of Jesus to the Tempter are all given in sentences from the book of Deuteronomy. In a wider sense, the whole story corresponds typologically to the central theme of the first part of Deuteronomy — the demand for whole-hearted, undivided allegiance to the one living and true God, on the one hand; and the testing of Israel's loyalty by the trials of life in the wilderness, on the other. Jesus is himself Israel; the people of God is represented in the person of Israel's appointed King; and he recapitulates in himself the spiritual experience of Israel, with the perfect obedience and the unbroken loyalty to God which Israel had failed to exhibit. He was tempted in all points like as we are, but without sin. He alone has steadfastly refused to worship other gods, or to tempt God; and he alone has obeyed entirely the command: 'Thou shalt love the Lord thy God with all thy heart, and with all thy soul, and with all thy mind.'

9. *The First Preaching in Galilee*

MATTHEW iv. 12-17   MARK i. 14-15   LUKE iv. 14-15

In all three Gospels, this section marks the opening of the public Ministry of Jesus in Galilee, and none gives the slightest indication that there has been an earlier period of activity in Judaea, such as is described in the Fourth

Gospel (John i. 35-51; ii. 13-iii. 36; especially iii. 24). The three accounts show little verbal similarity. Matthew has reworded the Marcan verses, and has taken occasion again to point to the fulfilment of prophecy. It is striking to observe that his citation of Isaiah (ix. 1-2) is independent of the LXX, yet handles the opening phrases of the Hebrew text somewhat freely. The oracle originally referred to the advance of the Assyrians to the Mediterranean ('the way of the sea'), and promised that a Deliverer would arise to free the territories from the marauders, and so to bring light into the dark shadows of their existence as captives. Matthew applies 'the sea' of the prophecy to the lake of Galilee, and sees the promise of the Deliverer fulfilled in the appearance of Jesus in Capernaum and the inauguration of his public ministry. 'To Matthew the words have a splendid application; the same district lay in spiritual darkness and death, and a new era dawned when Christ went thither' (McNeile, *St. Matthew*, ad loc.).

Both Mark and Matthew relate the opening of the Ministry of Jesus to the imprisonment of John; when one divine messenger is silenced, a greater takes up the message and carries it farther abroad. In Luke, the imprisonment of John is not mentioned at this point, and the section simply lays the groundwork for the narrative of the Rejection at Nazareth (§ 10).

General questions of the first importance for our whole understanding of the mission and message of Jesus are involved in the interpretation which we give to the terms of this first preaching. 'The time is fulfilled': Mark's phrase is not taken up by either of the others, but it will be recalled that Matthew has been sounding the note of fulfilment from the very beginning, and has used it here in a particular application (*v.* 14); and Luke is about to use it in another application in the following section (*v.* 21). It is one of the cardinal assumptions of all the New Testament writers that the coming of Jesus has taken place at the appointed time: 'When the fulness of the time came, God sent forth his Son' (Gal. iv. 4). It is the time of the fulfilment of God's promises of redemption: to quote St. Paul once again: 'All the promises of God are in him, Yes' — affirmed and confirmed, and acknowledged by us as true: 'Therefore through him the Amen is said to God, for his glory, through us' (2 Cor. i. 20).

'The kingdom of God (or, of the heavens) is at hand.' The Greek verb *ēggiken* means literally 'has come near'; but the perfect may have rather the sense 'is here'. The question is whether Jesus is represented as proclaiming that the kingdom of God is soon to be established ('is at hand'), or that it has actually been inaugurated with his appearance. Philology alone will not enable us to give a definitive answer; the Greek verb is capable of carrying either sense, and we are not greatly helped in this instance by an effort to go back to the underlying Aramaic in which the words were first uttered. The decision must rest upon the total interpretation of the teachings of Jesus and the beliefs of the early Church at which we finally arrive.

But what does Jesus mean by 'the kingdom of God', which according to the Synoptic tradition was the central theme of all his teaching? It is one of the conceptions which he inherited from Judaism, and it belongs in its earliest Christian usage to the pattern of thinking about God and the world which had developed in the last two or three centuries before Christ. In the canonical Old

Testament, it is represented chiefly by the book of Daniel – in its present form a product of the second century before Christ; but it is given expression in a wide range of apocalyptic works which never received canonical recognition. These apocalyptic writers, building upon the foundations of classical Hebrew prophecy, and influenced by Persian (Zoroastrian) dualism, in an historical situation which afforded no grounds for hope for the restoration of Israel as an independent state, rose above despair by an unquenchable faith in God. They saw the present age as an age governed by powers of evil – great world-empires which kept the people of God under the yoke and were themselves the instruments of the rule of Satan (or Beliar; the name given to the prince of evil varies) and the hosts of demons whom he controlled. But the future lies with God. This age is given over to the rule of Satan and the demons; but 'the age to come' is the age of God's triumph. At the end of this age, God will intervene to overthrow the entire dominion of evil; and then he will give the kingdom to his saints. There is no thought here of positive elements of good gaining the upper hand over the elements of evil in human society, to bring order and peace and plenty and justice for all through the processes of human history; the apocalyptists entertain no hope of this kind at all. They despair utterly and absolutely of history, and put their hope wholly in a catastrophic intervention of God who will bring this age to an end in final judgment, and will then establish his own kingdom on earth. The expectation does not always include the figure of a Messiah; some of the seers think of God himself as ruling without any intermediary.

The proclamation that 'the kingdom of God is at hand' (or 'is here') must be understood against this background of apocalyptic eschatology. It means the end of history – the near approach (or, the actual inauguration) of 'the age to come'. It is accordingly a message at once of hope and of warning: the good times promised by the ancient prophets are at the door, but the people of God are not worthy to have part in them. The proclamation of the kingdom must therefore be also a call to repentance, made all the more urgent by the shortness of the time that remains.

10. *The Rejection at Nazareth*

Luke iv. 16-30

Luke here departs from the Marcan outline, and uses a version of the story which appears to have been transmitted independently. Mark, with Matthew following him, does not introduce the story of the Rejection of Jesus at Nazareth until much later (see § 108). In Luke it follows immediately upon the Temptation, and is thus made the opening scene of the public Ministry. It is evident from the story itself that Luke's arrangement is chronologically wrong; for reference is made to a ministry at Capernaum – a city which Luke has not yet mentioned – which has been marked by works of healing (*v.* 23). We must therefore seek the motive of Luke's rearrangement in something other than chronology; and we may even remark that it is one of our first indications of a certain indifference to chronology on the part of the Evangelists. The motive is probably literary, and even more, theological. In Luke's treatment, the story becomes a preview of the whole mission of Jesus, foreshadowing the refusal of his own people of Israel to respond to his Gospel, and the transference of the blessing to the Gentiles. It may be designed as a companion piece to the Temptation, the two stories constituting a kind of double frontispiece — the one depicting the victory over Satan in the fundamental spiritual conflict; the other symbolizing the extension of the Gospel to the Gentile world in contrast with its rejection by the Jews.

There is almost no verbal similarity between the Lucan story and the narrative of Mark, so that we have no reason to hold that Luke has drawn upon Mark here at all. Yet there can be no doubt that it is the same incident; we have the same picture of Jesus' preaching in the synagogue of his home town; the same objection, that this local boy, this child of the village carpenter, cannot be taken seriously; and the introduction of the same proverb, that no prophet is honoured at home. Luke's version adds local colour (*vv.* 16-17), supplies (perhaps out of Luke's own imagination) the text of the reading from the prophets and of the sermon; the rather puzzling proverb; 'Physician, heal thyself', with its incongruous interpretation as meaning a challenge to heal people in Nazareth as he has in Capernaum; the whole of the analogy with the experience of Elijah and Elisha as prophets whose ministry extended beyond Israel; and the heightening of the hostility to Jesus into the attempt to murder him. It will also be observed that there is something awkward about the transition from the friendliness and admiration of the people which is first indicated (*v.* 22), to the implication in the words of Jesus which immediately follow, that he is in fact encountering doubt and even scorn. This suggests strongly that Luke has conflated two stories of the mission of Jesus in Nazareth, one of which represented him as winning the plaudits of his townsfolk, while the other (in agreement with Mark) told of a frosty reception. The furious climax of the story, in the attempt of the mob to throw him over the edge of a cliff, with the vague suggestion of a miraculous escape from their hands, has no parallel in the Marcan story, and is probably to be viewed as a bit of legendary enhancement.

11. *The Call of the First Disciples*

MATTHEW iv. 18-22 MARK i. 16-20

Matthew here keeps to the order and very closely to the wording of Mark; Luke again uses a different version of the story and transfers it to a different place in his account of the ministry (see § 17).

The version which we have here is strangely succinct. No indication is given of anything leading up to the call; there is no suggestion that any of the called have seen or heard Jesus before. He calls them to follow him; and they obey, without hesitation, abandoning their business, their gear, and their families. Probably for the Evangelists and for the Christian circles which preserved the story for their use, no more was necessary — they were not interested in the psychology of conversion, or of the call to the apostolate, but only in the power of the word of Jesus to call men into his service and in the response of obedience. In the Fourth Gospel, James and John are never mentioned; but the first disciples, who include Peter and Andrew, are directed to Jesus by John the Baptist, and there is no reference to this call from the lakeside in Galilee. But there is nothing to suggest that Mark (and Matthew) had ever heard of this earlier meeting between Jesus and these disciples. Nothing of the sort is presupposed or felt to be necessary.

'I will make you fishers of men.' The figure is not used elsewhere of the apostolic office; it is replaced by that of the shepherd. It belongs to the immediate situation, to the occupation of the individuals concerned, and it does not pass into Christian usage. It is not clear in what sense the task which the disciples are to undertake is analogous to fishing. This is one of many instances in which the familiarity of the words keeps us from realizing that their significance is not at all clear. It is perhaps legitimate to interpret the figure here in the light of the parable of the Drag-net (§ 102), which Matthew takes to be a parable of the Last Judgment, but which may have been in the first instance a parable of the appeal of the Gospel to all sorts and conditions of men. In that case the task of the disciples as fishers will be a parallel to the figure of the reapers sent out to gather in the harvest.

Note, however, that in Jeremiah xvi. 16, the sending of fishers (and hunters) is a threat against Israel — a figure of the execution of divine judgment upon the nation that has polluted the land.

It seems to me to be in the highest degree unlikely, as both Dibelius and Bultmann hold, that the tradition preserved only the words of the Call, with some indication of the persons addressed, and that Mark has constructed an ideal scene to fit the words. This strange figure — 'fishers of men' — to which there is no real parallel in earlier literature and which was never taken up into general Christian usage, could not have survived except as a fragment of genuine reminiscence and could hardly have been transmitted except in the context of the scene to which it belongs — a scene of fishermen at their daily tasks. Nor is there any justification for Lohmeyer's assertion that 'it is written in the style of an Epiphany-story' (*Markus*, p. 33); this can be nothing but an unconscious transference of sentiment from the Lucan version of the Call (§ 17).

12. *Christ in the Synagogue at Capernaum*

MARK i. 21-28 LUKE iv. 31-37

Before taking up § 12 in itself, we must first observe that the material which follows is handled quite differently in Matthew and in Mark. In Mark we now come upon a series of stories which are fairly closely linked together (§§ 12-16), as the account of a day in Capernaum which makes Jesus famous as a healer throughout the whole countryside and leads to his departure from the city by the lake to undertake a preaching tour through all Galilee. With this, § 45 is closely connected also, as the story of the healing of a leper, which so enhances the reputation of Jesus as to make it impossible for him to go into the villages, because of the numbers that gather round him. The whole sequence gives a brilliant picture of a swift and growing popularity — an outburst of popular enthusiasm occasioned by the miracles of healing, which Jesus appears to find more embarrassing than gratifying. In Matthew some of this material is not used at all, and the rest of it is rearranged. The first incident — the exorcism at Capernaum — is omitted; and the Sermon on the Mount (Matt. v-vii) is introduced at that point; § 16, Mark's account of the preaching tour in Galilee which follows the events of the day at Capernaum, is advanced to follow directly upon the call of the first disciples, and becomes a setting for the delivery of the great Sermon. § 15 is omitted. §§ 13 and 14 are retained, but transferred to a later stage of the ministry (§§ 47 and 48); and the story of the healing of the leper becomes the immediate sequel to the Sermon.

Luke, we find once again, follows Mark where Matthew diverges from him; through §§ 12-16 he keeps to the Marcan sequence with minor verbal changes. In § 17, he gives us a different version of the call of the first disciples, and places it *after* the events of the day in Capernaum and the preaching tour through Galilee.

The story of Christ in the Synagogue (§ 12) is not used at all by Matthew; he takes only one verse from it and uses it in a different context, as a concluding comment on the Sermon on the Mount. The Marcan story speaks of the impression made by the teaching of Jesus: 'they were astonished by his teaching; for he was teaching them as one with authority, and not as the scribes' (Luke alters this to: 'for his word was with power'). But Mark gives no inkling of the substance of this teaching which gave such an impression of power — he passes on at once to his account of the exorcism of an evil spirit. Matthew seems to have felt that before mentioning the effectiveness of the teaching, he should give his readers a comprehensive sample of it. He therefore introduces at this point the great collection of sayings of Jesus which is known to us as the Sermon on the Mount; and it is only after this has been put before us that he brings in the phrases of Mark to describe its effect upon the hearers (§ 44, Matt. vii. 28-29).

The alterations made by Luke in the Marcan story are mainly stylistic. He omits Mark's repeated *euthus* ('immediately'), changes the phrasing which describes the man's affliction ('spirit of an unclean demon' for 'an unclean spirit'), and makes a few other slight variations in the wording; but the greater part of the passage follows Mark word for word.

The exorcism itself is puzzling to the modern reader, in that it presupposes the ancient belief that illness, especially mental illness, was caused by demon possession. The belief in demons was all but universal at this time; it had extended from the Oriental world into the Greek, and was by no means confined to the uneducated but was held even by men of philosophical training. Jesus is a child of his time and takes for granted this notion of a world filled with demons. The nature of the man's affliction is not evident. Evidently he feels himself to be inwardly divided; so that he speaks of himself in the plural, as if a number of personalities were fighting within him. The presupposition of the story is that he is possessed by a number of demons. They recognize Jesus as the divine agent of their destruction, 'the Holy One of God'. The words of

Jesus are spoken as to a single demon, and the demon is regarded as responsible for the loud shout which the man utters as he falls on the ground in a fit of some kind. It will be observed that the narrator takes no further interest in the man, who is apparently still lying on the floor of the synagogue; but notes only the effect upon the people, who are lost in admiration and wonder.

13. *The Healing of Peter's Wife's Mother*

(MATTHEW viii. 14-15) MARK i. 29-31 LUKE iv. 38-39

Matthew has transferred this Marcan story to a later stage, and has abbreviated it. The changes made by Luke are mainly stylistic, but his postponement of the story of the call of the first disciples has led him to cut out the mention of Andrew, and of James and John, who have not yet appeared in this gospel. Simon is here mentioned for the first time; Luke evidently assumes that he will not need any introduction to the readers. The change of wording made by Luke in *v.* 39a indicates that he thinks of the fever as evidence of the presence of a demon, which Jesus rebukes; but the same notion is latent in Mark's expression, 'the fever left her', which Luke retains unchanged. The healing is instantaneous and complete; the woman feels no weakness from the effects of the fever, but is able to take up her tasks at once.

14. *The Sick healed at Evening*

(MATTHEW viii. 16-17) MARK i. 32-34 LUKE iv. 40-41

Mark is clearly again the source of both Matthew and Luke. Matthew has transferred the story, together with the one which precedes it, to another place (see §§ 47 and 48), and has abbreviated it; he has also added, after his way, a reference to the fulfilment of prophecy in the ministry of Jesus (*v.* 17). Luke has rewritten the passage with some freedom; like Matthew, he has omitted some of Mark's colour, notably the picture of the whole town gathered at the door; he has added the feature of the laying on of Jesus' hands, and has heightened the effectiveness of the cures, from the 'many' of Mark to 'each one' (cf. Matthew's 'all'). He has also made more graphic the recognition of Jesus by the demons, who shriek before him and cry 'You are the Son of God.' His last phrase 'they knew him to be the Christ' (i.e. Messiah) indicates that he takes 'Son of God' and 'Christ' to be equivalent titles. His changes are substantial enough to raise the question whether he has not in fact had at his disposal an independent version of the story; but the fact that he is here keeping to a Marcan sequence inclines us rather to conclude that he is simply rewriting Mark.

15. *Jesus departs from Capernaum*

MARK i. 35-38 LUKE iv. 42-43

Matthew omits this section entirely. The changes made by Luke are occasioned in great part by the fact that he has not yet provided Jesus with a band of disciples. In Mark, 'Simon and those with him' (i.e., the other fishermen whom Jesus has called to follow him) are already assuming a closer relationship to him, and make themselves the spokesmen of the people generally. In Luke they have not yet acquired this distinctive position, and it is 'the multitudes' who seek him out and beg him not to go away. The same consideration determines the change in the words of Jesus as reported: to his disciples Jesus can say, 'Let us go elsewhere ... that I may preach there also': to 'the multitudes' he can only say, 'I must go ... to preach the kingdom of God.' At the end, Luke changes Mark's verb, 'I came forth' to 'I was sent'; this is an interpretative alteration, which makes clear what was probably intended by Mark also, that Jesus is acting as the envoy of God. It is significant that even in Mark, who seems occupied chiefly with the miraculous healings which Jesus is accomplishing, the tradition reflects almost without his awareness of it that Jesus himself regarded the ministry of preaching and teaching as his primary task. He will not remain in Capernaum to exploit the fame that has come to him through the swift-spreading report of his healings. In fact he seems almost embarrassed by the acquisition of such a reputation, and is eager to get back to the main task of preaching. Note that Luke again interprets Mark by changing the simple verb 'preach' (the verb actually means 'make proclamation' as a herald) to the more specific 'preach the good news of the kingdom of God'.

16. *A Preaching Journey in Galilee*

MATTHEW iv. 23 MARK i. 39 LUKE iv. 44

together with

MATTHEW iv. 24-25 MARK iii. 10, 7, 8 LUKE vi. 18, 19, 17

In Mark and Luke, only the one verse of this section is used at this point of the story, and it is really the conclusion of the preceding section, noting simply that Jesus carried out the programme of preaching which he had proposed. Luke surprisingly alters the scene of the preaching from Galilee to Judaea; this is probably a matter of inadvertence, since Luke's next story is again laid in Galilee. The manuscript evidence shows that a number of good scribes have corrected the text to conform with the situation. The verses from Mark iii and Luke vi which are included in the section are given as parallels to the additional material introduced by Matthew, who has here suggested a wide enlargement of the area to which the news of Jesus has spread. 'Into the whole of Syria' is probably somewhat hyperbolical, though it is a fact that rumours of the appearance of a great new *hakim* can spread far and rapidly in the eastern countries to this day. (Rumour would also exaggerate the scope of the healings.) Of the additional Matthaean material found here, only *v.* 25 shows clear verbal dependence on the later Marcan passage (Mark iii. 7-8); but his phrase 'the whole of Syria' (*v.* 24) may represent Mark's 'around Tyre and Sidon.' Note that the words of Matthew's *v.* 25 are used by him again, with the one change of 'in the whole of Galilee' to 'all the cities and villages', in ix. 35, where it becomes part of his introduction to the sending out of the disciples (§ 58). Here his purpose seems to have been to frame an introduction to the Sermon on the Mount; 'the multitudes' who have gathered to hear Jesus are represented as coming from all parts of the Holy Land and even beyond. Note further that in Matthew we have not yet encountered any narrative of a healing; but he makes here some sweeping statements about the number and variety of the healing activities of Jesus; the particular episodes are held in reserve until after the Sermon.

17. *The Miraculous Draught of Fishes*

Luke v. 1-11

This is Luke's version of the story of the call of the first disciples, which has been told by Mark and Matthew in a different form and introduced at an earlier point (§ 11). This is the first appearance of Simon in this gospel, though Jesus has already been in his house and has healed his wife's mother of a fever (§ 13 – Simon is not said to be present). None of the other disciples has yet been named.

The picture of Jesus teaching from the prow of a fishing-boat while the crowds stand listening on the shore is used by Mark (and in dependence on him, by Matthew also) as the setting for the Parable of the Sower (§ 90); as Luke has used it here, he omits it at that point. The legend of the Miraculous Draught of Fishes is found in a different form in the Fourth Gospel, where it opens a cycle of Resurrection-narratives (John xxi). In both forms it is primarily a Peter-story; the role of the other disciples is subordinated to that of Peter (Simon, as he is called here). In Luke's story, Simon holds the centre of the stage along with Jesus; Jesus addresses his words to him alone, and he alone speaks to Jesus. The other disciples are silent, and all but anonymous; Andrew is not mentioned at all, and James and John are mentioned by name as a kind of afterthought, when the story is over (*v.* 10); it may well be that the story as Luke found it did not mention them except as 'the partners in the other boat' (*v.* 7), and that the names are the one element which Luke has taken from the Marcan story of the Call.

In the Lucan as in the Johannine form, this is clearly the story of an epiphany. Jesus reveals himself as a divine being, and therefore Simon is seized with terror and with the sense of sinfulness which makes him unfit to bear the divine presence (*v.* 8). Compare Isaiah vi. 4: 'Woe is me, for I am undone, for I am a man of unclean lips ... and mine eyes have seen the King, the Lord of Hosts.' In the Marcan narrative, the divinity of Jesus remains hidden from the disciples until a much later stage; he is recognized only by the demons, and he commands them to be silent.

THE SERMON ON THE MOUNT

§§ 18-44

MATTHEW v, vi, vii

If we glance rapidly through the Index of Parallels of these 27 sections (Huck-Lietzmann-Cross, p. xiv), we cannot fail to be struck with the distribution of the parallels in Mark and Luke. First of all we note that several large sections have no parallel in either of the other Gospels (§§ 21, 22, 23, 25, 28, 29, 31, 37); and in several other sections the parallelism which exists extends to only a part of the Matthaean material. A substantial portion of the great Sermon is drawn from a source, or sources, used by Matthew alone. Secondly, we note that Mark's gospel includes no such sermon at all; the Marcan parallels that can be cited (two verses in § 24 and one [possibly two] in § 30; together with a few brief partial parallels to vv. 13a, 15; vi. 29-30) are found in quite different contexts. Thirdly, and most important, we find that in Luke there is a Sermon which begins in the same way, with a group of Beatitudes; ends in the same way, with the Parable of the Two Houses; and includes, with no more than minor differences of order, large parts of six of the intervening sections (§§ 26, 27, 36, 39, 41, 42; cf. §§ 73-78). But there is a great deal more parallel material which Luke has employed in entirely different contexts, in chapters xi, xii, xiii, xiv, and xvi, and in a quite different sequence.

These considerations would be enough in themselves to show us that the Sermon on the Mount is a *compilation* of sayings, which Jesus delivered at different times and at different places. The time and the circumstances of the delivery of any particular saying or group of sayings can no longer be determined. (We shall have to take into account the possibility that sayings from other sources than Jesus might be included in such a compilation.) Even the general setting is different in Luke, who transfers the scene from the mountain to the plain (Luke vi. 17a), and postpones its delivery until after the appointment of the Twelve, which Matthew will recount at the beginning of his tenth chapter. It appears, then, that in the Sermon on the Mount we have a collection of sayings put together for the first time in this form by Matthew, as a comprehensive account of the ethical teaching of Jesus (though this is a loose and inaccurate description). He probably had before him as its core a collection roughly comparable to the 'Sermon on the Plain' of Luke vi. 20-49. But he was preparing a work which was to serve (among other purposes) as a manual for Christian instruction; and he therefore brought together all the sayings which seemed to him to bear upon the general theme — the life of man under the Rule of God; the New Law of the Christian society. Jesus is to him, under one aspect at least, the new Moses; and as the old law was given through Moses from Mount Sinai, so the New Law is given by Christ from 'the mountain' (v. 1). If we ask 'what mountain?' we shall receive no answer; for this mountain is not a geographical location, but the place of revelation. As well send a mountaineering expedition to look for the 'Vulture Peak' in Nepal, from which the Buddha delivered the Sutras.

We shall find, as we go on, that Matthew has carried through this conception of Jesus as the new Moses, and his teaching as the New Law, to the point of arranging his gospel in five books, centring around five discourses or groups of sayings, corresponding to the Five Books of Moses, which constituted the Jewish 'Torah'. Each of these five discourses ends with a formula, akin to that which Matthew uses at the end of the Sermon: 'When Jesus had finished these sayings' (vii. 28; cf. xi. 1; xiii. 53; xix. 1; xxvi. 1).

To whom are the sayings of the Sermon addressed? The question is of no little moment, for it raises the problem of whether we are to understand the teaching of Jesus as a general ethic, universally applicable, or as a way of perfection, intended only for those who have already become his disciples and have pledged themselves to his obedience. Unfortunately both the Evangelists leave some ambiguity. Matthew tells us at the beginning that 'his disciples came to him, and he opened his mouth and taught them'; but he has already told us that Jesus, 'seeing the multitudes, went up on the mountain', and at the end he will use Mark's phrase: 'the multitudes were astonished at his teaching, for he was teaching them as one having authority, and not as their scribes' (vii. 28; from Mark i. 22, word for word). Accordingly Jesus is said to be addressing his disciples, but 'the multitudes' evidently take it that his teaching has authority for them also. Similarly Luke seems to indicate even more specifically that the words are addressed directly to the disciples (vi. 20), but even so he notes at the conclusion that 'Jesus had completed all these sayings in the hearing of the people' (vii. 1). This at least may be said with confidence, that the whole ethical teaching of Jesus is fundamentally and basically *religious*; it is rooted and grounded, not in man, with his possibilities and his weaknesses, but in God. There is simply no basis here for a 'natural' morality, or for a 'scientific' ethic, which would have to begin with an examination of man and his life in himself and in the society of his fellows. For Jesus, the life of man is dependent upon God; the hopes which he sets before man as the supreme end of human life are hopes which only God can fulfil. Man must 'seek first the kingdom of God and his righteousness' (Matt. vi. 33), before even concerning himself with the elementary needs of food and clothing. The kind of life which Jesus commends is therefore only intelligible in a context of discipleship, and his teaching is bound to be regarded as inapplicable, as quite impracticable, as a pattern for a life that does not commit itself to God in faith and hope. The very ambiguity of the Evangelists has thus its own truth. Only those who will commit themselves to Jesus as his disciples can find meaning and direction in his counsels for life; and the notion that the Sermon on the Mount can provide the basis of a high morality independent of religion is nothing but hypocritical nonsense; yet at the same time this is no esoteric teaching, but a searching challenge also to the uncommitted 'multitudes' to turn and be healed.

In a more formal approach, of course, we might observe that once it is realized that the Sermon is not the report of a single discourse, but a compilation of sayings, it becomes unnecessary to suppose that all parts of it were originally intended for the same kind of hearer. The Beatitudes, especially in the Lucan form, are addressed primarily to the disciples; the concluding parable is equally clearly a warning to the uncommitted, to those who listen to Jesus but fail to accept his words as the foundation on which they will build their lives. Nevertheless, it will be found that the greater part of the teaching in the Sermon presupposes that the hearers stand in some degree of professed discipleship to Jesus.

But the most important observation that we are led to make as we examine the sayings in parallelism is that the words of Jesus were preserved and transmitted with a remarkable degree of freedom. They were not committed rigidly to memory. The Jewish rabbis, we are told, trained their disciples to memorize the wise words of their master; and there is a well-known tribute of a rabbi to one of his disciples, that 'he was like a well-plastered cistern that loses not a drop' (a left-handed compliment, but the good rabbi's sarcasm has missed fire). But Jesus did not impose upon his disciples any such technique of learning by rote, and it is seldom that any of his sayings have been reported in the same form of words by any two of the Evangelists. For examples, we may take the Beatitudes and the Lord's Prayer. The four Beatitudes given by Luke (vi. 20-23) are quite unmistakably a variant form of four of the (eight) Matthaean Beatitudes (Matt. v. 3, 6, 7, 10-12) even to the supplementary injunction to 'Rejoice, ... for great is your reward in heaven.' Yet the differences in the wording are very considerable, and far too great to be explained as the result of differences in the rendering of the Aramaic of Jesus into Greek. There is an *interpretative* element in the version which we find in Matthew; and the sayings have been generalized — all but the last one — by a shift from the second person (as in Luke) to the third. The Lord's Prayer, above all, which we might expect to preserve its original wording exactly, if anything did, we find before us in two surprisingly different versions (Matt. vi. 9-13; Luke xi. 2-4), that of Luke being substantially shorter. The followers of Jesus were never trained to rehearse a stereotyped tradition;[1] even the tradition of the words of Jesus was not stereotyped at any stage of its transmission for which we have any evidence.

18. *Introduction to the Sermon*

MATTHEW v. 1-2 LUKE vi. 12, 20

Note that the omission of the intervening verses of Luke (13-19) conceals the fact that in the Lucan version Jesus is no longer on the mountain; he has, in the meantime, appointed the Twelve and given them the title of 'Apostles'; and has then come down with them to take his stand upon a level place.

19. *The Beatitudes*

MATTHEW v. 3-12 LUKE vi. 20-23

We observe to begin with that the Matthaean sequence of Beatitudes is much longer than the Lucan. Not only does Matthew include more Beatitudes — eight (superficially, nine) in place of Luke's four — but he has also made

[1] There is a great saying of B. F. Westcott: 'Thank God, we are not called to rehearse a stereotyped tradition, but to unfold a growing message.'

significant additions to the first and second of Luke's sayings, and has given the fourth of them in a double form; for Matthew's eighth Beatitude (*v.* 10) is simply a generalized form of Luke's fourth, which Matthew repeats (*vv.* 11-12) in a form closer to the Lucan, adopting for this one saying the direct address in the second person, which Luke has used throughout the sequence. Luke's third Beatitude is probably to be regarded as the parallel to the second in Matthew's series; but either it rests upon a different translation of the Aramaic used by Jesus, or else once again Matthew has taken the freedom to interpret, in place of using a literal rendering. Without undertaking an analysis in detail, we may say that the comparison indicates that the main differences between the two sequences are probably to be attributed to the editorial work of Matthew. He has enlarged the collection from four to eight; he has transposed all eight into the third person, thus generalizing their application; and he has changed the wording in several instances, with a view to making the meaning clearer. The additional Beatitudes may have been found in the sources available to him as isolated sayings, which he has seen fit to bring together into his collection; or they may be fresh renderings, framed to bring out more fully the manifold meaning which he found in the somewhat obscure phrases that Luke has reported with no attempt at clarification.

The Beatitudes put forward a conception of human blessedness which completely reverses all the values of any social order that ever existed. They declare that those are blessed who are poor, mourning, hungry and thirsty, hated and maligned and persecuted. Matthew has felt it necessary to explain that 'poor' in this context means 'poor in spirit'. Even in this form the expression is difficult, in Greek as in English. It does not mean 'poor-spirited', but rather 'humble-hearted'. Matthew realizes that Jesus is using the word 'poor' as it is used in the Psalms, of the man of God who has no haughtiness, no pride of possession or of place, but is conscious only of his need. There is a tacit contrast with the self-righteousness which is capable of saying: 'I thank God that I am not as other men' (Luke xviii. 11-12; § 186). Matthew likewise is moved to explain that when Jesus pronounces blessed 'you that hunger', he speaks of the hunger and thirst *for righteousness*. But by this he does not mean a deep desire for personal holiness, but a longing for the victory of good over evil, for the 'righteousness' of God which is manifested in salvation, in the inauguration of the kingdom of righteousness and peace on earth. In all these sayings the blessedness is seen as based upon the fulfilment of the high destiny which God reserves for his people — to have part in his kingdom, to inherit the redeemed earth of the Golden Age that is to come, to be comforted and satisfied in every way by the eternal consolations of God, to receive mercy, to see God, to be called sons of God. The end will manifest the blessedness of the life which on earth has known only poverty and oppression and unsatisfied longings.

We may remark that the variant expressions given to the assurances of the future carry with them rich and manifold interpretations of the significance of 'the kingdom of God'. Every one of these promises must be understood as *eschatological*: they are promises of the age to come, not of improved social conditions in this age. Jesus has nothing resembling a social or political programme for the amelioration of the deep-rooted evils and injustices of human society.

Let us remark further that sayings such as these, however deep their appeal to the humble, could not fail to be infuriating to all in Israel who dreamed of freeing the nation by revolt, as in the glorious days of the Maccabees. It must be kept in mind that the spirit of rebellion was endemic. A sullen hatred of Rome and of those who served the Roman administration burned in the hearts of the people, and it was never difficult for a fanatical adventurer to gather a band of followers, eager to try conclusions with all the forces of Rome. The spirit that broke out forty years afterwards in the war against Rome was already abroad, and there had been a number of local uprisings which were crushed and punished with the utmost severity. (On one occasion, the legate of Syria crucified nearly six thousand Jewish rebels along the highway.) Into such an atmosphere the Beatitudes would fall like a torrent of cold water; and the counsel 'Love your enemies and do them good' would be still more unwelcome to those who looked upon active hostility to the occupying Romans as their patriotic and religious duty. 'Blessed are the peacemakers, for they shall be called sons of God' is not a sentiment calculated to appeal to men ardent for revolution.

20. *The Similes of Salt and Light*

MATTHEW v. 13-16 LUKE xiv. 34-35; xi. 33

In Luke these two similes are found widely separated, and neither is set in the framework of the Sermon. The simile of the salt is placed in the context of a series of warnings on the cost of discipleship (§ 171); and the simile of light is introduced twice — first in relation to the revelation of truth through parables (§ 94, Luke viii. 16, parallel to Mark iv. 21), and again in association with another saying about light (§ 153) which is used by Matthew in a later part of the Sermon. The linking of the two sayings, conveying the suggestion that there is also a linking of the thought, must therefore be regarded as an editorial device of Matthew's. We observe also that the two similes are found in Mark, again widely separated and in different contexts — the simile of salt in a short sequence of sayings which appear to be linked by nothing except the *word* 'salt' (§ 132; Mark ix. 49-50), where it is as enigmatic as the two sayings which accompany it; and the simile of light in the context of the interpretation of parables (Mark iv. 21, parallel to Luke viii. 16; see above), where it seems to be taken as an assurance that truth not now evident will later be made manifest. Only in Matthew are the two similes given as symbols of the role of the disciples in the world; and it must be regarded as possible, even as probable, that Matthew himself has made this explicit application by framing the phrases: 'You are the salt of the earth ... you are the light of the world.' He has also developed the sequence by introducing two other sayings of Jesus (*vv.* 14b, 16), which he found isolated in the tradition, or possibly in other contexts.

The comparison of the handling of these sayings by the three Evangelists throws a good deal of light upon the way in which they made use of the traditional materials which were transmitted to them. They felt free to combine isolated sayings into sequences, and even to transfer sayings to new contexts. This editorial arranging could not fail to have some effect upon the sense in which the sayings would be understood by the readers. The Evangelists thus make themselves in some degree – indeed, in no small degree – interpreters of the message of Jesus and not mere recorders or transcribers.

21. *Christ's Attitude towards the Law*

MATTHEW V. 17-20

This section forms the introduction to a portion of the Sermon (*vv.* 21-48) which states the contrast between the Old Law and the New, illustrated in respect of six particular commandments. Matthew appears to have found the nucleus of this sequence of sayings in a source which only he has used, and he has then built it up into a broader complex, partly by working into it some paragraphs from the Sermon, which he shares with Luke (§§ 26, 27); and partly by incorporating sayings from other contexts which seemed to him to be relevant to the theme (§§ 22, 24). Form-critical analysis indicates that the nucleus consisted of a triad of sayings, now found in *vv.* 21-22, 27-28, 33-37; and that Matthew has then brought under the same rubric ('It was said', or 'You have heard that it was said [to the men of old] ... But I tell you ... ') the pronouncements of Jesus on Divorce (§ 24), on Retaliation (§ 26), and on Love of One's Enemies (§ 27), which were not transmitted in the tradition under such a formula, as we see from the parallels in Mark and Luke. In §§ 22 and 23, he has also added sayings which have most tenuous links with the cardinal saying of the paragraph.

The material brought together in § 21 is found only in Matthew, except for *v.* 18, which appears to be a variant form of the saying as given in Luke xvi. 17. Matthew here combines sayings which were uttered at different times and in different contexts. These sayings are all *apologetic* in character; they are the defence against the charge that the teaching of Jesus is destructive of the basic religious traditions of Israel. The saying: 'Think not that I have come to destroy the law and the prophets' cannot be regarded as spoken merely to guard against a possible misinterpretation; it can only be the answer to a charge that has already been made by opponents. Controversy over the attitude of Jesus to the Law of Moses can hardly have arisen at the very beginning of his ministry; a certain lapse of time must be postulated before it would become necessary for him to reply to charges of this kind. For Matthew, of course, it is a standing charge in the controversy between Judaism and Christianity in his own time, some seventy years afterwards; and in the Jewish-Christian circles whose traditions are here employed, there was a natural tendency to minimize the differences between the teaching of Jesus and the traditional interpretation of the old Law – to emphasize the aspects of continuity. Even St. Paul, with his clear appreciation of the depth of the differences, will still affirm this continuity in the strongest terms: 'Do we then make void the Law through faith? God forbid! nay, we establish the Law' (Rom. iii. 31). The saying: 'I did not come to destroy, but to fulfil' is a saying capable of the widest application; we may legitimately apply it to the relationship of Christianity to all the higher religions, not to Judaism alone. Yet such 'fulfilment' involves a large measure of destruction — the destruction of all that would interfere with the full appreciation and apprehension of the highest and best of the old.

The second saying (*v.* 18) may well have been ironical though the Jewish-Christian source from which it came to Matthew has not so understood it. Taken as it stands, it would represent Jesus as a super-Pharisee; and indeed, the whole sequence would in itself represent Christianity as simply an improved Pharisaism, more thorough in its scrupulous adherence to the letter of the Law. It has been suggested by some critics that *v.* 19 actually originated as a bit of Jewish-Christian polemic against St. Paul, in resentment of his firm contention that 'by the works of the Law shall no flesh be justified in (God's) sight' (Rom. iii. 20). Certainly these two sayings are in themselves quite inconsistent with the passage which follows, in which Jesus adopts an openly critical attitude to some cardinal requirements of the Law; and with his notorious disregard of the rigid Sabbatarianism of the current Jewish piety. The fourth saying, in such a context, could only mean that Jesus was commending a quest for righteousness on the lines professed by the scribes and Pharisees, but requiring an even greater degree of achievement from his followers. In the light of the total teaching of Jesus, however, it must be understood as the radical repudiation of the kind of righteousness which the scribes and Pharisees had in view; and the best commentary on it is the words of St. Paul: 'They have a zeal of God, but not according to knowledge; for they, ignoring the righteousness of God and seeking to establish their own righteousness, have not made submission to the righteousness of God. For Christ is the end of the Law, for the attainment of righteousness, for every one who believes' (Rom. x. 2-4).

22. *On Murder*

Matthew v. 21-26

The caption given to this paragraph is misleading, for while it begins with the prohibition of murder, it continues with sayings which are related only by the theme of Disputes, Reconciliation and Judgment. The commandment: 'Thou shalt not kill' is extended to forbid hatred and enmity among men — the spirit which leads to murder; with the warning that the judgment of God falls upon the inward disposition and not merely upon the overt act. The law of an external commandment is deepened to the requirement of an obedience of the heart. Verses 23 and 24 have no bearing upon the theme of murder or even of the murderous disposition. They are linked with the preceding verses only as an extension of the thought of a dispute among brethren, with the warning (taking now the form of a principle of ecclesiastical discipline) that you must not approach the altar of God with enmity in your heart. Finally, *vv.* 25 and 26 are taken from a source which has been employed also by Luke, but in a different context; they are really a parable intended to impress upon men the necessity of coming to a reconciliation with God before the Day of Judgment.

It is quite evident that here Matthew has brought together materials of different provenance, and it would be unprofitable to attempt to interpret the two latter groups as corollaries of the pronouncement on the law of murder. There is a certain chain of ideas, but it is artificial, not grounded in a real sequence of thought.

23. *On Adultery*

MATTHEW V. 27-30

The primary element in this section, as in that which precedes it, is the deepening of the commandment to make it bear upon the inward disposition and not alone upon the overt act. To this, Matthew has again attached a pair of sayings (*vv.* 29, 30) which were spoken and transmitted independently, and are actually introduced by him, in a variant form, in another context (§ 131, About Offences), where it is part of a Marcan sequence that is not related to the law of adultery at all. We can only guess at what the new conjunction of sayings may have signified for Matthew — perhaps a recognition of the extreme difficulty of ridding the heart of unlawful desires, and a warning of the utter necessity of purging them at whatever cost.

24. *On Divorce*

MATTHEW V. 31-32

As the Synopsis indicates, this is a doublet of a passage which Matthew uses elsewhere in parallelism with Mark (§ 187); it is used also by Luke, in a different form and in a different sequence (Luke xvi. 18, § 176). Here Matthew has fitted the saying into the pattern of contrasts between the Old Law and the New by putting it under the rubric of *v.* 27: it becomes an extension of the law of adultery. A striking feature of the Matthaean form of the saying is the limiting provision 'except by reason of fornication', which is not suggested at all in Mark or Luke and has the appearance of a modification which transforms an enunciation of principle into a disciplinary regulation. It may be remarked that the principle of the indissolubility of marriage is as radical a departure from Jewish as from Greek or other pagan ethics and law. But Jesus is not offering legislation for a social order composed of all sorts and conditions of men, just as in the saying of verse 28, he is not proposing that the legal penalties applicable to adultery should be invoked against every lustful look.

The sayings of Jesus on divorce and re-marriage offer many problems of text and interpretation as well as of application within a non-Christian society. See further the Additional Note under § 187, for which I have had the invaluable assistance of my colleague, Dean C. R. Feilding.

25. *On Swearing*

MATTHEW V. 33-37

We shall find another sequence of sayings about oaths in § 210 (Matt. xxiii. 16-22), which reflects more pointedly the controversy over the casuistry of the matter as developed by the scribes and Pharisees. The question is not mentioned by Mark or Luke; this material belongs to Matthew's Palestinian (Jewish-Christian) source. Matthew has here used a form of his rubric to bring it into his pattern of contrasts between the Old Law and the New. The general thought is that the prohibition against breach of an oath is transformed into the positive injunction always to tell the truth; the resort to oaths is 'of the evil one', perhaps in the sense that it is an indication that the mere word of the speaker is not to be trusted.

26. *On Retaliation*

MATTHEW V. 38-42

In this section and that which follows, Matthew is clearly following the source which he shares with Luke ('Q'), which probably lay before him in a slightly different version — there are some differences both of phrasing and of order which can hardly be attributed to the editorial work of the Evangelists, besides some slight differences of content. Both sections have been brought by Matthew under his introductory rubric, thereby pointing them in relation to the contrast between the Law of Moses and the Law of Christ. For § 26, he uses the *lex talionis* as his point of departure. It should be kept in mind that the principle of 'an eye for an eye and a tooth for a tooth' was not initially a demand for peculiarly savage justice, but a *limitation* upon the custom of unrestricted revenge, which not only permitted but required an individual, a family, a clan, to avenge injuries not only upon the person of the wrongdoer but upon all connected with him. It was in its time a social advance of the first magnitude. But 'time makes ancient good uncouth', and Christ now deepens the old law by extending the principle of limitation to an absolute prohibition of revenge.

27. *On Love of One's Enemies*

MATTHEW V. 43-48

The phrase 'thou shalt hate thine enemy' is not found in so many words in the Old Testament. It is not part of the quotation, but is added to indicate the sense in which the command to 'love your neighbour' was commonly understood; hatred of enemies was taken to be the natural corollary of love of friends. Matthew, here as frequently elsewhere, has abbreviated the passage by omitting several clauses which Luke has retained (Luke vi. 27c, 28a, 34, 35a); and his phrase 'sons of your Father who is in heaven' (for Luke's 'sons of the Most High') is his own characteristic mode of expression. In the closing verse of the passage, however, it seems likely that Matthew's word 'perfect' (*teleios*; Hebrew, *tam*, *tamîm*) is a literal rendering of the underlying Aramaic used by Jesus; while Luke, realizing that his Gentile readers would hardly understand the word in its familiar Semitic sense, has interpreted it as 'merciful', at the cost of a considerable narrowing of its meaning. Note that in Luke these two sections are brought together under the general theme of 'love your enemies' (see § 75). In both versions the central teaching remains the same; the conduct and attitudes of the people of God must be determined by their relationship to him, not by the character and conduct of other people. As God is 'kind to the unthankful and evil', and 'causes his sun to rise on evil men and on good men, and sends rain upon righteous men and on unrighteous men', so men show themselves to be his 'sons' only when they show a like magnanimity.

§§ 28-31

On Almsgiving; On Prayer; The Lord's Prayer; On Fasting

MATTHEW vi. 1-18

In these four sections, Matthew brings together materials which bear upon another aspect of the contrast between the old order of Judaism and the new order of Christ. The distinctions now have to do not with the interpretation of commandments given in the Law, but with specific matters of religious practice. §§ 28, 29, and 31, and also some phrases of § 30 are found only in Matthew. The general theme — the contrast between deeds of 'righteousness' done ostentatiously, to win the approval of men, and deeds done 'in secret', seeking only the approval of God — is developed simply and consistently under the three heads of Almsgiving, Prayer, and Fasting, in *vv.* 1-6 and 16-18. Verse 1 states the theme: 'Take heed not to do your righteous deeds in the presence of men, to be seen by them; else you have no reward in the presence of your Father who is in heaven'; and the same theme is echoed in the double refrain of each section: 'They have their reward' — 'your Father who sees in secret will reward you'. The approval itself is the reward; the true piety is that which is concerned solely with the approval of God (cf. John v. 44, and 1 Cor. iv. 3-4). The 'reward' which God gives is his judgment which he will pronounce at the appointed time, the Day of Judgment; the thought is still eschatologically orientated; there is no suggestion of inward satisfaction or other compensation in the present.

In §§ 29 and 30, Matthew has attached some supplementary materials to the second of the three groups of sayings in this sequence. Verses 7 and 8 no longer bear upon the fundamental contrast between human approval and divine approval, between current Jewish (Pharisaic) piety and the piety which Christ requires of his followers, but upon the contrast between heathen prayers and prayers directed to the true God. Similarly, the Lord's Prayer does not enter into the general theme of contrast between true and ostentatious piety; Matthew introduces it here simply because he is putting together materials which have to do with Prayer. The Lord's Prayer was of course transmitted independently of any setting, in the liturgical and private usage of the Christian community. The comparison between the version of the prayer found in Matthew, and that which is given (in a quite different, but still artificially framed setting) by Luke (§ 146), indicates that the Matthaean additions have resulted from *liturgical* shaping. 'Who art in heaven' is, as we have seen, one of Matthew's own characteristic phrases (it does not occur in any other New Testament writer, except for one saying in Mark xi. 25 [26]). Verses 14 and 15 are a pair of detached sayings, introduced here by Matthew as a comment upon the petition for forgiveness; they are found in Mark, in a different form, somewhat incongruously attached to some words of Jesus concerning the significance of the withering of the fig tree (§ 201).

On § 31, we must note that Jesus takes for granted the practice of fasting, and speaks of it as a normal and presumably desirable aspect of piety, like almsgiving and prayer; like them, it must be done without ostentation, without any desire to make an impression on others, in singleness of heart that seeks only to please God. Yet we shall see (§ 54) that when the disciples of Jesus are reproached for not fasting, the reply of Jesus does not suggest that in fact they do fast, but in secret; on the contrary, his words concede the truth of the accusation — they do not fast, but they have good grounds for not fasting under the present circumstances, in the joy of his presence.

§§ 32-35

On Treasures; The Single Eye; On Serving Two Masters; On Cares

MATTHEW vi. 19-34

These four sections are closely related; they put before us a fundamentally new attitude towards personal possessions and the satisfaction of temporal needs. The followers of Jesus are to sit lightly to material treasures, to have no worries about the things that are commonly taken to be the primary necessities of life — food and clothing; their first and indeed their only concern is to be for heavenly things, to seek how they may please God and to prize his rewards above all earthly treasures; and worry is to be overcome by trust. There must be no attempt to make the best of both worlds; the service of God must be whole-hearted, with no division of allegiance.

For the detailed exegesis of these sections, the reader must consult the commentaries. Here we can do no more than point out that all four of these sections have their parallels in Luke, where §§ 32 and 35 are found together, but in reverse order; while §§ 33 and 34 are found in different contexts, widely separated; and none of the Lucan passages are found in his version of the Sermon. The closing verse of the chapter in Matthew is not represented in Luke at all; and in its place Luke gives a saying (xii. 32; § 157) which is not represented in Matthew: 'Fear not, little flock; it is your Father's good pleasure to give you the kingdom.' This is certainly not a variant of 'Do not worry about tomorrow; for tomorrow will worry about itself; its own trouble is enough for the day'. Both of these very different sayings appear to be detached *logia*, which the Evangelists have seen fit to append to the passage 'On Cares'.

The arrangement of the four sections in this sequence will thus be viewed as the work of Matthew, who will have seen in them a certain relevance to the theme of the first part of this chapter. The link is the theme of trust in God, and especially singlemindedness in the service of God.

The problem of the practical application of the words arises with special acuteness in connection with § 35. Does Jesus teach that the head of a family should be as little concerned over his food and clothing, and the food and clothing needed by his family, as if he were a thrush or a lily? It must of course be clearly understood that Jesus is not speaking of the necessary forethought of a prudent man, but of worry — worry about food and clothing that may so obsess a man that he cannot find place in his thoughts for the things of God. Against such an attitude Jesus first points to the futility of worry — no one can add an inch to his height or a minute to his life-span by worrying. But the worried man knows this perfectly well, and it does not help him to shake off his worries. The positive answer to them is given in the invitation to consider the bountiful providence of God, which extends even to the birds and the flowers. By an argument *a minore ad majus*, resting upon the presupposition that man is infinitely more precious than birds and flowers, Jesus bids us believe that the God who provides for them will all the more surely provide for us.

Let us recall that Jesus does not speak out of a sublime ignorance of the problems of poverty; he was himself brought up in the home of a workman in an obscure village; and most of his followers were drawn from the ranks of the poor and lowly. Every day of his life he looked upon scenes of destitution, and he was without any material resources other than those supplied by friends and well-wishers. He still insists that even for the destitute the first necessity is not the provision of food and clothing for his body, but care for the things of the spirit. He does not discount the material needs of man: 'Your heavenly Father knows that you need all these things' (*v.* 32); but he insists that the first necessity is to seek the kingdom of God.

In these passages Jesus speaks as a teacher of Wisdom, in the tradition of the Wisdom-literature of the Old Testament and the Apocrypha (Proverbs, Ecclesiastes, Wisdom of Solomon, etc.). It has been suggested (most forcibly by Professor R. Bultmann) that we can have little confidence in the authenticity of most of the sayings attributed to Jesus which fall within this general category (*History of the Synoptic Tradition*, pp. 101-105; and see his whole brilliant analysis under 'Logia (Jesus as the Teacher of Wisdom)', pp. 69-108). Most of them, in his view, reflect nothing characteristic of Jesus, nothing that rises above the level of the wise saws that are found in all societies, the common-places of popular proverbs and copy-book maxims. Concerning the passages now before us, he holds that while they do not belong to the category of this common wisdom ('profane Weisheit') but to the language of piety, their authenticity is still suspect; for the spirit of this piety is that of the popular ('volkstümlich') faith in God. Jesus may have made use occasionally of one or other of these proverbial sayings and given them a particular application; he may likewise have used the language of popular piety from time to time; but it is equally possible — and Professor Bultmann clearly regards it as infinitely more probable — that the Church took up into its tradition and attributed to Jesus most of the sayings of this type which have found a place in our Gospels. It is difficult to establish objective criteria for determining the authenticity of any particular sayings, once we seek to go beyond general considerations of probability; but it is held that there is no reason to accept as sayings of Jesus anything which does not reflect his cardinal message of repentance, of the swift approach of the kingdom of God, of the divine requirement of inward sincerity and truthfulness. Bultmann goes so far as to suggest that early collections of teaching material were prepared in and for the Church, which were not restricted to sayings of Jesus; but which combined with them, quite deliberately, and without attribution, sayings from other sources which were regarded as true and valuable for the instruction of converts; he raises the question of whether 'Q' may have been such a compilation. The attribution to Jesus of *all* the sayings in such a compendium would be a secondary stage.

It is impossible to dismiss out of hand the whole of this argument. We have already seen reason to suggest that certain sayings which we have examined have been wrongly attributed to Jesus, and that others have been given a sense which he can hardly have intended them to have. It is a fact, also, that in later Christian writings we occasionally find sayings from other sources cited as words of Jesus; and it is generally agreed that a fair proportion of the apocalyptic sayings in the Gospels belong to the common store of Jewish apocalyptic material and that they have been attributed to Jesus in the development of the tradition. There is, accordingly, no absolute barrier against the hypothesis that a certain number of maxims, proverbs and pronouncements on the life of piety may have been drawn from other sources (rabbinical or popular) and in one way or another attributed to Jesus. But it seems altogether unreasonable to hold that Jesus limited himself to the eschatological proclamation, and to suspect the authenticity of any saying that lacks the eschatological note or something that we have already taken to be characteristic of Jesus. If the tradition is faithful in representing Jesus as a teacher of Wisdom, as well as a prophet of things to come — and it would be arbitrary to challenge it in this respect — then we must expect that he will stand in the tradition of the Wisdom-teachers of his people, and will not shrink from incorporating into his teaching many sayings that were current before him and in his time. We may quite properly apply to him the saying: 'Every scribe schooled for the kingdom of heaven is like a householder, who brings forth from his storehouse things new and old' (Matt. xiii. 52).

Further, the present writer is much more sceptical about the curious genius which Professor Bultmann appears to attribute to the early Palestinian Church, and for that matter, also to the early Hellenistic Churches, than about the general authenticity of the sayings attributed to Jesus. There is really no reason to believe that Christian communities in Palestine and Syria in the first century were gifted with deeper religious insight and conspicuously greater creative powers than Christian communities in Yorkshire or in Pennsylvania in the twentieth century. It seems much more reasonable to suppose that they have transmitted to us a selection from a much more extensive store of sayings communicated in the first instance by the apostles and other companions of Jesus, than that they retained only the scanty remnants, of limited scope and theme, which will pass Professor Bultmann's scrutiny, and that they themselves in their communal life have brought forth the bulk of the wider-ranging and powerful body of teaching which is attributed to Jesus in the Synoptics.

§§ 36-44

The materials in Chapter Seven are heterogeneous and there is scarcely a thread of continuity between one section and another. It is hard to discern any principle of arrangement which may have guided Matthew here. We may indeed observe that the first four sections are given to injunctions on various themes, but one does not lead to another, or require the section which follows for its own completion. It is probable that the Golden Rule (§ 39) is intended to be a final summary of the whole tenor of the teaching; but we cannot feel that it stands in any particular relation to the encouragements to prayer which precede it or to the warnings which follow. The next four sections are all warnings, but again there is no association between one group of warnings and the next. The indications are that Matthew (and in some degree the compiler of the source which he had before him) has brought together materials which were originally detached — spoken at different times and to different people; some even drawn from other sources than the tradition of words of Jesus.

36. *On Judging*

MATTHEW vii. 1-5

The comparison with the parallel Lucan passage indicates that Matthew has once again abbreviated his source, and has thereby affected the sense in which the words are to be understood. His first two verses omit almost two-thirds of the corresponding matter in Luke; and then two Lucan verses are omitted by him entirely. The effect of the omissions in *v.* 2 is to bring the saying: 'With what measure you measure, it shall be measured to you' into collocation with the initial injunction: 'Judge not', and thus to treat it as giving the sense in which the injunction is to be understood. Matthew reinforces this by framing a similar phrase (almost certainly of his own making): 'With what judgment you judge, you shall be judged', to ease the transition from the thought of judgment to the metaphor of measurement, which is really much more apt in relation to the saying: 'Give, and it shall be given to you', with which it is associated in the Lucan version. It is a question whether this rearrangement has not actually denatured the initial saying of Jesus, which does not bid us judge others generously, but forbids us to act as judges of our fellows at all. The whole profession of the follower of Jesus is not to judge (whether harshly or generously), but to forgive; and this is the shape of the thought as it is put before us in the Lucan version. By the omission of the two following verses of Luke (vi. 39-40), Matthew also brings the figure of the Log in the Eye into closer relation with the initial saying. Certainly the point of this figure is that by reason of our own imperfections we are not competent to judge the conduct and character of others; but we are prone to overlook gross faults in ourselves while we look meticulously for the most trifling faults in others. We may remark in passing that this extravagant figure — what we might describe as a titanic hyperbole — is characteristic of Jesus; it is hard to find anything to compare with it elsewhere. A log in the eye is of course a literal impossibility;

there is something almost grotesque about the picture; but there can be no question of its force as an illustration. Similar figures are that of the camel trying to pass through the eye of a needle; of the hypocrites who strain out a gnat and swallow a camel; and even, in a certain sense, of such injunctions as: 'If your hand offends you, cut it off and throw it away; if your right eye gets you into trouble, knock it out and throw it away.'

On the Lucan treatment of these sayings, see the notes on § 76.

37. *On Casting Pearls before Swine*

Matthew vii. 6

This is an isolated logion of uncertain provenance. Certainly it has no bearing upon what goes before or what follows, and it is difficult to find in it a meaning consonant with the general teaching of Jesus. The ecclesiastical interpretation, found as early as the Didache, interprets it as justification for the exclusion of unbaptized persons from the Eucharist; but this is wholly inconceivable as a possible meaning on the lips of Jesus. It must also be said that it is difficult to imagine Jesus speaking of unreceptive hearers, or even of opponents, as 'dogs' and 'swine', in any context. Nor is there anything elsewhere in the Gospels to suggest that Jesus would have regarded any part of his teaching as esoteric, or as so 'holy' that it must not be imparted to the unworthy. The Great Physician would surely not have his medicines withheld from those most in need of them. We are inclined, accordingly, to regard this saying as spurious — 'a bit of apocalyptic Jewish exclusiveness, adopted by extreme Jewish Christians, and incorporated among the sayings of Jesus' (Manson, *Sayings*, p. 174).

38. *The Answer to Prayer*

Matthew vii. 7-11 Luke xi. 9-13

In Luke this section is not included in the Sermon, but in a sequence on Prayer (§§ 146-148), beginning with the Lord's Prayer; it is not included in the narrative of the Galilean ministry, but in the Travel Narrative. The wording in the two versions is almost identical. Matthew omits one Lucan verse (Luke xi. 12); but the one striking variation is found in the closing verse, where for Matthew's 'good things', Luke reads 'holy spirit'. In this instance it seems likely that it is Luke who has adapted the words of the source (preserved more literally by Matthew), to bring it into relation with the petition which seems to have stood in his version of the Lord's Prayer: 'May thy Holy Spirit come upon us and cleanse us.' In the Synoptic tradition Jesus seldom speaks of the gift of the Holy Spirit; and in this context his thought is not limited to prayers for one specific gift.

It is interesting to note that Jesus finds in human fatherhood a valid though imperfect analogy to divine fatherhood; and that the generous gifts of God are not alone for those who have a special claim upon him, as children upon their father, but for all who ask of him.

39. *The Golden Rule*

MATTHEW vii. 12 Luke vi. 31

The variant wording is not of any great significance; it probably goes back to different Greek renderings of an Aramaic original. The Matthaean addition: 'for this is the law and the prophets', may very well be borrowed from the anecdote of the great Rabbi Hillel, who is said to have given the negative form of the saying ('What you would not have others do to you, do not you do to them') in response to a questioner who challenged him to state the substance of the Torah while standing on one foot. In the negative form this rule is attributed to wise men of many lands. The positive formulation, attributed to the Jesus of the Gospels alone, cannot be regarded as a chance differentiation (*pace* Bultmann); it is wholly in keeping with the insistence of Jesus that virtue does not lie in what a man does not do, but in what he does (cf. the Parable of the Talents). In neither form is it properly described as 'the moralism of a naive egoism' (Bultmann).

40. *The Narrow Gate*

MATTHEW vii. 13-14 LUKE xiii. 23-24

Luke introduces the saying in a different context, and at a much later stage of the narrative (§ 165), as Jesus is on his way to Jerusalem. He has provided it with an artificial setting — an abruptly introduced question: 'Are the saved few?'; but he appears to preserve a more primitive form of the saying itself than that which we find in Matthew. The figures of the narrow gate (or door) and the hemmed-in road are found again in the Ezra Apocalypse (4 Esdras vii. 7), which is also obsessed by the small numbers of those that are to escape destruction. The 'gate', in the context, can hardly be anything other than the entrance to heaven, or to the realm into which God admits the faithful, however it be conceived; 'life' and 'destruction' are likewise used without explanation, as familiar terms of the religious vocabulary. But the thought is without any real parallel elsewhere in the recorded teaching of Jesus, and there is nothing to help us understand what he might mean by 'the narrow door'. It is tempting to feel that we have here an echo of the mournful feelings of the circles which produced 4 Esdras, rather than a genuine saying of Jesus (cf. Manson, *Sayings*, p. 175: 'The whole saying takes a very gloomy view of human life and destiny. In this respect it comes near to the spirit of 4 *Ezra*'). Yet it is conceivable that Jesus, if confronted with this pessimistic attitude, might reply with the challenge: 'If the gate is so narrow and the way so hemmed in, make it your business to see that you succeed in entering, without vain speculations about the numbers that succeed or fail.' But the saying conveys an impression of preoccupation with individual destiny, without thought of the redeemed *community* or of the social and universal aspects of redemption, which is hardly characteristic of Jesus. More often he puts the emphasis not on the narrowness of the door or the way, but on the urgency of making the great decision before it is too late — the time is short, and the Master of the house will shut the door for the night; enter now, without delay, while the door stands open for you. This is the thought of the corresponding passage in Luke (§ 165).

41. *The Tests of Goodness*

Matthew vii. 15-20

The structure of this section is exceptionally complex. It centres in a saying, or a group of sayings, about the correspondence of trees and their fruit — inward character and outward manifestation. In the parallel passage in Luke it is applied specifically to *words* (Luke vi. 45: 'Out of the abundance of the heart, his mouth speaks'); so also in Matthew's second use of the sayings (xii. 33-35). The 'fruit' of the good tree is in both those passages the good *words* which a man speaks, and there is no suggestion of a contrast between words and deeds. In our passage, however, Matthew has attached the sayings to a warning against false prophets. Here we have an initial awkwardness in the violent mixture of metaphors; in *v.* 15 the false prophets are wolves, while in the next verse they are trees. But how then are we to think of the 'fruits' of these 'trees'? They are certainly not the *words* spoken by the false prophets. There must be a latent contrast between words and deeds — the false prophets give good words but create havoc among the flock. McNeile points out that 'false *Christian* prophets did not appear until after the Lord's death, when the struggles with Judaizing Christians began' (*St. Matthew*, ad loc.). We are bound to feel that Matthew has made a secondary application of the sayings, and that *v.* 15 — itself perhaps an isolated logion — owes its place here to the editorial work of the Evangelist. Verse 17, again, which has no counterpart in Luke, appears to be a kind of homiletic repetition or underlining, which may also be a Mathaean addition; and *v.* 19 is taken verbatim from the report of the preaching of John the Baptist (§ 2), where it is more in keeping with the context than here. T. W. Manson (*Sayings*, pp. 24-5) warns us that a certain amount of 'adulteration' from the teaching of John has been introduced into Matthew's accounts of the teaching of Jesus, especially from 'M' (which is here combined with material from 'Q').

42. *Warning against Self-Deception*

Matthew vii. 21-23

Here again Matthew has brought together two fragments which are found in two different contexts in Luke. Verse 21 appears to be an elaboration of the simpler saying of Luke vi. 46. But in both forms the saying has this difficulty, that it implies that to address Jesus as 'Lord' (*Kyrie*) is to give him the honour which he was to receive in the Church as 'the Lord Jesus' (or, 'Christ the Lord'). But in Greek usage *Kyrie* as a form of address implied no more than 'Sir' implies in English. In the vocative, it does not carry with it a religious connotation; and it will be found that in the Synoptic tradition generally, Jesus is not given the title of *Kyrios* — the few exceptions (most of them in Luke) are easily understood as unconscious reflections of the later ecclesiastical practice. 'During his lifetime not only the Jews ... but also the disciples ... probably addressed Him only as *didaskale*, i.e. Rabbi ... *Kyrie* was the later title of worship, adopted in consequence of the Resurrection' (McNeile, *St. Matthew*, ad loc.). So we must look upon the use of the title here, with the full sense of authority, as an effect of ecclesiastical usage; but at the same time we shall feel that it is the form, not the substance, of the saying that comes into question. Jesus is not the leader of a discussion group, and he does call for disciples who will 'follow' him, who will give him their obedience. To profess oneself his disciple is to pledge oneself to do what he says, to do the will of his Father in heaven. The second part of Matthew's section is paralleled, with substantial differences of wording, in Luke xiii. 26-27 (§ 165; notice that there it is found in a sequence which includes the exhortation to 'strive to enter through the narrow door'). Matthew makes it specifically a reference to the Last Judgment ('in that day' — *v.* 22); and while in Luke it is 'the master of the house' (i.e. God) who shuts the door and refuses to hear the pleas of those excluded, in Matthew it is Jesus himself who pronounces the sentence. This is clearly a secondary development, but one that may well have occurred within the transmission of the tradition before it came to Matthew. See also the notes on § 165.

43. *Hearers and Doers of the Word*

MATTHEW vii. 24-27 LUKE vi. 47-49

Matthew and Luke both use this parable as the end of the Sermon. The differences in the wording are so great as to indicate that it has come to them through independent channels of transmission.

44. *The End of the Sermon*

MATTHEW vii. 28-29

Now only does Matthew make use of the one sentence which he retains of Mark's story of the exorcism at Capernaum (see notes on § 12). The contrast with the scribal teaching is manifest. The scribes viewed themselves wholly as interpreters of the authoritative traditions of Israel, written and oral; and much of their work has come down to us in the form of the opinions given by leaders of the different schools (especially those of Hillel and Shammai) on a number of specific questions of doctrine or practice. Jesus is far from a mere interpreter of a revelation communicated through others, in the past; he bears the word of God himself, and declares it directly to his hearers. The authority of his message is the reflection of the authority committed to him himself, as the one whom God has sent — not of the authority which belongs only to a tradition transmitted to him.

Miracles and Controversies
§§ 45-70

MATTHEW viii. 1-xii. 14 MARK i. 40-iii. 6 LUKE v. 12-vi. 11

Before attempting to examine these sections one by one, it will be worth while to look rapidly over the whole arrangements of the materials in the Synopsis, comparing the editorial work of the three Evangelists.

In Mark this part of the Gospel consists of a collection of controversy-stories

(§§ 52, 53, 54, 69 and 70), to which the miracle-story of § 45 forms a kind of introduction. This collection may well have been made before Mark. The sequence is not chronological, but topical. In Mark, the events of the Day in Capernaum have brought to Jesus a swift popularity, which proves embarrassing; he leaves the scene to work in other parts of Galilee. Now the healing of a leper (§ 45) brings him a still greater notoriety; masses of people so throng around him that he cannot enter a settlement. But another side of the picture begins to appear. In the very midst of the teeming throngs, voices of criticism make themselves heard. Jesus is accused of blasphemy (§ 52), of keeping bad company (§ 53), of failing to train his disciples to practise fasting (§ 54), of breaking the Sabbath (§§ 69, 70). The last of these charges stirs the spirit of murder in his critics, and the shadow of the cross falls across the narrative (Mark iii. 6 and parallels). In two of these sections (52, 70) the controversy arises out of circumstances connected with the exercise of miraculous healing power by Jesus; in the others we have to do with questions of conduct, of practical piety.

These six sections are taken over by Luke in the same sequence, unbroken, without rearrangement or interruption, with no more than slight verbal and stylistic modifications. But in his narrative, this Marcan group is separated from the stories of the Day in Capernaum (Luke iv. 31-44) by the story of the preaching by the lake and the call of the first disciples. Consequently it no longer has the effect of foil which we have noted in Mark — it does not bring out the contrast between the swift growth of Jesus' fame as a healer and the appearance of hostile criticism. Luke had in any case introduced the theme of hostility at a still earlier stage (The Rejection at Nazareth, § 10), before Jesus had even called his first disciples. Further, Luke's introductory phrases to the several sections almost seem designed to emphasize the independence of each one, rather than any thread of continuity.

In Matthew the general picture is far more radically changed. The Marcan order of the sections is preserved, but the association between them is broken by the insertion of large amounts of other material, much of it non-Marcan. The six sections taken from Mark are found in Matthew viii. 1-4 (§ 45), ix. 1-17 (§§ 52-54), and xii. i-14 (§§ 69 and 70). Between the first two Marcan stories, Matthew introduces four miracle-stories, a summary of healing activities, and a report of Jesus' responses to candidates for admission to the ranks of his followers. Between the fourth and fifth of the Marcan stories, he introduces three more miracle-stories, an account of the choice of the Twelve and the Charge addressed to them by Jesus, and some miscellaneous material, bearing upon various responses to the mission, with pronouncements of judgment upon the unresponding and invitations to the weary and burdened. Some of these Matthaean additions are taken from Mark, but from other parts of his narrative; a small amount is found only in Matthew; and the remainder is 'Q' material, which Luke has preferred to place in other contexts.

The long compound insertions of Matthew not only interrupt the Marcan sequence but destroy its unity. The original Marcan pattern is discernible still, but it has been overlaid by a new and quite different design of Matthew's own creating. The materials that fall within the limits of the six Marcan stories are now arranged in three great complexes and part of a fourth. Chapters 8 and 9 form the first of these, made up of three groups each containing three miracle-stories (§§ 45-47; 50-52; and 55-57), broken by the insertion of materials of a different character. In the first group of three, Matthew brings together the first story of the Marcan sequence with a 'Q' story (which Luke will introduce at a later stage), and a story from Mark's 'Day at Capernaum', which both Mark and Luke have used earlier. In the second group he uses the second story of the Marcan sequence together with two other Marcan stories which will appear in the other two Gospels at a later stage. Two of Mark's controversy-stories occupy the interval between Matthew's second group and his third. In the third group he uses the twofold miracle-story of Jairus' Daughter and the Woman with the Issue of Blood, which Mark and Luke hold for a later part of the narrative, along with two stories which are found only in Matthew's Gospel. This complex of miracle-stories is the counterpart to his Sermon on the Mount; he first presents Jesus in his mighty words, then in his mighty works. The two together develop on a grand scale the twofold theme which he has announced above: 'He went abroad in the whole of Galilee, teaching ... and preaching the gospel of the kingdom, and healing all disease and all infirmity' (iv. 23). His second complex (§§ 58-63) is constituted by the collection of sayings from different sources which he has woven together into the second of his five main Discourses of Jesus: it takes the form of a Mission Charge, with its introduction. The third complex (§§ 64-68) is diverse in character, but seems to have a certain unity of theme as reflecting conflicting judgments about the person and mission of Jesus — the doubts of John the Baptist (§ 64); the criticisms of John now matched by criticisms of Jesus, on contrary grounds (§ 65); the failure of the Galilaean cities to respond to the Gospel (§ 66); followed by Jesus' own affirmation of his divine mission (§§ 67, 68). The last two of Mark's controversy-stories (§§ 69 and 70), in which Jesus' attitude to the Sabbath is challenged, form the commencement of a fourth complex, which will be completed by another miracle-story (§ 85), and a series of controversy-discourses (§§ 85-89). If we were dealing with Matthew alone, therefore, we would gather under the heading 'Miracles and Controversies' the whole of Chapters 8 to 12. It is the Marcan pattern which imposes upon us the necessity of making the division after Matthew xii. 14 (= Mark iii. 6).

45. *The Healing of a Leper*

MATTHEW vi. 1-4 MARK i. 40-45 LUKE v. 12-16

Both Matthew and Luke have provided a setting for the miracle, which in Mark has no indication of place or time. Matthew links it with the descent of Jesus from the Mount of the Sermon, as if to suggest the association of word and work in the mission of Jesus; Luke sets it vaguely 'in one of the cities'. As a rule these stories of Jesus would be transmitted in oral tradition without indication of names and places and times — not as incidents in a continuous story, but as detached, self-contained anecdotes. Obviously Matthew and Luke do not feel in the least bound to use them in the same connection as that found in Mark; they exercise the same freedom of arrangement as Mark had used in the first instance.

The most striking changes made by Matthew and Luke are the omission of the participle (*splagchnistheis* — 'moved with compassion'; variant *orgistheis* — 'moved with anger') of Mark i. 41; and the omission of the entire *v.* 43: 'And raging at him, he straightway cast him out.' In *v.* 41, we must certainly regard *orgistheis* — 'moved with anger' — as the original reading; the change from 'moved with anger' to 'moved with compassion' is easily comprehensible, whereas no scribe would think of altering 'moved with compassion' to 'moved with anger'. We can also see that Matthew and Luke must have found *orgistheis* in the text of Mark which they had before them; they too would have no reason to omit *splagchnistheis* if it had been the reading of Mark as known to them. These two astonishing and difficult expressions, which the other two evangelists have been moved to omit, indicate that in the primitive tradition which Mark follows, the cure of the leper was regarded as the exorcism of a demon; the anger of Jesus is obviously not directed against the leper (for him, indeed, Jesus could only be 'moved with compassion'), but against the demon of disease who has possessed him.

In all three versions of the story the leper is charged to tell his story to no one, but to carry out the prescriptions of the Mosaic Law for lepers that have been cleansed; that is, to show himself to the priest and obtain his certificate of freedom from the disease, and to offer the prescribed sacrifice. This is to be done 'for a testimony to them'. The purport of this phrase is not immediately clear. In the story taken by itself, repeated as a detached anecdote, it could hardly have anything more than the surface meaning: 'as proof of your cleansing'. In its place in the Marcan sequence it may be an initial refutation of the charges that are to be brought against Jesus in the series of controversy-stories which follow: Jesus in fact is faithful to the Mosaic Law and bids others to fulfil its requirements. In Matthew no such connection of thought is possible, since he does not take up the Marcan sequence until much later (§ 52); but the words may well have for him much the same fundamental sense; the incident affords a practical demonstration of the claim that Jesus 'came not to destroy the Law and the prophets ... but to fulfil' (Matt. v. 17).

Luke follows Mark in his account of the upshot — the man's disobedience to the command of Jesus that he should not speak of the matter to anyone, and the increased numbers that flock about Jesus as a result. Luke changes the tone and sense of the situation — he quietly subdues Mark's intimation that this excess of popularity is an embarrassment to Jesus; if Jesus goes into desert places, it is not to escape from the throngs, but to pray. We shall have occasion to note quite often that it is characteristic of Luke to mention the praying of Jesus; this has already left its mark in the Lucan version of the Baptism (§ 6) — Jesus is praying, after being baptized, when the Dove appears (Luke iii. 21f.). Matthew omits this part of the Marcan story altogether, perhaps for no other reason than to abbreviate; he abbreviates nearly all the stories that he uses. But it is possible that he felt it pointless to speak of Jesus as 'in desert places' in one verse, and in the next to picture him as entering Capernaum; yet Mark also lays his next scene in Capernaum, though it is not the same incident.

The question of credibility of course remains the same, whatever changes are made in the telling of the story or its placing in the structure of each Gospel. Even though we are told that the disease which we know as leprosy was not found in ancient Palestine (see the article '"Leprosy" and the Bible', by K. P. C. A. Gramberg, with bibliography, in *The Bible Translator*, vol. XI, no. 1 [Amsterdam: Netherlands Bible Society], Jan. 1960); and even though the provisions of the Mosaic Law presuppose that the disease in question is curable and that evidence of cure can be accepted by the priests, the intrinsic difficulty of the story for the reader of our times is not thereby alleviated to any significant extent. We find it relatively easy to accept the notion that Jesus had some extraordinary gifts of healing mental disorders (even though we do not ordinarily consider the task of the psychiatrist any easier, to say the least, than that of the physician who treats bodily illness), but we are reluctant to believe stories such as this, of the sudden and complete healing of a loathsome skin disease by a mere word, even though it be the word of Jesus. Our doubts are reinforced by the reflection that wonder-tales of the same type were told of many others in the Hellenistic world, so that the miracle-story becomes a sub-literary type, with characteristic features which are almost invariably present—features which mark the Synoptic stories also (see Bultmann, *History*, pp. 218-44).

The writer cannot undertake to offer here anything like a general discussion of the problem of the miraculous element in the gospels.[1] He will remark only that no purpose is served by attempts to rationalize the miracle-stories of the Gospels, to make them appear as distorted reports of remarkable but perfectly natural occurrences. It appears to him to be beyond question that Jesus effected a number of healings; that not only his disciples but his opponents admitted the reality of his powers, though they explained them differently; and that Jesus himself believed that the Spirit of God acted through and in him to vanquish the demons and to heal diseases. How these events would be described by a trained scientific observer of our own times, or how the healings would be explained by a physician or psychiatrist today, it is impossible to say. That the stories have grown in the telling, that the popular imagination of the early Christians created new wonder-tales, or borrowed and adapted old ones from other sources (the Old Testament, the repertoire of Hellenistic aretalogists, 'lives' of Pythagoras or of Herakles, etc.) is only what we should expect under the circumstances. 'To wish such things away, for the sake of getting a more objective account of the facts, would be to wish the narrators not human at all or so highly trained in the sifting of *Wahrheit* from *Dichtung* as to belong neither to their country nor their age ... The impression made, on my mind at least, is that we are dealing, both when we examine the existing Evangelists and when we try to reconstruct their sources, written or oral, with thoroughly honest people, who told a story they entirely believed with no more than a minimum of the distorting medium through which every narrator, according to his date

[1] See the excellent chapter on 'Miracles and Miracle Stories' in *Mysterious Revelation*, by T. A. Burkill (Ithaca: Cornell University Press,) 1963, pp. 41-61.

and environment, must see the events which he tries to record'.[1] Finally, let us remark that the Christological question is not at stake in the matter. Certainly no one would feel obliged to give more credit to the miracle-stories of the Gospels than to those of Apollonius of Tyana or to those which Aelius Aristides attributes to Asklepios, unless in the feeling that the divinity of Jesus makes credible things that would otherwise be incredible; that is, no one will regard the miracle-stories of the Gospels as credible at all unless he has the prior conviction that they are congruous with the belief which he holds concerning Jesus on quite other grounds. But this proposition cannot be stated in reverse; it does not follow that anyone who holds to the Christian belief in Jesus as the incarnate Son of God must regard the miracle-stories as entirely credible. He must also consider the whole question of the nature of the materials, the time and circumstances of those who transmitted the tradition, and the impossibility of imagining men of the first century telling the story of Jesus without miracles. He will be entirely justified in concluding that the Church's faith in Jesus does not depend in the slightest on the credibility of the stories which were told of him in the first generation of Christian believers.

46. *The Centurion's Servant*

MATTHEW viii. 5-13 LUKE vii. 1-10

This story is not found in Mark; and in Luke it is used immediately following the Sermon on the Plain (Luke's version of the Sermon on the Mount). The differences in the two versions are more than merely verbal, and at first sight suggest that it has come to the two Evangelists through different channels of transmission. In Luke's version, the centurion never puts in an appearance; first he persuades Jewish elders to approach Jesus on his behalf (*v.* 3), and then he sends friends to bid Jesus not to take the trouble to come in person — the centurion has no doubt that Jesus can effect his purpose by word of command, as he himself can (*vv.* 6ff.). In Matthew neither of these groups of intermediaries appears. The centurion himself approaches Jesus directly, first to tell of his 'boy's' sickness, then to dissuade him from coming to the house in person to effect the cure. In keeping with this, Luke tells us that 'the friends who had been sent found the slave healed when they returned to the house', while Matthew is content to say that 'the boy was healed in the very hour' when Jesus spoke to the centurion (*v.* 13). The variation 'boy' — 'slave' is not significant, since the Greek word *pais* (used by Matthew) can have either sense according to the context; in the very different version used in John, it is interesting to note that it is interpreted as meaning 'son' (*huios* — John iv. 46-53). In *vv.* 11 and 12 Matthew has attached to the story a separate saying of Jesus, which Luke has used in a different context.

On further examination, however, we shall probably come to the conclusion that both stories are drawn from a single source, but that Matthew has abbreviated to the point of sacrificing much of the vividness of the underlying

[1] H. J. Rose, 'Herakles and the Gospels', *Harvard Theological Review*, vol. 31, no. 2 (1938) pp. 141-2.

narrative. The words of the centurion (spoken by himself in Matthew; conveyed to Jesus through his friends in Luke) are given with hardly the change of a vowel; and again the words which describe the effect upon Jesus and those which report his words of comment are given with almost equal similarity of expression (Matt. viii. 8-10 and Luke vii. 6-9 differ only in so far as is made necessary by Matthew's removal of the intermediaries; more than sixty of the words used in Luke occur again in Matthew in these few verses). It will be found that Matthew makes equally radical abbreviations in the double story of Jairus' Daughter and the Woman with the Issue of Blood (§ 107) and in the story of the Gadarene [Gerasene] Demoniac (§ 106), and in neither of the latter cases would we be inclined to postulate a different source. We shall see here, accordingly, one aspect of the literary methods of Matthew.

In §§ 106 and 107, we have to do with Matthew's treatment of a Marcan story; here it is a 'Q' story which he handles in the same drastic fashion. It would be difficult in the face of these observations to suppose that Matthew has been used as Luke's source for this story; and we shall find a number of other instances which tell strongly against the apparently simple hypothesis that the 'Q' material can be regarded as drawn from Matthew by Luke. Here certainly the case for a common source is much the more probable.

Let us add that it is precisely the passage in which the differences of the two versions are at the minimum that the central interest of the story lies. Not the miracle in itself, but the dialogue of the centurion with Jesus and the culminating words of the Lord form the heart of the story. It is told as an illustration of a faith found in a Gentile which exceeded that of any Israelite; thus it is related to the historical situation of the time of the Evangelists, when the Church was largely Gentile in composition and the gospel was finding almost no response from Jewish hearers. Even in the lifetime of Jesus, during a ministry almost wholly directed to Israel, there were intimations such as this that he and his message would find a readier response among Gentiles than among his own people. Matthew has driven home this point by introducing here the detached logion of verses 11 and 12.

§§ 47 and 48 — see under §§ 13 and 14, where we have drawn attention to Matthew's characteristic abbreviation of Mark and his equally characteristic attachment of a prophetic oracle (viii. 17) to the Marcan narrative — an oracle which again, as frequently in Matthew, is given a sense that hardly belongs to the Hebrew text.

49. *Two Claimants to Discipleship*

MATTHEW viii. 18-22

Matthew here introduces a pair of sayings from 'Q', supplying a setting for them (18a); Luke uses them in a different setting, along with a third saying (§ 138). They are grouped as stressing factors which discourage any half-hearted discipleship. The first saying gives us our first instance of the use of the phrase 'Son of Man' in Matthew. In the mind of the Evangelist it is undoubtedly a title of Jesus, and he takes the words to mean that the 'Son of Man' of apocalyptic expectation — the glorious heavenly being who shall descend to judge the earth and to inaugurate God's kingdom — has appeared on earth in the person of Jesus, in a destitute condition, lacking even the shelter of the birds and beasts. It is probable, however, that the words, if actually spoken by Jesus at all, were not spoken in this context or with this sense. The Aramaic phrase *bar-nasha*, literally 'son of man', will here have had the ordinary sense of 'man', 'human being', in keeping with a common Semitic idiom; and the saying will have been a somewhat morose popular proverb, a comment on the social situation of the times in which human beings lacked even the shelter from the elements which foxes and birds could find for themselves. In 'Q', this proverb, already applied to Jesus in the tradition by the misunderstanding of the phrase 'son of man', had been provided with an artificial introduction in the words of the scribe; to this, Matthew and Luke have each given a setting — Matthew placing the petition and response on the way to the boat; while Luke places them 'on the road' in Samaria. See also the notes on § 138.

On the problem of the use of the term 'Son of Man' in the Gospels, see the discussion in *The Names of Jesus*, by Dr. Vincent Taylor (London: Macmillan, 1953), pp. 25-35.

The placing of this group of sayings does not seem particularly appropriate to the context, and leaves us with the feeling that Matthew has introduced them at this point merely to separate his first two triads of miracle-stories — 46-48 and 50-52. To form his second triad, he has brought forward two Marcan stories, and grouped them with the first of Mark's sequence of controversy-stories. Treatment of the first two (§§ 50 and 51) may be postponed until we come to them in the Marcan order (§§ 105 and 106).

52. *The Healing of a Man sick of the Palsy*

MATTHEW ix. 1-8 MARK ii. 1-12 LUKE v. 17-26

A quick glance at the Synopsis will show us that Matthew has again abbreviated the Marcan story. As frequently, he has sacrificed some of Mark's vivid scene-painting for the sake of conciseness; thus he omits the whole picture of the circumstances of the healing — the packed dwelling, the determined friends who make a hole in the roof and lower the sick man through it on his bed. Both Matthew and Luke have altered Mark's colloquial word *krabaton* ('bed, pallet') for the more literary terms *klinè*, *klinidion*. An interesting change is to be noted in Luke, in his introduction of *tiles* on the roof; for roof-tiles were not used in Palestine, and Luke has contributed this detail, mistakenly, out of his acquaintance with buildings in the Greek provinces.

This is a double story; the account of the miracle is interwoven with a dialogue between Jesus and his opponents ('some of the scribes' — Mark; 'the scribes and Pharisees' — Luke) over his authority to forgive sins. The scribes make their appearance somewhat surprisingly — have they forced their way through the throngs and into the packed house, with a determination equal to that of the friends of the paralytic? Once the dialogue is concluded, they disappear equally surprisingly, and the story takes no further account of them: they are certainly not included among those who glorify God when they have witnessed the healing. The controversy-portion of the pericope, accordingly, is an interpolation, which disturbs the structure of the basic miracle-story; all the words that fall between the phrase 'he says to the paralytic' of Mark ii. 5 and its repetition in *v.* 10 must be regarded as secondary. It is unlikely that they are derived from an independent controversy-story; rather, the story of the paralytic has been expanded in the tradition by the insertion of this little dialogue. In this developed form, the miraculous element in the story is subordinated to the apologetic. The authority to forgive sins is exercised in the Church, as a continuing function; by the Jews this is assailed as blasphemy; and the fact of the healing is adduced as evidence that God has in fact 'given such authority to men' (Matt. ix. 8).

The Marcan introduction to the story implies that Jesus is at home, and that he has transferred his regular residence from Nazareth to Capernaum. The fact that he has a regular residence anywhere is at variance with the saying which Matthew has given in § 49, in the sense which he has given to it: 'the Son of Man has nowhere to lay his head'. Matthew accordingly omits all mention of a house as the scene of the healing, saying only that Jesus 'came to his own city'. Luke's changes in the introduction are occasioned by his feeling that something is needed to prepare the reader for the appearance of 'Pharisees and teachers of the Law' in the company: he explains that they have 'come from every village of Galilee and Judaea, and from Jerusalem'.

The problem of the meaning of the phrase 'son of man' again confronts us. Here it may be simply a surrogate for the personal pronoun 'I'; but it may equally well have been used in the first instance in its primary sense 'man'. It could never be taken to suggest that the authority to forgive belongs to man as man, but only to man as commissioned by God — that is, in the Christian sense, to the authorized ministers of the Church. The thought oscillates between the authority of Jesus himself to forgive, and the power of absolution committed to the Church; just as it links together healing and pardon. The concluding words in the Matthaean version suggest rather the collective interpretation, speaking as they do of the authority that God has given to *men* — not to Jesus alone. Thus the story as a whole illustrates strikingly the principle that the materials preserved in the Gospels are those which were relevant to the continuing mission of the Church. In recounting Jesus' reply to the charge of blasphemy, the Church defends itself also against the same charge, and claims that its own power of absolution is confirmed by the reality of its ministry of healing. The divine power that is present to heal the diseases of the body can also heal the troubles of the soul. The man in his entirety — body and soul — is made whole.

53. *The Call of Levi*

MATTHEW ix. 9-13 MARK ii. 13-17 LUKE v. 27-32

In Matthew this section and the next are used as the break between his second and his third triad of miracle-stories. In Mark and in Luke they form part of the collection of controversy-stories, as we have noted above.

The section is composite. In Mark, it consists of three elements: (1) an editorial link with the preceding section (*v.* 13) — this is omitted in Matthew and a briefer phrase is substituted for it in Luke; (2) the story of the call of an apostle, framed on the same lines as the call of the fishermen (*v.* 14; cf. § 11); here Matthew substitutes the name Matthew for that of Levi the son of Alphaeus and Luke adds the phrase 'forsaking everything'; and (3) a 'pronouncement-story' (to use the classification of Dr. Vincent Taylor), which is artificially attached to the story of the call (*vv.* 15-17).

Interest attaches chiefly to the third part, though it is of course interesting to learn that one of the detested tax-collectors ('publicans') was brought by Jesus into the apostolic band which he was forming. Here, however, the story of the call is told not for its own sake, but merely as a peg on which to hang the controversy-story, which in turn is no more than a vehicle for the great saying of Jesus: 'They that are well do not need a physician, but they that are sick; I did not come to call righteous men, but sinners.'

Note that in Mark and Matthew, the scene is laid in Jesus' house, while Luke sets it in the house of Levi and thus makes it natural for the company to consist of tax-collectors, people of his own profession whom Levi has invited. The setting is in any case artificial; it is impossible to imagine where the scribes and Pharisees of the story are standing, when they make their criticisms — obviously they are not following the example of Jesus in eating with tax-collectors and sinners! And we can hardly suppose that they address their reproachful query to the disciples over the garden wall. It is the saying that matters; the setting has been created to frame it. Here again we have a fragment of Christian apologetic: in repeating these words, the Church is not merely defending the memory of Jesus against Pharisaic slurs, but is directly defending its own practice of opening its gates to all sorts and conditions of men — like Jesus, it has a mission to heal and to save. Luke's addition of 'to repentance' is interpretative; it involves a certain narrowing of the force of the saying. The addition made by Matthew (ix. 13) may be derived from a variant form of the story with which he was acquainted; note his introduction of the same citation from Hosea into the controversy over Sabbath-observance (§ 69 — Matt. xii. 7).

54. *The Question about Fasting*

MATTHEW ix. 14-17 MARK ii. 18-22 LUKE ix. 33-39

Again we have before us a section compounded of several elements. Its kernel is the saying of Jesus: 'Can the wedding-guests fast when the bridegroom is with them?' (Mark ii. 19a). It is obvious that this rhetorical question could only be framed in response to criticism of the disciples of Jesus, for their failure to observe the practice of fasting. The introduction to the section suggests that they were unfavourably compared in this respect with the disciples of John the Baptist; the mention of the Pharisees (or the disciples of the Pharisees) is probably secondary. But this introduction as it stands gives an indistinct picture of the circumstances. The words in Mark suggest that the disciples of John (and the Pharisees) were actually fasting at a time when the disciples of Jesus were not; this could apply to a special fast of some kind, which was observed not by the whole community of Israel, but by devout groups. In Matthew and Luke, on the other hand, the position is generalized: it is suggested that the disciples of Jesus do not observe the practice of fasting at all; and the question of Jesus really presupposes this. The additional words — 19b (Mark only) and 20 (paralleled in Matthew and Luke, with verbal alterations) are probably secondary, justifying the practice of fasting in the life of the Church of the Evangelists' time, in spite of the recollection that Jesus himself and his disciples did not fast while he was with them on earth. To this Mark has added a pair of sayings originally detached — the parabolic sayings on Patches and Wineskins, which have no immediate relevance to the question of fasting, but make a general defence of the Christian innovations in religious practice and forms of community life. The Gospel of Christ cannot be simply attached to the venerable structure of Judaism, like a new patch on an old garment; the new life which it brings cannot be contained within the ancient forms; the attempt to keep it subordinated to Judaism can only result in disaster for both. To this Luke has added a third saying (*v.* 38), which may well be authentic but is certainly out of context here. It is not a defence of innovation, but a plea for conservatism — the old is better than the new.

The figure of the Bridegroom belongs to the imagery of the Kingdom of God as a wedding-feast, which is rooted in the Old Testament and is frequently employed in later Jewish literature. The words of Jesus carry the challenging implication that he is himself to be the central figure in the coming Kingdom; indeed, that the promised Kingdom is in some sense present, when he is on the scene, and that his disciples are appointed to have places at the great feast of God. It will be seen that the words are of crucial significance in relation to the whole question of eschatology in the teaching of Jesus, and to his understanding of his person and his mission.

§§ 55-57

Jairus' Daughter and the Woman with the Issue of Blood; Two Blind Men Healed; The Healing of a Dumb Demoniac

MATTHEW ix. 18-34

These three sections form the third of Matthew's triads of miracle-stories. The first of them is a Marcan story, greatly abbreviated; even the name of Jairus does not occur here, but is imported into the title from Mark. It will be more convenient to defer the analysis until we meet the same (twofold) story in its Marcan sequence (§ 107).

Sections 56 and 57 belong to the material found only in Matthew; but the former is manifestly a doublet of the Marcan story of blind Bartimaeus (§ 193), which Matthew also gives in its Marcan place, at the departure of Jesus from Jerusalem (there too he turns the single blind man of Mark's story into two); and the second of them is a doublet of the 'Q' passage (healing of a blind and dumb demoniac, followed by the accusation of the Pharisees that Jesus casts out demons by powers which derive from the prince of the demons — § 85). It would appear that Matthew includes these two stories at this point in order to complete his picture of the mighty works of Jesus in all their diversity, and to lay the groundwork for the words to be spoken in answer to the query of John the Baptist (Matt. xi. 5 — § 64).

§§ 58-63

The Appointment of the Twelve Apostles and the Mission Charge

MATTHEW ix. 53-xi. 1

At this point in his Gospel, Matthew introduces the second of the five main discourses in which he presents the teaching of Jesus. It takes the form of a Mission Charge to the Twelve, ostensibly delivered at the time of their appointment, as Jesus sends them out on a mission to preach and to heal, in Galilee. But it quickly becomes evident that the setting is a literary frame created by Matthew, not an historical reminiscence transmitted in the tradition. Like the Sermon on the Mount, the Charge is a compilation of sayings which have been transmitted through many channels, and have been brought together by Matthew from several sources and from other contexts. If we glance through the Synopsis we shall see that it presents much the same general appearance as we observed in the examination of the former Sermon. Some of it has no parallels in the other Gospels — it is drawn from Matthew's own fund of tradition. The greater part of it (some of § 58, and nearly all of §§ 60, 61 and 62) is paralleled in Luke, but in his work is scattered over several chapters (chapters 10, 12, 14 and 17), and much of it is set in quite different contexts; clearly Matthew did not find it gathered into this discourse in 'Q', however 'Q' may be conceived. A small part of it is derived from Mark, partly from Mark's own brief Mission Charge, which is, however, placed by him at a much later stage of the ministry, almost at the close of the Galilean period (§ 109 — Mark vi. 6-11); partly from Mark's account of the appointment of the Twelve, which follows soon after his sequence of Controversy-stories (Mark iii. 13-19; § 72); and partly from Mark's Apocalyptic Discourse, which is set in the last days in Jerusalem (Mark xiii; § 215); and a single verse is transferred from Mark's account of the Feeding of the Five Thousand (Mark vi. 34; § 112). It would scarcely be possible to imagine a more complicated rearrangement.

58. *The Sending out of the Twelve*

MATTHEW ix. 35-x. 16

The opening verses of this section in Matthew make a little introduction to the account of the appointment of the Twelve, and the mission on which they are to be sent. Verse 35, itself an enlargement of Mark's succinct introduction to the story, is at the same time a repetition in almost identical words of the sentence which precedes the Sermon on the Mount (see § 16; Matt. iv. 23), and is probably designed to mark off the portion of the Gospel that lies between these two verses, as a twofold picture of the mission of Jesus, first in word (the great Sermon), then in action (the three triads of miracle-stories). Verses 36 and 37 then suggest Jesus' sympathy with the masses in their need and lack of leadership, and so prepare the way for the provision which he is about to make in creating the apostolic band to guide these 'sheep without a shepherd'.

The list of the Twelve is identical with Mark's, except for two changes in the order of the names; in Luke's list, the name of Thaddaeus is replaced by that of Judas, son of James. It is surprising how little is known of the Twelve – of most of them, nothing at all; even the names are not entirely certain. They never functioned as a group, except perhaps in the very earliest days of the Jerusalem Church, after the Resurrection. Except for Peter, they are the shadowiest of figures; so much so that it has been questioned whether such a group was ever actually formed by Jesus (J. Wellhausen, J. Weiss, R. Bultmann and other critics of the highest rank; against this scepticism, see especially V. Taylor, *St. Mark*, p. 229 and the Additional Note 9, on 'The Twelve and the Apostles', pp. 619-27). However, it must be said that they are rooted in the earliest strands of tradition that have come down to us. The number twelve has communal and eschatological significance; they are the representatives of the twelve tribes of Israel and thus are mystically conceived as the ancestors of the new Israel which Jesus is forming about his own kingly person.

Matthew is alone in reporting the strange words with which Jesus opens his charge (x. 5-6), forbidding his disciples to go to Gentiles or Samaritans and commanding them to confine their mission to 'the lost sheep of the house of Israel'. With this we may compare the words of Matthew xv. 24, where Jesus affirms that his own mission is similarly confined. Though neither these words nor anything corresponding to them is to be found in the other Gospels, this must not be taken as an indication that the sayings are not authentic. It is natural enough that they should be preserved in the Jewish-Christian circles which provided Matthew with much of his material; and it is equally natural that they should have disappeared from the tradition current in the Gentile Churches, for which Mark and Luke were writing, in view of the fact that they had ceased to be relevant. St. Paul himself, the Apostle of the Gentiles, recognizes that 'Jesus Christ was made a minister of the circumcision for the truth of God' (Rom. xv. 8); and the long hesitancy of the primitive Church to carry the Gospel to Gentiles is more easily understandable if its tradition contained a flat injunction of Jesus, forbidding his disciples to go among Gentiles and Samaritans. The risen Jesus, through his Spirit, led his Church into a wider mission than he had attempted or counselled in the days of his flesh. Matthew reflects the facts of the historical development when he introduces the charge to evangelize the world only after the Resurrection (Matt. xxviii. 19).

The 'lost sheep' are the disinherited masses (the *Am-ha-arez* – 'people of the land') for whom the established religious leadership was accepting no concern, leaving them 'as sheep without a shepherd' (ix. 38, above); 'no Am-ha-arez is pious' said Rabbi Hillel.

The mission entrusted to the disciples is conceived as paralleling in every way the mission of Jesus himself — they are to take up his proclamation of the advent of God's Kingdom, and to exercise his powers of exorcism and healing and even of giving life to the dead.

It will be observed that most of the non-Marcan sayings which we find in Matthew in this Section are paralleled in Luke, but in the Charge to the Seventy (§ 139), of which neither Mark nor Matthew makes any mention. Both Matthew and Luke appear to have independent versions of the Charge, in addition to a source which they have used in common. Matthew has conflated the brief Marcan Charge with materials drawn from both 'Q' and his own special source, into a single discourse; Luke has kept the Marcan materials where he found them — in the Charge to the Twelve; and has conflated the 'Q' materials with a Charge to the Seventy, which he found in his special source. The Lucan handling of these materials will be examined when we come to them in his own sequence, in § 139.

Besides the command to confine the mission to 'the lost sheep of the house of Israel', Matthew has two sayings which have no parallel in either of the other Gospels: (i) 'Freely you received, freely give' — *v.* 8b; and (ii) 'Be therefore prudent as the serpents and harmless as the doves' — *v.* 16b. Both of these may well have circulated in the tradition as detached sayings. The second, in particular, strikes an incongruous note; the mixture of metaphors, which moves from the precarious situation of 'sheep in the midst of wolves' to the counsel to combine the sagacity of the serpent with the harmlessness of the dove, is decidedly violent. It is hard to see how the combined qualities of serpent and dove are to save the sheep from the fangs of the wolves.

In the brief Marcan charge, Jesus forbids the apostles to take food, wallet, money (bronze coins) in the belt, or a change of clothing (no second *chiton*); but he permits them to carry a staff and to be shod with sandals. In Matthew's version, staff and sandals are both forbidden; and the description of the coins (which must not be carried) is enlarged to include gold and silver as well as bronze. Luke mentions only silver, and forbids the staff; in his second charge (x. 4) the sandals too are forbidden. This would appear to indicate that in 'Q', the charge forbade staff and sandals, and perhaps read 'take no gold or silver', in place of 'take no bronze'. In Luke and Matthew the language of 'Q' has occasioned modifications in the wording of the Marcan charge. Luke may have omitted mention alike of the 'gold' of 'Q' and of the 'bronze' of Mark from a feeling that the disciples would be unlikely in any case to have gold coins in their possession, but that they might well have something a little more valuable than bronze coins — silver would probably be available to them, but hardly gold. The prohibition of staff and sandals, going beyond the demands of the Marcan charge, appears to be secondary. Perhaps, as W. L. Knox suggests, it may be prompted by a desire to show that the Christian missionaries can endure hardness as severe as that of the wandering Cynic preacher, who took pride in getting along without even the simplest equipment; he needs nothing but the meagre clothes in which he stands.

Matthew enlarges the brief Marcan injunction about lodgings by adding materials which seem to be drawn from a source shared by Luke (Matt. x. 10b, 11-13, 15, 16a); the variations from Luke's order and wording (Luke x. 3, 5-6, 7b, 12) are not so great as to suggest the use of a separate source. It will be observed, however, that Luke uses these supplementary sayings in the context of the Mission of the Seventy (-Two); the question is thus raised, whether 'Q' reported this second Mission, or whether it was found only in Luke's special source. See the discussion under § 139.

59. *The Lot of the Disciples*

Matthew x. 17-25

The Charges as given in Mark and Luke contain no parallel to these verses. Much of the material, however, is drawn from the Apocalyptic Discourse of Mark xiii (§ 215). Verses 17 to 22 are quite unmistakably copied from Mark xiii. 9-13, with only trifling alterations in the wording. The most significant change is the addition 'and to the Gentiles', in *v.* 18 – strangely out of place in the context of a commission that explicitly excludes 'the way of the Gentiles' (*v.* 5). Verses 21 and 22 are word for word identical with Mark xiii. 12-13, apart from the first connective (*de* for *kai*); and in *vv.* 17-20 there are no less than 35 words identical with those of Mark xiii. 9-11, without even a variation in order. A couple of sentences of the same Marcan passage are used again by Matthew in his own version of the Apocalyptic Discourse (Matt. xxiv. 9, 13).

It is evident that these verses (17 to 22) are out of place here. On this Galilean mission the disciples were not in fact haled before local sanhedrins or flogged in synagogues or (most definitely) haled before governors and kings; nor was there such division in households as is here described. Matthew here allows himself to be anachronistic. His vision goes beyond the Galilean mission, with which he is ostensibly dealing, to the conflicts of the Church's early days, when households were bitterly divided against themselves, even to the point of delivering the Christian members over to death; when the missionaries were indeed flogged in the synagogues (St. Paul tells us that no less than five times he was given the 'forty stripes less one' at the command of the synagogue authorities – 2 Cor. xi. 24); and even beyond the Jewish mission to the still more distant days when apostles were to be put on trial before Roman governors and before Emperors ('kings'), for a testimony to the Gentiles. See the remarks of B. W. Bacon in his *Studies in Matthew* (New York: Holt, 1930), pp. 196-201.

We have here a particularly striking instance of the tendency of all the Evangelists to subordinate historical exactitude to the concerns of the living Church. For Matthew, the Jesus who delivered the mission charge to the Twelve in Galilee is incorporated into one portrait with the Jesus who governs his Church from heaven, and still calls his disciples to bear the Gospel message to all the world without fear either of the consequences to themselves or of the social disturbances which are sure to follow. And he does not feel it incumbent upon him to confine his report of the Charge to the words which Jesus actually spoke on that particular occasion. He is not attempting to write as a scientific historian or a painstaking biographer; and we must not make the mistake of judging him, or of seeking to interpret him, by canons by which he is not himself guided — any more than we would judge El Greco or Picasso or Dufy by the standards of colour photography or even of Rubens or Titian.

Verse 23 offers problems of its own. It is found only in Matthew, and bears the distinctively Jewish-Christian cast of his special source. 'This city' can only mean 'Jerusalem', and the words (like those of *vv.* 5 and 6) intimate that the mission will not extend beyond Palestine — there will not be time even to make the circuit of the Holy Land before the great Day dawns. If Jesus spoke words like these, we must conclude that he expected the advent of the Son of Man to take place very shortly, and that he entertained no vision of an extension of the gospel to the Gentiles. It has been suggested, accordingly, that what we have here is an oracle delivered in and for the early Church in Jerusalem, received and preserved by it as a command of the risen Jesus. In what sense it was interpreted by Matthew himself we find it impossible to say; for he certainly believed that the risen Jesus sent his apostles into all the world to preach to all nations, and did not hold that the advent of the Son of Man would take place before they could make the round of the cities of Israel.

The sayings of *vv.* 24 and 25 are partly paralleled in Luke, though in a different context and probably with a different sense (Luke vi. 40, § 76, in the 'Sermon on the Plain', *q.v.*). A still closer parallel is found in the Fourth Gospel (John xiii. 16; xv. 20), in the context of the Farewell Discourses of Jesus at the Last Supper. In neither case is there any indication of the use of a common source; we have three independent lines of transmission of Jesus' warning to his disciples that they must not expect any gentler treatment than was accorded to him.

60. *Exhortation to Fearless Confession*

MATTHEW x. 26-33 LUKE xii. 2-9

The material of this section has been drawn almost entirely from a source used in common by Matthew and Luke (Q). Matthew has incorporated it into his mission charge, and has thus pointed it as a warning and encouragement to Christian missionaries. Luke has used it in a totally different context (§ 155; Luke xii. 2-12); he places it immediately after the Discourse against the Pharisees (reserved by Matthew for the controversies of the Days in Jerusalem — Matt. xxiii. 1-36; § 210), and under the warning to 'beware of the leaven of the Pharisees, which is hypocrisy'. This affects the meaning considerably; and directs the exhortation no longer to missionaries but to the whole body of believers, specifically, indeed, to believers living in a Jewish environment.

Two of the *logia* found in the passage are used separately and in different contexts by Mark. The first two verses of the 'Q' material are paralleled in Mark iv. 22, where they bear upon the interpretation of parables; the last two are paralleled in Mark viii. 38, in association with the call to the disciples to take up the cross, following the Petrine confession at Caesarea Philippi. It seems probable, therefore, that these two *logia* were transmitted independently in the oral tradition, and that their incorporation into this catena of sayings was done by the editors of the 'Q' source. We can no longer determine the context in which this catena was placed in 'Q', still less the situations in which Jesus first spoke the several *logia* which it contains. There is no necessary connection between the sayings. We have before us four *logia*, intrinsically independent of one another (*vv.* 26-27; 28; 29-31; and 32-33), and Jesus may well have uttered them on four different occasions. None of the contexts in which we now find them is compellingly appropriate.

The differences in wording which we observe in comparing Matthew with Luke may go back to differences in the text of the source which they have used, or may be attributed to the freedom which one or both of them exercised in reproducing it. Such a question cannot be decided by the examination of this one passage; our answer would depend upon the general views which we are able to form concerning the style and methods of the two Evangelists, and upon the degree of variation that the 'Q' source may have exhibited in different copies. If 'Q' was originally an Aramaic collection, the differences could point to independent Greek translations from the Aramaic. Professor T. W. Manson suggested that the two explanations should be combined. 'There is nothing improbable in the supposition that several Greek versions of such a document might be made ... We have two versions of Q – Q according to Matthew and Q according to Luke. The differences between them can be explained in part as editorial – stylistic or other "improvements" carried out by the Evangelists. But after we have allowed for these there is still a certain amount of difference in wording, and some of it at least can be explained on the supposition that we have before us two different renderings of a single Aramaic original' (*Sayings*, p. 18).

A third factor may be suggested. We find that in our manuscripts of the Gospels, scribes have a tendency to assimilate – to substitute the words of one Gospel for those of another, in parallel passages. It was easy for the scribe, if his attention flagged for a moment, to put down familiar words almost mechanically, without checking the wording of the text which he was copying. Is it not possible, and even likely, that these Evangelists, who show clearly enough in any case that they felt no obligation to reproduce exactly the words of their sources, would from time to time substitute – now by inadvertence, now by design – a form of words familiar to them *from oral repetition* for the variant form of such and such a saying which they found in Mark or in 'Q'? This would, for instance, offer a plausible explanation of the difference between Luke and Matthew in the third *logion* of the passage – 'two sparrows for a penny', in Matthew; 'five sparrows for two pence', in Luke. (In this particular instance there is also the prosaic possibility that each Evangelist 'corrected' the saying in keeping with the market price for sparrows at his own dealer's.)

61. *Division in Households*

MATTHEW x. 34-36 LUKE xii. 51-53

Again we have a 'Q' logion, which Luke has set in another context (§ 160). Matthew has abbreviated his source, as he so often does; but has completed the citation from Micah vii. 6, at the end. See the notes on the Lucan parallel.

62. *The Conditions of Discipleship*

MATTHEW x. 37-39 LUKE xiv. 26-27; xvii. 33

The three sayings which are here brought together by Matthew are paralleled in Luke, but in two different and widely separated contexts, and with such great differences in their wording as to indicate that the Evangelists have not drawn them from a common source. The first saying has no Marcan parallel; the Lucan version probably stands closer to the original form of the saying, as it reproduces a peculiarly Semitic locution. 'Hate' is not meant to be taken in the positive sense, but in the comparative sense of 'love less', as frequently in O.T. and Talmud (see the note of T. W. Manson, *Sayings*, p. 131). Matthew's version renders the underlying Aramaic more freely, but conveys the sense better in Greek (and in English). The second and third sayings are transmitted independently in the context of Peter's Confession (Mark viii. 34-35 and parallels), where Matthew and Luke follow the Marcan wording closely.

The first two sayings are found in Luke as part of a catena on 'The Cost of Discipleship' (§ 171), addressed to 'great multitudes' (Luke xiv. 25). There also the setting is editorial, and the passage is a collection of sayings that were not connected in their original delivery or in the earlier stages of oral transmission. The third saying was not found by Luke in the same collection, but in the middle of an Apocalyptic Discourse (§ 184, 'The Day of the Son of Man'), where it is not a general 'condition of discipleship', but a specific warning of the impossibility of finding safety in flight when the hour of Judgment strikes. We have here another illustration of the extent to which the point of a saying can be changed by the context in which it is placed, whether by the Evangelist or by the compiler of his source.

63. *The End of the Discourse*

MATTHEW x. 40-xi. 1

Matthew closes the Charge with a short catena of sayings which are linked by the theme-words 'receive' and 'reward'. Probably he has brought them together himself. Mark, followed by Luke, has used the *logion* of *v.* 40 in association with the 'Dispute about Greatness' (§ 129); Matthew omits it at that point (Matt. xviii. 5) because he has already used it here. A parallel to this logion, with a negative emphasis (consequences of rejecting the messengers) is used by Luke in the Mission Charge to the Seventy (§ 139). Bultmann (*History*, p. 147) suggests, plausibly enough, that *v.* 41 is an example of Christian appropriation of inherited Jewish material; in itself, the saying requires no distinctively Christian frame of reference, but receives it from the context in which it is placed. The third saying is found in a slightly different form in Mark ix. 42, loosely (and inappropriately) attached to the counsel of Jesus to refrain from interfering with an exorcist who uses the Name of Jesus though he does not belong to the band of disciples. T. W. Manson argues that in several sayings in which Jesus spoke of 'little ones', meaning simply 'little children', the tradition has transferred them in application to the disciples: 'there is a steady movement in the direction of turning "little ones" into "disciples"'

(*Sayings*, p. 138). In the mouth of Jesus, the saying will have meant that kindness to a little child will be rewarded by God; in Matthew's adaptation (probably not made by him, but already reflected in the tradition on which he drew), the thought is that everyone who befriends a disciple of Jesus 'in the name of disciple' — that is, because he holds the status of disciple — will receive a reward (from God).

The last verse of the section (xi. 1) is the formula which Matthew uses (with appropriate variations) at the conclusion of each of his five main Discourses (vii. 28; xiii. 53; etc.).

Notice that Matthew has nothing more to say of the Mission. He has told us (x. 5) that Jesus sent out the Twelve after delivering the Charge which we have just been studying; but now it is Jesus himself who goes elsewhere to resume his teaching and preaching, and we hear nothing of the missionary activities of the disciples and of their return. Contrast with this, Mark vi. 12-13 = Luke ix. 6; and Mark vi. 30 = Luke ix. 10. The Charge remains, but the Mission which it was to govern disappears from the narrative.

Mixed Reception of Jesus in Galilee
§§ 64-68

MATTHEW xi. 2-30

A glance at the Synopsis will show that the greater part of the material in these sections is paralleled in Luke; but Matthew has again brought together into a sequence materials which Luke has chosen to use in three different contexts (and one verse in a fourth context). A very few verses are peculiar to Matthew, but all the rest is 'Q' material, in which the Matthaean version, apart from excisions, follows the Lucan word for word. Now we have already had occasion to observe that it is characteristic of Matthew to abbreviate, but it is no habit of Luke to pad things out. Accordingly, the evidence points to the use of a common source by Matthew and Luke, not to the use of Matthew by Luke.

64. *The Baptist's Question*

65. *Christ's Testimony to the Baptist*

MATTHEW xi. 2-19 LUKE vii. 18-35

These two sections in Luke form part of his 'Little Insertion' (vi. 20-viii. 3; §§ 73-84), where he breaks into the Marcan framework to introduce materials derived mainly from 'Q' but partly from his own special source. The two Evangelists are obviously following a common written source, for they agree almost word for word, even to details of word order. The introductory phrases are editorial, linking the story of John's question and the reply of Jesus loosely (indeed vaguely) to the preceding sayings and stories, with which there is no intrinsic connection. The common source 'Q' has already brought together a number of fragments of tradition concerning the relations between John and Jesus, in a form in which genuine reminiscence is already coloured by the continuing rivalry between the Church and the sect which revered the memory of John.

The attitude of the Church to John and to the movement which he founded reflects a certain ambiguity. On the one hand it could never be forgotten that Jesus himself had received baptism at the hands of John, however great the difficulties that this occasioned for Christian thought. It seems likely, too, that some of the first disciples of Jesus had been disciples of John, as the Fourth Gospel tells us (John i. 35ff.; cf. Acts i. 21-22), and that there was a continuing drift of converts from the Johannine sect to the Church (John iii. 22-30; Acts xix. 1-7). Accordingly, the Church looked with friendly eyes upon the rival movement, and sought to win its adherents by persuading them that their founder himself had pointed to Jesus as one greater than himself. On the other hand there was the awkward fact that John himself had never become a disciple of Jesus; therefore, though his greatness was fully recognized, it could be said that 'he that is least (literally, "lesser") in the kingdom of heaven is greater than he'. It is reported several times that Jesus himself saw John as fulfilling the role appointed for Elijah in the End Time, and the tradition attributed to John himself the same view of his mission. In accordance with this testimony of the Gospels, John is still honoured in the liturgy as 'The Forerunner'.

In § 64, there are no significant differences between the two versions. Apart from the independently constructed introductions, both editorial, Matthew has cut out two verses (Luke vii. 20-21) which are repetitious. The doubts of John probably arose from his perception that the mission of Jesus showed no signs of issuing in the devastating judgment by wind and fire that he had predicted. These doubts were not to be removed by an exhibition of miraculous powers. There is even something incongruous in the notion that Jesus would put on a spectacular display of his gifts for the benefit of John's messengers. The real point of the reply is that the mission of Jesus is not to condemn but to save; and John must not be offended that things are not developing in accordance with his expectations and predictions.

There is a profound difference between the spirit of John's preaching and the mission of Jesus, yet there are important links between them. This is the general theme of § 65. Both have been sent by God; John has come as the herald of Jesus; and both have been rejected by the nation at large. Luke suggests in an aside (*vv.* 29-30 – sayings used only by him, perhaps as a footnote by way of comment) that the respectable and pious 'Pharisees and lawyers' turned a deaf ear to John, but that the masses and the despised tax-collectors were moved to repentance. But the concluding Parable of the Children at Play makes no such distinction. It presupposes that both missions have met with the same disappointing reception. John has been rejected because he was too austere; Jesus, because he is too lax.

'The Son of Man' here, as often, carries no more weight than the personal pronoun 'I' (see T. W. Manson, *The Teaching of Jesus*, pp. 217ff.).

66. *Woes on the Cities of Galilee*

MATTHEW xi. 20-24 LUKE x. 13-15

The sayings of this section are used by Luke in the Charge which he attaches to the Mission of the Seventy. Matthew has preferred to introduce them here, where they carry on the theme of the rejection of Jesus. Nothing is known of a mission in Chorazin or in Bethsaida, and we have no account of the 'mighty works' which ought to have sufficed to move those towns to repentance. We have here an incidental reminder of the great gaps in our knowledge of the ministry of our Lord. Even the reproach to Capernaum surprises us, for the stories of Jesus' activity in that city have suggested rather that he met with an enthusiastic response (Matt. ix. 8; cf. Mark i. 27-28 – these verses, however, are not taken up by Matthew). The last sentences of the Matthaean passage (23b, 24; not found in Luke) appear to have been constructed by him on the analogy of *vv.* 21-22, on the foundation of the saying of *v.* 24, which occurs in a modified form in the context of the Mission Charge (Matt. x. 15 = Luke x. 12).

67. *Christ's Thanksgiving to the Father*

MATTHEW xi. 25-27 LUKE x. 21-22

68. *Comfort for the Heavy-laden*

MATTHEW xi. 28-30

Luke connects the Prayer with the return of the Seventy and the report of the successes which have attended their mission; Matthew prefers to set it here, after the 'Woes', indicating that he thinks of it as continuing the theme of rejection. Thus in the Lucan setting, the emphasis is laid on the revelation to 'babes'; in the Matthaean it falls rather on the hiding of the revelation from 'wise and prudent'.

The two sections are rhythmic in structure, consisting of three strophes, of which Luke has used only the first two. Perhaps the third was missing in his copy of the source. There is nothing distinctively Matthaean about it, and we would be less positive than Professor Manson, that 'the absence of these verses from Lk. is a fatal objection to the theory that they stood in Q' (*Sayings*, p. 185). At the same time, the association of the three strophes is literary (or pre-literary) rather than original. The first and third are Semitic in tone and character, and are almost certainly translations from Aramaic. The second 'sounds like a Hellenistic revelation-saying' (Bultmann, *History*, p. 159). The third is closely akin to utterances of the personified Wisdom of Hebrew literature (cf. Prov. viii. 4-11; 32-35; Ecclus. xxiv. 19-22; etc.). This has led some critics to hold that it is a citation from an otherwise unknown Jewish book of Wisdom, which in the development of the tradition has been attributed to Jesus, conceived as the incarnate Wisdom of God. We could equally well think of it as an oracle composed in the same spirit by a Jewish-Christian prophet. But there is no absolute compulsion upon us to hold it unauthentic. If we attribute it to Jesus, as the Gospel does, it will of course carry weighty implications for his 'Messianic' self-consciousness. We shall then be inclined to adopt the interpretation of T. W. Manson, who holds that Jesus speaks 'as the representative, not of the divine Wisdom, but of the Kingdom of God' (*Sayings*, p. 186). 'My yoke' will then be 'the yoke of the Kingdom' (contrasted with 'the yoke of the Law', which lay like a heavy burden on the neck — Acts xv. 10).

On the form of this group of sayings, see especially E. Norden, *Agnostos Theos*, pp. 277-308; and W. L. Knox, *Some Hellenistic Elements in Primitive Christianity*, pp. 6f.

'Wise and prudent' means, in Rabbinic parlance, those learned in the Law; the 'babes' will be the unlearned, the fishermen and peasants who have responded to the message that has left the learned cold. Jesus is perhaps the only great teacher in history who has had to communicate his thought to people so far below his own intellectual level. The bright young men of the rabbinical schools followed their masters in rejecting him. Jesus does not feel chagrin over this, or deplore it as a misfortune. It is the good pleasure of God, and he can only give thanks. In the same spirit, St. Paul reminds us that 'God has chosen the foolish things of the world, that he may put the wise to shame ... that no human flesh may glory in his presence' (1 Cor. i. 27-29).

The language of the second strophe is unique in the Synoptic tradition, in that nowhere else[1] does Jesus speak of himself absolutely as 'the Son', or claim the possession of a knowledge of God which others can receive only through his mediation. It recalls the language of the Fourth Gospel; see especially John iii. 35f; v. 19ff. Jesus certainly addressed God as 'Father' (as in the Thanksgiving above), and there is good reason to hold that he spoke of him as 'my Father' in a peculiar sense, and that he conceived of his relationship to God in terms of sonship. But the terminology of this passage goes beyond anything that we can find in the language which we can confidently ascribe to Jesus himself; it reflects an early stage of the Hellenistic mystical theology which comes to fruition in the Johannine writings. Jesus speaks here as the mystagogue, the '*Exēgētēs*' (cf. John i. 18), the Revealer who communicates to others the knowledge of God which he alone possesses.

There is a possibility (which must be regarded as remote) that Jesus spoke in this mystical way of his relationship to the Father and his function as Revealer; and that we have here a stray fragment of an aspect of the teaching which is much more amply represented in the Fourth Gospel. We would then have to think of Jesus as somehow imbued with a Hellenistic mysticism (from what point of contact?) which was utterly strange and incomprehensible to his immediate disciples. It seems far more reasonable to see in the passage evidence for the early emergence of Hellenistic influences in the thought of the Church — early enough to be accepted by the compilers of 'Q' as something that could be attributed to Jesus.

69. *Plucking Corn on the Sabbath*

MATTHEW xii. 1-8 MARK ii. 23-28 LUKE vi. 1-5

With this pericope, Matthew picks up the thread of the Marcan narrative, and we return to the sequence of controversy-stories which began with § 52.

[1] There is one partial exception in Mk. xiii. 32 (Matt. xxiv. 36) — 'nor the Son'; but there Jesus *disavows* any special knowledge.

There is nothing to indicate that either Matthew or Luke has combined another version of the incident with that which lay before him in Mark. Apart from minor verbal changes in the introduction, we note that both Matthew and Luke have removed the erroneous reference to Abiathar (Mark ii. 26), and the entire saying of Mark ii. 28; and Matthew has made a considerable addition (*vv.* 5-7).

It is not hard to see why the two later Evangelists have eliminated the saying: 'The sabbath was made for man, not man for the sabbath.' As it stands, the words imply that man is the measure of all things, and that the observance of God's law is to be subordinated to the passing needs of the individual – he need not keep the law if it imposes upon him a trifling hardship. It is in fact impossible that Jesus should have expressed himself to this effect. If we now take into consideration the underlying Aramaic, we shall observe that the phrase *bar-nasha* (literally 'son of man') would represent both the 'man' of Mark's *v.* 27 (twice) and 'the Son of Man' of his *v.* 28. But it is not conceivable that the same phrase should have had one sense in the first saying and another sense in the second; either it meant 'man' all the way through, or 'the Son of Man' all the way through. As it is utterly inconceivable that Jesus should have declared that 'Man is Lord of the sabbath', it follows that the proper rendering of the first saying was: 'The sabbath was made for the Son of Man, not the Son of Man for the sabbath.' In such a context, 'the Son of Man' is clearly used as a self-designation of Jesus, not in any apocalyptic sense but as an equivalent of 'Messiah'; and the saying, so understood, would be akin to the rabbinical affirmation that 'the world was made for the Messiah'. Verse 28 (Mark), which is retained by Matthew and Luke, is then seen to be a parallel expression, and it is not necessary to regard it, as do many critics, as a later and somewhat inconsequential addition to *v.* 27. Matthew and Luke, having the erroneous Greek rendering of the first of this pair of sayings before them, have dropped it, recognizing that the point was sufficiently made by the second saying alone.

This saying, or rather the pair of sayings which Mark gives us, is the Christian reply to the Pharisaic challenge of Mark ii. 24 (and parallels). It was not unlawful to pluck a handful of grain to satisfy one's hunger; indeed, the Law even provided that the landowner should leave a little grain standing for the poor to glean. The offence lay in doing so on the sabbath; plucking the grain was interpreted as harvesting; and rubbing it out to eat, as threshing. To us this seems pettifogging; and indeed there is a saying in the Mishnah (Tractate *Hagigah* I. 8), that 'the rules about the sabbath ... are as mountains hanging on a hair, for Scripture is scanty and the rules many'. But the Christian reply makes no attempt to reject the tradition of interpretation elaborated by the scribes; it appeals solely to the higher authority of Jesus, who is Lord of the sabbath as of all the life of the community.

The appeal to the example of David is clearly secondary. This will appear if we notice that the scenery is artificially contrived. The appearance of the Pharisees is as inexplicable here as is that of the scribes, or scribes and Pharisees, in §§ 52 and 53. Are we to imagine them as out for a sabbath stroll in the country, where they happen to spot the disciples just as they are plucking a few heads of grain? Or that the disciples are regularly accompanied by a number of Pharisees? But such a scene could not have been contrived, or such a question framed, as an introduction to the saying about David. For the action of David was not a breach of the sabbath-law, nor was there any question of the disciples eating the 'bread of the Presence', which was permitted only to the priests. The appeal to the example of David is an anomalous intrusion into the basic framework of the controversy-story. We might add that the sayings of *vv.* 27 and 28 (Mark) are altogether irrelevant to the citation of David's action in eating the shewbread.

The Matthaean supplements (*vv.* 5 to 7) are themselves secondary to the introduction of the reference to David, to which they are linked by the theme-word 'priests'. Only the priests are permitted to eat the shewbread; and the priests likewise do their work on the sabbath without incurring guilt. This appeal is relevant only on the premiss that the disciples are in some sense exercising priestly functions as they walk through the fields on the sabbath – a premiss that would certainly not be allowed by the Pharisees, to whom the justification is offered! Verse 6 is yet another accretion, framed (perhaps by Matthew himself) in words analogous to the sayings of *vv.* 41 and 42 below. Verse 7, in turn, is a further accretion, linked to *v.* 5 by the theme-word 'guiltless'; it could well be an authentic saying of Jesus, transferred from another context (cf. Matt. ix. 13).

Form-critical analysis thus indicates several stages in the formation of the pericope. It is doubtful whether the saying, or pair of sayings (Mark ii. 27-28), from which it all began, can be regarded as authentic. As Bishop Rawlinson remarked (*Commentary on St. Mark*, ad loc.), 'Our Lord would not have been likely to say that "man" was "lord of the sabbath", which had been instituted by God. On the other hand, it is almost equally unlikely that He would have emphasized his personal lordship of the Sabbath.' We take it, accordingly, that the saying originated not with Jesus, but with the apostolic Church of Palestine, in controversy with the Pharisees, who took exception to the failure of Christian Jews to observe the sabbath. Some support is given to this hypothesis by the fact that the accusation is brought against the disciples, not against Jesus himself (cf. Mark ii. 18-22; vii. 5; and parallels – in all these controversies we must ask whether Jesus himself maintains a different standard of observance from his disciples; see the remarks of R. Bultmann, *History*, pp. 48-49). The Christian reply to the accusation (Jesus, the Son of Man, the Messiah, is Lord of the sabbath) has then come to be regarded as a saying of Jesus himself, and the little story of the disciples in the grainfields has been created as a frame for the saying. The successive supplements – first the appeal to the example of David; then the appeal to the exercise of duties by the priests – enlarge the area of the claim. Not only the law of the sabbath, but the whole system of Jewish observances is subordinate to the authority of Jesus: something greater than David, something greater than the Temple is here. The followers of Jesus are in the train of 'great David's greater Son', and are occupied in the priestly service of the Kingdom of God.

We look upon this pericope, accordingly, as based indeed upon some reminiscence of the action and attitudes of Jesus, but as owing its present form and most of its substance to complex adaptations in the course of transmission, in the service of Christian apologetic against Jewish (Pharisaic) criticism.

See further my article, 'The Sabbath was Made for Man?' in *JBL*, 79, Pt. II (June, 1960), pp. 130-6.

70. *The Healing of the Man with the Withered Hand*

MATTHEW xii. 9-14 MARK iii. 1-6 LUKE vi. 6-11

This is the last incident of Mark's series of controversy-stories. The miracle is not the centre of attention; the man who has been healed is of no interest to the narrator except as the necessary instrument of the action of Jesus, and nothing is said of the impression made on the people. The spotlight falls on the conflict between Jesus and his opponents, and the cause of controversy is not the healing as such, but the fact that it is done on the sabbath. Criticism has hardened into open hostility; the opponents of Jesus are looking for something that can be made the basis of a charge against him, presumably a formal charge to be laid in the Sanhedrin. All this suggests a situation for which nothing in the previous narrative has prepared us, and indicates that the story belongs to one of the last stages of the Ministry, probably as part of the final conflict with the authorities in Jerusalem. The association of Pharisees with Herodians, supporters of the rule of the Herod family in Israel, can hardly be imagined except as the last depth of hatred.

The Herodians have disappeared from the versions of Matthew and Luke, probably because this party had long ceased to exist by the time they wrote. Even in Mark, the reference to Pharisees and Herodians may be secondary, for in the introductory words of *v.* 2 the hostile observers are not identified, and there is a general tendency for adversaries of Jesus to be turned into scribes, Pharisees, or (more often) both, in the transmission of the tradition (see the remarks of R. Bultmann, *History*, pp. 52f.). But if so, they cannot have been introduced by Mark, for there could be no party of Herodians after the death of Herod Agrippa in A.D. 44 — there was no longer any Herodian pretender to the throne. We have here, then, an indication that the pericope had attained its present form before A.D. 44, and it is at least possible that the same early dating may be assigned to the whole collection of which it forms part (cf. W. L. Knox, *Sources*, I, p. 9). Yet there are indications that it had already passed through Gentile hands, even though the question would only be raised in Jewish circles; in particular, there are two Latinisms (!) — *sumboulion* in the sense of 'counsel' when it properly means 'council' (a confusion of *consilium* and *concilium*); and *sullupoumenos* in the sense of 'being grieved' — the Latin *contristari* — when its proper Greek meaning is 'to sympathize'. Thus W. L. Knox can suggest: 'It looks as though Mark or his source was drawing from a Latin version and retranslating it pretty badly' (*Sources*, I, p. 9, n. 2).

Both Matthew and Luke have eliminated Mark's *sullupoumenos*. Luke has also got rid of the barbarous *sumboulion*; the plot to destroy Jesus has been reduced to a conference to discuss what may be done about him. He has also transferred the mention of the Pharisees from the end of the story to the beginning, and added that Jesus 'knew their thoughts' (*v.* 8). Both Evangelists have removed Mark's reference to the emotion of Jesus — anger and grief — as part of a general tendency to avoid ascribing human emotions to him.

Matthew has added an isolated saying (*vv.* 11-12), which appears in a much modified form in Luke in the context of another story, which may be a doublet of this one (Luke xiv. 1-6, § 168). At the same time, he has cut out the challenge propounded by Jesus (Mark iii. 4). This may be an indication that he has had before him a version of Luke's other story, and has conflated the two while Luke has kept both.

The Call of the Twelve and the Great Sermon §§ 71-78

MATTHEW xii. 15-21 MARK iii. 7-19 LUKE vi. 17-49

At this point, the Gospel narrative seems for a time to lose coherence. Mark's material does not offer any clear divisions. Miscellaneous scenes are brought before us with little or no connection; they are linked together in a loose way by recurrent references to the lake ('sea') of Galilee, until at vii. 24 Jesus moves away to 'the region of Tyre and Sidon'. The material consists chiefly of miracle-stories and controversy-stories, together with a small collection of parables. With Matthew we are in the midst of a controversy-sequence, which has begun with the two stories of sabbath-disputes, and will continue with the accusation that Jesus is empowered by the devil (xii. 22-35). In Luke the next two sections form the introduction to his version of the great Sermon (§§ 73-78), which Matthew has already reported. With this, Luke in his turn departs from the Marcan narrative to insert a large amount of material, partly shared with Matthew, partly derived from sources used only by himself (§§ 73-84). We observe again that Luke does not mix Marcan material with 'Q' and 'L'; he uses Mark in solid blocks, alternating with blocks in which 'Q' and 'L' materials are combined. For the time being we shall be guided by the Lucan arrangement.

71. *Christ Heals the Multitudes*

MATTHEW xii. 15-21 MARK iii. 7-12 LUKE vi. 17-19

Note that Luke has transposed this section and that which follows.

In Mark this section gives a summary picture of the activity of Jesus during a period of great and growing fame. It is generally taken to be a construction of Mark himself, but there is much to be said for the view that it is the beginning of a 'Twelve-source', an early compilation of traditions concerning the Twelve (W. L. Knox, *Sources*, I, c. II, pp. 17ff.). The last phrase of *v.* 7 and the whole of *v.* 8 have all the appearance of secondary elaboration, widening the circle from which Jesus is drawing his crowds. The use of the boat to escape the pressure of the crowd anticipates the setting of the parabolic teaching of chapter iv, suggesting that the teaching from a boat anchored a little off shore was a regular practice of Jesus. As Luke has changed the scene from 'the sea' (that is, the lake-shore) to a 'level place' at the foot of 'the mountain' where Jesus appointed the Twelve, he must dispense with the boat; he has in any case used the picture in connection with the Miraculous Draught of Fishes (v. 1-11; § 17). There is sufficient coincidence of language to indicate that both he and Matthew are making use of Mark here, in spite of the freedom with which they have reshaped his material. The description of crowds from far and near has been used already by Matthew in his setting for the great Sermon (iv. 25). Apart from that, he omits mention of the lake, and speaks of Jesus' move as a withdrawal occasioned by his knowledge of the plot to destroy him; and he has abbreviated Mark drastically. In compensation for the abbreviation, he adds a characteristic appeal to prophecy (*vv.* 16-21).

By transferring the section to its place after the appointment of the Twelve, Luke has made it the stage-setting for the great Sermon, which in Matthew is delivered on 'the mountain', but in Luke on a 'level place' to which Jesus descends after a night of prayer on 'the mountain'. All these indications of place are as vague as can be, and give us no real information about the movements of Jesus.

72. *The Call of the Twelve Apostles*

MATTHEW x. 1-4 MARK iii. 13-19 LUKE vi. 12-16

Matthew has already used this material as part of the introduction to his Mission Charge (§ 58). There is little to add to the remarks made at that point. The chief changes made by Luke are the addition of *v.* 12, telling us that before appointing the Twelve Jesus spent the night in prayer; the note that Jesus himself named the Twelve, 'apostles'; and the omission of the nickname given to the sons of Zebedee ('Thunderbolts', as Austin Farrer renders it). We have already observed Luke's fondness for mentioning the praying of Jesus (on § 45). The term 'apostles' does not seem to belong to the earliest tradition, and was not at first applied exclusively to the Twelve; Luke's introduction of the title at this time is probably an anachronism. Mark's picture of the great and growing popularity of Jesus leads naturally enough to the appointment of associates to share the tasks. If we are right in thinking of this as the commencement of a 'Twelve-source', we would go on to suggest that the source continued with the Mission Charge and some account of the doings of the Twelve after their appointment; but Mark has seen fit to postpone this until after the rejection of Jesus at Nazareth (vi. 6-12).

The Sermon on the Plain
§§ 73-78

LUKE vi. 20-49

In examining the Sermon on the Mount (§§ 18-44) we observed that it was built round a smaller collection of sayings of Jesus, which is found here in

Luke as the Sermon on the Plain. The relationship between the two versions of the Sermon was discussed in that place and we shall now confine ourselves to drawing attention to the elements in the Lucan version which were not used by Matthew. It seems probable that the many differences in wording are in part attributable to differences in the sources which they employed, and in part to recasting by one (or conceivably in some instances, both) of the Evangelists. More is involved than different renderings of the underlying Aramaic of the sayings, though this will account for some of the variations in the wording.

73. *The Beatitudes*

LUKE vi. 20-23

In the four beatitudes which he shares with Matthew, Luke retains a stark simplicity which is probably original. Difference of substance is found only in the fourth, where Luke speaks of four kinds of hostility that the disciples must encounter in place of the three mentioned in Matthew. The first clause, 'when men hate you', embraces all that follow. Most of the differences in wording here are easily explained as different Greek renderings of the same underlying Aramaic. 'Cast out your name as evil', for instance, looks like an over-literal rendering of a common Semitic expression which Matthew has given as 'say all manner of evil against you falsely'.

74. *The Woes*

LUKE vi. 24-26

The four woes are the converse of the four beatitudes. Only the fourth is addressed to the disciples; the first three are addressed to the absent, in what can only be called a rhetorical denunciation. This passage is a secondary composition, introduced as the pendant to the beatitudes; they make necessary a new start in verse 27: 'But to you I say, you that hear.'

75. *On Love of One's Enemies*

LUKE vi. 27-36

The section in Luke has a well-defined poetic structure, employing the parallelism characteristic of Semitic poetry; it has been argued that on retranslation into Aramaic it is rhythmic and even rhymed (C. F. Burney, *Poetry*, p. 169). Nevertheless, such unity as it possesses is redactional; it cannot be regarded as going back to the utterance of our Lord himself or even to the common source of Luke and Matthew. This is shown in part by the very different arrangement of the sayings in Matthew, who can hardly be supposed to have found them in the Lucan order and then dispersed them, even to the point of moving the 'Golden Rule' entirely out of context to set it in a place where it has no particular relation to the preceding or the following words. It is shown still more clearly by the change from the plural (*vv.* 27-28) to the singular (*vv.* 29-30) and back to the plural again (*vv.* 32-36). As T. W. Manson has put it: 'The change (in 29f.) ... indicates that we have here a separate saying. The sermon consists of such utterances on various occasions brought together and topically arranged to show the general character of the preaching of Jesus' (*Sayings*, p. 51). Apart from the differences of arrangement, Matthew has as usual abbreviated his material, cutting out two of the clauses of *vv.* 27 and 28, the whole of *v.* 34, and the first half of *v.* 35 (as they stand in Luke). Against this he has added a word of general introduction to the second group of sayings (Matt. v. 38-39b), to work them into his series of antithetical statements of the differences between the Old Law and the New. His terms 'tax-collectors' and 'Gentiles' are probably original, as against Luke's 'sinners' (twice, *vv.* 32-33); Luke has generalized them for the benefit of the Gentile readers for whom he writes. Similarly, his word 'merciful' in *v.* 36 looks like an attempt to clarify the sense of the Semitic 'perfect' (*teleioi* = *tamîm*) for readers to whom *teleioi* would hardly be even a term of the ethical vocabulary. But 'merciful' is a much narrower word then *teleioi.*

76. *On Judging*

LUKE vi. 37-42

In the Lucan arrangement it is probable that *v.* 36 should be taken as the commencement of this section rather than as the conclusion of § 75. On the change in the significance of the first group of sayings (*vv.* 37-38) by Matthew's abbreviation, see the notes on § 36 above. We may now observe that *vv.* 39 and 40 are not used by Matthew in this context at all, but are introduced separately in his Gospel; the first (xv. 14) is brought into the Marcan passage concerning the ritual of washing hands (§ 115), which Luke has not included; and the second (x. 24-25) has been given a place in the Mission Charge (§ 59). It seems probable that these two sayings were not found by the two Evangelists in a common source, but came to their attention as isolated sayings which each has introduced at the point which he himself felt to be appropriate. For Luke, the saying 'Can the blind lead the blind?' seemed to form a natural parallel to the theme: 'Can the unworthy judge the unworthy?', especially in relation to the picture of the man with impaired vision (a log in his eye) seeking to aid one with a minor impairment (a speck in his eye). To Matthew it suggested rather the futility of the Pharisees in seeking to instruct people in the law of God, when they are themselves nullifying that law through their elaborate network of interpretation. In this context the following saying (*v.* 40) can only mean that those who accept the teaching of the Pharisees are bound to fall into the same errors as their masters. In Matthew (and in John xv. 20) it means that the disciple of Jesus cannot expect better treatment than was given to his Lord. A still different meaning is given to the same saying in John xiii. 16 (the follower of Jesus must not think himself too good to do the humble service to others that Jesus has done).

77. *The Test of Goodness*

LUKE vi. 43-46

It will be noticed that Matthew has two parallels to this passage, one in the Sermon on the Mount, and the other in the counter-attack of Jesus against the Pharisees who have accused him of working miracles by the power of Beelzebul (§ 86). The second parallel is sometimes closer to Luke's wording than is the first. Matthew xii. 34b-35 corresponds almost word for word to Luke's *v.* 45, with a transposition of clauses; and Matthew xii. 33 corresponds very closely to Luke's *vv.* 43, 44a. Against this, Matthew vii. 16b is clearly a rephrasing of Luke's *v.* 44b, or vice versa. There is no particular connection with the preceding section. Matthew has drawn upon a version of the Sermon which retained the same order as that used by Luke, but had some differences in wording and a certain repetitiousness (16a, 20; 17, 18); and he has incorporated a sentence from the preaching of John the Baptist (Matt. vii. 19 = Matt. iii. 10b). The passage in Matthew xii. 33ff. was perhaps found by Matthew in another source.

The last verse, at least in Luke's construction, seems more pertinent as an introduction to § 78 than as a conclusion to this section. In Matthew, however, it is separated from the closing parable by another group of sayings. In Luke the figure of the trees and their fruit is not used as a warning against the failure to match words with deeds.

78. *Hearers and Doers of the Word*

LUKE vi. 47-49

It is obvious that in substance this is the same parable as that which concludes the Matthaean version of the Sermon, but the differences in the wording are more striking than the coincidences, and are not such as could be attributed to an independent translation of the one Aramaic source. The parable has been recast in the history of its oral transmission. In Matthew the disaster to be apprehended is that from heavy rains and high winds together with the overflowing of rivers; in Luke, only the flooding of the river is mentioned. Luke's version suggests the spring torrents of the mountain streams in Greece; Matthew's is more Palestinian, keeping to the thought of 'the former and the latter rains'. The differences illustrate the way in which the tradition could be modified through transmission in a non-Palestinian environment. The essential lesson is not affected.

The Lucan 'Little Insertion'
§§ 79-84

LUKE vii. 1-viii. 3

Through these six sections, Luke introduces the first and smaller of his major insertions of material into the Marcan framework. The story of The Centurion's Servant (§ 79) follows closely on the Sermon in Matthew's arrangement also, and may well have followed it directly in the source which both are using.

§§ 81 and 82 have already been before us in Matthew's order (see notes on §§ 64 and 65), and no further discussion will be attempted at this point. The three sections which remain are found only in Luke, and each must be considered briefly.

80. *The Widow's Son at Nain*

Luke vii. 11-17

The story has several points of contact with the Old Testament stories of Elijah and Elisha, both of whom restore life to a young boy, an only son (1 Kings xvii. 17-24; 2 Kings iv. 18-37). In the Elijah story the mother is a widow, as here, and Luke actually quotes the Septuagint phrase: 'he delivered him to his mother' (1 Kings xvii. 23). The language of the people (*v.* 16) is likewise Septuagintal, and the scene is laid in a specific Palestinian locality, the village of Nain, which has a gate and consequently must have a wall; and the burial-practice as described is thoroughly Jewish. Yet the story as it stands is a classic example of the form of the Hellenistic wonder-tale, even to the detail of the thaumaturge meeting the funeral procession and raising the corpse from the bier. We have here, then, a story that has arisen on Palestinian ground but has been recast through transmission in Hellenistic circles. Luke has introduced it at this point to prepare the way for the response of Jesus to John the Baptist, which follows in the next section (especially the words: 'the dead are raised' — *v.* 22). Verse 17 is not part of the story proper, but an editorial addition which relates it to the carrying of the news of Jesus to John in his prison; otherwise we should expect to read 'in all Galilee', rather than 'in all Judaea and the country round about'.

83. *The Woman that was a Sinner*

Luke vii. 36-50

This story is not wholly independent of the Marcan tradition; it has several points of contact with the story of the Anointing at Bethany (§ 232), which Luke has omitted, probably because he recognized it as a doublet of this. But Luke's story is much more than a variant of the Marcan incident. There appears to be here a conflation of the story of the Anointing at Bethany with a parable of Two Debtors (*vv.* 41-43), and fragments of a controversy-story concerning the authority of Jesus to forgive sins (*vv.* 48-49), akin to that which is embedded in the story of the Healing of the Paralytic (§ 52). Probably Luke found the materials already conflated in his source.

The following coincidences with the Marcan story may be noted: the name of the host — Simon; the entrance of a woman from outside, to anoint Jesus; Jesus is reclining at table during the anointing; the phrase *alabastron murou* — 'an alabaster flask of ointment'. On the other hand, the place and time are different; in Luke, there is no thought of anticipation of the burial of Jesus; the objection raised is not based on the waste of costly ointment, but on the character of the woman; the moving detail of the woman wetting the feet of

Jesus with her tears and wiping them with her hair has no counterpart in the Marcan story; and there are no parallelisms in the dialogue of the two stories.

It may be remarked that the Johannine story of the Anointing (John xii. 1-8) appears to conflate the Lucan story with the Marcan (with some new touches added).

The Lucan story is related to its context (i) as an illustration of the charge that Jesus is 'a friend of ... sinners' (*v.* 34), and (ii) as a justification of the contrast between the response of the Pharisees and that of 'the whole people and the tax-collectors' to John's preaching of repentance, now seen again in the response to the merciful goodness of Jesus.

84. *The Ministering Women*

LUKE viii. 1-3

Luke can hardly mean that this band of women accompanied Jesus and the Twelve on their peregrinations. Having introduced the woman of the streets in the story of the anointing in the house of Simon, he takes occasion to mention other women of a different social status who have the same devotion to Jesus, having experienced his healing power. The implication is that they are women of some wealth, out of which they are able to provide for the needs of Jesus and his company. There is no suggestion here that Mary of Magdala is to be identified with the 'woman who was a sinner' of the preceding story; demon-possession is not a matter of sexual licence.

Hostility towards Jesus
§§ 85-89

MATTHEW xii. 22-50

MARK iii. 20-35 LUKE xi. 14-26, 29-32

Matthew is following the Marcan order here, but is drawing his material from a different source, and some of it (§§ 87, 88) has no parallel in Mark at all. Luke has used the same source as Matthew, but has departed from the Marcan order, holding most of the material for his 'Travel Narrative' (§§ 149, 150 and 152), where it is interwoven with materials drawn from his own store ('L'); a few of the verses which Matthew uses here are scattered widely in Luke (vi. 43-45; viii. 19-21; xii. 10). Even in the sections in which Matthew offers parallels to the substance of Mark, and in Mark's order, he has preferred to substitute for the Marcan version the account which he found in 'Q'; except for the placing of the materials, Matthew stands much closer to Luke in these sections than to Mark.

In the arrangement of Matthew, these sections continue the account of the attacks of the Pharisees which began with the sabbath-controversies of §§ 69 and 70. In Mark the summary of healing activities and the call of the Twelve (§§ 71 and 72) intervene, with indications of growing popularity and a widening of the mission, serving to set in relief the pictures of misunderstanding and bitter hostility which are now to be brought before us. On the one hand vast crowds are flocking to Jesus from all parts of the Holy Land and even beyond, and he is choosing men from among his followers to share the growing tasks; on the other his own family hears that he is out of his mind, and seeks to put him under restraint, so that he is obliged to disown them and to recognize only the ties of spiritual kinship; and the recognized leaders assert that he owes his powers to the devil.

Both Matthew and Luke have discarded the reference to the family's lack of sympathy with him in his mission, though they have retained the saying of Jesus that his mother and brethren are those who do the will of God, which really implies a repudiation of the ties of earthly kindred — implies, indeed, that his own family are not among the responsive hearers of his message.

85. *The Pharisees' Accusation*

MATTHEW xii. 22-24 MARK iii. 20-22 LUKE xi. 14-16

The differences between Mark on the one hand and Matthew and Luke on the other are substantial. Mark's opening verse is an editorial link with the scene of the call of the Twelve, which was set on 'the mountain'. The locale remains vague. The phrase *hoi par' autou* — 'his friends' (AV, RSV) undoubtedly means 'his family' (see the excellent note of Taylor, *St. Mark*, ad loc., with illustrations from the papyri); and there can be little doubt that it originally stood in immediate association with *vv.* 31-35 (or the nucleus of these verses, which themselves appear to have undergone some expansion). Mark (or his source) has interwoven a story of the unsympathetic family and Jesus' repudiation of natural ties with an independent story of Jesus' response to the accusation that his powers are given to him by the devil.

Matthew and Luke have followed a source which supplied an exorcism-story as the introduction to the accusation in place of the story of the unsympathetic family. The story of the dumb (in Matthew, blind and dumb) demoniac is as bare of particular detail as could be imagined, and is clearly told not for its own sake, but to pave the way for the accusation of the scribes.

The general terms of the accusation are alike in all three accounts, even to the use of the unusual name Beelzebul (or Beezebul, or Beelzebub — all three spellings occur in the manuscripts) for 'the prince of the demons'. In Luke the accusers are not defined; his 'some of them' (*v.* 15) is probably the wording of the source ('Q'), for there is a tendency in transmission for opponents of Jesus who are at first unidentified to be turned into scribes or Pharisees or both. In this instance at least, 'Q' is more primitive than Mark — an indication, for what it is worth, that the 'Q' material was compiled relatively early.

It is possible that the words in Mark should be understood as carrying two distinct charges: (i) that 'he has Beelzebul' — that is, he is insane — another way of putting the rumour that has stirred up his family: 'he is beside himself'; and (ii) 'in the prince of demons (that is, by means of powers given to him by the prince of demons) he casts out demons'.

86. *The Beelzebub Controversy*

MATTHEW xii. 25-37 MARK iii. 23-30 LUKE xi. 17-23

In all three accounts the first part of the reply is in substance the same: the accusation is nonsensical, for it would mean that the kingdom of demons is rent by civil war. Once again, Matthew holds to the Marcan order but uses a version of the material which he has drawn from the source that he shares with Luke. The same source continues with a second reply, a *tu quoque*: you have exorcists whom you acknowledge as your own ('your sons'); by whose power do they cast out demons? This looks much more like a retort of the apostolic Church to Jewish belittling of its exorcisms than a possible quip of Jesus himself. All three join again in the positive explanation which Jesus offers: his exorcisms are clear proof that he has overthrown the 'strong man', the head of the kingdom of demons. In this verse (Mark iii. 27 = Matt. xii. 29), Matthew adopts the wording of Mark while Luke keeps to 'Q' (Luke xi. 21-22), but both continue with a verse from their common source which sits loosely to its context (Matt. xii. 30 = Luke xi. 23); the linking is secondary. Luke here continues with a further passage on the theme of demon-possession (§ 88), which probably stood at this point in his source; but Matthew again draws upon Mark for the sayings about the sin against the Holy Spirit (Mark iii. 28-29 = Matt. xii. 31-32b), though there is enough difference in wording to suggest the possibility that he has another source at his disposal — this view is strengthened by the observation that he introduces an additional clause (*v.* 32a). Verse 30 in Mark is probably a note of his own, explaining the point of the saying.

The sayings already show signs of being an assemblage of utterances which were at an earlier stage of transmission preserved in isolation or in other associations, and Matthew now enlarges the group by a series of warnings to the effect that charges such as have been uttered reveal an inward wickedness in the accusers, for which they will be called to account by God (*vv.* 33-36). Verse 33 is a 'Q' saying, which Luke has used in his Sermon on the Plain; *v.* 34a may be a fragment of teaching of John the Baptist — at least, the phrase 'offspring of vipers' is attributed to him in § 2; *vv.* 34b and 35 are drawn again from the source which Luke has used for the Sermon.

In this section, then, Matthew has made a conflation of Mark with 'Q' and with a source of his own, while Luke has stayed with 'Q' throughout.

It is very difficult indeed to suppose that Luke has here drawn his parallel material from Matthew!

87. *Against Seeking for Signs*

MATTHEW xii. 38-42 LUKE xi. 29-32

Mark has a brief account of a Pharisaic demand for a 'sign', and the refusal of Jesus to meet it, but he introduces it at a much later stage (§ 119; following the Feeding of the Four Thousand). Matthew uses the Marcan version at that point (with some adaptation), though Luke does not. Here Matthew and Luke are drawing upon their common source, 'Q', from which § 88 also comes; but Matthew has reversed the order of the two for reasons best known to himself.

To us, at least, the Lucan order seems to give more coherence to the materials, as it keeps to the general theme of the preceding sections — exorcisms and demon-possession. Matthew has framed his own introduction to the section (*v.* 38), whereas Luke has paved the way for it (in this he was probably following the source) by coupling the demand for a sign with the accusation that Jesus is using powers conferred by the devil (*vv.* 15-16, § 85). Luke omits the adjective 'adulterous' (*moichalis*), probably because his Gentile readers would not understand the Jewish use of this word to express infidelity to God. The interpretation given to 'the sign of Jonah' is probably secondary. It has even been suggested that the words of Jesus were 'the sign of John', in the sense that the preaching of John the Baptist was the only 'sign' that was needed or would be given. It is still more likely that the answer of Jesus was substantially that of the little Marcan pericope: 'No sign shall be given to this generation' (Mark viii. 12). The mention of Jonah (or of John) would itself be secondary; and all the rest would be elaboration by way of attempts to interpret what was meant by the 'sign of Jonah'. The Lucan version would then be an intermediate stage — 'As Jonah was a sign to the Ninevites, so shall the Son of Man be (a sign) to this generation.' But these words still fail to make clear in what sense Jonah was a 'sign'. The version of Matthew, accordingly, adds the desired precision: the three days and three nights which Jonah spent in the belly of the whale are a symbol of the three days and three nights which 'the Son of Man' — Jesus — is to spend 'in the heart of the earth' between the Crucifixion and the Resurrection (Matthew, according to his custom, quotes from the Septuagint version of the book of Jonah). It is doubtful if an early Christian reader, or writer, would pay any heed to the inconsistency between the 'three days and three nights' and the tradition (uniformly attested) that Jesus rose 'on the third day' — that is, after only two nights in the grave.

The remaining two verses (there is again an inversion of order) are not intrinsically connected with the refusal of a sign; they are linked to it by the theme-word 'Ninevites'. The two sayings form a pair; they are akin to those of § 66.

88. *The Return of the Evil Spirit*

MATTHEW xii. 43-45 LUKE xi. 24-26

In itself, this little fable would suggest that exorcisms had no lasting effect; after a temporary relief, the patient is found to be in worse shape than before. Such an observation could well have been made by any cool-headed critical observer; but if it were originally taken from some Jewish writing, as R. Bultmann suggests (*History*, p. 164), it is hard to see how it ever was taken up into the tradition of the sayings of Jesus — the mere fact that it deals with 'demonological matter' is not sufficient, seeing that it reflects unusual misgivings about the efficacy of exorcisms. If we start, however, with the reminder that the fable was conceived and first transmitted independently of its present context, we may suppose that Jesus commented in this way on certain cases of exorcisms performed by himself, which had not proved lastingly effective; or that his attention had been drawn to relapses of demoniacs whom others had healed. But it must be noted that the fable does not itself distinguish between exorcisms that were lasting in their effects and those that were not.

Nevertheless, it is probable that the Evangelists read such a distinction into it. In Luke, especially, its direct attachment to the saying: 'he that is not with me is against me, and he that does not gather with me scatters' (xi. 23) is probably meant to suggest that exorcists who work independently of Jesus are unable to effect lasting cures, because they bring no new life to the sufferer to take the place from which the demon has been expelled. Jesus, who casts out demons 'by the finger (Matthew — "by the Spirit") of God', does not leave the house empty for other demons to occupy, but makes it a habitation of the divine Spirit.

89. *Christ's Real Brethren*

MATTHEW xii. 46-50 MARK iii. 31-35 LUKE viii. 19-21

In Mark this paragraph is the sequel to *v.* 21, which tells us that the family of Jesus came to put him under restraint, taking him to be beside himself. In such a context, the words of Jesus amount to a repudiation of the natural ties of family. We must keep in mind, however, that the significance of the saying is not to be narrowed to mere vexation over the lack of appreciation. Jesus calls upon all his followers to put their allegiance to him above the requirements of filial piety; for him as for them, the demands of service to the kingdom of God take precedence over family obligations, and the ties of spiritual brotherhood are closer than those of natural affection. Compare Luke ix. 59-62, xii. 51-53, xiv. 25-26; Mark x. 29-30; and parallels. Both Matthew and Luke have omitted the reference to the hostility of the family, and in their versions the words of Jesus are taken as conferring on his followers the high honour of recognition as members of his family. See also the notes on § 104.

In keeping with a tendency akin to that which turns unspecified opponents into Pharisees, Matthew here turns the 'crowd' of Mark's setting into 'his disciples' (*v.* 49). His *v.* 47 (omitted in RSV and in *Gospel Parallels*) has inferior manuscript attestation.

A Collection of Parables
§§ 90-104

MATTHEW xiii. 1-52 MARK iv. 1-34 LUKE viii. 4-21

In Matthew these sections constitute the third of the great discourses in which this Evangelist has presented the teachings of Jesus. Like the others, it is a compilation. Part of it is drawn from Mark, part of it from 'Q', and part from sources which have not been employed by his fellow-Evangelists. The much smaller collection of Mark has provided him with a nucleus which he has supplemented by the addition of materials drawn from his other sources. He has omitted the sayings of Mark iv. 21-25 (§ 94, 'The Right Use of Parables') at this point, and transferred them to other contexts; and for Mark's parable of the Seed growing Secretly (§ 95), he has substituted the parable of the Tares with its interpretation (§§ 96, 100). This and three more of the parables of this chapter are found in neither of the other gospels. Luke, on the other hand, has broken up the Marcan collection. At this point he has retained only the parable of the Sower, with its accompanying catena of sayings about the Reason for Parables, the 'Interpretation', and the sayings about the Right Use of Parables. The Parable of the Mustard Seed he has transferred to his Travel Narrative, where it appears in association with the parable of the Leaven, as in Matthew (§ 164). None of the other parables of this section have been used by him at all.

It is interesting to observe that all seven of the parables of the Matthaean collection are found in the newly-discovered (Gnostic) *Gospel of Thomas*.

The Parables of Jesus: Approaches to their Interpretation

There is hardly an area of New Testament study which has witnessed such far-reaching changes in this century as our understanding of the parables of Jesus. From the second century to the nineteenth it was taken for granted that the parables were allegories and that every feature in them must have its own spiritual significance. This approach, erroneous as we now perceive it to be, has left its mark even upon the Gospel records. St. Mark, the earliest of our Evangelists, has brought it into his presentation in the interpretation of the parable of the Sower (§ 93), and has even attributed it to Jesus. The seed sown is 'the word'; the trodden path, the rocky soil, the thistles represent different types of hearers who fail to make a lasting response; the good soil represents those in whom the word brings forth fruit abundantly. As we shall see, this 'interpretation' misses the point and gives an application which was not in the mind of Jesus. Matthew and Luke have followed Mark at this point and have applied the method more widely. Later, as the teachers of the Church resorted more and more to allegorical interpretations of the scriptures generally, the parables offered a particularly fertile field for their imaginations. Origen of Alexandria leads the way which the Greek and Latin Fathers generally will follow, and we find sober and learned theologians offering interpretations which we can only regard as strained, extravagant, and curious. The 'five yoke of oxen' of the parable of the Great Supper (Luke xiv. 19) are the five senses which by their imperious solicitations draw men away from the things of the spirit (Augustine); in the parable of the Good Samaritan, the man who goes down from Jerusalem to Jericho is Adam, who forsakes the abode of heavenly peace (Jerusalem) for the change and decay of our mortal life (Jericho); the brigands who rob and beat him are the devil and his angels; the Samaritan who rescues him is our Lord; the inn is the Church and the innkeeper is the Apostle Paul; the two pence which the Samaritan leaves with the innkeeper are the two commandments of love, or perhaps the promise of this life and that of the life to come (Augustine again, and this outline omits much of the detail). If the leaven is put in three measures of meal, Archbishop Trench (to come now to one of the leading interpreters of the nineteenth century) feels obliged to find some significance in the number 'three'. It must represent body, mind, and spirit, all to be sanctified by the Gospel; or perhaps the three sons of Noah — Shem, Ham and Japheth — from whom stem all the branches of the human race (Gen. ix. 19). It must be understood that these are not isolated oddities; they are fair samples of the approach to interpretation of the parables which prevailed through all the centuries of the Church, until our own times.

The radical rejection of this entire method was initiated by Adolf Jülicher in a work that truly deserves to be called epoch-making — *Die Gleichnisreden Jesu*, published in 1899, and followed by a second edition in 1910. It is not too much to say that all serious study of the parables in the twentieth century has been based upon the method proposed by Jülicher. He succeeded in demonstrating that the parables are not allegories and that the attempt to find an allegorical significance in all the details is a fundamental error. It is not merely that this or that interpretation is fanciful or extravagant, but that the whole method is erroneous and based upon a mistaken conception of the nature of the parable. The interpreter must not seek for a hidden significance in the details, but must view the parable as a whole and look for the one point which it is designed to make clear. Thus the parable of the Good Samaritan is not an allegory of the history of salvation; it is a story told to give a new dimension to our notion of the 'neighbour' to whom we are to manifest our love. The parable of the Sower is not an allegory of the different kinds of people who hear the Gospel of God; it is an illustration of the fact that in the realm of the spirit as in agriculture, a bounteous harvest is to be garnered even if some of the seed goes to waste on unreceptive soil.

The weakness of Jülicher's work was not in the method of approach, but in the application. His interpretations usually lead to a moral generalization of some kind, as if the parables of Jesus were no more than brilliant illustrations of the principles of conduct which are inculcated in the Ten Commandments. As Professor C. H. Dodd has remarked: 'This method of interpretation makes the parables to be forcible illustrations of eminently sound moral and religious principles, but undeniably its general effect is rather flattening'; and he asks: 'Was all this wealth of loving observation and imaginative rendering of nature and common life used merely to adorn moral generalities? Was the Jesus of the Gospels just an eminently sound and practical teacher, who patiently led simple minds to appreciate the great enduring commonplaces of morals and religion? This is not the impression conveyed by the Gospels as a whole' (*The Parables of the Kingdom*, p. 25).

Professor Dodd has been one of the leading exponents of an advance beyond Jülicher, which seeks to relate the parables less to moral generalities and more to the immediate situation of crisis which the mission of Jesus itself inaugurated. He has made a thoroughgoing effort to interpret a number of them, those which bear upon the Kingdom of God, in the light of his hypothesis of 'realized eschatology', or, to put it more accurately, 'eschatology in process of realization'. (This cumbrous phrase is an attempt to do justice to the German expression of Ernst Haenchen and Joachim Jeremias — 'sich realisierende Eschatologie';

see Dodd's *Interpretation of the Fourth Gospel* [Cambridge: C.U.P., 1953], p. 447, n. 1.)

Still more important is the work of Joachim Jeremias, *The Parables of Jesus*, which likewise seeks to find the setting of the parables in the particular situation of the Ministry of Jesus, but shows how they have been modified in the transmission to make them pertinent to the very different situation of the apostolic Church. He has noted seven 'principles of transformation' which have left their marks on the parables as they have been recorded in the Gospels. The modifications sometimes affect only the form of the parable, but very frequently they result in substantial changes in the sense. In many cases, perhaps in most, the parable has been transmitted without its context, and a new context has been supplied by the Evangelist or by the tradition upon which he draws. In some instances the parable has one context in Matthew and another in Luke, and the change of context carries with it a change in the point of the parable itself. Sometimes the movement of the Christian mission into a Hellenistic environment, the transference from Jewish to Gentile soil, has led to changes in the form and in the application of parables. The tendency to allegorize has had far-reaching effects. A number of parables have been transmitted to us in pairs; sometimes the pairing goes back to Jesus and provides a real clue to the sense which he intended for both of them; but sometimes the pairing is secondary, and makes a false connection which may take both parables in a different sense from that of the Teller. Sometimes the Evangelists themselves have provided introductions and conclusions to parables, which have the effect of imposing a particular interpretation upon them which may not be original. The working of these principles of transformation must be considered in relation to particular parables as we come to them. For the moment, we are content to note that we cannot too readily assume that the sense in which any given parable is understood by one or other of the Evangelists is identical with that which Jesus intended, but must in each case subject it to critical examination, with this very question open in our minds.

Finally, let us observe that the meaning of the parables is seldom self-evident. Nearly always they require to be interpreted in relation to the teaching of Jesus as a whole; and the interpretation at which we arrive will be largely determined by the conception which we have already formed of the general substance of that teaching. As we have already remarked, the seven parables of Matthew xiii are all found in the *Gospel according to Thomas* (together with several other parables of the Synoptic tradition and a few otherwise unknown). It follows that a Gnostic teacher of the second century could use them with some modifications — sometimes trifling, sometimes far-reaching — as illustrations of the doctrines of his sect; even when he makes no significant changes in the wording, he assumes that the parable is a vehicle of teachings which none of us would recognize as teachings of Jesus or of the Christian Church. The Evangelists, standing firmly within the sound tradition of the apostolic faith, could none the less use the parables as vehicles or illustrations of the developed teaching of the Church, which was far from a mere reproduction of the teachings of Jesus himself. To this day, even among those who adopt the same general approach to the parables, it will be found that surprisingly different interpretations are offered by different scholars, in keeping with the different ways in which they envisage the central themes of the teaching of Jesus. The parables do not of themselves convey a well-defined body of teaching; they illustrate and elicit response to teaching which is more directly put before us by other means. For us, they remain in a measure enigmatic.

90. *The Parable of the Sower*

MATTHEW xiii. 1-9 MARK iv. 1-9 LUKE viii. 4-8

The Marcan passage, which is certainly the source of Matthew's version and probably also of Luke's, is given in a literal 'translation-Greek', which betrays in numerous details the wording of the underlying Aramaic (M. Black, *Aramaic Approach*, pp. 45, 119ff.). This is not characteristic of the parables generally; most of them are translated with a fair degree of freedom, into idiomatic Greek. Luke especially allows himself to make 'literary productions' of his parables; in the story of the Good Samaritan, for instance, we shall have occasion to note that it is given in good colloquial Greek, without a trace of Semitic locutions or constructions (see notes on § 144). Here, too, the great differences in wording between his version and those of Mark and Matthew do not suggest the use of an independent source but simply reflect the remarkable freedom with which he recasts the parables generally. This view is confirmed by the observation that Luke's version of the Interpretation of the parable presupposes the Marcan wording, even where Luke has abandoned it in the recasting of the parable itself; in the parable, he tells us that the new growth withered on the stony ground because it lacked moisture, but in the interpretation it is because of the lack of roots, as in Mark. (*See* Creed's note, ad loc.).

The phrase 'by the wayside' (Gk., *para tēn hodon*) is a mistranslation of the ambiguous Aramaic phrase *'al 'urha*, which in this context certainly means 'on the road', that is, on the path which has been worn through the stubble. So understood, the whole picture is seen to be perfectly true to life. In Palestine, the field is sown *before* it is ploughed, and the sower tosses seed on the path because he knows that it will be ploughed under. So too will the patches of thorns; and the rocky outcroppings will hardly be visible to him beneath the stubble. Luke's addition, 'it was trodden down', shows that he has understood the words correctly; and it is interesting to find that the version of this parable in the *Gospel according to Thomas* actually uses the rendering 'on the road'.

The description of the scene — Jesus seated in a fishing-boat a little off shore, while the crowds throng about him at the waterside — is probably of Mark's own sketching at this point; in iii. 9, he has intimated that this was a regular practice of Jesus in his teaching by the lake. Matthew has kept the Marcan setting, but has made the connection with the preceding section much closer; the teaching by the lake is given on the same day as the dispute with the Pharisees and the repudiation of family ties. Possibly Matthew thinks of the parable as a reflection of the mixed reception which he has been describing — the enthusiastic multitudes and the receptive disciples on the one hand, representing the good soil which is bearing an abundant crop; the hostile Pharisees representing the rocks and thistles. Luke has transferred the substance of § 89 to a point immediately following the parable and the sayings associated with it, and it may be that he too sees a connection between the parable and Jesus' recognition of responsive hearers as his 'mother and brethren'. No such connection is suggested in Mark. Unlike Matthew, Luke abandons the Marcan setting altogether; he has used the picture of Jesus teaching from the boat as the setting for his version of the Call of the First Disciples (§ 17; v. 1-3) and here he does not even hint that the teaching is given by the lakeside.

But what is the lesson of the parable, in the intention of Jesus himself? It will be found that the commentators give surprisingly different answers to this question. They are all agreed that the 'interpretation' of § 98, although the Evangelists attribute it to Jesus, does not in fact go back to him, but is a bit of early allegorizing. The emphasis in the parable is not on the few handfuls of seed that are wasted, but on the abundance of the harvest that is reaped in spite of the waste; the good ground will include nearly all the area that is sown – the hard path, the rocky patches and the thistles will occupy only a few square rods in all, and are negligible in the final result. The parable is basically a parable of assurance. Accordingly many commentators take it that Jesus is encouraging his disciples to be confident that God will abundantly bless the work that he and they are doing; they must not be dismayed if some of it appears to be wasted effort. Professor F. C. Grant, however, takes it more as a warning to inattentive hearers. 'Its purpose is to show how various hearers respond to the message of the Gospel – in the first instance to Jesus' own message ... Like the parable of the two houses, at the conclusion of the Sermon on the Mount, this parable was doubtless intended to be an admonition to responsive hearing, and was not a mere reflection of the experience of the teacher' (*IB*, 'Mark', ad loc.). Professor Dodd, on the other hand, in keeping with his doctrine of 'realized eschatology', takes it as illustrating, under the figure of harvest, the theme that the kingdom of God has arrived with the ministry of Jesus. God has done the sowing in ages past, through the ministry of the prophets, and lately through the ministry of John the Baptist. Much of this work has seemed to end in failure. 'True, says Jesus, but no farmer yet delayed to reap a good crop because there were bare patches in the field. In spite of all, the harvest is plentiful; it is only the labourers that are lacking' (*Parables*, pp. 181-3). The parable thus becomes an appeal to men to go forth and reap the harvest that stands ripe for the sickle. The interpretation of J. Jeremias is not greatly different from this, but is less rigidly shaped to the doctrine. He speaks of it as 'a contrast-parable'. 'On the one hand', he writes, 'we have a description of the manifold frustrations to which the sower's labour is liable; there lies the fallow land, whose picture includes the tale of weeds, bad weather, plundering birds, and all the other enemies of the seed. In contrast to this the parable paints the picture of the ripening field bearing its rich guerdon of harvest. ... To human eyes much of the labour seems futile and fruitless, resulting apparently in repeated failure, but Jesus is full of joyful confidence; he knows that God has made a beginning, bringing with it a harvest of reward beyond all asking or conceiving. In spite of every failure, the Kingdom of God comes at last' (*Parables*, p. 92).

The present writer must confess that none of these interpretations seems to him to be wholly satisfactory. He has passed them in review at this point chiefly in order to make the student aware of how widely the doctors can differ, even in their treatment of this familiar and apparently simple figure of agricultural life.

91. *The Reason for Parables*

MATTHEW xiii. 10-15 MARK iv. 10-12 LUKE viii. 9-10

Mark here advances — and attributes to Jesus — the incredible theory that Jesus used parables not to make his teaching clear, but to veil its meaning from all but his own disciples. The underlying assumption is that the parable is not an illustration, but a riddle, so that its meaning cannot be unravelled except by those who possess the key. Taken with the 'interpretation' of the parable of the Sower, which in Mark follows immediately, these sayings reflect the notion that parables are allegories. Now, as Professor Dodd has pointed out, such a misunderstanding could hardly have arisen except in a non-Jewish environment (*Parables*, p. 15). We have here a striking testimony to the fact that Mark drew upon forms of the tradition which had undergone a long shaping in Hellenistic circles; it follows that this Gospel does not stand in any close relationship to the Apostle Peter. For the Jewish Church, and Jewish Christians generally, would have been in no danger of mistaking the nature of parables. 'Among Jewish teachers the parable was a common and well-understood method of illustration, and the parables of Jesus are similar in form to Rabbinic parables' (Dodd, loc. cit.). On the other hand, the Hellenistic world was not acquainted with this technique of teaching; while it was thoroughly accustomed to the use of allegory. It was almost inevitable that converts who stood in the Greek tradition would be misled into taking the parables as allegories, and seeing in them veiled representations of profound spiritual truths.

It will be observed that in Mark these sayings are represented as esoteric. The scene of the teaching by the lake is set aside for the moment while Jesus explains the Reason for Parables, and gives the allegorical interpretation of the parable of the Sower to 'those who were around him, with the twelve, when he was alone' (*v.* 10). This device of introducing a private conversation of Jesus with the disciples is used by Mark several times, when he wants to explain something in the tradition for the benefit of his readers (vii. 17; ix. 28; x. 10-11; perhaps we should include xiii. 3). The circle of initiates who are entrusted with the 'mystery of the Kingdom of God' are explicitly distinguished from 'those that are without'. This in itself is contrary to everything else that we learn from the Gospels; it comes very close to a Gnostic division of mankind into the *pneumatikoi* ('spiritual') who alone are capable of attaining salvation, and the masses of *hylikoi* ('material'?) who lack any such capacity. As Professor Grant has remarked: 'Such conceptions of esoteric revelation were common in the Greco-Roman world of the first century; what Mark has done is to apply such a principle to Jesus' teaching by parables. But the principle will not apply; Jesus' teaching was not esoteric, and he was no Gnostic mystagogue' (*IB*, 'Mark', ad loc.). But Mark has compounded the difficulty by combining with this theory of an esoteric revelation through parables a doctrine of the reprobation of Israel akin to that which is expounded by St. Paul in Romans ix-xi. The unbelief of Israel has been decreed by God, as is shown by the oracle which Mark cites from the book of Isaiah. The teaching is conveyed in enigmas, *in order that* the hearers may not understand it, 'lest they should be converted and be forgiven'.

It is often pointed out by the Aramaists that the Greek particle *hina*, 'in order that', may here be a mistranslation of the Aramaic particle *di*, which can be used to express purpose but was here probably used as the relative pronoun. It is worth noting that Matthew has substituted the particle *hoti*, 'because'; and both he and Luke have removed the 'lest' clause in Mark, thus avoiding the suggestion that the purpose of the teaching was to make repentance and forgiveness impossible. Strangely, the form of Mark's citation appears to be dependent upon the Targum of Isaiah; it departs both from the Hebrew text and from the Septuagint. 'No such Greek reading ever existed, for it is not a variant but a characteristic Targumic paraphrase of Hebrew *rapha*', peculiar to the Targum of Isaiah' (Black, *Aramaic Approach*, p. 156; his entire discussion of the passage should be read, pp. 153-8). Luke makes no use of the citation at all; but Matthew introduces it and gives the complete text of the oracle (from the Septuagint, verbatim, substantially differing from the Hebrew Masoretic text); but he gives it as an oracle that has been fulfilled in the failure of the people generally to repent at the teaching of Jesus, not as an indication that the preaching was given in parables with the intention of hiding its significance and thus making repentance impossible.

It is held by a number of scholars that the logion of Mark iv. 10-11 is an authentic saying of Jesus, but that it is out of context. Mark, it has been suggested, has been led astray by the translation of the Aramaic word *mathla* (Hebrew *mashal*) as 'parable', whereas in this saying it has the meaning of 'riddle'. Originally, then, it will have been a much more general comment upon the inability of many to understand the teaching of Jesus because of their unwillingness to respond to his call to repentance and faith. 'The secret of the present Kingdom is disclosed to the disciples, but to the outsiders the words of Jesus remain obscure because they do not recognize his mission nor repent ... The passage affords no criterion for the interpretation of the parables, nor any warrant for seeking to find in them by means of an allegorical interpretation some secret meaning hidden from the outsiders. On the contrary, Mark iv. 11f. asserts that the parables too, like all the words of Jesus, announce no special "secrets", but only the one "secret of the Kingdom of God", to wit, the secret of its contemporary irruption in the word and work of Jesus' (Jeremias, *Parables*, pp. 15, 16). We would then have a saying of Jesus conveying much the same thought as the words of St. Paul: 'We have received not the spirit of the world, but the spirit which is from God, that we might know the things that are graciously bestowed upon us by God ... But the natural (*psychikos*) man does not receive the things of the Spirit of God; for they are folly to him, and he cannot know them, because they are spiritually discerned. But the spiritual man discerns all things' (1 Cor. ii. 12, 14, 15).

92. *The Blessedness of the Disciples*

MATTHEW xiii. 16-17

Matthew has transferred to this point, with some changes in wording and a complete change of sense, a saying which Luke has linked with Christ's prayer of thanksgiving to God that the things which have been hidden from wise and prudent people have been revealed to 'babes' — that is, to the humble people who responded to Jesus with faith and love while the learned rejected him. This is not inappropriate in association with the sayings of the preceding section here, but it is probable that Luke's version retains the original meaning of the saying and that Matthew's interpretation is secondary. See the notes on § 142 (the Lucan parallel).

93. *The Interpretation of the Parable of the Sower*

MATTHEW xiii. 18-23 MARK iv. 13-20 LUKE viii. 11-15

Mark has again been used as the source of the versions of Matthew and Luke, who have abbreviated to some extent and have removed some of Mark's more glaring Semitisms; as in the parable, Luke has rewritten his material rather freely.

The interpretation cannot be regarded as deriving from Jesus himself, despite its markedly Aramaic flavour. Considerations of vocabulary alone tell strongly against it. In this short passage of Mark, there are no less than ten words which either do not occur elsewhere in the Synoptic Gospels, or are not used in them with the signification which they have here (see especially the discussion of Jeremias, *Parables*, pp. 61f.); and two others occur in other places only once, and that in passages which are regarded as secondary. But even more decisive is the fact that the 'interpretation' misses the central point of the parable. It focuses attention chiefly upon the seed that goes to waste, and fails to bring out the thought that the harvest is so bountiful as to make negligible the few handfuls of seed that are unproductive. 'The emphasis has been transferred from the eschatological to the psychological aspect of the parable' (Jeremias). The interpreter is chiefly interested in the analysis of the different types of men who fail to respond to the Gospel. He regards the parable as an allegory and seeks to interpret all its details allegorically. And as Vincent Taylor remarks: 'The vocabulary and subject matter of 17b-19 clearly reflect the interests and experiences of a primitive Christian community' (*St. Mark*, ad loc.).

Professor Günther Bornkamm, while agreeing that the 'Interpretation' is a later formation, suggests that it 'very properly ... shows that the role of spectator does not suit the hearer in this story. He is not the spectator who, as it were, can watch the sower at his work from the edge of the field or the boundary path; quite otherwise, he is part of the story himself: he is the ground on which the seed falls. Thus the parable speaks with full confidence of the fate of the word of God, and no less clearly of the fact that this word is the fate of the hearers for time and eternity' (*Jesus of Nazareth* [London: 1960] p. 74). But surely this is again a sermonic application of the parable, and indeed a relapse into allegory, not something which is 'clearly' in the parable itself.

94. *The Right Use of Parables*

MARK iv. 21-25 LUKE viii. 16-18

One verse of this group has been brought forward by Matthew into his version of § 91, above; and the others have been used by him in other contexts. The Marcan grouping is clearly artificial. The sayings about the lamp (*v.* 21) and the measure (*v.* 24) are parabolic in character; that is to say, they would come within the broad range of the *mashal*, which includes similes and metaphors and even riddles, proverbs, and maxims, as well as the more developed type of illustrative story which we think of as a parable. Mark might well feel, accordingly, that they would be suitably placed in his collection of parables. The saying of *v.* 22 was transmitted independently and is used elsewhere by both Matthew and Luke in two different senses (see note on Luke xii. 1-2, § 155). Luke here adds to it the phrase which he has used in his version of the parallel 'Q' saying, in xii. 2: 'that those who are entering may see the light' — the light is kindled in us to aid others to find the way. Mark may have thought of these verses as modifying the starkness of the notion of reprobation of § 91; the hiding of the revelation is not for ever, but is to issue in a fuller manifestation. So St. Paul concludes his dissertation on the reprobation of Israel with the assurance that blindness has come upon Israel partially and temporarily — at the last, all Israel shall be saved (Rom. xi. 25f.).

95. *The Parable of the Seed growing Secretly*

MARK iv. 26-29

This is one of the few passages in Mark which is not paralleled in either Matthew or Luke; some scholars regard the parable of the Tares, which is substituted for it in Matthew's collection, as a greatly modified version of Mark's parable. The variety of interpretations is truly astounding. To some commentators *v.* 29 is secondary; to others it is the key to the central thought. To some the emphasis lies in the thought that the earth brings forth the crop 'of itself' (*automatē* — certainly the position of this word in the sentence lends it great emphasis, in the Greek text). The central idea would then be that Jesus by his ministry has set in motion a process which must go on to completion, inevitably, without dependence upon human effort. Others are inclined to lay stress on the stages of growth — 'first the blade, then the ear, then the full grain in the ear' — suggesting the gradual development of God's Kingdom in visible form. Still others direct attention above all to the words 'he knows not how', and think of the mysterious process by which the Kingdom grows. Men preach the Gospel, and in ways that they know not, God gives the increase. But when the closing verse is retained, and treated not as an irrelevant supplement but as conveying the central thought, the whole meaning of the parable is transformed. Now the sower is God, and the whole picture sets forth the thought that the time of his harvest has come, the time to put in the sickle. Long ago, he planted the seed; for ages and for generations he seemed to be unmindful of his own cause, like the farmer who 'sleeps and wakes, night and day, and the seed springs up and grows, he knows not how'; but now, with the ministry of Jesus, the fields are white with the ripened grain, and the time has come to reap. 'In terms of this parable', Professor Dodd tells us, 'we must conceive Jesus not as sowing the seed, nor yet as watching the growth and predicting a harvest in the future, but as standing in the presence of the ripe crop, and taking active steps to "put in the sickle" ' (*Parables*, p. 179). It would be hard to offer a clearer example of allowing the interpretation to be determined by the idea of the doctrine which has been previously formed. In spite of the skill with which Dr. Dodd presents his argument, we shall feel that this is a strained interpretation, even though it is accepted (in substance) by that other great student of the parables, Professor Jeremias (*Parables*, pp. 91f.).

In part at least, this parable is a rebuke to those who imagine that the Kingdom of God will be brought in by a Messianic uprising. But we are inclined to ask also if it is at all compatible with the notion that it will come by an apocalyptic catastrophe of any kind. On the whole it would appear best to regard the parable as complete with the close of *v.* 28; *v.* 29 will then be a secondary addition, introduced solely for the sake of the citation from Joel iv. 13 ('an apocalyptic appendage to the parable'. F. C. Grant, op. cit., ad loc.).

The Parable of the Tares (§ 96) may be deferred for consideration together with its Interpretation (§ 100).

97. *The Parable of the Mustard Seed*

MATTHEW xiii. 31-32 MARK iv. 30-32 LUKE xiii. 18-19

In both Matthew and Luke this parable is paired with the parable of the Leaven, and there is reason to hold that this pairing goes back to the common source ('Q') and possibly even to Jesus himself. In Mark, however, it forms the third in a sequence of parables which begin with the figure of a man sowing seed and end with the completion of its growth. In the first (the Sower), we have the assurance that the abundance of the harvest makes the trifle that goes to waste insignificant; in the second (the Seed growing Secretly), it is the hidden but certain growth to maturity despite the sower's occupation with other matters and his ignorance of how the growth takes place; here in the third, it is the contrast between the smallness of the seed and the greatness of the plant which grows from it. The school of 'realized eschatology' puts the main stress on the picture of the birds which take shelter under the shadow of the full-grown shrub (Mark), or lodge in its branches (Matthew, Luke). This, they point out, is used in the Old Testament as a figure for great nations taking shelter under the protection of a renewed and glorified Israel (Ezek. xvii. 23; in Dan. iv. 12, it is a figure of subject nations under the protection of Nebuchadnezzar's Babylon). They suggest, then, that the parable really points to the emergence of the Kingdom of God in the ministry of Jesus; the Gentile nations are already flocking to its shelter. But surely this detail in the picture is there only to emphasize the size of the shrub. It is agreed that in any case, Mark takes it to be a parable of great growth from small beginnings.

Comparison of the three versions suggests that Luke and Matthew have used a common source apart from Mark; Matthew has conflated his two versions, and has recast the introductory phrase — 'the Kingdom of heaven is like ... ' in place of the double question of Mark and Luke, which evidently stood in the 'Q' source. The change in Luke from 'earth' or 'field' to 'garden' is an indication of Luke's familiarity with the Hellenistic world, and his unfamiliarity with Palestine; for in Palestine it was forbidden to sow mustard seed in a garden.

98. *The Parable of the Leaven*

MATTHEW xiii. 33 LUKE xiii. 20-21

In Matthew and Luke this parable, which is not found in Mark, is paired with the parable of the Mustard Seed. If this pairing goes back to Jesus, as it may, it must again be interpreted as a parable of contrast, pointing on the one hand to the littleness of the leaven and on the other to the immense amount of meal which is transformed by it. If the pairing has come about in the transmission, and the two were originally given independently, it would appear more natural to adopt a different explanation. We might then take the working of the leaven as a symbol of the manner in which the teaching of Jesus, or more broadly his whole ministry, is working in the mass of Judaism. 'There was in it no element of external coercion, but in it the power of God's Kingdom worked from within, mightily permeating the dead lump of religious Judaism in His time' (Dodd, *Parables*, p. 193). The emphasis would then be not on great growth from small beginnings, but on the inwardness of the power of the Kingdom.

The writer would venture to suggest a wholly different interpretation. If we once abandon as secondary the connection with the parable of the Mustard Seed, there would seem to be no reason to avoid the consistent biblical usage of leaven as a symbol of evil. We should then regard the introduction also as secondary, and hold that this was not originally a parable of the Kingdom of God at all but a warning against the growing corruption which is caused by the tolerance of apparently trifling evil. When St. Paul warns the Corinthians that 'a little leaven leavens the whole lump' (1 Cor. v. 6), he is certainly speaking of the danger that the whole society may be corrupted if it fails to purge out the evil that it is tolerating. Is it possible that St. Paul is our first commentator on this parable, and that he knew it in a form which did not make it a figure of the Kingdom of God at all? It will be recalled that elsewhere in the teaching of Jesus, leaven is a symbol of evil that may corrupt his own disciples — 'the leaven of the Pharisees and the leaven of Herod' (Mark viii. 15; cf. Luke xii. 1, Matt. xvi. 6).

99. *The Use of Parables*

MATTHEW xiii. 34-35 MARK iv. 33-34

In Mark these verses form the conclusion of his collection of parables. The two sentences are independently conceived, and hardly compatible in thought. The first represents the parables (rightly) as aids to understanding; the second appears to renew the theory of § 91, that the parables were incomprehensible apart from the explanations which were given privately to the disciples.

On the Stages in the Construction of Mark iv. 1-34

We have now come to the end of the parable-collection as it stands in Mark, and may stop to sum up what we have learned about the stages by which it was put together. The three parables which form the heart of the collection — the Sower, the Seed growing Secretly, and the Mustard Seed — are drawn ultimately from authentic tradition, but it is most unlikely that they were all spoken on the same occasion. They have been linked together in the transmission, and may well have come to Mark in this form in a written source. The Interpretation of the Parable of the Sower, which cannot go back to Jesus himself, will also have been found by Mark in his source, seeing that there is nothing distinctively Marcan in its vocabulary or style. Mark himself will have enlarged the collection by the addition of the two similes ('parables' in the wider sense) of Light and Measure (*vv.* 21-25). The question of *v.* 10, abruptly shifting the scene from the public discourse by the lakeside to a private session with an intimate circle, marks the introduction of a new element, the 'theological' explanation of the use of parables by Jesus as a device for hiding the revelation from outsiders (*vv.* 11, 12). This passage presupposes that the meaning of the parables is veiled, and requires to be unfolded by the teacher; whereas the question put by Jesus in *v.* 13 clearly intimates that the meaning of the parables ought to be transparent. Verse 33 may well have been the conclusion of the parable-collection in the source, but *v.* 34 is a Marcan addition, picking up the reprobation-theology of *vv.* 11-12. As Jeremias remarks: 'The three stages of the tradition (Jesus ... the primitive Church ... Mark) are recognizable throughout the whole of Mark's Gospel, but nowhere so clearly as in ch. iv' (*Parables*, p. 12, n. 11). See also the analysis of W. L. Knox, *Sources* I, ch. iv, 'The Book of Parables'.

96. *The Parable of the Tares*

100. *The Interpretation of the Parable of the Tares*

MATTHEW xiii. 24-30, 36-43

We may begin by observing that the 'Interpretation' of this parable, like that which was offered for the parable of the Sower, cannot be attributed to Jesus himself, but must be regarded as a secondary construction which treats the parable as an allegory, attaches a hidden meaning to all the details, and fails to mention the central point, the danger of attempts to anticipate the judgment of

God in the effort to purge the holy community of unworthy members. The linguistic evidence is decisive. The passage contains several expressions which Jesus himself can hardly have used, seeing that the corresponding Aramaic words are never found with the sense that their Greek equivalents carry here. Still other phrases, though found elsewhere in the recorded teaching of Jesus, are used here in a quite different sense. Here, for instance, 'the sons of the Kingdom' are the true and faithful members of the Church; elsewhere, they are those who as Jews are the natural heirs of the Kingdom, but who through their lack of faith are threatened with expulsion (Matt. viii. 12). Professor Jeremias lists no less than thirty-six examples of expressions which exhibit the linguistic characteristics of the Evangelist himself, and holds that 'it is impossible to avoid the conclusion that the interpretation ... is the work of Matthew himself' (*Parables*, pp. 64-7).

In our own approach to the parable, accordingly, we must not allow ourselves to be led astray by Matthew's allegorizing. His 'Interpretation' has indeed an interest of its own, not as an indication of the thought of Jesus, but as a reflection of Matthew's conception of the Church as a mixed society, faced with the problem of internal discipline. He quite legitimately applies the teaching of Jesus to the situation of the Church of his own time. But he is less concerned with the danger of premature judgments, which may cast out true followers of Jesus in an excess of zeal for expelling unrighteous members, than with the insistence that the Church will assuredly be subject to the divine judgment 'at the end of the age'. He has indulged in flights of allegorical fancy, which reveal to us some of his own theological ideas, or more broadly those of his school. He thinks of the Church as 'the kingdom of the Son of Man', that is, of Jesus; it now contains sons of the devil as well as children of God – the devil himself has planted his servants in the midst of the Church; the ministers of the divine judgment are to be the angels – it will be recalled that Paul, on the other hand, speaks of 'the saints' as destined to judge the angels (1 Cor. vi. 3). After the evil men have been cast out of the kingdom of the Son of Man by the angels, the righteous will 'shine forth as the sun in the Kingdom of their Father'. Thus the Kingdom of the Father is conceived not as the rule of God on earth, the establishment of an order in which God's will is done on earth as in heaven, but as the glorious abode to which the righteous are admitted after the Last Judgment. And the burning of the weeds in the furnace is interpreted as an allegory of the fate of the wicked.

The parable itself is not an allegory, though it has acquired some allegorical touches corresponding to the Interpretation. The presence of weeds in a field is not in itself surprising – the surprising thing would be a field which contained no weeds. The suggestion that an enemy had come by night and sowed the weeds has all the appearance of allegorizing retouching. If we remove this, together with the unimaginable dialogue of *vv.* 27 and 28a, we are left with a clear and consistent picture of a field of grain with its inevitable admixture of weeds, which is used as a figure of the community of Israel with its mixture of good and bad members. John the Baptist had envisaged the mission of his greater Successor as a mission of judgment; but Jesus teaches that the time for making the separation of the righteous from the wicked has not yet come — it must await the judgment of God. Just as the farmer allows weeds and grain to grow together until the harvest, so God allows righteous and wicked to live side by side in his own Chosen People, and men must not anticipate his judgment by seeking to form a community of the pure. Probably the parable was in some measure at least a defence of his own welcome to tax-collectors and sinners — his refusal to form a separatist group of holy and righteous people after the manner of the Pharisees and the Essenes.

It has been argued that the parable as a whole is not authentic, but is nothing more than a drastically modified version of Mark's parable of the Seed growing Secretly, with which it has some coincidences of language and which it replaces in the Matthaean reproduction of Mark's parable-sequence. As T. W. Manson puts it: 'It is an allegory constructed out of material supplied by Mark's parable (iv. 26-29) combined with the eschatological teaching of the Baptist, ... an allegory composed for the sake of the explanation which is to follow. It is not to be regarded as a genuine parable of Jesus' (*Sayings*, p. 193). Against this we must repeat that in fact the explanation misses the central point of the parable, the injunction to 'let both grow together until the harvest'; if the allegory was framed for the sake of the explanation, it is impossible to suppose that it would give such emphasis to a point which the explanation entirely neglects. It seems more likely that Matthew has remodelled an independent parable of Jesus, conflated it to some extent with the Marcan parable (as indicated by the coincidences of vocabulary), and added some allegorical embellishments which detract from the realism of the original parable.

101. *The Parables of the Hidden Treasure and of the Pearl of Great Price*

MATTHEW xiii. 44-46

These two parables, which are found only in Matthew, are similar in both form and significance. The emphasis is not upon the possessions that must be surrendered if the kingdom of heaven is to be won but on the surpassing worth of the kingdom of heaven. Once it is found, the finder gladly parts with everything he possesses that he may gain it. Christian interpretation soon came to take the Pearl of Great Price as a figure of Christ himself, not of the kingdom, in the spirit of St. Paul's ardent words: 'What things were gain to me, those I counted loss for the sake of Christ; not only that, but I count everything as loss for the sake of the supreme good, the knowledge of Christ Jesus my Lord, for whose sake I have suffered the loss of everything, and count it all worthless rubbish that I may gain Christ and be found in him' (Phil. iii. 7-9).

102. *The Parable of the Drag-net*

MATTHEW xiii. 47-50

The interpretation (*vv.* 49-50) is again secondary, being clearly modelled on that of the Tares, from which it borrows the figure of the 'furnace of fire', which is appropriate to the bundles of weeds but not to the unsaleable fish. The parable has thus been turned into a forecast of the Last Judgment. It seems probable that the parable proper (*vv.* 47-48) has been drastically modified to make it capable of such an interpretation. The picture of fishermen sorting their catch and discarding the fish for which there would be no market is true to life, but it is hard to see how the double role of the fishermen is to be viewed as analogous to the workings of the kingdom of heaven. If the sorting is a figure of the judgment, the ministers of judgment would appear to be identified with the missionaries as the 'fishers of men'. But since the appeal of the Gospel is made precisely to sinners — the net is cast for the bad as well as the good — it would seem that the main purpose of the missionary work is frustrated if the bad are cast away as soon as they have been caught. We are inclined, therefore, to accept the suggestion of T. W. Manson (*Sayings*, p. 197), that the original parable consisted solely of *v.* 47: 'The kingdom of heaven is like a net which was cast into the sea and gathered fish of every kind.' It was not intended as a parable of judgment at all, but as a parable of missionary work, suggesting the appeal of the Gospel to all sorts and conditions of men. But in its present form it has been reshaped into a warning that the Church, a mixed body which includes bad men as well as good in its membership, will be purged at the end of the age. This is a theme which receives repeated attention in Matthew; see especially his incongruous addition to the parable of the Marriage Feast (§ 205; Matt. xxii. 11-14).

There is in any case no warning here against *premature* judgment, as in the parable of the Tares — no suggestion that we must wait patiently for the appointed time of God's judgment (against the interpretation of J. Jeremias). If we recognize the secondary character of the allegorical interpretations appended to the two parables, there is no reason to take them for a pair. If *v.* 48 is part of the original parable, the emphasis in our interpretation will be shifted from the indiscriminate appeal of the Gospel to the process of selection which accompanies it — not the Last Judgment, as in Matthew's allegory (and in the non-allegorical interpretation proposed by Jeremias), but the judgment which men bring upon themselves when they count the cost of accepting the invitation. This is the line of interpretation taken by C. H. Dodd (*Parables*, pp. 187-9). It is in keeping with his underlying doctrine of 'realized eschatology', but it is not clearly appropriate to the imagery of the parable. It recalls the Johannine theology. There is really no suggestion of the reaction of the fish; the parable is wholly concerned with the actions of the fishermen. For that reason, we prefer the analysis of Manson.

103. *The End of the Parables*

Matthew xiii. 51-52

In *vv.* 34-35, Matthew has used the Marcan conclusion of the collection of parables. He has represented the interpretation of the parable of the Tares, and the three short parables which follow it, as addressed to his disciples alone, after the dismissal of the crowds. The little dialogue of *v.* 51 is artificially contrived as an introduction to the saying of *v.* 52, which is not particularly relevant to the teaching of this chapter.

It is hard to imagine that Jesus himself compared his disciples to scribes who had added to their knowledge of the ancient Law a like accumulation of knowledge of the principles of the Gospel. The saying is indeed susceptible of interpretation as a companion-piece to Matthew v. 17. Just as Jesus came not to destroy the law and the prophets, but to fulfil them, so the follower of Jesus keeps in his treasury all that the Law has to teach men of the will of God, while he enriches it with the treasures of the kingdom of heaven. But there is much to be said for the view of T. W. Manson that the saying represents rather a Jewish-Christian attempt to formulate a mediating position towards the traditions of Judaism, less radical than that of Jesus or that of Paul. Matthew may himself have been a 'scribe who had been made a disciple to the kingdom of heaven.' As Manson remarks: 'It is beyond doubt that the sharpest and most obvious conflict in the ministry of Jesus was that between His teaching and the scribal interpretation of the written Law. Matthew, more than any other Gospel, emphasizes this fact. But Matthew also attempts, here and elsewhere, to suggest that the conflict goes no deeper than that; that it is a dispute about the exegesis of the Law, and that the Law itself is not in question. Both Jesus and the scribes knew better than that ... The bitter hostility of the scribes is not mere professional jealousy. It is based on the recognition that the logical end of Jesus' teaching is the end of the Law.' And he concludes: 'This saying expresses perfectly the Jewish-Christian ideal; it may well be doubted whether it represents the conviction of Jesus Himself' (*Sayings*, pp. 198-9).

104. *Christ's Real Brethren*

LUKE viii. 19-21

This is Luke's version of the Marcan passage which immediately precedes the parable collection (§ 89). In that area, Luke is not following the Marcan order; he rejoins Mark for the parable of the Sower after inserting a long series of sayings and incidents drawn from 'Q' and 'L'. By introducing this pericope at this point, following the parable of the Sower and its interpretation, he treats it as an illustration of the seed which falls on the good ground, understood as figuring 'those who in an honest and good heart, having heard the word, keep it and bring forth fruit with patience' (*vv.* 8, 15). The phrasing of Jesus' reply is altered accordingly: 'Whoever does the will of God' becomes 'those who hear and do the word of God'.

Miracles by the Lake of Galilee
§§ 105-112

105. *The Stilling of the Tempest*

MATTHEW viii. 18, 23-27 MARK iv. 35-41 LUKE viii. 22-25

In this and the two following sections, Mark introduces four miracle-stories which are linked together by a double crossing of the lake, or perhaps it would be better to say, by the boat which had served for the delivery of the parables (iv. 1) and now becomes itself the theatre of the first miracle and the means of transportation to the scenes of the others (iv. 36ff., v. 2, 21). Luke follows the Marcan order, but Matthew has transferred all three sections to an earlier stage of the narrative and has separated the twofold story of the third section from the first two, working it into a grouping of his own. Thus it comes about that neither Matthew nor Luke associates the boat of the storm-scene with the boat of the teaching. Luke, having employed the picture of the teaching from the boat for his version of the call of the first disciples (§ 17), did not mention it in his introduction to the parable of the Sower, and must now frame an independent setting for the trip across the lake (*v.* 22); it is not even laid in the late evening of the day of parables, as in Mark, but vaguely 'on one of the days'. It will be noted once again that neither Luke nor Matthew feels obliged to take the Marcan time-indications seriously. The variations in wording of the three versions are considerable, but not such as to suggest that the other two Evangelists have used another source besides Mark.

The story, especially in its Marcan form, is clearly conceived as the exorcism of a storm-demon; the same verb (with a change of tense) is used as in the story of the exorcism at Capernaum (*pephimōso*, *phimōthēti* — Mark i. 25). This impression is somewhat obscured in Matthew and Luke by the omission of the words of command, but Jesus still rebukes the raging winds and waves. The terrified reproach of the disciples' appeal as given in Mark: 'Teacher, don't you care that we are perishing?' is softened in the other versions; and the rebuke of Jesus: 'Why are you so cowardly? How is it that you have no faith?' is softened even more. Here, as in several other places, the growing veneration for the apostles has led the later Evangelists to remove or conceal in some degree the blemishes which Mark portrays more frankly.

One is tempted to suspect that the whole story has been created to represent Jesus as fulfilling the testimony of the Psalms to the 'God of our salvation ... who stills the roaring of the seas, the noise of their waves, and the tumult of the peoples' (Ps. lxv. 5, 7; cf. Ps. lxxxix. 9). But it is at least possible that a miracle-story has grown out of an actual incident, in which the disciples were astonished by the undisturbed calmness of Jesus in the midst of a storm which made them fear for their lives, and attributed the ensuing calm to his power over nature. If we are impressed by the parallels with the story of Aeneas (*Aeneid* iv. 554ff.; see notes of V. Taylor, ad loc.), it is not necessary to ask if Mark had read Vergil; it would suggest rather that both Vergil and Mark were following a pattern of sea-wonders.

106. *The Gadarene Demoniac*

MATTHEW viii. 28-34 MARK v. 1-20 LUKE viii. 26-39

The Marcan story is again the source employed by Matthew and Luke. Matthew has abbreviated drastically, removing much of the picturesque detail of Mark in the process. For some reason he has turned the one demoniac of the Marcan story into two; compare his similar doubling of the blind man of

Jericho (§ 193). Luke has likewise abbreviated Mark's graphic account of the demoniac's wild behaviour, but the substance of it is transferred to his *v.* 29b; otherwise he makes only trifling verbal alterations. His change of 'out of the country' to 'into the abyss' (*v.* 31) reflects popular beliefs about the abode of demons.

The central feature of the story is the exorcism, with its emphasis on the dangerous character of the mania – the strength and violence of the man, and his feeling that not one demon but an entire legion has taken up its abode in him. In the dialogue (Mark v. 7-9), the man is represented as speaking in the person of the demons, reverting at times to the singular ('I adjure you' ... 'My name'). The story of the destruction of the herd of swine is secondary, and has 'the appearance of typical elaboration in folk tales' (F. C. Grant). In Jewish (or Jewish-Christian) circles, the destruction of a herd of unclean animals belonging to a pagan farmer would even have an element of rough humour.

The locality of the incident cannot be determined. Manuscripts vary between the country of the 'Gerasenes', the 'Gadarenes', and the 'Gergesenes'. The third of these readings is traceable to Origen, who pointed out that neither Gerasa nor Gadara corresponded to the description, and suggested a place called Gergesa, which was on the lake of Galilee, with an overhanging cliff near by. In Mark, by far the best-attested reading is 'Gerasenes', but Gerasa is in fact thirty miles south east of the lake. Matthew almost certainly wrote 'Gadarenes', perhaps as a deliberate correction, based on his knowledge that Gadara was much nearer to the lake – though it was still six miles away. Neither of these towns could be said to be 'opposite Galilee' (Luke viii. 26). But as F. C. Grant remarks: 'The original text of Mark is not to be settled by topography' ('Mark', ad loc.). The shore of the Gentile region of the Decapolis, in the territory ruled by Philip, is intended in any case (cf. Mark v. 20).

Despite these difficulties in detail, and the obviously legendary character of the story of the swine, there is no reason to doubt that underneath it all is a true story of the restoration of a maniac to sanity by our Lord. The episode of the swine may be explained as 'one of the numerous aetiological myths which were current in the hellenistic world to explain the rite of precipitating a victim or victims from a cliff into a river, lake or sea as a means of removing the contagion of sin or ritual impurity acquired since the rite was last performed. ... On the assumption that a story of this kind has been attached to Jesus by the floating popular tradition of Transjordan the details ... are easily explicable' (Knox, *Sources* I, pp. 39-40). This has been combined with exploitation of the recurrent motif of the demon duped (their request is granted, but results in their own discomfiture – they perish in the lake along with the swine). There is no need to invent rationalistic explanations for the mass suicide of the swine, on the supposition that we are dealing with the recollections of eye-witnesses. But the affirmation that the story of the demoniac 'shows every sign of being an extraneous interpolation into the Gospel tradition' (Knox, loc. cit.) is not applicable to the exorcism itself.

107. *Jairus' Daughter and the Woman with the Issue of Blood*

MATTHEW ix. 18-26 MARK v. 21-43 LUKE viii. 40-56

We have here an interweaving of two miracle-stories in a manner that has no parallel in the Synoptic tradition. It seems likely that they were originally independent, and that the story of the woman has been intercalated here through word-association – 'twelve years' – *vv.* 25, 42; 'made well' (or 'saved' – rendering various forms of *sōzō*) – *vv.* 23, 28, 34; *pistis*, 'faith', and *pisteue*, 'believe' – *vv.* 34, 36. Further, it allows time for the arrival of the messengers with the word that the girl has died; this of itself would hardly lead to the interweaving of the stories.

Matthew has again drastically abbreviated the Marcan account, even to the extent of changing the whole situation. In Mark the ruler comes to ask Jesus to heal a little girl who is at the verge of death; in Matthew she is dead already, and the father asks Jesus to restore her to life. This obliges him to delete the coming of the messengers (Mark, *vv.* 35-37). The story of the woman with the haemorrhage is shortened even more, at the cost of much of its vivid colour and pathos. When we observe the magnitude of the changes that could be made in a *written* record as late as the time of Matthew, we cannot fail to perceive that the tradition would be liable to still more radical change during the years of oral transmission.

Luke's changes are trifling, in comparison. The name Jairus seems to have been introduced by him; it is not used by Matthew, and though it has weighty textual attestation in Mark, it may none the less have been introduced there by way of assimilation to Luke (it is omitted in Codex Bezae and in the Old Latin of Mark). It is exceptional, in these stories, to find the characters named. The interest of the narrator is in Jesus, and after him in the apostles. Even the apostles are seldom mentioned by name; the names of others are often a mark of legendary elaboration. In the story of the woman, Luke has characteristically softened the brusque wording of the disciples' remonstrance (*v.* 36), and has made Peter the spokesman.

It is possible that the miraculous element in both these stories is secondary. Mark certainly presents the story of Jairus' daughter as an account of the reanimation of a dead person; but the words actually attributed to Jesus (*vv.* 36, 39) will bear the sense that he does not credit the report that the girl is dead, and that he rouses her from a coma. The story of the woman, likewise, might conceivably have grown out of an incident in which Jesus felt a hesitant touch in the midst of a crowd, and realized that someone was making a diffident appeal to him for help and comfort; there is no indication of how it became known that she was suffering from a haemorrhage, and this feature could be regarded as secondary. Such attempts to find a natural explanation of the miracle-stories are not really convincing. We shall, however, agree with V. Taylor that 'what really happened is a much more difficult question to answer ... It is hard to resist the conclusion that the evidence that the historical Jesus raised the dead is far from being decisive' (*St. Mark*, pp. 285-6). In such a question, could any 'evidence' be decisive? The question is rather whether any historical occurrence lies behind the story, or whether it is simply part of the cult-legend of Jesus, like the infancy-narratives.

108. *Christ is Rejected at Nazareth*

MATTHEW xiii. 53-58 MARK vi. 1-6

Matthew here takes up again the thread of the Marcan narrative, and follows it with few omissions or transpositions, though with many additions of new material, till the end of the Gospel. Luke has already used the story of the Rejection at the very beginning (§ 10), as an enunciation of one of his leading themes, and consequently he omits it at this point, but rejoins Mark in the following section and follows him, with substantial omissions, through most of the next chapter. A full discussion of the incident and of the significance attached to it by the three Evangelists is offered by the late R. H. Lightfoot in the seventh of his Bampton Lectures (*History and Interpretation in the Gospels*), 'The Rejection in the Patris'.

We have to observe first of all an apparent inconsistency in the Marcan story, which is reflected in the Matthaean version and becomes still more conspicuous in the Lucan. It begins in much the same tone as the first story of Jesus' preaching in a synagogue (Mark i. 21-22), with indications that the hearers are filled with admiration; but this impression turns immediately into scorn and indignation. As Lightfoot points out, even the expression 'the son of Mary', so full of tenderness for us, is 'presumably meant to be derogatory in the highest possible degree. No man in the East, whether his father were living or not, would be known familiarly by reference to his mother'. For this reason, both Matthew and Luke have felt it unbearably insulting in tone, and have altered it, Luke to 'the son of Joseph'; and Matthew to 'the son of the carpenter; is not his mother called Mary?' It is probable that in its original form the story was wholly one of hostility, and that Mark has added in *v.* 2 the conventional note of astonishment and admiration (cf. Knox, *Sources* I, pp. 48-9). It seems likely, also, that the story was originally one of complete failure: 'He could do no mighty work there, ... and he marvelled because of their unbelief' (*vv.* 5a, 6), and that Mark himself has qualified this by the somewhat inconsistent addition of 5b: 'except that he laid his hands upon a few sick people and healed them'. Matthew has removed all suggestion of Jesus' *inability* to heal, contenting himself with saying that 'he did not do many mighty works there because of their unbelief'. In Luke, the lack of miracles at Nazareth is mentioned only by implication, in the words of Jesus: 'You will surely repeat to me this proverb, Physician, heal yourself. The things that took place in Capernaum, as we have heard, do here in your own country also' (Luke iv. 23).

For all three Evangelists, the story is a symbol of the wider rejection of Jesus by Israel. The ministry which opened amid scenes of enthusiasm at Capernaum is drawing to its close amid tokens of repudiation and scorn. It is undoubtedly significant that in the Marcan story, Jesus never enters a synagogue again.

109. *The Sending Out of the Twelve*

MATTHEW ix. 35, x. 1, 9-11, 14   MARK vi. 7-13   LUKE ix. 1-6

Matthew has used this Marcan material, conflated with materials drawn from 'Q' and from his own Jewish-Christian source, in the second of his discourse-compilations, the Mission Charge (ch. x). Mark, by placing the pericope immediately after the story of the Rejection, may intend to suggest that Jesus now adopts new methods; the Rejection at Nazareth leads to a widening of the mission, just as the rejection of the Gospel by Israel was to lead to expansion into the Gentile world. In Luke there is no trace of any such connection.

Many critics have questioned the historicity of this mission, on the ground that 'the Twelve merely make an experiment and remain afterwards as lacking in independence and as passive as before, although the experiment succeeds' (J. Wellhausen, *Evangelium Marci*, p. 44). It is then taken to be a reading back into the days of the Ministry of the missionary activity of the primitive Church. It is in any case difficult to attach to it the great importance attributed to it by Taylor, Branscomb and others. Mark himself passes over it lightly; Matthew gives the charge, but tells not a word about how the mission was executed; Luke adds an account of a mission of Seventy (or Seventy-two), which is probably a mere doublet in the tradition, and may even be a construction of his own, but even he makes no great event of it. Taylor himself admits that 'at the time the Gospels were written, the significance of the mission had long been forgotten' (*Life and Ministry*, p. 110); it must then be precarious to lay emphasis 'upon the crucial importance of the mission and its decisive importance for Jesus himself' (ibid., p. 107). There is simply no justification for imposing upon our documents a construction for which they offer no evidence whatsoever.

110. *Herod's Opinion of Christ*

MATTHEW xiv. 1-2   MARK vi. 14-16   LUKE ix. 7-9

The Herod of this pericope is Herod Antipas, son of Herod the Great, who received the administration of Galilee and Peraea at the death of his father (4 B.C.) and remained in charge of these territories until he was banished by Caligula in A.D. 39. His official title was 'tetrarch' (correctly given in Matthew and Luke); Mark's use of 'king' (*basileus*) may reflect popular usage.

Matthew has again abbreviated the Marcan passage, keeping only his report of the opinion of Herod and omitting the views of the people, perhaps because they will be mentioned later (xvi. 14, § 122). Luke, on the other hand, has kept Mark's report of popular opinions but has made Herod expressly reject the notion that Jesus could be John *redivivus*. This is certainly a deliberate revision of Mark, not an independent version drawn from another source. We may notice further that Luke omits the following section, concerning the death of the Baptist, but borrows from it the mention of Herod's perplexity (*ēporei* — Mark vi. 20; *diēporei* — Luke ix. 7). There is no suggestion here that Herod's interest in Jesus is hostile or menacing.

111. *The Death of the Baptist*

MATTHEW xiv. 3-12 MARK vi. 17-29

This passage, omitted by Luke, is little more than a footnote to the reference to John's execution in the preceding sentence. It need not be dismissed as the gossip of the bazaars; see Taylor's discussion (*St. Mark*, pp. 310-33), and Knox's remarks on the unreliability of Josephus at this point (*Sources* I, pp. 50-1). It is the only story in Mark which is not about Jesus in any degree.

Without examining it in detail, we shall note the characteristic abbreviation of Mark by Matthew. The closing phrase in Matthew – 'they came and told Jesus' – provides an editorial link with the episode that follows.

112. *The Return of the Twelve and the Feeding of the Five Thousand*

MATTHEW xiv. 13-21 MARK vi. 30-44 LUKE ix. 10-17

The introduction is in each case an editorial construction, and shows substantial differences in the three versions. In Mark the apostles return to Jesus to make their report on their mission, and Jesus takes them off to a 'lonely place' by boat for a period of rest; but the crowds pour out from the 'cities' and run on foot to the other shore, and arrive before the boat is beached. There is a certain incoherence in the account; it is not clear where Mark takes Jesus to be when the apostles return to him, nor where the 'lonely place' to which they sail is to be found, nor how the crowds from the 'cities' (whatever cities they be) manage to assemble and run around the lake so much more quickly than the boat can sail. In Matthew, the departure by boat to the lonely place and the crowds following on foot are retained, but in place of the motive of rest after the preaching tour the incident is connected with the news of John's execution. In Luke the incident follows directly upon the return of the apostles with their report, but there is no suggestion that the withdrawal is for the purpose of seeking rest, nor that it is to a lonely place – they go to the city of Bethsaida, in the territory of Philip. As Bethsaida was a good ten miles from the nearest point in Galilee, the crowds which followed them would have a long walk. This may be taken as another indication that Luke is not familiar with the topography of the area. Bethsaida is introduced from Mark vi. 45, a passage which Luke omits; in Mark's account, it is 'on the other side' of the lake from the scene of the Feeding, and the disciples go there by boat *after* the miracle. Luke then forgets that he has brought Jesus and the disciples to a city, and reverts, in *v.* 12, to a 'lonely place' as the scene of the teaching and the miracle. Mark mentions the teaching of Jesus, but as usual does not feel it necessary to say anything about what he taught; Luke gives the theme of the teaching as 'the kingdom of God', and adds that Jesus healed those that were in need of healing; Matthew says nothing about teaching, but speaks of the healing of the sick.

It is evident that for all the Evangelists, the details of the setting are of little importance. Mark has invented freely, being concerned only to provide a scene in which Jesus is surrounded by hungry throngs, in a place where food is not readily obtainable; and Matthew and Luke have felt perfectly free to alter his picture.

The story of the Feeding of the Five Thousand is a miracle-story with Eucharistic overtones, and it has often been suggested that the miraculous element is secondary. We shall of course dismiss out of hand the preposterous notion that we have before us the story of a picnic on the grass, at which the hearers opened their own lunch-baskets when Jesus and his disciples had set the example, and so found that there was enough for everyone, and to spare. It is reasonable, however, to take into account the fact that in Oriental tales the numbers tend to be exaggerated. Even in the versions before us, we may note that Matthew is not satisfied with Mark's 'five thousand men', but adds 'besides women and children'. Apart from the question of the numbers involved, and the legendary embellishment that after all had partaken there was far more food left than when they began, we must entertain the possibility that underneath the miracle-story there may lie a non-miraculous account of a *ritual* meal, conceived as a symbol and foretaste of the Messianic banquet. The most notable exponent of this interpretation is Albert Schweitzer. 'The supper at the Lake of Gennesareth was a veiled eschatological sacrament. Neither the disciples nor the multitude understood what was happening, since they did not know who He was who thus made them His guests. This meal must have been transformed by tradition into a miracle, a result which may have been in part due to the references to the wonders of the Messianic feast which were doubtless contained in the prayers, not to speak of the eschatological enthusiasm which then prevailed universally' (*Quest of the Historical Jesus*, pp. 377f.). In support of this approach we may point to the frequent use of the bread and fish in early Christian art as Eucharistic symbols, and recall the elaboration of the Eucharistic discourse of John, ch. vi, in dependence upon the story of the miraculous feeding. We may remark further that none of the versions make any reference to the astonishment of the disciples or of the crowd at the multiplication of the loaves and fishes; yet the effect upon the witnesses is an almost invariable element of the miracle-story.

But are we really justified in accepting an explanation which is certainly not in the mind of the Evangelist, and was not grasped at the time by either the disciples or the multitude? The story as told has Eucharistic overtones, and was always understood as having Eucharistic significance, but does this justify the conclusion that the miraculous element is secondary and that some remembrance of a non-miraculous ritual meal lies beneath it? It is perhaps more probable that the Eucharistic aspects are secondary, and that the whole narrative was primarily an epiphany-story, in which the divine Dispenser of blessings revealed his presence by the miraculous multiplication of the loaves and fishes, just as Dionysus reveals his divine presence in numerous myths by the miraculous provision of wine and oil and honey.

St. Luke's 'Great Omission': Miracles and Controversies §§ 113-121

MARK vi. 45-viii. 26

At this point Luke omits almost two chapters of the Marcan narrative and moves directly from the Feeding of the Five Thousand to the Messianic Confession voiced by Peter. This 'Great Omission' has been explained in different ways. Some critics have argued that Luke must have been using an earlier version of Mark (*Urmarcus*), which did not contain these sections; or that he had a mutilated copy from which these pages were missing. Others hold that Luke recognized that much of the omitted material consists of doublets; thus Creed remarks: 'His critical instinct will have led him to regard the feeding of the four thousand and the feeding of the five thousand as doublets' (*St. Luke*, p. lxi). More broadly, the whole of Mark viii. 1-26 is generally recognized as a variant version of the same cycle of events that has been reported in Mark vi. 30-vii. 37. The controversy over the Washing of Hands (§ 115, 'The Tradition of the Elders' — Mark vii. 1-23) would be largely unintelligible to Gentile readers, and Luke might well feel that he would be touching upon it sufficiently in his introduction to the Discourse against the Pharisees (§ 154; Luke xi. 37ff.). Something must also be allowed for the necessity of reducing his material to fit the space available on a papyrus roll, which would not ordinarily exceed 35 feet. 'An idea of the amount which a roll could contain may be given by saying that a roll of about 32-35 feet would hold, in a medium-hand, one of the longer books of the New Testament (Matthew, Luke, Acts), or a book of Thucydides, but no more' (F. G. Kenyon, *Books and Readers in Ancient Greece and Rome*, 2nd ed. [Oxford: Clarendon Press, 1951], p. 64). Both Luke and Matthew were obliged to shorten their Marcan material substantially in order to leave room on the roll for the additional material which they wished to introduce from their other sources. Matthew has achieved his end by using nearly all the Marcan stories, but abbreviating them in drastic fashion; Luke has preferred to omit a number of the Marcan stories outright.

113. *The Walking on the Water*

MATTHEW xiv. 22-33 MARK vi. 45-52

The story is linked to the miracle of the Feeding of the Five Thousand. In the Johannine narrative we have the same association, and it is worth noticing that the story of the Feeding of the Four Thousand is likewise followed by a lake-crossing. This would indicate that the two incidents were linked at a very early stage in the formation of the tradition.

The story is quite different in character from the narrative of the stilling of the storm. It is essentially an epiphany-story, with more than a touch of the uncanny. It has frequently been proposed to take it for a misplaced Resurrection-story, and it has in fact certain formal features which justify this conclusion. It has been remarked, on the other hand, that 'the Marcan rendering of this incident is farther away from the type of the post-resurrection narratives' than the Johannine; and that 'the incident is firmly welded into its context, more firmly, indeed, than most of the *pericopae* belonging to the Galilaean Ministry' (C. H. Dodd, 'The Appearances of the Risen Christ: An Essay in Form-Criticism of the Gospels', in *Studies in the Gospels*, ed. D. E. Nineham [Oxford: Blackwell, 1955], p. 24). Professor Dodd concludes that either a Resurrection-narrative has been transplanted into a different context, or that an incident of the Galilean ministry has been influenced in its form by the post-resurrection narratives.

The closing sentence in Mark reflects his theory of the 'Messianic secret'. Jesus is revealed in his true supernatural person, but the disciples fail to grasp the significance of the revelation because 'their hearts were hardened'. The thought is that their lack of perception is supernaturally induced (by Jesus himself, or by God), because the divinity of Jesus must remain hidden until the appointed time. This notion is discarded in Matthew, who makes the scene an occasion for the recognition and worship of Jesus as 'Son of God'.

It is unprofitable to seek for some commonplace event that may have served as the nucleus around which the miracle-story grew, to justify the supposition 'that the narrative has a factual basis, and is not merely a product of fancy and imagination' (Taylor, *St. Mark*, p. 326). Once we have abandoned the notion that the story must be taken *au pied de la lettre*, there is no need to suppose that its presence in the Gospel is a guarantee that it embodies some remembrance of actual events. It is best understood as a transference to Jesus of a typical marvel, which has many parallels in the Hellenistic literature of the period, and indeed in folk-tales from many other parts of the world. There is no more justification for assuming that the tale must have some 'factual basis' when it is told of Jesus than when it is told of Lucian's Hyperborean magician or of a Buddhist devotee. The only question that concerns the investigator is the question of meaning: what did such a story mean to the Evangelist who incorporated it in his Gospel or to the Christian who heard it read in the liturgy? He would undoubtedly take it at its face value, in a way that is impossible for us; but he would also take it to his heart as a picture of the Jesus whom he worshipped as Lord, who was present with him, invisible but no mere phantom, when the night was dark around him and the winds contrary.

Matthew's supplement (*vv.* 28-31) is one of a very few Peter-legends. Its presence here reflects the particular interest taken in Peter by the Church (of Antioch?) in and for which this Evangelist wrote. It is obviously secondary to the epiphany-story in which it is embedded, and is indeed inconceivable without it. If we think of the primary story as a transferred Resurrection-narrative, we may conclude that Matthew knew it in a form in which it was accompanied by an account of a special manifestation of the risen Christ to Peter on the waters by night. But the style and language of the verses are distinctively Matthaean, and the story may be a composition of the Evangelist himself.

114. *Healings at Gennesaret*

MATTHEW xiv. 34-36 MARK vi. 53-56

According to Mark vi. 45, Jesus had 'compelled the disciples to embark on the boat and to go before him to the other side, to Bethsaida'; but it turns out that they land at Gennesaret and anchor there. Matthew has removed the discrepancy by omitting both place-names. There is a tendency among commentators to reconcile the conflicting statements of Mark by supposing that the 'contrary wind' (*v.* 48) had made a change of course necessary. This presupposes a degree of accuracy in the transmission of the tradition that is hardly justified by the facts. Mark was 'certainly unfamiliar with the geography and topography of northern Palestine' (F. C. Grant, 'Mark', *IB*, VII, p. 631), and may have thought that the plain of Gennesaret was near Bethsaida; or he may simply have drawn upon two different sources without being conscious of their discrepancy.

It will be noticed that Matthew, according to his custom, has abbreviated the little Marcan summary at the cost of its more vivid touches (the pallets of the sick, the placing of the sick in the village market-squares, etc.).

115. *The Tradition of the Elders*

MATTHEW xv. 1-20 MARK vii. 1-23

The Marcan passage is again the basis of the Matthaean. Except for verses 12 to 14, which bring together an independent logion (*v.* 13) with a 'Q' saying which Luke has used in another context (*v.* 14; cf. Luke vi. 39, § 76), under an editorial introduction composed by Matthew himself, the whole section in Matthew is drawn from Mark, with abbreviations and one transposition — Mark's 'Qorban' passage (*vv.* 9-13) is placed by Matthew before the Isaiah citation instead of after it. Only one of the abbreviations is significant. In *v.* 19, Matthew's list of the defiling things which come out of the heart is 'reduced to a list of actionable offences' (apart from the first term — 'evil thoughts') 'and the dispositions are omitted. A principle of morals is thus converted into a precept of law' (Kilpatrick, *Origins*, p. 36).

The Marcan passage is itself composite, and the analysis is exceptionally difficult. The central elements of the complex are: (i) a Pronouncement-story, in which the disciples of Jesus are accused of violating 'the tradition of the Elders' — that is, the oral law, as defined by the scribes — in the matter of washing the hands before eating, with the counter-attack of Jesus, who charges that the scribes and Pharisees themselves nullify the commandment of God by their insistence on the scribal tradition (*vv.* 1-8); (ii) an illustration of this nullification — the commandment to honour father and mother is effectively set aside by the tradition of 'Qorban' (*vv.* 9-13); (iii) an independent saying of Jesus, which bears upon the general question of 'defilement', though not on the particular matter of the washing of hands, is added as an *ex parte* declaration to 'the crowd', which has not hitherto come into the picture (*vv.* 14-15); (iv) an explanation of the significance of the appended saying is given privately to the disciples (*vv.* 17-23).

The terms of the controversy are not easily grasped by the modern reader, as they have to do with peculiarities of ancient Jewish law and custom. The washing of hands before eating is not in the least a sanitary precaution, or a matter of personal cleanliness, but a ritual action; it was not designed to remove dust and dirt, but to take away ceremonial 'defilement'. The hands could be 'defiled' in numerous ways – as, for instance, by touching a roll of the sacred scriptures; the books of the heretics do not defile the hands, strange as it may seem, but the canonical scriptures do. A tractate of the Mishnah, called *Yadaim* – 'Hands' – gathers together the opinions of Jewish authorities. It begins with the question of how much water is necessary for the fulfilment of the ritual requirement. The opening paragraph runs as follows:

'[To render the hands clean] a quarter-*log* or more [of water] must be poured over the hands [to suffice] for one person or even for two; a half-*log* suffices for three persons or for four; one *log* or more suffices for five or for ten or for a hundred.'

The *log*, the unit of measurement used here, is given as a volume equivalent to the contents of six eggs.

A further paragraph tells us that 'if water was [so polluted that it was] unfit for cattle to drink, if it was in vessels it is invalid [for the washing of hands] but if it was on the ground it was valid' (Danby).

The phrase 'that is, unwashed' (*v.* 2) and the whole of *v.* 3 are editorial notes added by Mark to make the point of the dispute clearer to Gentile readers. The reference to 'the Pharisees and all the Jews' is plainly derogatory, almost sneering in tone. The account of Jewish customs is not in accord with Palestinian practice of the time; the strict rules of ceremonial purity were applicable only to the priests. It is possible that Jews in the Diaspora – perhaps specifically at Rome – observed such purifications, from the feeling that they incurred defilement from their contacts with Gentiles in the market-place. But there is something artificial about the entire *mise en scène*. The elaborate introduction, bringing in as it does a party of scribes from Jerusalem as well as the (presumably local) Pharisees, is out of proportion to the complaint which they make, that the disciples of Jesus are not observing the traditional rules of purification. Again, that the charge is levelled against the disciples and not against Jesus himself is an indication that the dispute has arisen in the Palestinian community of the early Apostolic Age, not in the days of Jesus himself (cf. Mark ii. 23f., § 69, notes). There is no indication of time or place, or of the circumstances in which the disciples are eating under the eyes of their critics. The setting, then, is an artificial construction, devised for the sake of the 'pronouncement' of Jesus in *vv.* 6 to 8. The Jewish Christians defend themselves against the charge that they do not observe 'the tradition of the Elders' by appealing to the judgment of Jesus, that reverence for the scribal tradition has the effect of nullifying the commandments of God.

The 'Qorban' passage is added as a conspicuous example of the way in which a specific commandment could be effectively nullified by a scribal application which had acquired the status of 'tradition', and it is charged that many such examples could be given (*v.* 13). It thus becomes clear that the real issue goes far beyond the comparatively trifling question of the ritual washing of hands, and involves the entire problem of the Christian attitude towards the oral Law. For the primitive Church, in its Jewish environment, there was no more crucial question. The radical rejection of the 'tradition of the elders' set the Christian community free to give a new interpretation to the Old Testament scriptures in their entirety, and, in particular, to put forward a totally different conception of purity and of the basis of the moral life.

The new principle, in turn, is enunciated formally, as a public declaration of Jesus to 'the crowd' which he has called to him to hear it: 'There is nothing from outside man that can enter into him and defile him; but it is the things that come out from man that defile man.' The saying is then expounded in private to the disciples. The terms of this exposition make it directly pertinent to one of the most bitterly disputed problems of the early church — the table-fellowship between Jews and Gentiles. It has been suggested that this exposition must have received its form in a Gentile community, on the ground that 'we cannot account for the early disputes at Jerusalem and Antioch if Jesus spoke so directly' (Taylor, *St. Mark*, p. 342; he refers particularly to *vv.* 18-19). It may be remarked, however, that inherited prejudices are not easily removed, and that Jesus may well have been more radical than his followers. The cardinal saying of *v.* 15 certainly required something in the way of exposition.

116. *The Syro-Phoenician Woman*

MATTHEW xv. 21-28 MARK vii. 24-30

Here we find for the first time a story which is longer and more vivid in Matthew than in Mark. We can hardly imagine that in this one instance Matthew has expanded his Marcan source, after consistently abbreviating it up to this point. The explanation is rather that he has had at his disposal a second account of the same incident, independently transmitted, and has conflated this with the Marcan story.

The chief differences are the following: (i) in Mark, Jesus is alone and is seeking seclusion; in Matthew, he is accompanied by his disciples; (ii) in Mark, the woman is 'a Greek, a Syro-Phoenician by race'; in Matthew, she is described as 'a Canaanite'; (iii) in Matthew, but not in Mark, the woman addresses Jesus as 'Son of David'; (iv) the final saying is totally different in the two versions. All these features indicate the use of a second source by Matthew; most of the other differences between the two versions reflect the usual Matthaean abbreviation of the Marcan source, and some unimportant changes in the wording.

The centre of interest is not the miraculous healing of the woman's child, which is merely incidental to the dialogue, but the attitude of Jesus to Gentiles. It lacks virtually all the formal features of the miracle-story (description of the illness, actions of the healer, evidences of the reality of the cure, amazement of the bystanders). Like the story of the Centurion's Servant (§ 46), with which it has much in common, it depicts the faith of a Gentile and foreshadows the extension of the salvation of Christ beyond the limits of Israel to all who have faith. The harshness of the saying of Jesus: 'It is not good to take the children's bread and cast it to the dogs' still puzzles the Christian reader, who finds it impossible to imagine Jesus addressing a distraught mother in such terms. It is hardly less difficult to imagine the mother accepting the description of her and her people as 'dogs' who hope only for crumbs from their masters' table. Dare we see in all this a reflection of the reluctance with which the primitive Church embarked upon the Gentile mission?

The geographical setting is extremely vague, and can hardly be regarded as solid evidence for a journey of Jesus into the regions north of Palestine. The statement that he 'went away into the regions of Tyre [and Sidon]' is probably an editorial introduction devised by Mark himself, prompted by the description of the woman as 'a Syro-Phoenician'. No motive is given for this journey, with or without the disciples. Mark's account of the return (*v.* 31) brings Jesus 'from the region of Tyre, through Sidon, to the sea of Galilee, through the midst of the regions of the Decapolis'. This would be like going from New York to Albany through Philadelphia, by way of the Laurentians; or like going from London to Birmingham through Southampton by way of the Lake country! Matthew seems to represent Jesus as remaining in the Holy Land ('the parts of Tyre and Sidon' probably being taken to mean the border districts of north-western Galilee), so that the woman comes 'from that region' (i.e. Phoenicia) to seek his aid.

117. *The Healing of Many Sick Persons* (Matthew) – *of a Deaf Mute* (Mark)

MATTHEW xv. 29-31 MARK vii. 31-37

Matthew has abandoned Mark's impossible itinerary for the return to the lake. Neither of them indicates to what point of the lake Jesus came, but they probably intend to convey that he is on the north shore; 'the mountain' of Matthew cannot be identified. The story of the Deaf Mute was probably transmitted without any indication of time or place; again, there is no mention of the presence of the disciples, and Matthew does not introduce them. It is not likely that Matthew is making use of another source. His reasons for dealing so drastically with the Marcan story can only be conjectured; perhaps he disliked the attribution to Jesus of the use of magical means (spittle) and actions. Or again, the closing comments of the people, in the Marcan story, imply that this is not an isolated healing but an illustration of the general activity of Jesus, and Matthew has acted on this hint to substitute a generalizing summary.

The use of magical means and actions by Jesus is paralleled (in the Synoptic Gospels) only in Mark's story of the Blind Man of Bethsaida, which closely resembles this story in vocabulary also. Further consideration of these features may be deferred till we come to the second of the pair (§ 121 – Mark viii. 22-26).

118. *The Feeding of the Four Thousand*

MATTHEW xv. 32-39 MARK viii. 1-10

This story is an independently transmitted version of the story of the Feeding of the Five Thousand (§ 112), which Mark – and following him, Matthew also – has taken for a separate incident. The variations are all of a kind that would come about inevitably in the process of oral transmission. The notion that 'St. Mark's reason for writing the second story as the mere shadow of the first was to concentrate our attention on the sole significant novelty, the variation in the numbers; and in addition, that he intended the numbers to be not the numerical expression of a bathos but the symbolical expression of a mystery' (A. M. Farrer, *St Matthew and St Mark* [London: Dacre Press, A. & C. Black, 1954], pp. 62-3) can only be regarded as a curiosity of criticism. Nothing is in fact less 'significant' than the variation in the numbers, which is simply the reflection of variation in the two sources employed.

The remark that the crowds have been with Jesus for three days, and the reappearance of the disciples without any preparation (in Mark, Jesus has been by himself during the long journey into Phoenicia and back), are probably to be taken as 'signs that at an earlier stage in the tradition the story stood in a fuller context which it is now impossible to recover' (Taylor, *St. Mark*, p. 357).

As in the story of the Five Thousand, the feeding of the multitudes is followed by the dismissal of the crowds and the crossing of the lake, though here the miraculous incident of the crossing is not repeated. The place of landing is given in Mark as Dalmanoutha, and in Matthew as 'the region of Magadan' (with variants, of which 'Magdala' is the best attested). After the Feeding of the Five Thousand, the disciples are directed to make for Bethsaida, but they actually land at Gennesaret; in the sequence before us, they eventually reach Bethsaida (*v.* 22). But the details of the itinerary are not to be pressed; Mark is not really interested in topography, and takes the place-names from his sources without bothering to locate them on a map. Probably he was not familiar with the topography of Palestine; but W. L. Knox reminds us that Josephus can set down equally inconsistent topographical data, even though he was well acquainted with the region (*Sources*, I, p. 46, n. 1).

119. *The Pharisees Seek after a Sign*

MATTHEW xvi. 1-4 MARK viii. 11-13

The passage appears to be out of context; it may be that Mark has placed it here as an introduction to the 'Discourse on Leaven' which follows, and which is evidently conceived to be spoken aboard the ship. It is not clear where the Pharisees are, when they make their demand for 'a sign from heaven'. The Matthaean passage is taken from Mark, apart from the sayings of *vv.* 2 and 3, for which the textual attestation is poor. We are told that the signs of the weather in the Lucan passage (Luke xii. 54-55) are true to Palestinian conditions, but that the Matthaean sayings are more doubtful as grounds for prediction (T. W. Manson, *Sayings*, p. 201). Matthew has a doublet of the passage in xii. 38-39 (§ 87; see notes). Matthew's addition to Mark at this point ('except the sign of Jonah the prophet') is probably derived from his other version of the saying.

120. *A Discourse on Leaven*

MATTHEW xvi. 5-12 MARK viii. 14-21

This whole passage appears to have been constructed around the saying of Jesus: 'Take care, beware of the leaven of the Pharisees and the leaven of Herod.' As the Herods had long passed from the scene, Matthew has substituted the more familiar combination 'Pharisees and Sadducees'. The meaning of the saying had evidently been forgotten. Mark does not attempt to explain it, but suggests that it is related in some way to the miraculous feedings; Matthew indicates that by 'leaven' here, Jesus meant 'teaching', though it is far from clear what the recollection of the miracles of feeding has to do with the teaching of the Pharisees and Sadducees. Luke uses the saying by itself, following a Discourse against the Pharisees (Luke xii. 1 — § 154), and represents Jesus himself as explaining that 'the leaven of the Pharisees' is hypocrisy.

It will be observed that Matthew tones down the rebuke to the disciples, and removes Mark's suggestion that they do not understand Jesus even after his explanation

In the circumstances of the early Palestinian Church, this group of sayings may have been brought together as a warning to those who felt that they must compromise with the demands of the Pharisees or of Herod if they were to be able to go on earning their daily bread.

121. *The Blind Man of Bethsaida*

Mark viii. 22-26

This story has striking linguistic agreements with the story of the Deaf Mute in the preceding chapter (§ 117); and even more remarkable similarities in the description of the methods employed by Jesus. The removal of the patient, so that the cure may be worked in privacy; the use of spittle; the touching of the affected part with the hands — these features, common to the two narratives, are also typical of the techniques of magicians. The command 'Ephphatha' (to the Deaf Mute) is in itself an intelligible Aramaic word, but its retention here could hardly fail to suggest to a non-Semitic reader of the time the magic word in an unknown tongue, often enough quite meaningless, by which the wandering magician effected his cures. In general, we must recognize that these two stories are substantially indistinguishable from other Hellenistic miracle-stories, and that we are not justified in claiming for them any basis in fact. Matthew had good reason for discarding them, even in a section in which he is following Mark very faithfully.

We must suppose, however, that Mark saw a particular significance in *this* story when he placed it at this point of his narrative, immediately before the Messianic Confession and the instruction in the Way of the Cross. The unique feature of this story, among the Synoptic traditions, is that the blind man's cure proceeds by stages; at first, the men that he sees look like trees walking; then, after Jesus has laid his hands on his eyes, he sees all things clearly. So in the following scene, the disciples show that they have attained a measure of spiritual insight when they acknowledge that Jesus is the Messiah; but when they rebel at the teaching that he must attain his destiny by the Way of the Cross, they show that their vision is still distorted. In the Transfiguration, they will for a moment enjoy the dazzling vision of the glory that truly belongs to him — a foretaste of the fullness of insight that will come to them with his Resurrection.

This brings us to the end of Luke's 'Great Omission'. At this point he again picks up the Marcan narrative and follows it with only one brief omission through the following nine sections. Matthew continues to make use of the Marcan material.

Messiahship and the Way of the Cross
§§ 122-127 (128)

122. *The Confession at Caesarea Philippi and the First Prediction of the Passion*

MATTHEW xvi. 13-23 MARK viii. 27-33 LUKE ix. 18-22

In this passage Mark has provided the framework of the incident — the question of Jesus, the reply of Peter, and the prophecy of the Passion of the Son of Man. The second part of the Marcan story — the remonstrance of Peter and his rebuke by Jesus (*vv.* 32-33) — has been retained by Matthew, with some new elements of dialogue which are probably derived from a second source; but has been omitted by Luke, probably out of respect for the memory of the apostle. In the introduction, Matthew has retained the setting of Mark (in the neighbourhood of Caesarea Philippi) with minor changes of wording. This involves a rather long movement from Bethsaida, where the previous Marcan incident is located (*v.* 22), or from the vaguer 'other side' of Matthew's last reference to place (xvi. 5; § 120). Caesarea Philippi, founded by Philip, the brother of Herod Antipas, on the site of the ancient Paneas, lay in the foothills south of Mount Hermon, some twenty miles north of the lake of Galilee. Luke has omitted the place-reference entirely; characteristically, he adds the remark that Jesus was praying (as at the Baptism and again at the Call of the Twelve — iii. 21; vi. 12), as if to suggest that Jesus prepares himself for an act of particular significance by renewed communion with God. For Mark, the movement to a pagan neighbourhood, so far from Galilee, is probably a symbol of the transition from a public ministry to the private preparation of the disciples for the approaching Passion. At any rate, we are told that when Jesus returns from the north and re-enters Galilee, it is not to resume the public ministry, but to pass through the land incognito, to meet the final conflict in Jersualem. 'When he departed from there, he was passing through Galilee, and he did not wish that anyone should know; for he was teaching his disciples and telling them that the Son of Man is betrayed into men's hands, and they shall kill him ... and he shall rise again' (Mark ix. 30-32).

In the Marcan version of the incident, the centre of interest is not the Messianic confession itself. This is distinctly shown to be based upon a profound misunderstanding of the way in which Jesus himself views his mission, and Jesus forbids the disciples to speak of him in terms of Messiahship. In fact the verb *epitimaō* which Mark uses here (rendered 'charged' in our versions) is used twice immediately below (*vv.* 32, 33) in its ordinary sense of 'rebuke' (Peter begins to *rebuke* Jesus; Jesus *rebukes* Peter); elsewhere in this Gospel it is generally used of the injunctions which Jesus lays upon demons or demoniacs, with a note of rebuke, and it would seem that Mark uses it here also with a sense of rebuke. Jesus does not welcome the title, but repudiates it. If it were not for the Matthaean supplement (Matt. xvi. 17-19), which is certainly out of place in this context (if indeed it be authentic at all) we should never think of the story as suggesting that Jesus accepts the title and seeks merely to fill it with a new content. See the discussion of G. S. Duncan (*Jesus, Son of Man*, pp. 149ff.), and more generally his argument in chapter X of the book ('Did Jesus claim to be the Messiah?'), with the conclusion that 'in the Gospels there is singularly little evidence that Jesus specifically laid claim to be the Messiah'; that he 'certainly regarded Himself as entrusted by God with a commission which after His death His followers interpreted — and rightly interpreted — as Messianic', but that 'we cannot safely deduce from this that during His lifetime Jesus had either Himself openly connected His authority with Messiahship, or had allowed others to do so' (p. 133).

We are inclined, accordingly, to look upon the little dialogue of Mark viii. 27-29 as an artificially contrived introduction to the prophecy of the Passion. The Messianic Confession may then be a projection backwards, into the period of the ministry of Jesus, of the earliest Christology of the apostolic Church, a conviction based upon the Resurrection. It seems at least a possibility, however, and the present writer is inclined to look upon it as a probability, that the disciples entertained messianic conceptions of their Master during his ministry, and may even have expressed them. Recognition of the artificial character of the Marcan dialogue here does not of necessity lead to the thorough-going scepticism of Wrede and his followers. Just as there are many sayings of Jesus in the Gospels which are acknowledged to be authentic even though they have been transmitted out of their original context, so it may be that the disciples in fact attached naive and inadequately-conceived messianic expectations to Jesus before his death, even though our record preserves them only in a literary construction of the earliest Evangelist.

The Matthaean version puts a totally different interpretation upon the incident. First, the Confession itself is elaborated in terms of a 'Son-of-God' Christology; such a conception of Messiahship is certainly not conceivable in terms of Jewish expectation. Whatever may be said of the Marcan form, there can be no doubt that the Matthaean Confession: 'Thou art the Christ, the Son of the Living God', is a projection into the past of a Christology which could not have been formulated until the Apostolic Age. Still more striking is the long Matthaean insertion (*vv.* 17-19), in which Jesus pronounces Peter 'blessed', affirms that his perception of the Messiahship of Jesus has come to him by divine revelation, and proceeds to explain his new name Peter (Cephas, 'Rock') as indicative of the place that he is to hold in the founding of the Church.

There are strong grounds for questioning the authenticity of these sayings. The group is composite, and may have been brought together by Matthew himself (see Kilpatrick, *Origins*, p. 39). Some of the phrases reflect the peculiarities of the Evangelist himself — 'kingdom of the heavens', 'My Father who is in heaven'. The first saying recalls the words of St. Paul in Galatians i. 11, 12, 16. As St. Paul affirms that he did not receive his Gospel from man ... but through a revelation, and that he did not confer with flesh and blood, so Jesus himself affirms the divine origin of St. Peter's faith. 'The beatitude of this verse may well express the feelings of his Jewish fellow-Christians' (Manson, *Sayings*, p. 204). The principal arguments against the genuineness of the other sayings may be summarized from the discussion of Professor Manson (op. cit., pp. 202-3). (i) The word *ekklesia* ('church') never occurs in the Gospels except in this passage and in Matthew xviii. 17, which is itself suspect on other grounds, and in any case uses the word in a different sense. There it means the local community, conceived as exercising judicial authority over its members; here it means the whole Church. 'But this state of affairs – a great Church, whose constituent members are smaller communities – belongs to the period of Acts. In the Gospels we have a body of disciples with Jesus at their head expecting the coming of the Kingdom of God.' (ii) If the saying were genuine, Peter could hardly have failed to attain recognition as the authoritative ruler of the nascent Church. But the narrative of Acts shows clearly enough that he enjoyed no such status. He must answer to the Jerusalem Church for his conduct in preaching to Gentiles at Caesarea (Acts xi. 2ff.); he makes his contribution to the debate at Jerusalem over the question of the admission of Gentiles, but the sentence of the assembly is formulated by James; and at Antioch, Paul resists him to his face (Gal. ii. 11). 'There is no satisfactory answer to this objection.' (iii) There is nothing else in the tradition to suggest the notion that one of the Twelve is to have primacy over the others. In Matthew xviii. 18, the power of 'binding' and 'loosing' is conferred on the community, not upon an individual apostle; and in Matthew xix. 28 (cf. Luke xxii. 30), the Twelve are promised that they 'will sit on twelve thrones, judging the twelve tribes of Israel', with no thought that Peter will have a higher position than the rest. And in Mark x. 35-45 the request of James and John that they may sit on either hand of Christ is rejected, 'not on the ground that the primacy belongs already to Peter, but on the ground that it is not in the power of Jesus to confer such rank'.

Manson accordingly holds that 'we should not regard the saying as a genuine utterance of Jesus', and suggests (on the ground of certain passages in 1 Corinthians) that 'the kind of claim for Peter which we have in Matt. 16: 18 was being pressed in the fifties of the first century, and that Paul is resisting it in Corinth when he writes 1 Cor. It may also be conjectured that the challenge implied in the claim was directed against Paul himself. He was always suspect to the Palestinian Church; and it is possible that the elevation of Peter was meant to act as some kind of check upon Paul' (ibid., p. 204).

But it must be said that not all scholars would reject the words so decisively.[1] John Lowe, for instance, tell us that 'the scruples I once felt about the authenticity of Matthew 16:18 have been dissipated. I do not think it is in its right context, and I doubt if we can say positively where it belongs ... The uncertainty about the original context does not affect the genuineness of the saying itself' (*Saint Peter* [Oxford, 1956] ch. 3, 'The Primacy of Peter', p. 55). See also the discussion by K. L. Schmidt in his article (translated from Kittel's *Theologisches Wörterbuch*), *The Church* (London, 1950), pp. 35-50. The most complete

[1] There is a hint that Manson himself changed his mind in his later years. See his remarks in the (posthumous) volume of lectures, *Ethics and the Gospel*, p. 69.

treatment in English, in defence of the authenticity of the passage, but not its place in this context, is that of O. Cullman in his book *Peter: Disciple — Apostle — Martyr* (trans. F. V. Filson, Philadelphia, 1953), under Part II, 'The Exegetical and Theological Question'. He cannot believe that Jesus never *during his lifetime* explained the title 'Rock', and accordingly he thinks it probable that Matthew found the saying 'in an ancient oral tradition', as a separately transmitted unit. It is impossible to assume that it was spoken in this context, where 'Peter plays the role of one who does not understand the Messianic role of Jesus'. Cullmann is inclined to think that it was originally spoken in the context of the Passion-story. If it be accepted at all as a fragment of ancient tradition, it is probably better (with R. Bultmann and others) to think of it as part of a Resurrection-story (Bultmann, *History*, pp. 259, 406f.).

Authentic or not, the Matthaean sayings are out of context and must not be allowed to affect our interpretation of the Marcan story. There, as we have remarked, the centre of interest is not in the Messianic Confession, but in the prediction of the Passion which follows. The main question here is the significance which we are to attach to the title 'Son of Man'. Let us notice before we go any further with this inquiry that Matthew has introduced the title into the question put by Jesus: 'Who do men say that the Son of Man is?' (*v.* 13), where it replaces the personal pronoun of the Marcan version; and conversely, he now replaces Mark's 'Son of Man' by the personal pronoun. It would be hard to get clearer evidence that Matthew takes the phrase 'Son of Man' in this context to be no more than a surrogate for the personal pronoun. We are not justified, therefore, on the basis of this passage, in taking it as a *title* which Jesus deliberately chooses for himself, in preference to 'Messiah'. The Aramaic locution which he uses here means simply 'I must be betrayed ... and put to death'. The question of what the phrase means *as a title* does not arise at this point.

The authenticity of this prophecy has often been denied by critics; but unless we are to deny the very possibility of predictive prophecy, there seems to be no sufficient reason for challenging these sayings. It is surely not hard to suppose that Jesus was clear-sighted enough to foresee that the opponents of his ministry would sooner or later bring him to his death, and that his faith in God was so strong as to keep him calmly confident that his death would not be the end of the story. Certain forms of the prediction reflect, naturally enough, modifications introduced in the light of the actual course of events (especially in the Third Prediction, § 191, with its details of the transference from the Jewish to the Gentile authorities, and the mocking, spitting, and scourging), but these tend on the whole to set in relief the substantial genuineness of the basic prophecy as we have it here.

The variation 'after three days' (Mark) — 'on the third day' (Matthew, Luke) is not significant; there is abundant evidence that in the Greek of this period generally, and in the Septuagint particularly, the two phrases were identical in meaning. Commentators are inclined to hold that Jesus spoke less precisely of the *time* of his resurrection; but if it be granted that he confidently expected that God would raise him from the dead, the form of his prediction might well be determined by the recollection of 'the third day' in Hosea vi. 2.

The force of Mark's phrase, 'he began to teach them' (*v.* 31), is reinforced by Matthew's, 'from that time, he began to teach the disciples', as indicating that a new stage in the ministry is commencing. Hitherto the main theme of the teaching of Jesus has been the Kingdom of God; from this point on, it is the Way of the Cross — first the prediction of his own Passion, then the repeated call to his followers to renunciation, self-denial, the bearing each of his own cross.

123. *The Conditions of Discipleship*

MATTHEW xvi. 24-28 MARK viii. 34-ix. 1 LUKE ix. 23-27

We have here a catena of sayings, originally transmitted in isolation, which have been brought together in this grouping by Mark, who is probably also responsible for attaching them to the prophecy of the Passion. The scene is contrived by him, and is in a measure incongruous with the solitude presupposed by the preceding episode; both Matthew and Luke have omitted the summoning of the crowd, which is not easily imagined in that pagan environment. A variant version of the sayings of *vv.* 34 and 35, again in combination, is used by Matthew in a different context, in his Mission Charge (x. 38-39); and again, in separation from one another, in Luke xiv. 27 and xvii. 33 (the latter, in an apocalyptic context). In *vv.* 36 and 37 we have two sayings of a proverbial character (Wisdom-sayings), each capable of standing by itself. Verse 38 is even more clearly drawn from a different circle of ideas. In it, 'the Son of Man' is not a title of Jesus himself, but a glorious figure of apocalyptic expectation. Undoubtedly for Mark himself he was identified with Jesus, and all three Evangelists take the saying as a reference to the Parousia of the Lord; but in the saying as it stands (at least in Mark and Luke; the modification in Matthew is probably designed to remove the possibility of such an interpretation), the Son of Man is distinguished from Jesus. Without carrying the matter farther at this point, we may remark in passing that when 'the Son of Man' occurs in apocalyptic passages, the identification with Jesus is never explicit. The last of the sayings, which is provided with an introduction of its own — the peculiarly Marcan phrase: 'And he said to them' — forms the transition to the story of the Transfiguration.

Mark's arrangement brings out with great power the challenge to the followers of Jesus to be faithful even unto death, in the assurance that they will receive the crown of life. If, as we conjecture, he wrote his Gospel in Rome during or immediately after the persecution under Nero, these sayings could not fail to strike home to the hearts of Christians who had seen multitudes of their friends dragged off to torture, to crucifixion, to death in the most horrible forms that savagery could devise. Here the death of the Christian is linked with the death of his Master; and the assurance that 'he who loses his life for the sake of Christ and the Gospel will save it' is bound up with the prediction that 'after he has been killed, he will rise again'. On the other hand, there is the warning against apostasy in the face of the terror; for 'he who wants to save his life will lose it', and he who denies Christ on earth will himself be denied in the

Day of Judgment. Finally, there is the assurance that the coming of God's kingdom in power is near at hand, for Jesus had promised that some of those standing around him would live to see it. The present danger will pass; the triumph of God's kingdom will soon be seen; and those who now suffer with Jesus will be glorified with him. The vision of the transfigured Jesus is an anticipation of the heavenly glory to which all his faithful followers are called, though like him they must attain to it by the Way of the Cross.

124. *The Transfiguration*

MATTHEW xvii. 1-8 MARK ix. 2-8 LUKE ix. 28-36

There is probably no other pericope in the Gospels which has received such divergent interpretations as the story of the Transfiguration. As Vincent Taylor remarks: 'The interpretation of the narrative presents a very difficult problem and few will claim that they can give an explanation which completely satisfies them' (*St. Mark*, p. 386). After a short account of different hypotheses, ancient and modern, he writes: 'In sum, we may say that, while it is impossible to say exactly what happened on the mount, we may well believe that the confession of viii. 29 was deepened and confirmed in an incommunicable experience of prayer and religious insight' (ibid., p. 388). Or as G. S. Duncan puts it: 'This is not history in the ordinary sense of the term; and the precise significance of the story is not easily grasped' (*Jesus, Son of Man*, p. 151). A good many scholars renounce the attempt to look for any factual basis underlying the story, and treat it wholly as a product of theological symbolism. Even where a concrete historical experience is postulated, it is recognized that the narrative as it stands is charged with a most elaborate symbolism. Thus William Manson holds that it 'would seem to be of the nature of a vision seen in a trance ... While the Transfiguration narrative is thus, as it stands, highly symbolical, an historical basis is discernible in some experience, perhaps a vision of Christ in prayer, through which his words about the sufferings which awaited him flashed upon the disciples' minds with a new insistence and reality, recalling significant things which he had said about Moses and Elijah, and opening a momentary vista of what lay beyond the veil of time and sense. ... As the tradition stands, it implies that the disciples saw Jesus for the moment in the light in which his Church was to see him after the Resurrection' (*Luke*, pp. 113, 115).

A great many commentators have taken the view that this is a Resurrection-story brought back into the story of the earthly life of Jesus. However, Julius Schniewind pointed out that while the basic notion is that Jesus appears to the disciples in the glorified form that is to be his in the Resurrection, the story has elements which are not found in the Resurrection-narratives generally; in particular, the only visitants from the heavenly world in the Resurrection-narratives are angels, and even they do not appear in company with Jesus; and in none of them do Elijah and Moses appear. More broadly, Professor C. H. Dodd has examined the story in the context of a form-critical investigation of all the Resurrection-narratives of the Gospels, and has come to the conclusion that 'On formal grounds this theory (that the Transfiguration-story is an antedated post-resurrection appearance of the Lord) has no support whatever. On the contrary, the pericope in question contrasts with the general type of post-resurrection narrative in almost every particular.' He proceeds to note five major points of difference, and adds: 'To set over against these points of difference I cannot find a single point of resemblance. If the theory of a displaced post-resurrection appearance is to be evoked for the understanding of this difficult pericope, it must be without any support from form-criticism, and indeed in the teeth of the presumption which formal analysis establishes' ('The Appearances of the Risen Christ: An Essay in Form-Criticism of the Gospels', in *Studies in the Gospels*, ed. D. E. Nineham [Oxford: Blackwell, 1955], p. 25).

It would seem that the time has come to relegate this theory to the museum of antiquities. In general, we may say that the choice lies between postulating a visionary or mystical experience of the disciples which has been elaborated in terms of a complex symbolism, and treating the story wholly as the creation of an artist in religious symbolism. In either case, the chief interest for us must lie in the interpretation of the symbolism, and it must be said that the search for an historical basis of any kind is bound to rest upon speculations concerning the psychology of religious experience, in which our sources are not at all interested.

It is in fact difficult to point to a single detail that can be taken definitely to indicate historical reminiscence rather than religious symbolism. Much ingenuity has been expended in the effort to identify the 'Mount of the Transfiguration'. Mount Tabor, long the favourite, is now in disfavour because it is 'not more than 1000 feet high' (V. Taylor), and there is a tendency to prefer Mount Hermon (9200 feet); but three Tells in the neighbourhood of Caesarea, each over 4000 feet, are also mentioned. But it is probable that 'the Mount' is simply a symbol of the place of revelation, like the mount of the great Sermon. There may be some significance in the location of the epiphany on a mountain in pagan territory, not on Mount Zion or any of the holy mountains of Old Testament revelation. 'There may be a consciousness here that "neither on this mountain nor in Jerusalem shall they worship the Father" (John iv. 21). The holiness of Zion is thereby shattered, and another land and another mountain receive a new dedication' (Lohmeyer).

Nor is the phrase 'after six days' rightly construed as a reminiscence that about a week elapsed between the Confession at Caesarea Philippi and the Transfiguration. It probably comes directly from the story of Moses on Sinai: 'The glory of the Lord settled on Mount Sinai, and the cloud overshadowed it for six days; and on the seventh day he called to Moses out of the cloud' (Exod. xxiv. 16). More generally, it is pointed out that six days of fasting preceded the great Feasts, and that the priest passed six days in the Temple before the Day of Atonement, to purify himself. 'Six days are thus the time of preparation for a divine revelation' (Lohmeyer; cf. the remarks of Austin Farrer in *St Matthew and St Mark*, pp. 111f.). There are in fact not less than seven details of the story of Exodus xxiv which have their parallels in the Transfiguration story. These are (i) the scene — a mountain of revelation; (ii) the six-day interval; (iii) the overshadowing cloud — the relatively rare verb of the LXX version of this Exodus passage is used again here; (iv) the presence of Moses; (v) the Voice from the cloud; (vi) the transforming glory (here we must turn to the descent of Moses from the mountain, for the supernatural brightening of his face—Exod. xxxiv. 29-35); and (vii) Peter's proposal to build 'three tents' recalls the eschatological significance of the Feast of Booths (or, Tabernacles; in Greek, 'tent-pitching' — *skēnopēgia*), and also the fact that God speaks to Moses (Exod. xxv.ff.) to give instructions for the making of the Great Tent which was conceived to be the prototype of the Temple. It is difficult to find anything in what remains that savours any more of concrete historical fact.

Both Luke and Matthew follow the Marcan story closely. In place of Mark's 'after six days', Luke has put 'about eight days after these things'. As the eighth day is also the first day, Luke may have wished to suggest the Resurrection. Luke changes the Marcan verb *metemorphōthē*, perhaps to avoid any thought of similarity to pagan stories of 'Metamorphoses'. Mark's description of the transformation in Jesus is somewhat surprisingly confined to the clothes; both Matthew and Luke speak first of the changed appearance of the countenance, and both have omitted Mark's homely comparison: 'as no fuller on the earth could whiten them'. The Lucan addition (*vv.* 31-32) introduces a new element of significance into the narrative, which will be discussed below. Matthew's addition (*vv.* 6, 7), on the other hand, seems to be designed merely to mediate the transition to the conclusion of the scene — the discovery that the heavenly visitants have faded out of the scene, leaving Jesus alone. Luke's closing sentence takes the place of the conversation between Jesus and the disciples as they come down from the mountain, which Luke omits (§ 125).

The significance of the Lucan addition has been well indicated by H. Conzelmann. Moses and Elijah, appearing in glory, speak of 'the Exodus' which Jesus is to accomplish in Jerusalem. Their words are not for the disciples, who are 'heavy with sleep'; but when they awake, they see the glory of Jesus and the two men standing with him. (The rendering of *Gospel Parallels* [RSV] is quite wrong here; the Greek words cannot possibly be construed as meaning that they 'were heavy with sleep but kept awake'.) Mark says nothing of the *content* of the colloquy between Jesus and the glorified saints of the old dispensation. Luke, by his addition, makes the scene into a heavenly proclamation, to Jesus himself, of the meaning of the sufferings which he has already foreseen. They will be the central action of the New Exodus, bringing the redemption of the people of God. The Transfiguration is thus a companion-piece to the story of the Baptism. At the Baptism, Jesus received the assurance that he is the Son of God; at the Transfiguration, he receives the assurance that his sufferings are coming upon him in accordance with the will of the Father. The scene has thus a twofold significance in the Lucan version: for Jesus, a heavenly revelation of the necessity of his Passion; for the disciples, a revelation of the divine and heavenly nature of Jesus, and of his precedence over the Law and the Prophets. In this context, the injunction to the disciples to 'Hear him!' has the special sense, that they must heed his proclamation of suffering. (*Die Mitte der Zeit: Studien zur Theologie des Lukas*, 3rd ed., Tübingen, 1960, pp. 50-2.) See also the remarks of Archbishop Ramsey, *The Glory of God and the Transfiguration of Christ* (London, 1949), pp. 121-3.

125. *The Coming of Elijah*

MATTHEW xvii. 9-13 MARK ix. 9-13

This passage is omitted by Luke in keeping with his consistent removal of all suggestions that John the Baptist is the Elijah of prophetic expectation. Matthew makes some revisions in the Marcan wording, chiefly designed to clarify the thought of a rather obscure passage. 'St Matthew is St Mark's closest interpreter, and his characteristic attitude to St Mark is the desire to expound and expand. He finds his predecessor's thought too packed, too pregnant' (Austin Farrer, *St Matthew and St Mark*, p. 4). There is a lack of connection in the Marcan passage, which is only partly remedied by Matthew. The question about the coming of Elijah does not follow in any obvious way upon the command to say nothing about the experience on the Mount of Transfiguration until after the resurrection of the Son of Man; and it is hard to see the relation between the affirmation that 'Elijah first comes and restores all things' and the question 'How is it written concerning the Son of Man, that he should suffer many things and be set at nought?' (Mark ix. 12). There are missing links here, and they are not easily restored. There is probably something in Farrer's suggestion that Mark 'was writing for men who could take up easily references which we track down painfully. ... It is unfair, then, to suggest that St Mark's paragraph required as full a paraphrase to make it intelligible to his first readers as it requires to make it intelligible to us' (ibid., pp. 5, 6). Even so, he remarks that the unravelling of the meaning of the paragraph 'is beyond what St Matthew or St Luke is prepared to ask of his readers'. Under the circumstances, we may well doubt whether Mark's readers were really able to make for themselves the expansions which Dr. Farrer uses, to explain the movement of the thought.

In any case, the authenticity of the dialogue is more than doubtful, and the effort to reconstruct it in a fuller form is misdirected effort. 'Apart from all difficulties of word-connection and sentence-connection, this dialogue does not seem to be possible in the mouth of Jesus and his disciples ... Question and answer have developed out of the discussions of the primitive church with Jewish opponents' (Lohmeyer, *Markus*, pp. 183-4).

126. *An Epileptic Child Healed*

MATTHEW xvii. 14-21 MARK ix. 14-29 LUKE ix. 37-43a

In Mark, this story is unusually full of detail, some of it repetitive, some irrelevant. The desire to prune away some of this exuberance is sufficient to account for the drastic shortening of the Matthaean and Lucan versions, without the hypothesis of another source or of a different edition of Mark. In the Marcan version, the opening verses sound like the introduction to a controversy-story; they picture the disciples, surrounded by a throng, engaged in argument with some scribes; and the first question of Jesus is 'Why are you arguing with them?' But with that, the scribes vanish from the story, and we never learn anything about the argument. Instead, a man in the crowd begins to describe to Jesus the symptoms of his son in the fits of epilepsy to which he is subject, which the father takes to be the work of a demon; and the remainder of the narrative is an exorcism-story. Both Matthew and Luke have removed all mention of the scribes and the argument, perceiving them to be irrelevant, and have thus confined attention to the exorcism. Again, though the symptoms of epilepsy have been described with great fullness by the father, they are repeated by Mark in his account of a seizure which the lad suffers as Jesus approaches; this is much abbreviated by Luke and omitted entirely by Matthew. Both of them omit the striking little dialogue between Jesus and the father (Mark ix. 21-24), and proceed directly to the exorcism. Here again they both omit the words of Jesus' charge to the demon and the account of the demon's final fling, which causes the spectators to think that the boy is dead (Mark ix. 25b-26). Luke omits the closing question and answer (Mark ix. 28-29); while Matthew substitutes a different reply of Jesus. Probably neither of them thought that the answer found in Mark was at all conceivable. It is remarkable that in the Marcan narrative nothing is said of the effect upon the witnesses (the stock conclusion of the miracle-story). Luke has repaired the omission (*v.* 43), but Matthew has not. Both of them have rewritten Mark's account of the symptoms, each in his own words; we note especially Matthew's characteristic verb *selēniazō* (from *selēnē* — 'Moon', hence literally, 'moon-struck', 'lunatic', as in Matt. iv. 24), and Luke's *monogenēs* ('only'), as in the story of the Widow's Son at Nain (Luke vii. 12). The addition to the exclamation of Jesus of Mark ix. 18 ('O faithless *and perverse* generation'), common to Matthew and Luke, is a reminiscence of Deut. xxxii. 5. This entire saying can hardly be authentic in this form; it implies that Jesus is conscious that he is a divine being out of his true environment, 'who has appeared for a brief interval in human form, and is soon to withdraw again to heaven' (M. Dibelius).

The placing of the story, to follow the Transfiguration, must be ascribed to the editorial work of Mark, not to the tradition as it came to him. Scribes would hardly be found in a story which was laid in the foothills of Mount Hermon; and 'the disciples' are mentioned without any trace of a distinction between the three who have witnessed the Transfiguration and the nine who remained below. In Mark's arrangement, the healing of the epileptic completes a threefold sequence, the first scene being laid on the mountain, the second on the descent, the third at the foot; the first pictures Jesus in his heavenly form of glory, the second speaks of his sufferings, the third makes manifest his power to help and save. Such a construction is clearly literary and theological, not merely biographical.

The question of the disciples: 'Why could not we cast it out?' is given a surprising answer in the Marcan version. 'This kind cannot be driven out by anything except prayer.' Does this imply that the demon of epilepsy is especially hardy? or again, does it imply that the disciples do not pray? It is no wonder that Luke omits the passage, and that Matthew substitutes a different answer, which declares that the secret is to be found not in prayer, but in faith. The conclusion is secondary in any case, representing an attempt to deal with the difficulty raised by the statement that the disciples had tried in vain to exorcise the demon. Perhaps the most significant thing is that Jesus does not ascribe his power to his own divine nature. Whether the secret lie in prayer (or, as later manuscripts put it, prayer and fasting) or in faith, it is presupposed that such exorcisms can be accomplished by men of God, not by Jesus alone. He does not profess to exercise powers which are not available to his followers, if only they will pray, if only they will have faith.

The answer given in Matthew is a variant form of a saying which is used by Luke in a different context (Luke xvii. 6), almost indeed without context, as a detached saying. It appears in a still different form in Mark xi. 22-23 (with a parallel in Matthew), in connection with the Cursing of the Fig Tree (§ 201); and it appears to underlie the words of Paul in 1 Corinthians xiii. 2. The tradition of this saying is curiously involved; see the analysis of T. W. Manson (*Sayings*, pp. 140f.), with his concluding remark: 'This word of Jesus does not invite Christians to become conjurers or magicians, but heroes like those whose exploits are celebrated in the eleventh chapter of Hebrews.'

127. *The Second Prediction of the Passion*

MATTHEW xvii. 22-23 MARK ix. 30-32 LUKE ix. 43b-45

This second prediction is the least elaborated of the three. It makes no mention of repudiation by the official leaders of Judaism, as in the first prediction; or of sufferings to be inflicted by the Romans, as in the third. Mark makes this the beginning of the journey from the north to Jerusalem, and represents the approaching Passion as the theme of Jesus' teaching, given privately to his disciples, as he passes through the land as it were secretly ('He did not want anyone to know' — *v.* 30). In keeping with this conception of the journey, Mark introduces no more incidents of public ministry until Jesus is leaving Jericho by the Jerusalem road (x. 46f. — § 193). The crowds appear again, in the region beyond the Jordan (x. 1), but no incidents follow. The whole journey is given over to miscellaneous fragments of teaching, mainly on humility, renunciation, self-sacrifice; and even when outsiders are introduced (the Pharisees, in x. 2; the wealthy man of x. 17) the answers of Jesus are developed in private instruction of the disciples immediately afterwards (x. 10 and x. 23f.).

In Matthew, this picture of a private ministry is not so definitely indicated; there is no suggestion that Jesus is leaving Galilee for Jerusalem until xix. 1, or that he is seeking to avoid attention; but the part of his Gospel between this prediction and the departure from Jericho is again given over almost wholly to teaching, partly drawn from Mark, but even more from 'M'. Luke makes far more drastic changes. He does not suggest that the Passion now becomes the central theme of the teaching, nor does he ever put forward any notion of a period of withdrawal from public activity to engage in a more or less private ministry to the disciples. He makes no reference to the journey to Jerusalem till ix. 51, and then his emphasis is laid, not on any preparation of the disciples for the approaching Passion, but on the fixed purpose of Jesus: 'He steadfastly set his face to proceed to Jerusalem.' And his account of the journey is filled with the same alternation of incident and discourse, virtually all in the presence of crowds and hostile critics, just as before.

128. *The Temple Tax*

MATTHEW xvii. 24-27

The story in itself is in no way on any higher level than the conjurer's tricks which are ascribed to Jesus in the apocryphal Infancy Gospels, and the argument of the dialogue 'reflects so strong an anti-Jewish feeling that its genuineness must be considered extremely doubtful' (McNeile, *St. Matthew*, ad loc.). Modern systems of taxation have made the question of Jesus sound strange in our ears, now that 'the kings (and still more, the parliaments) of the earth' tax their own people and let foreign legations go free! Naturally we do not interpret a first-century text in the light of twentieth-century practices. But the thought here is that the Jews pay the temple-tax to God, the King of Kings, as foreigners; and rightly, Jesus and his followers, as 'sons of the Most High' should be exempt. The argument is pushed a long step further in an addition found in two late minuscules and in the Arabic Diatessaron (11th century): 'Simon said unto him, Yes. Jesus said, Do you then pay it as a foreigner.' (following *v.* 26). In this version, only Jesus is the 'son', and therefore exempt from the taxes paid to God for the upkeep of his Temple; Simon is a 'foreigner' like the Jews generally, and must therefore pay. But to avoid offence, he is told to pay for both.

In its odd way, the story reflects the fact that Jesus conformed to the ordinary prescriptions of law governing the Jewish people. He was 'born under the law' (Gal. iv. 4), and 'did not please himself' (Rom. xv. 3).

The Ordering of the Christian Community
§§ 129-136

MATTHEW xviii. 1-35 MARK ix. 33-50 LUKE ix. 46-50

In Matthew this chapter constitutes the fourth of the discourses which he has formed to carry his presentation of the teaching of Jesus. A glance at the index of parallels will show that he begins with two Marcan sections, keeping them in Mark's order, but omitting § 130 ('The Strange Exorcist') and § 132 ('About Salt'); part of the latter has already been used by him in the Sermon on the Mount (§ 20). The Parable of the Lost Sheep (§ 133) appears in a variant form, in a different context and with a different point, in Luke's Gospel, in the framework of his Travel Narrative (§ 172). The remaining three sections are found only in Matthew, apart from three sayings, widely separated (*vv.* 6-7, 15 and 22) which Luke has brought together in a different context (Luke xvii. 1-4 — §§ 178, 179), again in his Travel Narrative. Thus we have the familiar grouping of materials from 'Q' and 'M' around a Marcan nucleus.

This discourse, like the others, is a compilation of materials diversely transmitted, brought together by Matthew himself to give a comprehensive account of the principles which are to govern the life of the followers of Jesus in the community of his Church. There is to be no rivalry among them (§ 129); they must at whatever cost to themselves avoid causing trouble to others (§ 131); they must take every measure to prevent the loss of a single one of those entrusted to their care (§ 133); they may expel an offender from their fellowship, but only after they have made every possible effort to win him over (§ 134), and there must be no limit to their forgiveness (§ 135); the lesson of forgiveness is enforced by a parable (§ 136). To Matthew, the Church is above all a society of unlimited forgiveness of sins — the forgiveness which we have been granted by God must lead us to grant the same full and free forgiveness to our fellows.

129. *The Dispute about Greatness*

MATTHEW xviii. 1-5 MARK ix. 33-37 LUKE ix. 46-48

In Mark, the section is composite. Verses 33 to 35 constitute a Pronouncement-story, complete in itself, and *vv.* 36 and 37 make a supplement which conveys a different lesson. The first part is a rebuke to ambition; the second, an injunction to give a welcome to children. But there are further difficulties. In the first part, *v.* 35 was apparently transmitted independently of the Marcan setting of *vv.* 33-34; if Jesus is in the house, asking his disciples about their recent conversation, how should he *call* the Twelve? They are already around him. Again, the saying of the second part 'gives a rule for the time when Jesus no longer dwells on earth himself, but can receive tokens of love only through his representatives, for his Name lives on among them' (Wellhausen, *Evangelium Marci*, ad loc.). This would suggest that we have here a saying which in its basic thought goes back to the historical Jesus, but in its present form has been recast as an utterance of the Risen Lord. Further, it may be suggested that *v.* 37 'really has to do with disciples and not with children', and that *v.* 36 'is a mistaken attempt to provide a narrative preparation' for it (Manson, *Sayings*, p. 206). Thus we would have here two sayings of Jesus, transmitted in the tradition as isolated *logia*, which owe their narrative settings to the Evangelist.

Luke has recast the Marcan section in his own words, removing some of the vividness of Mark, and combining the two sayings. But it must still be said that the two sayings are intrinsically unrelated. 'He who is least among you is great' is hardly a corollary to the injunction to welcome children as Christ himself.

Matthew has revised his Marcan source much more radically. First he has suppressed all suggestion of the dispute over precedence among the disciples; they simply ask the general question: 'Who is greatest in the Kingdom?' This is part of his general pattern of removing or toning down anything that would seem to reflect unfavourably upon the disciples (cf. Matt. xx. 20, *note* — § 192). Then he introduces two entirely different sayings upon the object-lesson of the child (*vv.* 3-4). The child is now treated as an example of humility. Mark's first saying is omitted. Verse 3 is a variant of Mark x. 15 (omitted by Matthew in his parallel section – xix. 13-15); *v.* 4 is probably secondary – perhaps framed by the Evangelist himself as a commentary, to explain in what sense those who would enter the Kingdom must become like little children.

130. *The Strange Exorcist*

MARK ix. 38-41 LUKE ix. 49-50

This is one of the few Marcan stories which are omitted by Matthew (except that he has already used the saying of *v.* 41 in his Mission Charge – x. 42). Luke omits the last of the Marcan sayings, which is clearly out of place. It may be that the omission reflects a certain ecclesiastical narrowness on the part of Matthew – that he cannot really believe that Jesus himself sanctioned the work of unauthorized ministers. However, it is more likely that he omitted it simply because it did not fit into the general theme of the chapter, which is concerned with the internal ordering of the community, not with questions of its attitude to outsiders.

Note that a definitely hostile view of unauthorized exorcists is reflected in the picturesque story of Acts xix. 13-16.

131. *About Offences*

MATTHEW xviii. 6-9 MARK ix. 42-48 LUKE xvii. 1-2

On the opening verses of this section, T. W. Manson remarks: 'A comparison of these passages shows how complicated, not to say confused, these sayings have become in the course of tradition' (*Sayings*, p. 138). The trouble arises out of the tendency in the tradition to confuse sayings about 'little children' with sayings about disciples. It may well be that the sayings of the opening verses were originally spoken about little children, but they have been interpreted as bearing upon Christian believers – 'these little ones who believe [in me]' (this sense is implicit in the Lucan context also). The sayings which follow (Mark ix. 43-48) are not used by Luke. They have already been used, in a variant form, by Matthew, in the Sermon on the Mount (v. 29-30). If he repeats them here, it is probably because he finds in them a special relevance to the theme of the whole chapter. Christian believers must avoid becoming a cause of offence to their fellows, and must discipline themselves without waiting for the Church to pronounce sentence, out of fear of the inescapable judgment of God.

132. *Concerning Salt*

[MATTHEW v. 13] MARK ix. 49-50 [LUKE xiv. 34-35]

A Marcan catena of three sayings, linked by the theme-word 'salt'; it appears to be linked to the preceding verses by the word 'fire' (the connection is merely verbal). V. Taylor remarks that 'the structure of the whole is artificial and must be set down to the work of a pre-Marcan compiler who sought to assist catechumens in committing the sayings to memory ... Distaste for such artificial methods of compilation is more than compensated for by the knowledge we gain of catechetical practices in the pre-Gospel period. Moreover, it is to these very methods that we are indebted for the preservation of the sayings' (*St. Mark*, pp. 409f.).

Matthew and Luke omit these Marcan sayings, but have used a 'Q' version of a saying akin to *v.* 50a in different contexts.

133. *The Lost Sheep*

MATTHEW xviii. 10-14 LUKE xv. 3-7

We have here a striking instance of the manner in which the whole point of a parable can be altered through a change of context. It is not likely that the two Evangelists have drawn upon a common source, for the two versions have scarcely a word in common apart from the numbers. In Matthew it is introduced by an injunction to the disciples, addressed as the responsible leaders of the Church: 'Take heed that you do not despise one of these little ones.' In this context, it is taken as a solemn warning to the ministers of Christ, that they must spare no effort to bring back into the fellowship the brother who has gone astray; however unimportant he may seem to be, he is precious in the sight of God. The conclusion is: 'It is not the will of your Father in heaven that one of these little ones should perish.' But in Luke, with changes in the introduction and in the closing comment, the same parable is given a quite different purport. It is presented as the answer of Jesus to the criticism of the Pharisees and scribes: 'This man receives sinners and eats with them.' In this context, it becomes a defence of the Gospel as good news for the outcast. Jesus receives sinners because he is the Shepherd of God's flock, and God rejoices over the recovery of the lost. Jesus is not concerned to keep clear of disreputable company, whatever respectable people may say. He is concerned to bring them back to God, for 'there is joy in heaven over one sinner who repents more than over ninety-nine righteous men who have no need of repentance'.

It is probable, indeed almost certain, that Jesus told the parable originally in the sense that it has in the Lucan context, and that Matthew has given it a secondary application. 'The change of audience has resulted in a shift of emphasis; an apologetic parable has assumed a hortatory character' (Jeremias, *Parables*, p. 29).

The same tendency is seen at work in the transmission of a number of other parables; examples could be drawn from all three Gospels. See the list offered by Jeremias (op. cit., p. 31), with his warning that 'we must always ask who were the original hearers, and what a parable would mean if we take it as addressed to opponents or the crowd'.

This parable seems to have had a curious appeal to Gnostic teachers. In the *Gospel of Thomas*, it is told as a parable of the Kingdom; the sheep that has lost its way is the largest (this is apparently the reason for the shepherd's eagerness to recover it); and when he finds it, he says to it: 'I love you more than the ninety and nine.' There is no thought of joy in heaven or of the will of the Father. The point is probably that the Gnostic is the choice soul for whom the Redeemer is concerned. In the *Gospel of Truth*, a Valentinian meditation of about the same date as *Thomas* (A.D. 140-150), the interest rests upon some numerological fancy; the addition of one to ninety-nine makes one hundred, and this number is more perfect than those from one to ninety-nine; it is counted on the right hand. This is not very enlightening to us.

134. *On Reproving one's Brother*

MATTHEW xviii. 15-20

The passage as it stands cannot be authentic, for it presupposes an organized Church of the followers of Jesus, exercising discipline over its members – a situation that did not exist until after the Resurrection. Jesus speaks here as the Risen Lord. In *v.* 20 it is clear that the presence of Jesus is conceived spiritually, not physically, so that he can be with those who gather together in his Name at any time and in any place. We might add that it is contrary to all that we know of Jesus that he should speak of Gentiles and tax-collectors as outcasts, excluded from the company of his followers (*v.* 18). This phrase is an echo of a narrowly exclusive Jewish Christianity, not of the true voice of one who called a tax-collector to the inner circle of disciples, and was rebuked for eating with tax-collectors and sinners (Mark ii. 13-17 and parallels; § 53).

The first saying has a partial parallel in Luke xvii. 3; but in the Lucan form, 'your brother' is your fellow-man, while here it means 'your fellow-Christian'.

There is probably a nucleus of genuine sayings of Jesus here, but they have been reshaped by Matthew into laws for the discipline of the Church. 'It is the most distinctly ecclesiastical passage in Matthew's Gospel' (McNeile, *St. Matthew*, ad loc.). Note that the power to bind and loose is here taken to mean the authority to excommunicate or to absolve; and it is given to the *ecclesia* – the local congregation of the faithful – not to St. Peter alone (as in xvi. 19) nor even to the apostles as a body. Compare 1 Corinthians v. 3-5; vi. 1ff.

135. *On Reconciliation*

MATTHEW xviii. 21-22

The corresponding saying in Luke (xvii. 4) is not put as the answer to a question, and it is probable that Matthew has himself devised the question of Peter as an introduction to the saying (Bultmann, *History*, p. 141). It would then be another instance of this Evangelist's particular interest in Peter. In its Matthaean form, the saying is framed as a counter to the threat of unlimited revenge of Genesis iv. 24: 'If Cain shall be avenged sevenfold, truly Lamech shall be avenged seventyfold.' Among the followers of Christ, there is to be no limit set to forgiveness. In the context, Matthew presents this not simply as a rule for individual conduct, but as a principle to govern the exercise of discipline by the Church; its doors are never to be shut against the offender; he is never to be reduced to his 'last chance'.

136. *The Parable of the Unmerciful Servant*

MATTHEW xviii. 23-35

This parable is not an illustration of the principle laid down in the preceding saying, for it does not bear upon the limitless granting of forgiveness, but upon the necessity of responding to God's forgiveness of our sins by forgiving the comparatively trifling offences of our brethren. The details of the parable are not to be pressed, as if it were an allegory; it is not to be taken as implying that God keeps a corps of torturers. The parable has nothing to do with punishments after death. The central lesson is the warning that God's great and free forgiveness will be withdrawn, if those whom he has forgiven go on to treat their brethren harshly. Within this, there is the reminder that our debt to God, which he has freely remitted, is infinitely greater than any debt that a brother has incurred towards us. Everything else belongs to the furniture of the story. The king is an Oriental despot; the first servant, whose debt is remitted, is a high official, for the amount of the debt is enormous — the equivalent of millions of dollars; while the debt which he insists on collecting amounts to no more than a month's salary. The difference in the status of the two servants has no bearing upon the point of the parable, nor has the intercession of his comrades, nor yet the kind of penalty exacted by the king — whether the sale of the defaulter's wife and children, as in the first action (*v.* 25), or the delivery to the tormentors, as in the final disposition (*v.* 34).

The discourse is followed by Matthew's familiar closing formula: 'When Jesus had finished these sayings' (xix. 1; § 187).

II. THE LUCAN TRAVEL NARRATIVE §§ 137-186

LUKE ix. 51-xviii. 14

At this point Luke abandons the Marcan narrative to make room for a rich collection of materials from other sources which he weaves loosely together into an account of the journey of Jesus with his disciples from the north to Judaea. Through these fifty sections he makes no use of Marcan materials; in four sections, Marcan parallels are cited, but in all of them Luke is clearly drawing upon another source. In twenty-eight sections, Matthaean parallels are cited, but in at least ten of them Luke appears to be drawing upon a source of his own, not upon that used by Matthew. In twenty-two sections, no parallel to the Lucan material is to be found in either Mark or Matthew. The material peculiar to Luke, in this portion of his Gospel, includes some of the very greatest treasures of our tradition, such as the Parables of the Prodigal Son, the Good Samaritan, and the Pharisee and the Publican.

The travel-framework in which all this material is cast is artificial in the last degree. No one has been able to reconstruct the itinerary. Jesus starts on his way to Jerusalem by way of Samaria (§ 137), and there are occasional references to Samaritan settings along the way; but at the end he approaches Jerusalem by way of Jericho (as in Mark and Matthew), although the passage through Samaria would not take him near Jericho. The Evangelist has made no effort to adapt the incidents of the journey to a Samaritan environment, and there are in fact occasional touches which imply that Jesus is still in Galilee. His presence in synagogues and his contacts with Pharisees are hardly compatible with the Samaritan scene. The parallel passages in Matthew are laid either in Galilee or in Judaea. It would appear that the material which Luke has brought together here was found by him without anything to indicate a time or a place for the sayings or the incidents, and he has arranged it as seemed good to him, unaided by anything in the tradition.

It is only by dint of reference to the structure of Mark that we treat this 'Travel Narrative' as a unit. Within Luke's own structure it is not self-contained, as it does not bring us to the end of the journey from the north to Jerusalem. § 137 is clearly intended to mark the beginning of a distinct stage in the ministry of Jesus. The close of this stage is not so clearly indicated. In one sense we might take the position that it is not completed until the Ascension, at the very end of the Gospel (xxiv. 50-53); but an intermediate break may reasonably be made at the approach to Jericho (§ 193); or perhaps better, at the end of § 195 (the Parable of the Pounds), which is still marked as belonging to the journey (xix. 11). In either case, we would find four Marcan pericopes included by Luke in the last part of his 'Travel Narrative' (§§ 188-9, 191, 193).

137. *The Samaritan Villages*

Luke ix. 51-56

This section is peculiar to Luke. The first verse is probably an editorial introduction, framed by Luke himself as the key-note of the narrative that is to follow. 'The days of his taking up' will include the whole process by which Jesus goes to the Father — Crucifixion, Resurrection, Ascension envisaged as one event; Luke's word *analēmpsis* — 'taking up' — is close in significance to the Johannine *hypsōsis* — 'lifting up'. *Analēmpsis* and the cognate verb *analambanō* are used in reference to the Ascension only in the Lucan writings and in the creedal formula of 1 Timothy iii. 16.

A glance at the apparatus criticus will draw attention to three remarkable additions to *vv.* 54 and 55 which are found in different manuscripts. The short text which lies before us is attested by the Beatty Papyrus, Codex Vaticanus, Codex Sinaiticus, the Latin Vulgate, two early Syriac versions, and the Sahidic. In *v.* 54, a number of excellent witnesses add 'as Elijah did'; the uncials which support this addition are slightly inferior in quality to Vaticanus and Sinaiticus, but the weight of testimony in the versions is very great, including as it does the Old Latin and the Bohairic. The question of the true reading here could not be decided on the basis of the testimony of manuscripts and versions alone; but we would be inclined to regard the additional words as an explanatory comment introduced by an early scribe, rather than as the original reading which has somehow been dropped from so many excellent witnesses. In *v.* 55, the short reading is attested by the same group of witnesses, with the exception of the Latin Vulgate and the Curetonian Syriac, and by three important uncials (Codex Alexandrinus, the Freer Codex, and Codex Ephraemi Syri) which include the additional words in *v.* 54. The great bilingual Codex Bezae adds: 'And he said, You do not know what spirit you are of.' Besides this phrase, a further group of witnesses adds, with some minor variations: '[For] the Son of Man did not come to destroy [men's] lives, but to save them.' The evidence which supports these additions is much less weighty than that which is against them. Yet they are not at all the ordinary type of scribal enlargement, and they cannot lightly be dismissed from consideration. It has been suggested that they stood in the original text of the Gospel, but were removed in the course of the controversy with Marcion, from the feeling that they lent too much support to Marcion's rejection of the Old Testament. Others have taken the contrary view, that they did not stand in the text originally, but were introduced through Marcionite influence, precisely to adduce the support of Jesus for the Marcionite doctrine that the Old Testament was fundamentally incompatible with the spirit of the new faith. Critics of very conservative tendencies are found supporting both these conjectures; Zahn for the former, Lagrange for the latter. It will be noted that either explanation involves the admission that the text of the Gospels could be tampered with as late as the middle of the second century in the interests of a party. William Manson, however, feels that 'the longer text may be due simply to homiletical elaboration of the incident in some early Christian quarter' (*Luke*, p. 120). The closing sentence of the addition: 'The Son of Man did not come to destroy men's lives, but to save them' has all the appearance of a 'pronouncement' of Jesus, akin to the words addressed to Zacchaeus (Luke xix. 10); it may have been preserved in an independent pronouncement-story, which was conflated with this Samaritan-village story in an early copy of Luke's Gospel. At all events, we shall take note that the problem of the true text cannot always be settled by the evidence of the texts and versions alone.

138. *Claimants to Discipleship*

LUKE ix. 57-62; cf. MATTHEW viii. 19-22

See also the notes on § 49. The three sayings of the Lucan group were probably found together in his source, but they are intrinsically independent. Only the first two are used by Matthew (with little change); if he identifies the first 'claimant to discipleship' as a scribe, this is in keeping with a general tendency to give greater definition to the 'someone', which Luke has retained from the source. The phrase 'as they were proceeding on the way' is Luke's editorial introduction, framed to fit the sayings into the context of the journey. The third saying is found only in Luke. It recalls the story of the call of Elisha (1 Kings xix. 19-21); Elijah permits his disciple to say his farewells and even to offer a banquet to his friends, but the call of Jesus will permit no delay.

In Luke's arrangement, the setting of the catena has a double appropriateness. The first saying has just received an illustration in the refusal of hospitality (*v.* 53); and the whole concern with the conditions of discipleship forms a fitting preface to the mission that is to follow.

139. *The Sending Out of the Seventy*

Luke x. 1-16

The Mission of the Seventy is found only in Luke, but most of the Charge (*vv.* 2-12) is paralleled in Matthew's version of the Mission of the Twelve, and its concluding verses (13-16) are used by Matthew in other contexts.

Analysis of the Lucan Charge leads to the conclusion that it is a conflation of 'Q' materials with materials drawn from Luke's special source, 'L'. In Matthew, as we have seen (§ 58), the Charge has been formed by a triple conflation of Mark, 'Q', and materials drawn from Matthew's special source, 'M'. Luke has used the whole of the brief Marcan Charge in his own version of the Charge to the Twelve (§ 109), and does not draw upon it here.

The comparison with Matthew indicates that 'Q' provides *vv.* 2, 3 and 13 to 16 of the Lucan Charge. Verses 4 to 7 show almost no coincidence of wording with Matthew, but are presupposed by the wording of the 'L' passage in Luke xxii. 35f., and are therefore regarded as deriving from 'L'. Verses 8 to 12 have a certain unity of their own, and *v.* 8 is little more than a doublet of *vv.* 6 and 7; it is probable that this section also may be ascribed to 'Q', and that the differences in the Matthaean version here are due to conflation with Mark. Verse 1 may be an editorial introduction framed by Luke himself, or in view of the reference to it in the 'L' section which follows (§ 140), it may be ascribed to the 'L' source. (So T. W. Manson, *Sayings*, p. 74.)

It appears, then, that four strands of tradition have transmitted a report of a Mission Charge addressed by Jesus to his disciples. In Mark the Charge was addressed to the Twelve; in 'L' it was addressed to the Seventy. Since the 'Q' material has been combined with the Marcan Charge to the Twelve by Matthew, and with the 'L' Charge to the Seventy by Luke, it would seem that the hearers were indicated vaguely in 'Q', or else not indicated at all.

The question is bound to arise, whether the Mission of the Seventy is a separate event in the career of Jesus, or whether it is no more than a doublet of the Mission of the Twelve. Our suspicions are aroused by the number Seventy (or Seventy-two – the evidence of the manuscripts is evenly balanced and makes a choice between the two readings virtually impossible). Professor B. M. Metzger lists no less than thirteen instances of seventy or seventy-two (men, nations, victims, angels, books) in Jewish tradition.[1] For the Evangelist and the circles which provided him with his materials, the seventy elders whom Moses appointed to assist him, to whom God gave a share of the spirit that was upon him (Num. xi. 16-25), would inevitably be regarded as a type of the chosen followers who shared the tasks of Jesus; and indeed it seems more likely that the story of the Mission should be reshaped in the telling to bring it into conformity with the Moses-story than that a story which lent itself so readily to the Exodus-typology should disappear from the strands of tradition which were received by Mark and Matthew, if it was grounded in history. The variant Seventy-two would correspond to the addition of the absent Eldad and Modad (Num. xi. 26-30) to the seventy who gathered about the Tent with Moses.

[1] 'Seventy or Seventy-Two Disciples', *NTS*, V, pt. 4 (July, 1959), pp. 299-306.

Many of the other instances of Seventy or Seventy-two which Metzger cites indicate that the number stands for the nations of the world, according to Jewish reckoning. Genesis x reckons seventy nations, according to the Hebrew text, seventy-two according to the Septuagint. Seventy (or Seventy-two) translators made the first Greek version of the Torah, according to Jewish tradition, for the benefit of the Gentile world. At the Feast of Sukkoth ('Tabernacles'), a sacrifice of seventy bullocks was offered on behalf of the Gentile nations. It is not far-fetched, then, to see in the Mission of the Seventy a foreshadowing of the great Gentile mission, and the fact that Luke has placed it in Samaria would in itself suggest that he thinks of it as a token of expansion beyond the bounds of Israel.

Dr. Farrer insists strongly on the prefigurative character of the Lucan mission. 'It is difficult to understand St Luke's rehandling of the Marcan story', he writes 'except on the supposition that he was convinced that a double ministry of apostles and elders belonged to the nature of things, and was prefigured in an act of Christ's own.' In his view, Luke is here giving us the myth of the institution of the Christian presbyterate. He is persuaded that Luke is a typologist who 'makes the facts of the New Testament antitypical to those of the Old' ('The Ministry in the New Testament,' in *The Apostolic Ministry* [ed. K. E. Kirk], pp. 135ff.). The observation that Moses first chooses Twelve as representatives of the Twelve Tribes (Num. i. 4-16), and then Seventy of the Elders to share his burden (Num. xi) would be quite sufficient to account for his introduction of a band of Seventy to be commissioned by a second Charge. We might add that if the Seventy foreshadows the Gentile mission, there would be a particular pertinence to the words (found only in Luke); 'Eat what is set before you' (*v.* 8). For it is clear that problems of food quickly arose when the Gospel was carried to the Gentiles — first over the propriety of Jews eating with Gentiles (Gal. ii. 11-14; Acts xi. 1-18), and then over Christians eating meat offered to idols (1 Cor. x. 25ff., which seems to echo our passage).

The words of the Charge 'are clearly coloured by the belief that the final crisis is imminent' (Manson, *Sayings*, p. 76). The injunctions to travel light, without staff or sandals or even a change of clothing, and especially the saying, 'Greet no one on the way' (*v.* 4 — only in Luke) create the impression that there is no time to spare. Did Jesus then think that the great Day would arrive before the disciples could complete the mission on which they were now sent; was this the original sense of the Matthaean prediction: 'You will not have completed the circuit of the cities of Israel before the Son of Man comes' (Matt. x. 23)? This is the view of Dr. Vincent Taylor. 'What Jesus expected, and what he sent forth the Twelve to announce, was the speedy coming of the rule of God and the setting up of the Messianic community of the Son of Man ... It was not for simple evangelistic activity that they were charged to ignore the traditional salutations of the east, to travel surprisingly light, to receive without comment the barest sustenance, to hurry on from place to place, to reject even the dust of unresponsive towns, always announcing the imminence of the Kingdom of God' (*Life and Ministry*, pp. 107f., 110). See also the interpretation of Albert Schweitzer, in *The Quest of the Historical Jesus*, pp. 357f. On this view, the Mission marks a significant turning-point in the ministry of Jesus, leading him to the conviction that he must suffer death before the Kingdom could be inaugurated. It did not meet with the response for which he had hoped, and he became increasingly aware that the crowds which flocked to him were not dedicated to the ways of the Kingdom. From this time, accordingly, he withdraws from public teaching and gives himself chiefly to the preparation of his disciples for the Cross and for the gospel of victory through rejection and death and resurrection from the dead.

It is very doubtful if our sources are capable of sustaining this bold construction. It is far from clear that Jesus expected great results from the Mission of his disciples or that he considered it a failure. Above all, there is no solid evidence in the documents to support the thesis that the doctrine of the Cross developed in the mind of Jesus as a consequence of the failure of his people to respond to the Gospel of the Kingdom. We must refrain from such attempts to squeeze out of our sources information which they have not preserved.

On the Woes of *vv.* 13-16, see the notes on § 66. These verses were probably not transmitted as part of the Charge, but as a separate group, and were attracted into this place by their similarity of subject-matter to *v.* 12.

The closing saying of the Charge (*v.* 16) is paralleled in Matthew (see notes on § 63), in an abbreviated form and with a change of verb ('receive' in place of 'hear'). A kindred saying in Mark ix. 37 puts 'one of such little children' in the place of the disciples. T. W. Manson suggests that all three passages rest upon a common original, and points out that 'the Aramaic verb *qabbēl* means both "to receive" and "to hear" in the sense of "obey" ' (*Sayings*, p. 78). The words have great significance for the understanding of the apostolic office, in that they apply to the messengers of Jesus the principles of representative honour and authority which belonged to the Jewish *shaliach*. On this, see the remarks of Dom Gregory Dix, in *The Apostolic Ministry*, pp. 228ff.; and K. H. Rengstorf's article *Apostleship* (trans. J. R. Coates; London: A. & C. Black, 1952).

140. *The Return of the Seventy*

Luke x. 17-20

The account of the Return does not correspond to the sending, except in the number of disciples. According to *v.* 1, Jesus 'sent them in pairs before him, to every town and place where he himself intended to go'. But now all thought of his following where they have paved the way is forgotten; they return to report the triumphant completion of their mission, not two by two, but all together. The Charge has said nothing about exorcisms (though in the parallel Matthaean Charge there is the injunction: 'Cast out demons' – Matt. x. 8), but the report mentions nothing except their success in exorcizing demons. It would appear, then, that the whole of *v.* 17 is an editorial construction of Luke's own devising, framed to introduce the group of sayings which follow. The grouping of the three sayings is itself artificial; they are linked by the common reference to victory over the demons. We cannot feel confident of the authenticity of any of them. The first is commonly called an 'apocalyptic' image, but it is in fact astrological; the downfall of Satan has already taken place in the higher realm, and its realization on earth is certain. The second saying (*v.* 19) is modelled on Psalm xci. 13, and is closely akin to the words of the longer spurious ending of Mark (Mark xvi. 17-18). The third is in itself a sober warning against over-valuing 'spiritual gifts' and against the danger of becoming intoxicated with the powers that God has committed to us. If we may suppose that the disciples successfully practised exorcisms during the lifetime of Jesus, as they did later (Acts viii. 7, etc.), we may also hold that Jesus himself cooled their excitement with this warning.

On § 141, see the notes on § 67.

142. *The Blessedness of the Disciples*

LUKE X. 23-24

In Matthew, the passage is attached to sayings about the general failure to understand 'the secrets of the kingdom of heaven'. Matthew has changed the wording of the source, to point the contrast between the disciples who see and hear, and the many who are blind and deaf to the truth of God. In the Lucan context, there is no such contrast; the thought is wholly of the privilege of the disciples, not of the insight that has been given them. The distinction is not between those who use their eyes to good effect and those who do not, but between those who are on earth to see the manifestation of the Kingdom in the works and words of Jesus, and those men of old who lived too soon to see the fulfilment of their hopes and longings. Matthew's 'righteous men' is secondary; the 'kings' of the saying of course denotes the kings who were regarded as pious in Jewish tradition, above all David in his legendary character of psalmist and prophet of the Messianic Age.

143. *The Lawyer's Question*

LUKE X. 25-28

In Mark and Matthew, the parallel to the dialogue between Jesus and the lawyer is set in Jerusalem, in the last days of the Ministry, and is used as the third in a series of controversy-stories which bring Jesus face to face successively with Pharisees, then with Sadducees, then with a scribe (§§ 206-208); in a fourth pericope which completes the series, it is Jesus who asks the question and no answer is given (§ 209) — thus Jesus conclusively demonstrates his superiority over all his challengers. Luke follows Mark at that point in respect of the first two of the series and in the fourth; but he omits the third, because he has used a parallel story here. The question is whether the Lucan story is a different incident altogether, or a report of the same incident which has been transmitted through different channels, or a deliberate recasting of the Marcan story by Luke himself, to fit it for use as the introduction to the parable of the Good Samaritan.

The decision really lies between the second and third of these three suggestions; the first may be confidently dismissed as involving too many coincidences

— a scribe as the questioner, and the linking of the two commandments of love to God and to our neighbour as the answer, together with the fact that Luke himself clearly took his version to be a doublet of the Marcan story and therefore cut it out of the Marcan sequence. But it is hard to show that the great variations from the Marcan version can be attributed to Luke's rewriting. The change from 'scribe' to 'lawyer' could be regarded as Luke's preference for a word which would be more intelligible to Gentile readers; and the change in the question, even though it involves substance as well as form, might be explicable on similar grounds, as Luke's attempt to spare his Gentile readers a debate over the (to them) academic question of the relative importance of commandments in the Jewish Law. But when this has been granted, how much evidence of literary dependence upon Mark is left to us? Apart from the commandments, there is scarcely any coincidence in the wording — nothing, in fact, except the verbs 'say' and 'answer', and even here there are differences. We conclude, therefore, that Luke has found the incident in an independently transmitted version, in a non-Marcan source. We may go further still. Matthew's version follows that of Mark in the main, but it has some significant points of correspondence with Luke's. Like Luke, he uses *nomikos* 'lawyer' in place of Mark's *grammateus* 'scribe' — and this change is not habitual with Matthew, as it is with Luke; again, he uses the phrase 'testing him', which is found in Luke but has no equivalent in Mark; and he agrees with Luke in using the preposition *en* 'with', throughout the first commandment, against Mark's *ex* 'out of'. This would indicate that the Lucan version comes from 'Q', the document which he shares with Matthew; and that Matthew has conflated Mark with the 'Q' story.

The Lucan story may well be closer to the facts of the incident. The linking of the two commandments to love God and to love our neighbour is not original with Jesus, for it is found twice in the Jewish *Testaments of the Twelve Patriarchs*[1] and may be regarded as a commonplace of scribal lore. 'It is not surprising that the source should have represented Jesus as himself testing the questioner by returning the question to him. It is most unlikely that the Evangelist should have conceived the idea of putting the good response in the mouth of the lawyer, if the source had attributed it to Christ. The story originally presented Jesus as setting the seal of his approval on the answer most in keeping with his own spirit, which would have been given by the Jewish doctors in their discussion of the great commandment; later it will have seemed more desirable to attribute the good answer directly to Jesus himself' (Loisy, *Évangile selon Luc*, p. 303). For the defence of the contrary view (priority of the Marcan form), see Klostermann on Mark xii. 28-34 (after Wellhausen), and V. Taylor, *St. Mark*, pp. 484-5.

144. *The Parable of the Good Samaritan*

LUKE X. 29-37

In Mark and Matthew the story of the Lawyer's Question is complete in itself; in Luke it is subordinated to the Parable, which is offered in response to

[1] These Jewish writings of the Hasmonaean period have come down to us in a form which shows Christian interpolations; but there is no reason to suspect the passages in question (Zeb. v. 1, 2; Iss. vii. 6; Dan. v. 3) as interpolations.

the demand for further definition of the sense in which 'neighbour' is to be taken. The preponderance of weight is thus transferred from 'the great and first commandment', the Jewish *Shema*', to the second. It is to be noted that St. Paul twice quotes the commandment 'Thou shalt love thy neighbour as thyself', as alone summing up the whole of the law (Rom. xiii. 8-9; Gal. v. 14); and that to the apostolic writers generally love for God is inseparable from love for our brother. See especially 1 John iv. 20-21.

Strictly speaking, the Parable of the Good Samaritan does not answer the question: 'Who is my neighbour?', but rather, 'How does one prove himself a neighbour?' Jesus asks, 'Who showed himself neighbour of the man who fell among the thieves?'; and the lesson of the story is certainly not that 'the neighbour whom you are to love as yourself is the one who has first helped you in your time of need'. The basic thought is rather that the question 'Who is my neighbour?' is not rightly put; the true spirit of love does not seek to classify and delimit the objects of its compassion, but pours itself out on anyone who is in need.

But with this observation, it becomes clear that the parable is not too appropriate to its context. Not only does it require a radical restatement of the question to which it professes to give an answer, but it introduces irrelevant elements into the contrast between the man who behaves as a neighbour and the two who do not. To the contrast in behaviour there is added a difference in status and in nationality. It is surely not intended to suggest that Samaritans were characteristically kindhearted and generous, and that priests and Levites were uniformly hardhearted and unkind. The very sequence — priest, Levite, Samaritan — has something unnatural about it; we ourselves may tell a story about an Englishman, a Scotsman, and an Irishman, but hardly about an Englishman, a Scotsman, and a Unitarian; or, say, about a bishop, a priest, and a Buddhist. The natural sequence would be priest, Levite, layman of Israel; and the lesson, that the layman who is kind to a man in need is more faithful to God than a priest or Levite who shows no compassion. Such a lesson is intrinsically independent of the question of how the term 'neighbour' is to be applied in relation to the commandment, and it is probable that the connection is the work of Luke himself. He has found this parable in a collection which stood in his source 'L', and has thought fit to attach it to the story of the Lawyer's Question, with which it had originally nothing to do. It is probable, however, that the 'Samaritan' already was in the story, and it was this that led Luke to work it into the 'Travel-Narrative' with its intimations of a Samaritan itinerary.

Let us observe further that the story could come only out of a Palestinian background. In pagan religions generally, the priest was not expected to set a moral example; priestly functions could perfectly well be exercised in Greece and Rome alike by men who were themselves atheists in belief and libertines in conduct. This story clearly presupposes that a high standard of conduct was expected of the priest and the Levite. The secondary feature of the Samaritan would of course only be significant in circles which were aware of the intense hostility between Samaritans and Jews. Yet the story as Luke tells it has not a single phrase which betrays translation from an Aramaic original; it is cast in fluent colloquial Greek from start to finish. It affords an excellent example of the freedom with which Luke renders the parables. Like another which M. Black discusses, 'so far is it from being a literal translation, that it is doubtful if we have the right to call it a translation at all; Luke's parables are literary productions' (*Aramaic Approach*, p. 132). He does not as a rule avoid Semitisms; indeed, he seems at times to affect a conscious Semitizing of diction, to give his narrative a Septuagintal flavour.

145. *Martha and Mary*

LUKE x. 38-42

The opening words are editorial, serving to remind the reader of the journey. For the moment, Jesus appears to be unaccompanied by his disciples.

The story is peculiar to Luke. The variations in the text make it difficult to be sure how he intended it to be understood. The Sinaitic Syriac and the Old Latin versions omit the whole reproach to Martha, reading simply, 'Martha, Martha, Mary has chosen the good part, which shall not be taken away from her'. To this Codex Bezae adds only the one word *thorubazēi* 'you are troubled'. All the other witnesses support the reading of the text which lies before us, but differ on the wording of the first clause of *v.* 42; 'there is need of one thing', or 'there is need of few things, or of one'. The passage has lent itself to allegory, taking the two sisters as symbols of the contemplative life and the active life, respectively; and even today critics tend to read into it symbolism of one kind or another. According to Loisy, Martha is a symbol of Jewish Christianity, with its earnest devotion to the works of the Law; Mary, of Hellenistic (Pauline) Christianity, seeking salvation by faith alone. All this is too elaborate; probably the thought is simply that no preoccupation with worldly affairs, even with the most necessary duties of hospitality, is to be allowed to interfere with devotion to Christ the Lord.

146. *The Lord's Prayer*

LUKE xi. 1-4

The next three sections in Luke form a sequence on the theme of Prayer. The Lord's Prayer is not given in Mark; in Matthew it is given in a different wording and is made part of a different prayer-sequence, in the Sermon on the Mount (§ 30). Luke has provided it with an introduction (*v.* 1). As often, he depicts Jesus himself as praying. It is not unlikely that John the Baptist had composed a form of prayer for his disciples — Jewish teachers often did this, and it is possible that the sect which revered the memory of John was known to use a prayer which he had prescribed. It is less probable that the Lord's Prayer owed its composition to the request of a disciple who appealed to the example of John. The setting appears to be wholly artificial.

The differences between the Lucan and the Matthaean versions of the Prayer are generally explained as reflecting liturgical development in the form adopted by Matthew. This would account adequately for the expansion of the address, 'Father' into the characteristically Matthaean formula, 'Our Father who art in heaven', and for the addition to the second petition of the clause, 'Thy will be done, as in heaven, so also upon earth'; and perhaps also for the addition to the concluding clause: 'Deliver us from the Evil One.' Variations in translation from the Aramaic original would account sufficiently for the minor differences in wording in *v.* 4. It is astounding to see that no alternative rendering is found for whatever Aramaic word underlies the Greek word *epiousion*, which is otherwise unknown to us and was altogether unknown even to Origen. Its meaning remains uncertain. Unusual as it is, it must have become established very early in the usage of the Greek-speaking Churches – so firmly that no one could think of having recourse to the Aramaic to find a more intelligible substitute.

Great interest attaches to a striking variant which was known to Marcion and is found in a few Greek witnesses at the beginning of the Lucan version of the Prayer: 'May thy Holy Spirit come upon us and cleanse us.' Tertullian also appears to have used this petition in the Prayer, for it is presupposed by the wording of his challenge to Marcion: 'To whom shall I say "Father"? From whom shall I ask for the Holy Spirit? Shall I pray for his kingdom to come, when I have never heard of him as the King of Glory? Who will give me daily bread? Who will forgive me my sins? Who will not suffer us to be led into temptation?' (*Against Marcion* IV, 26). Thus there is good evidence for the early existence of this variant, and it is even possible that it may have stood in the original text of Luke's Gospel. For on the one hand, the strong tendency to assimilation would help it to disappear; and on the other hand, its presence here is suggested by the fact that in *v.* 13 below, Luke substitutes 'Holy Spirit' for the 'good things' of the parallel verse in Matthew.

147. *The Friend at Midnight*

LUKE xi. 5-8

This parable, found only in Luke, is used by him as an introduction to the sayings of the following section, which encourage us to make our petitions to God in the confidence that he will not refuse to grant what we need. As a vignette of contemporary life, it is singularly vivid, and has a touch of humour. The thought is that if your neighbour, even though he may grumble at the inconvenience to which you are putting him, will none the less yield to your importunities and give you what you need, how much more can we count upon God to respond to our petitions. There is no suggestion here that the prayer must be importunate.

148. *The Answer to Prayer*

LUKE xi. 9-13

This passage, with some differences of wording, is used by Matthew in the Sermon on the Mount (Matt. vii. 7-11; § 38), where it has no connection in thought with what precedes or with what follows. It would appear, therefore, that in the source it was found with no indication of context. In place of Matthew's 'bread' and 'a stone', Luke uses a different illustration – 'egg' and 'a scorpion'; possibly the source contained three illustrations, of which each Evangelist has selected two. Here again the comparison tells in favour of the use of a common source and against the use by one Evangelist of the other. See also the notes on § 38.

On §§ 149 and 150, see the notes on the parallel sections where they occur in the Matthaean order, §§ 85, 86, 88.

151. *The Blessedness of Christ's Mother*

Luke xi. 27-28

The section-heading is misleading. Luke substitutes these verses at this point for the Marcan-Matthaean section on 'Christ's Real Brethren' (§ 89), which he has used in a different context (following the sayings about the Right Use of Parables, §§ 94 and 104). The story of the Annunciation would be sufficient to show that Luke himself thinks of the Virgin Mother as blessed above all women; but here the saying which pronounces her blessed is virtually brushed aside as a gush of superficial piety. The true blessedness belongs to 'those who hear and keep the word of God'. In the saying as it stands, there is no implication that the Mother of Jesus is included in the number of those who are thus blessed, and it is possible that the saying is a variant tradition of the repudiation of the family as reported in Mark iii. 33-35. For Luke, however, it probably had rather the sense: 'The blessedness of Mary is open to all , if only they hear and keep the word of God as she did.'

A better heading is given to the section by T. W. Manson: 'Flattery Rebuked' (*Sayings*, p. 88), with the succinct comment: 'Jesus was not deluded by people who made pious noises, and He brought them back to realities by the shortest possible route.'

On § 152, see the notes on § 87.

153. *About Light*

Luke xi. 33-36

This catena of sayings is linked in Luke by the catchwords *luchnos* ('lamp') and *phōteinos* ('full of light'). The same connection is not made in Matthew, where there is no parallel to the last saying (*v.* 35), and the first is widely separated from the second group, being transferred to a different section of the Sermon on the Mount (§§ 20, 33).

Luke makes a characteristic change in the first saying. In the Matthaean form, the words picture a simple house of only one room, and the lamp is lit to give light to those who are within; in Luke the picture is that of a Graeco-Roman house with a vestibule (and a cellar), and the lamp is lit in the vestibule, not to illuminate the interior of the house, but to give light at the entrance as people come in. In Matthew, accordingly, the words bear upon the illumination of the Jewish people by the Gospel; in Luke the thought is that the Gospel lights the entrance into the household of God for Gentiles who seek to enter from outside.

Luke's final verse is unintelligible as it stands, but the difficulty is probably due to an error in translation from the Aramaic original. C. C. Torrey has proposed to correct the rendering as follows: 'If however your whole body is full of light, with no part dark, then all about you will be light; just as the lamp lights you with its brightness' (*The Four Gospels*, p. 309). The general thought will then be that the followers of Jesus have received the light in order that they may give light to others; but they are warned that if they are to bring others to the knowledge of the truth, their own vision must be clear. If they are blind or half-blind themselves, they cannot give sure guidance to others.

Following as it does the rejection of the demand for a 'sign', the words suggest that the real sign is the Gospel itself and the lives that it has filled with the light of truth.

There is a logion in the *Gospel according to Thomas* which may represent an early form of this saying. 'Within a man of light there is light and he lights the whole world. When he does not shine, there is darkness' (Logion 24). Unfortunately, there is a measure of ambiguity in the Coptic text. See the notes of Jean Doresse, *The Secret Books of the Egyptian Gnostics* (London: Hollis & Carter, 1960), p. 373.

154. *Discourse Against the Pharisees*

LUKE xi. 37-xii. 1

The sayings of this passage are found in Matthew, with many differences of order and of wording, as part of a much larger collection of Woes pronounced by Jesus against the scribes and Pharisees at Jerusalem, in the last days of the Ministry (Matt. xxiii. 1-36; § 210).

The general structure of the section in Luke may be analysed as follows. First there is a pronouncement-story (xi. 37-41), followed by three 'Woes' against the Pharisees, loosely (and, under the circumstances, inappropriately) attached to it (*vv.* 42-44). Next, a transitional verse (45) serves to introduce three 'Woes' against the scribes, or 'lawyers' as Luke terms them (*vv.* 46-48, 52); within this second series is inserted a prophecy of judgment (*vv.* 49-51). The two series of 'Woes' are rounded off by an indication of the hostile reaction of the scribes and Pharisees to these denunciations. Finally, an enigmatic logion of warning against 'the leaven of the Pharisees' is added, to serve as an introduction to the sayings of the following section (xii. 1).

It will be observed that in Matthew the words of criticism which Luke has embodied in his pronouncement-story are recast into a 'Woe', to bring them into the same form as the remaining sayings of the series. The pronouncement-story itself may be a variant tradition of the controversy concerning the Washing of Hands (Mark vii. 1ff., with its parallel in Matthew but not in Luke; § 115); or it is possible that Luke himself created the setting for the sayings by utilizing elements of the Marcan controversy-story. It is obvious, however, that the setting will barely serve for the sayings of *vv.* 39-41, and is altogether inappropriate for the denunciations which follow; we can hardly suppose that Jesus would employ his time at the dinner-table in denouncing his host and the circles to which his host belonged. We must observe further that the

Samaritan location of the journey seems to be forgotten, for a Pharisee would hardly have his residence in Samaria, among the 'foolish people that dwelt in Sichem', whom he would count with the 'nations which his heart abhorred' (Ecclus. l. 25-26). It would seem that the sayings against the Pharisees were transmitted without any indication of the time or place of their delivery, and Luke has felt free to bring them together in this setting, while Matthew has transferred them to the discourses of the last days in Jerusalem.

The pronouncement (*vv.* 39-41) which constitutes the reply of Jesus to the criticism of the Pharisee is difficult to interpret in detail, and it is probable that there is at least one error in translation from the Aramaic, and also a certain amount of confusion resulting from the combining of parabolic words of Jesus with their application. The unintelligible words of the Lucan version: 'Give alms of those things which are within' are represented in Matthew by the phrase: 'Cleanse first the inside'. The Lucan words have been plausibly explained as the result of a confusion between the Aramaic *zakki*, 'give alms' and *dakki*, 'cleanse' (the two initial consonants are easily mistaken for one another). But the difficulty of the passage goes deeper, and it seems probable that the words of Jesus were a parable about pots and pans: 'it does no good to wash the outside of the pot while you leave the inside dirty' — a biting criticism of the insistence on rituals of external purification which do nothing to cleanse the inward parts of man; and somehow in the transmission, the application to human life has become mixed up with the simple and direct words of the parable. The general teaching is clear enough, and is substantially that of the Marcan controversy-story: it is not external defilements that make a man unclean, but the defilements of the heart (Mark vii. 16-22). It must be understood that the washing of hands to which the story refers has nothing to do with hygiene; it is a ritual washing, for which a half-teaspoonful of water was reckoned sufficient. See the tractate *Yadaim* ('Hands') of the Mishnah, which reports the solemn debates of noted masters concerning the quantity that was required.

The three 'Woes' which follow differ in order and in a considerable number of significant words in the versions of the two Evangelists, and it would seem that they have come through two independent lines of transmission. In the third 'Woe', the whole picture is different, though it is probable that we have before us variant versions of the one saying. In Matthew the tombs are seen and admired, and the contrast is between the beauty of the outside and the unseen corruption within — the basic thought is parallel to that of the pot which has been polished on the outside while the inside remains filthy. In Luke the tombs are not seen at all; men are walking over the bones of the dead without being aware of it; and the thought is that the Pharisees constitute a danger of which men are not conscious. Here the Matthaean saying is clearer; it cannot be assumed that it is for that reason closer to the original. The tendency in transmission would be rather to lend clarity to a saying of doubtful meaning than to turn a clear saying into an enigma.

Verse 45 introduces a complementary series of three Woes, directed against the scribes. In Matthew's version, scribes and Pharisees are grouped together, and all the Woes are addressed to them jointly, as 'hypocrites'. Luke is hardly likely to have separated the two groups; it is much more probable that his sources contained the two series, divided between Pharisees and lawyers. But it is not easy to see why the scribes should be the objects of these particular criticisms; only the last ('You have taken away the key of knowledge') would seem capable of an interpretation that would apply to their professional functions. The accusation that they build the tombs of the prophets and thus show themselves true sons of those who killed them is strange enough in itself — the builders of the later Canterbury cathedral are not commonly regarded as indicating their approval of the murder of Thomas à Becket — but it is equally strange that the *scribes* should be held particularly responsible in the matter. Scribism was commonly taken to begin with Ezra, after prophecy had ceased. The saying leads up to the menacing prediction which follows, which would seem to apply rather to the entire nation than to one professional class within it, and it may be that the malediction on the scribes (or on the scribes and Pharisees, as in Matthew) was originally conceived as a more general denunciation of Israel.

The prophecy (*vv.* 49-51) is put in the mouth of Jesus himself by Matthew; but in Luke it is attributed to 'the Wisdom of God'. This formula certainly suggests that it is a citation from a book bearing this title. If this conjecture be accepted, we would have before us documentary evidence of the transference to Jesus of words drawn from another source. But as there is no other evidence for an apocryphal book called 'the Wisdom of God', it is perhaps better to look for another interpretation. Loisy proposes to regard it as the utterance of a Christian prophet in the early Palestinian Church, who speaks in the name of Jesus as the incarnate 'Wisdom of God'. T. W. Manson suggests that Jesus himself may have used the Lucan formula in the sense: 'God in his wisdom says'; he recalls that Jewish teachers often personify the attributes of God and represent them as speaking to men. By the time of the Evangelists, Christians generally looked upon the disasters of the Jewish War and the fall of Jerusalem as punishments brought upon the nation for its persistent rejection of God's messengers and especially of his Son. The form of the prophecy, especially in Matthew's version, reflects a specifically Jewish outlook; Luke's 'prophets and apostles' is secondary to Matthew's 'prophets and wise men and scribes'. Probably Luke saw a certain incongruity in naming scribes among the messengers of God who are victims of persecutions for which scribes are held primarily responsible.

It will be observed further that Matthew, by attributing the prophecy directly to Jesus, makes it refer to the persecution of *Christian* 'prophets and wise men and scribes' — those who are sent by Jesus; whereas in the Lucan form, where God or 'the Wisdom of God' is represented as the sender, the reference would be more generally to the fate of messengers sent by God to the Jews. The sufferings of the Gentile mission are not envisaged; as in the parable of the Wicked Tenant-Farmers (Mark xii. 1-12 and parallels; § 204), the thought is concerned with the reprobation of Israel.

The prophecy makes a natural conclusion to the denunciations and it is so used in Matthew; the third Woe against the scribes seems curiously out of place after it. A possible explanation is that Luke has conflated two sources. In the one ('L') he has found the sequence of three Woes against the scribes, without the prophecy; in the other ('Q') he has found the second Woe with the prophecy attached to it, as in Matthew, and has brought it into his series at this point, without concern for its climactic effect. In the third Woe, Luke's 'key of knowledge' is less appropriate to what follows than Matthew's version of the saying; the accusation that they neither entered themselves nor permitted others to enter belongs rather to the thought of 'locking the kingdom of heaven in men's faces' than to taking away 'the key of knowledge'. Luke's phrase has a Hellenistic sound, as Creed and others have remarked; 'knowledge' (*gnōsis*) is one of the key words of Hellenistic religious thought, but is never found in our Gospels except here and in Luke i. 77 ('knowledge of salvation'); it is avoided even by the Fourth Evangelist, even though he makes much use of the corresponding verb. It is all the more significant that in the (Gnostic) *Gospel according to Thomas* (Logion 39), the saying is transmitted, independently of Luke (?), in a form which mentions 'the keys of knowledge'.

In Matthew and in Thomas, the rebuke is addressed to Pharisees and scribes together. In Luke's form, the thought is probably that the key to the saving knowledge of God is the right interpretation of the Old Testament scriptures (cf. John v. 45-47); and the scribes have 'taken away the key' by imposing erroneous interpretations upon the people as the authoritative tradition. In the Matthaean version we have the more general thought of the leaders using all their influence to deter people from responding to the Gospel.

The vocabulary of *vv.* 53 and 54 is classical rather than colloquial; this leads us to attribute the little paragraph to Luke himself. It serves both as a natural conclusion to the denunciations and as an intimation of the atmosphere of menace which prompts the 'Exhortations to Fearless Confession' of the next section. The last verse (xii. 1) is more awkward. The sudden appearance of a crowd numbering tens of thousands, stepping on one another's toes around Jesus as he emerges from the Pharisee's house after lunch, is strangely linked with a warning against 'the leaven of the Pharisees' which is addressed primarily to the disciples. The words of the following section are probably meant to be taken as addressed to these crowds. But does Luke intend to suggest that such teeming throngs attended Jesus all the way from Galilee to Jerusalem? The saying about the leaven of the Pharisees is used by Mark, with Matthew following him, in a part of his narrative which Luke omits (§ 120); Mark does not indicate how the 'leaven' is to be understood; Matthew takes it to mean 'the teaching of the Pharisees and Sadducees' (Matt. xvi. 12). W. L. Knox holds that it 'was originally a warning against *agents provocateurs* who might entrap the disciples into fatal indiscretions' (*Sources* II, p. 68; cf. *Sources* I, p. 57). See also the notes on § 120.

155. *Exhortation to Fearless Confession*

Luke xii. 2-12

The greater part of this passage has already been discussed in its Matthaean context (§§ 59 and 60), where it is incorporated in the complex structure of the

Mission Charge. Verse 10 appears to be out of context, and it is probable that the Greek as it stands is the result of a misinterpretation of the Aramaic. The parallel in Matthew is found in the context of Jesus' refutation of the charge that his powers are the powers of evil (Matt. xii. 32; § 86). The Marcan form of the saying, which may be regarded as a better rendering of the Aramaic, says nothing about blasphemy against the Son of Man, but declares that 'all manner of sins and blasphemies shall be forgiven the sons of men' (except blasphemy against the Holy Spirit). The phrase 'Son of Man' in the text common to Luke and Matthew should have been rendered simply 'man', giving the sense: 'Insults against a man will be forgiven, but there is no forgiveness for blasphemy against the Holy Spirit.'

Notice that the sayings of *vv.* 2 and 3 are given an altered meaning by being attached to xii. 1. They now become a warning that hypocrisy is sure to be exposed. The parallel sayings in Matthew are an exhortation to proclaim in public all that Jesus has revealed in private teaching. Again, the opening phrase of *v.* 4 indicates that in Luke's view the following words are not addressed to his disciples, but to the multitudes, the 'tens of thousands' of *v.* 1, who now become the representatives of the countless Christians of later times. The whole passage, though less conspicuously than in Matthew, is coloured by the experience and outlook of the Church of the Evangelist's own time.

156. *The Parable of the Rich Fool*

Luke xii. 13-21

This section is taken from Luke's special source. In it the parable has been linked with a pronouncement-story (*vv.* 13-15), in which a detached saying of Jesus (*v.* 15) is provided with an artificial setting – the abrupt request of an individual in the throng, who ventures to interrupt the discourse of Jesus, strikes an incongruous note and can hardly be envisaged as a fragment of reminiscence. The parable is self-contained and does not require the pronouncement-story to introduce it. In itself, it contains nothing distinctive of the teaching of Jesus, and appears to be nothing more than a popular tale which has been attached to the tradition in the course of transmission. Variants of the same tale are found elsewhere in Near Eastern collections (*The Thousand and One Nights*, for instance), where there is nothing to suggest derivation from Christian sources. It occurs in a simpler form, without the introductory setting of *vv.* 13 to 15 or the moralizing comment of *v.* 21, in the newly discovered *Gospel according to Thomas* (Logion 63). Note that verse 21 is omitted in some Latin witnesses, and is bracketed as doubtful by Westcott and Hort. The phrase 'Take your ease, eat, drink' together with the clause immediately preceding ('laid up for many years') is omitted in Codex Bezae and in the Old Latin. It recalls the Epicurean phrases that are often found in epitaphs, such as 'Eat, drink, play, and come to me'; it may be a reminiscence of Ecclesiastes viii. 15.

Oddly enough, the little dialogue which Luke uses to introduce the parable is also found in the *Gospel according to Thomas* (Logion 72), without the pronouncement of *v.* 15, and without context.

157. *Cares about Earthly Things*

LUKE xii. 22-34

See the notes on §§ 32-35, where nearly all these sayings are found, with one change of order, as part of Matthew's Sermon on the Mount. It is linked with the preceding parable by the word *psychē* ('soul', or 'life', perhaps better, 'self'), and by the general similarity of theme. Verse 32 is found only in Luke, and may be drawn from his special source, which has probably given him also his version of the saying of *v.* 33, where the wording differs so substantially from the parallel in Matthew that it can hardly be attributed to the common source. The counsel 'Sell your possessions and give alms' (*v.* 33), as Luke understands it, is intended as a general rule for the followers of Jesus. Possibly the Matthaean version represents a weakening of the radical demand, reducing it to advice against hoarding in place of the positive requirement of renunciation. There is a tendency in Matthew to mould the precepts of Jesus into legislation for the Christian society, and this sometimes requires a modification of their original rigour. Notice, for example, his modification of the saying about divorce (Matt. xix. 19 and parallels; § 187; cf. Matt. v. 32).

158. *Watchfulness and Faithfulness*

LUKE xii. 35-46

159. *The Servant's Wages*

LUKE xii. 47-48

The sayings which are here gathered together are dominated by the conviction that a crisis is at hand which will break suddenly and unexpectedly. It reflects the early Christian expectation that 'the day of the Lord will come like a thief in the night'. It will be a day of reckoning, and the servants of the Lord are warned that they must always be prepared, seeing that it will come without notice and no time for preparation will be given. The significance of the Day is here envisaged wholly in terms of rewards and punishments.

Part of Luke's material (*vv.* 39-46) is paralleled in Matthew with such close coincidence of language that we must suppose them to have been drawing upon a common source ('Q'). Verses 35 to 38 and 47-48 are peculiar to Luke, but it is probable that they were derived by him from the same source. For the various sayings appear to be linked by the theme-word *doulos*, 'slave'; and Luke is so far unconscious of this that in *v.* 42 he has actually used *oikonomos*, 'steward', in place of *doulos*, and in *v.* 45 he has replaced Matthew's 'fellow-slaves' by 'menservants and maidservants'. The association around the word *doulos* would therefore seem to be attributable to the source, not to the editorial work of Luke; and this observation inclines us to attribute the non-Matthaean sayings of the Lucan sequence to 'Q'.

The sayings of the first group (*vv.* 35 to 38) imply a good deal that is left unexpressed. The figure of the master who 'returns from the marriage-feast' is hardly self-explanatory, and it may be that these sayings were at one time attached to a parable like that of the Ten Virgins (Matt. xxv. 1-13). Verse 37b is probably secondary in this context, though it may be an adaptation of a saying of Jesus. It is clearly not true to life, in terms of the general picture: the master of the house does not, as a rule, serve supper to the servants who wait up for him when he comes home late! The words are allegorical, representing the thought of Christ as the Servant-Messiah; but elsewhere in the Gospels this thought is not attached to the Parousia, but to the historical ministry of Jesus (cf. Luke xxii. 27, Mark x. 45, and especially the story of the Washing of the Disciples' Feet in John xiii. 1ff.). Verse 38, again, reflects disappointment over the delay of the Parousia, and is thereby marked as secondary. It is in keeping with a tendency to supplement warnings that the Day will arrive at any moment with somewhat incompatible suggestions that it may be delayed so long as to take the edge off anticipation and lead to slackness. Verses 45 and 46 sound the same note even more distinctly: 'My master is delayed in his coming.'

The insertion of Peter's question in *v.* 41 makes it explicit that the sayings which follow are intended specifically for the apostles, to whom responsibilities of administration have been given. Certainly there is a break in thought between the sayings of *vv.* 39 and 40, with their picture of a householder on guard against the coming of a thief, and the sayings of *vv.* 42 to 48 which rest upon the figure of the master's dealings with his steward. The transition is somewhat awkwardly mediated by the insertion of the question, which is retrospective (concerning the application of a 'parable' already given), but is answered by another parable which introduces a different theme.

The sayings of § 159 are not intrinsically connected with the figure of the steward, but were in all probability in origin a warning to Israel in the spirit of Amos iii. 2: 'You only have I known of all the nations of the earth; therefore I will punish you for all your iniquities.' Transferred to this context, Luke transforms them into a warning to the apostles, supplementary to the warnings of the preceding paragraph. Because they have enjoyed the privilege of receiving the clear revelation of the divine will from Jesus, they will be judged all the more severely if they are unfaithful. More generally, it becomes a warning to all the followers of Christ, whatever their station.

The whole catena of sayings in these two sections is undoubtedly composite, and it is not easy to determine how much we can attribute to the teaching of Jesus himself and how much represents the results of adaptation and reinterpretation in the usage of the Church. For Luke himself, the *kyrios* ('lord') of the first passage, whose return from the marriage is awaited, is a figure of Christ; so is the Son of Man of *v.* 40, and the 'master' (or 'lord'; the word again is *kyrios*) of *vv.* 42-48. But all these passages are in themselves susceptible of interpretation without this identification, though in their present form they have been adapted to the early Christian expectation of the Parousia of Jesus and even to the growing disappointment over the delay of the Parousia. In their primary form they may well be warnings of the swift and unexpected coming of the Son of Man as Judge, and exhortations to be prepared for his coming at any moment. From that point on, our interpretation will be affected by, and will in turn have bearing upon, our general conception of how Jesus couched his teaching about the future, especially in relation to the question whether he identified himself with the Son of Man of apocalyptic expectation or whether this identification was made by the early Church, which interpreted the predictions of the coming of the Son of Man in terms of the Parousia of the crucified and risen Jesus. See also the notes on §§ 52 and 184.

160. *Signs for this Age*

Luke xii. 49-56

The section is composite, and it is not easy to see a thread of connection between its several parts, or any clear relationship with the sections that precede and follow. The first two verses appear to express the mood of Jesus, as if he were weighed down with the burden of his mission and eager to have it over and done with. It will set the world aflame, and will involve his own suffering and death, figured as a 'baptism' that he must undergo. The 'fire' has been variously interpreted as a figure of judgment, of holiness, of faith, and of the divisions which are to be described in *vv.* 51-53. It is doubtful whether we are justified in allowing the present context to determine our interpretation; the context is almost certainly secondary, and may help us to make out how Luke understood the sayings, but not what they meant in the first instance, on the lips of Jesus. Verse 49 appears in a curious variant in the *Gospel of Thomas*: 'Jesus said, I have cast fire upon the world, and see, I keep it until it burns up' (Logion 10). Another Gnostic saying, long known to us and now found to be from the *Gospel of Thomas*, seems to use 'fire' in parallelism with 'kingdom', suggesting that the kindling of fire in the earth is a figure for the inaugurating of the kingdom. 'He that is near me is near the fire; and he that is far from me is far from the kingdom' (Logion 82). We have been told that John the Baptist looked for his greater Successor to baptize with (wind and) fire (§ 4); and this association may have led to the linking of the 'fire' saying of *v.* 49 with the 'baptism' saying of *v.* 50; these two sayings may have been quite independent of one another originally. It will be noted that Matthew has neither of them, but in his parallel to *v.* 51, he uses the strange phrase 'to cast peace' in place of Luke's 'to give peace'; this almost leads us to feel that he has had before him the saying containing the phrase 'to cast fire upon the earth', and has inadvertently carried its verb over to the other saying. Verses 51 to 53 are in any case a unit in themselves. The description of divisions that split families is drawn from the oracle of Micah vii. 6; Creed notes that in the Micah passage, and in Matthew, the words describe the revolt of the younger generation against their elders, while in Luke this is changed to a picture of mutual hostility.

Verses 54 to 57 form another unit. It has no intrinsic relation to its present context, and we are left with no clue to indicate what lesson the hearers should be learning from the historical situation. In the opinion of T. W. Manson, 'The work of Jesus is the sign of the time. From it they ought to infer that the Kingdom of God has come upon them and that the final consummation is near' (*Sayings*, 121). It is at least equally possible that Jesus is thinking of the social unrest in the land and of the simmering of revolt against Rome, and warning that the signs point to a national catastrophe. Pilate's massacre of the Galileans (Luke xiii. 1-3) was a clear enough indication of how Rome was likely to deal with the insurrection of which many were dreaming.

161. *Agreement with one's Adversary*

LUKE xii. 57-59

Matthew, by using this exhortation in a different context, has given it a different meaning. In Matthew it is subordinated to the extension of the commandment forbidding murder, to include anger and hostility towards our brethren (§ 22; Matt. v. 25-26). In Luke it is really a crisis-parable. If you were dealing with a creditor, you would make every effort to arrange a settlement out of court, before he secured a judgment against you and had you imprisoned (the law of the time, of course, provided for imprisonment for debt until repayment was made). Why then do you not acknowledge that you stand before God as an insolvent debtor, and come to terms with him before it is too late? We have here another example of the tendency to change the emphasis in a parable from the eschatological to the hortatory; an urgent warning to act to meet the approaching crisis is transformed into a piece of sage advice, a counsel of prudence, to settle your conflicts before they get you into serious trouble.

162. *The Call to Repentance*

LUKE xiii. 1-9

Nothing is known of the two incidents of which Jesus speaks. Both must have occurred in Jerusalem, and it is an obvious conjecture that the episode belongs to the ministry of Jesus in Jerusalem. We may note that the strange story of the Cursing of the Fig Tree (§§ 199, 201), which appears to be a transformation of this parable into a symbolic act, is laid by Mark and Matthew in Jerusalem. Luke is arranging his materials topically, not geographically or chronologically, and he is still keeping to the theme of the approaching crisis — the judgment of God which is to fall upon rebellious Israel and will not be long delayed. The twin sayings about the slaughtered Galileans and the people who were killed by the fall of the tower are used by the Evangelist as an introduction to the parable. These deaths are not a judgment upon conspicuously wicked individuals; they are a presage of the disaster that will engulf the whole nation, if it fails to repent. But the emphasis in the parable itself is not on the necessity for repentance, but rather on the concern of the gardener to save his fig tree from destruction; he intercedes for it, and undertakes to give it every possible care to make it fruitful. The setting must therefore be regarded as secondary, and it may be conjectured that the original point of the parable was that Jesus himself, like the prophets, interceded with God for Israel and sought through his ministry to make it fruitful. But certainly the parable in itself does not suggest the imminence of catastrophe, and therefore the urgency of repentance, but the deferment of the threatened disaster and the hope that the measures to be taken will obviate it entirely. It is only the context in which Luke has placed it that enables us to give it any connotation of a call to repentance, and it is impossible to regard this setting as original. We may recall the warning of Jeremias, of 'the necessity of always examining critically the context in which a parable has reached us, in order to see whether it agrees with the original meaning of the parable in so far as it is possible to recognize it' (*Parables*, p. 75).

163. *The Healing of a Woman with a Spirit of Infirmity*

LUKE xiii. 10-17

In this story the miracle is not the centre of interest, but merely the occasion for the controversy over sabbath observance. The nature of the woman's disability is not indicated; the phrase 'a spirit of infirmity' reflects the view that her trouble is caused by a demon, and the same thought is found again in the words of Jesus, that 'Satan has bound her for eighteen years'. The healing is thus looked upon as an exorcism. But basically this is a controversy-story, and the centre of interest lies in the reproach of the ruler of the synagogue (*v.* 14) and the reply of Jesus (*vv.* 15-16). The healing ministry of Jesus is part of his warfare against Satan, and the prince of evil is not to be left in possession on the sabbath day. There is an odd play on the verb 'loose' — first of loosing an ox or ass, then of loosing the bonds of Satan. Verse 17 is a characteristically Lucan comment on the effect of the words and deeds of Jesus. We again note the Lucan use of the title *ho kyrios* ('the Lord') in narrative — a reading back of the developed ecclesiastical usage.

This story is closely related to that of the healing of the man with the dropsy (Luke xiv. 1-6), and both of them may be variants of the story of the healing of the man with the withered hand (Mark iii. 1-6 and parallels).

On § 164, the Lucan version of the twin parables of the Mustard Seed and the Leaven, see under the Matthaean parallels, §§ 97 and 98.

165. *The Condemnation of Israel*

LUKE xiii. 22-30

The section is composite. All of it has parallels in Matthew, but they are scattered, and set in no less than five different contexts. In all but one case (Matt. viii. 11-12 = Luke xiii. 28-29), the wording is so different as to suggest that the Evangelists have drawn upon two different sources.

Verse 22 is an editorial introduction of Luke's own composition, recalling to us that Jesus is on his way to Jerusalem. Verses 23-24 differ not only in words, but to some degree in substance, from the corresponding Matthaean passage, which stands without relation to the passages which precede and follow it, in the Sermon on the Mount (Matt. vii. 13-14; § 34). In Luke we have a figure of a single door, which men are to strive to enter; in Matthew, we begin with the slight change from a 'narrow door' to a 'narrow gate', through which men are to enter; but the figure changes immediately to that of two roads, one of which leads to destruction and one to 'life', and the 'gate' becomes subsidiary to the roads. It looks very much as if the Matthaean form has been assimilated to the well-known 'Pythagorean Y' – the dividing of the ways which is expressed in the myth of the Choice of Herakles, and is symbolized by the 'Y' on tombstones (see F. Cumont, *Lux Perpetua* [Paris, 1949], pp. 278f.). This 'door' must be the entrance to the kingdom of heaven; there is no clue to indicate in what sense it is 'narrow'.

Verses 25-27 also employ a figure of a door, but do not follow up the thought of the previous figure. It is no longer a question of a door that is narrow, and thus difficult to pass through, but of a door which cannot be entered at all after a certain moment, at which it is shut by 'the master of the house'. It reflects some relationship with Matthew's parable of the Ten Virgins, but there is evidently a complicated history behind both passages, and the original form of the parable can no longer be discerned. There is no suggestion here of a bridegroom entering, and the door being shut as soon as he has entered. Here the master of the house is pictured as already at home; at a certain moment he rises and shuts the door, and no more visitors are admitted. This looks like the end of a parable of which the beginning is lost. The closing verses, however, are not appropriate to the imagery, but shift to an allegory of the Last Judgment; the Matthaean parallel to this part (*vv.* 26-27) is not found in the Parable of the Ten Virgins, but in the Sermon on the Mount, in a passage which pictures Christ himself as denying entrance to the kingdom of heaven, not to people who have made their decision too late, but to those who have made false professions of discipleship. In the Lucan passage they do not profess to be disciples, but only claim that they have eaten and drunk in his presence and that he has taught in their streets. The reference is clearly enough to the earthly ministry of Jesus, and he has come to be identified with the 'master of the house' of the parable, and with the Judge of all. But it is probable that the parable was one of those which sought to awaken men to the urgency of the crisis with which they were faced in the ministry of Jesus himself: the door of mercy is now open for all who will repent, but the patience of God is near an end, and the moment will come, and that speedily, when he will arise and shut the door and there will be no more opportunity to enter.

Verses 28-29, again, are intrinsically independent of this context, as is seen from the fact that in Matthew they are attached to the story of the Centurion's Servant (§ 46). In this Lucan passage it is not indicated who is addressed in the words 'You shall see'. It cannot be the questioner of *v.* 23, and no other audience has been mentioned. Obviously enough it is addressed to the leaders of Israel, or more generally to the nation as a whole; but this is further proof that it is out of context here.

Verse 30 is an isolated logion, probably authentic, which is used in different contexts by Mark and (twice) by Matthew.

166. *The Departure from Galilee*

LUKE xiii. 31-33

The incident is out of place in a Samaritan itinerary, for in Samaria Jesus would already be out of Herod's jurisdiction. The Pharisees are treated as lackeys of Herod, passing on their master's threats and bidden to carry back the scornful reply of Jesus. The general purport of the answer is clear enough: Jesus will continue his mission to the end, despite all threats; and his death will not be encompassed by Herod, since he must die at Jerusalem, like the prophets who went before him. In detail there are difficulties of interpretation, and a number of commentators suspect a corruption of the text (Wellhausen – interpolation of the words 'and on the third day I am perfected', followed by a secondary interpolation of 'today and tomorrow and', in *v.* 33; *Evangelium Lucae*, ad loc.). But the authenticity of the sayings (and of the whole incident) is doubtful: does Jesus think of his mission as consisting essentially of exorcizing demons and working cures? There may lie behind it a genuine reminiscence of the attitude of Jesus towards Herod – a 'fox' who skulks in the shadows but dare not come out in the daylight; Jesus is not to be intimidated by the threats of such as he.

167. *The Lament over Jerusalem*

LUKE xiii. 34-35

This saying owes its place wholly to the verbal association ('Jerusalem') with *v.* 33. In Matthew it forms the conclusion to the discourse against the Pharisees, which Luke has given in chapter xi, but which Matthew lays (with a number of supplements) in Jerusalem. On the basis of the Synoptic framework, which has not yet made room for a visit of Jesus to Jerusalem, the saying is oddly out of place here. Note that in the Matthaean context, the saying looks forward to the Second Advent, when Jerusalem will acknowledge and welcome the divine Emissary whom it now rejects; in Luke the saying anticipates the acclamations which will greet Jesus as he enters the city before his Passion. Jesus speaks here as the incarnate Wisdom of God, and the words may have been originally a continuation of the prophecy (attributed by Luke to 'the Wisdom of God' – xi. 49 – see notes on § 154) which precedes it in Matthew's version (attributed to Jesus himself – Matt. xxiii. 34ff., § 210). 'The entire verse is probably to be understood in relation to the myth of the divine Wisdom, who, after she has vainly dwelt upon earth and called men to herself, takes her leave of earth, so that men now seek after her in vain. Here she prophesies that she will remain hidden until the arrival of the Messiah; for only he can be meant by "He who comes in the name of the Lord"' (Bultmann, *History*, p. 115).

168. *Healing of a Man with the Dropsy*

LUKE xiv. 1-6

This and the two following sections are set in the context of a dinner in the house of a prominent Pharisee on a sabbath day. The setting is plainly a literary device employed by Luke to link materials that are intrinsically independent.

The healing of the dropsical man is a variant of the story of the healing of the man with the withered hand (Mark iii. 1-6 and parallels, § 70). The dinner-party setting has no bearing upon it; the man is not there as a guest, since he is dismissed as soon as he is healed. There is no real interest in him or even in the miracle; the central question is the dispute over sabbath-observance, one of the acute points of conflict between the early Church and Pharisaic Judaism. Bultmann suggests that the whole incident has been constructed (in the tradition prior to Luke) around the saying of *v.* 5 (*History*, p. 12); Luke has used the story as he found it, creating only the setting (*v.* 1).

The strange association, 'a son or an ox', in the challenge of *v.* 5, is undoubtedly the better-attested reading, and must be regarded as prior to the Byzantine reading, 'an ass or an ox' (*Gospel Parallels*, from RSV, with AV). There has probably been a primitive corruption, though the reading 'son' is defended by some of the best critics. The difficulty was felt early enough to affect the text of the Curetonian Syriac, which makes the conflation: 'a son or an ox or an ass'. The Matthaean parallel, introduced into the story of the man with the withered hand (Matt. xii. 11-12), perhaps by conflation with another version of this Lucan story, speaks of 'a sheep', and adds the corollary: 'How much better is a man than a sheep?' The comparison would hold with an ox or an ass, but not with a son. Despite the weight of textual evidence, therefore, we can hardly maintain that 'son' represents the original reading; but neither can we suppose that it has arisen out of an original reading 'ass'. The only remaining possibility is a corruption prior to all our existing texts.

169. *Teaching on Humility*

Luke xiv. 7-14

The section is composite. The first part is a bit of homely advice: 'Do not lay yourself open to humiliation by claiming honours to which you are not entitled.' This is presented as a criticism of the unseemly conduct of the guests, and is addressed to them (*vv.* 7-10). In itself it has no religious significance whatever, and it is doubtful if Jesus was concerned to teach men how to avoid public shame or how to win admiration from other men. Luke, however, has turned it into a parable (*v.* 7); and takes it as an illustration of the great principle of divine dealings with men, which is enunciated in *v.* 11: 'Everyone who exalts himself will be humbled; and everyone who humbles himself will be exalted.' In the kingdom of God precedence will not be granted to the self-seeking. This is certainly a secondary combination. In any event the circumstances of the utterance are incredible: would Jesus openly rebuke his fellow-guests in such a manner?

The second part (*vv.* 12-14) may well contain a genuine utterance of Jesus; here is no question of worldly wisdom, but quite the opposite. But we must again question the credibility of the circumstances. Would Jesus criticize his host's choice of guests, and in their presence?

170. *The Parable of the Great Supper*

MATTHEW xxii. 1-10 LUKE xiv. 15-24

The general discussion of this parable and the relationship between the two versions may be left for treatment when we reach it in the Matthaean order (§ 205, in the Jerusalem ministry). Here it will be sufficient to note the introduction (*v.* 15), by which Luke relates it to the (artificial) setting of the banquet in the house of the Pharisee. As in Luke xi. 27-28, Jesus gives short shrift to a person who utters pious noises. The sentiment of the guest is excellent, but he and his friends belie it by their attitude to the invitation which Jesus brings.

171. *The Cost of Discipleship*

LUKE xiv. 25-35

This is a catena of sayings, probably constructed by Luke himself out of diverse materials. The setting is abruptly changed from the house of the Pharisee to the open street, and the audience from the hostile dinner-guests to the enthusiastic crowds. The sayings warn against a too facile acceptance of the invitation to follow Jesus; thus the theme too is changed, from the reproach of the preceding parable addressed to those who are refusing the invitation to the caution addressed to those who may not be prepared to accept all the consequences of their first enthusiastic response.

The setting (*v.* 25) is created by the Evangelist. The first two sayings (*vv.* 26-27) are used by Matthew, in a different, somewhat freer translation of the underlying Aramaic, in his Mission Charge (x. 37-38; § 62). The two parables which follow (*vv.* 28-30; 31-32) are peculiar to Luke. Together they constitute one of those double parables which seem to be a feature of the teaching methods of Jesus. The 'tower' of the first parable is not likely to be a fortification; more probably it is a large farm building of some kind, since the question of Jesus implies that such a piece of construction falls within the experience of his hearers ('Which of you ... ?'). The farmer in his small way, the king in his military enterprises, must not embark on undertakings which are too great for his resources. The 'resources' needed by the follower of Jesus are the settled purpose and the will to commit all that he has, even to life itself. Verse 33, accordingly, though it may not have been the comment of Jesus himself on the twin parables, is needed to tie the thought of the paragraph together. The saying on salt (*vv.* 34-35) is found in a variant form in Matthew, in the Sermon on the Mount (*v.* 13; § 20), coupled with the saying; 'You are the salt of the earth.' Here it appears to be entirely out of context; perhaps Luke thinks of the half-hearted disciple as like savourless salt, but the figure does not really bear upon the theme of renunciation.

172. *The Lost Sheep and the Lost Coin*

LUKE xv. 1-10

We now come to a long block of material which Luke has drawn from his special source ('L'); it extends through the whole of the next two chapters, and consists mainly of five parables.

The parable of the Lost Sheep is found also in Matthew (xviii. 12-14), but in a totally different context and with a totally different application (see § 133, *notes*). The differences of vocabulary are so great as to indicate that Luke and Matthew have not found it in their common source 'Q', but that Matthew has taken it from 'M', and Luke from 'L'. In Luke it is coupled with the parable of the Lost Coin, and it is probable that they were originally framed as twin parables by Jesus himself, and as an answer to critics who challenged his approach to the outcast and the undeserving. The gospel of God is a gospel of redemption; the outcasts of society belong to him and he is actively concerned for them, for every single one. The note of joy is central. 'Joy in heaven' – 'joy in the presence of the angels' – these are Jewish paraphrases for 'Joy in the heart of God', framed to avoid ascribing human emotions directly to God. And God calls others to share in his joy.

The two concluding sayings (*vv.* 7, 10) are secondary; either Luke has framed them himself, or he has found them detached in the tradition and given them this place. They introduce a note which is not to be discovered in the parables themselves – the *penitent* disposition of the recovered outcast. The parables are not concerned with penitence; the recovery of the sheep depends on the unwearied search made for it by the shepherd, not on its own change of attitude; and even more obviously, the lost coin is found because the woman will not rest until she finds it, not because it has acquired the will to be found. Jesus probably framed the parables without putting the lesson into formal words – he left the hearers to draw their own conclusion. If God rejoices in the recovery of his lost possessions, how can they feel resentment that Jesus is searching out the lost and restoring them? The point is not the change of mind in the sinner, but the unchanging love of God that will not let him go, which is being manifested in the redemptive activity of Jesus.

The Matthaean version, as so frequently, lacks much of the vivid detail of the Lucan picture – the sheep carried home on the shoulders of the shepherd; the invitation to his friends and neighbours to share his joy.

173. *The Prodigal Son*

Luke xv. 11-32

It has been suggested that *vv.* 1-3 were originally designed as the introduction to this parable, and that Luke has inserted the twin parables of *vv.* 4-10 into the frame; note that *v.* 3 speaks of 'this parable', as if only one were to follow. However that may be, we shall ascribe to Luke's artistry the grouping of the three parables to make a trilogy.

The story of the Prodigal Son is a parable with a double point. The first part (*vv.* 1-24) develops the same theme as the twin parables of the preceding section. Here the element of repentance does come in – the return of the prodigal is dependent upon his own change of attitude, not upon the efforts of anyone sent to bring him back. But this is not the central interest of the story. The emphasis is laid not upon him, but upon the father, who welcomes him home without recriminations. But this first part is designed mainly as an introduction to the second (*vv.* 25-32); and the fundamental contrast is not between the two sons — the one who has gone to the dogs and the one who has stuck faithfully to the job — but between the father and the elder son in their attitude to the returning prodigal. The elder son, conscious of his rectitude and unrelenting in his judgment of his brother's past follies, is clearly a type of the Pharisees with their proud consciousness of fidelity to the Law of God and their censorious attitude towards their brothers who have fallen from the path of duty.

Note that here no formal lesson is appended; Jesus leaves the parable to speak for itself, to make its own appeal to the consciences of his hearers. He is no longer on the defensive (so Jeremias, *Parables*, p. 106); he hopes to move the Pharisees to abandon their harshness and pride, and to share the joy of God in the return of the outcasts of Israel.

174. *The Unjust Steward*

Luke xvi. 1-13

The section is composite, and the primary lesson of the parable is hard to discern. Verses 10 to 13 manifestly consist of a series of supplements which have been attached to the parable, perhaps by Luke, perhaps in the course of transmission; they are attempts to find interpretations — all different — of a parable which had already become obscure. Verses 8 and 9 are more difficult to classify. The first problem is whether 'the lord' of *v.* 8 is to be taken as the rich man of the story, or as 'the Lord' who is the author of the parable. Is it the conclusion framed by Jesus, or the comment of the Evangelist? It seems hard to believe that the parable would end with the rich man commending the steward who has defrauded him; it seems equally strange that Jesus should commend a man who secures his own immediate future by cheating his employer. In either case *v.* 8 appears to be the first interpretation offered. If it belongs to the parable, then the lesson is that men should show as much forethought in spiritual matters as in temporal. The steward is commended, not for his crooked dealings, but for his astuteness in providing for his future welfare before it is too late. 'The sons of light' — which on this basis can only mean 'the people of God' — should be showing the same astuteness in the face of the crisis which confronts them. The Day of the Lord is at hand; they should be making provision to meet it. The steward is *phronimos* ('prudent') in that he recognizes the crisis that confronts him, and takes prompt action to prepare for it. The morality of the action is irrelevant; the only point with which Jesus is concerned is that he takes the action which the situation requires. 'He did not let things take their course, he acted, unscrupulously no doubt, though we are not concerned with that, but boldly, resolutely, and prudently, with the purpose of making a new life for himself. For you, too, the challenge of the hour demands prudence, everything is at stake' (Jeremias, *Parables*, pp. 127-8).

This interpretation is attractive, but it seems to require us to take the phrase 'the sons of light' as meaning 'the people of God', that is, Israelites generally. But this is an unnatural sense. The contrast 'sons of this age' — 'sons of light' is surely not a contrast between Gentiles and Jews, but between those whose horizons are limited to the present world and those who are concerned for the things of eternity. But are these 'sons of light' the people who need the warning to take action to meet the impending crisis? If they are described as 'sons of light', it is surely because they have their hearts set on things unseen. Compare 1 Thessalonians v. 4-5: 'You are not in darkness, brethren, for that day to surprise you like a thief. For you are all sons of light and sons of the day.' It would seem, then, that *v.* 8b was not originally attached to the parable. It may have been transmitted as an isolated logion, a comment on the astuteness with which worldly men pursue their temporal ends in contrast with the fumbling and ineffectual ways of the pious in their pursuit of the highest.

Verse 9 offers a different interpretation, and the way in which it is framed ('And I tell you') seems to indicate that Luke takes it to be the interpretation intended by Jesus himself. It clearly refers back to *v.* 4: as the steward has used his position to secure entrance into the houses of his master's debtors, so the disciples are to use their resources to secure entrance for themselves into 'eternal habitations'. On this basis, the parable 'appears to be intended to commend prudence of a specific kind, namely prudence in the use of wealth' (Creed, *St. Luke*, p. 201). 'Make friends for yourselves by means of the unrighteous mammon' – that is, sell all your goods and give to the poor; 'that when it fails they (that is, God, as in vi. 38) may receive you in the eternal habitations' – you shall have treasure in heaven (cf. Mark x. 21 and parallels).

A brilliant suggestion was offered by C. C. Torrey (*Our Translated Gospels*, under the heading 'Questions Misunderstood as Declarations' – Chapter II, Exhibit XI c); its force is not dependent upon the translation-hypothesis. He takes *vv.* 8 and 9 as challenging *questions*: 'Did the lord of the estate praise the faithless steward? And do I say to you, Gain friends for yourselves with base lucre, so that when it is gone you may be received into the eternal abodes?'

The theme of the right use of wealth leads on to the supplementary sayings of *vv.* 10 to 12; the word *adikos* ('unrighteous') supplies a verbal link. Verse 10 is essentially an independent saying, the enunciation of a general principle; *vv.* 11 and 12 are particular applications. None of them have any real relation to the parable or to the interpretations of *vv.* 8 and 9. Worldly wealth is 'the unrighteous mammon', regardless of the means by which it has been acquired; there is something unreal about it, in comparison with 'the true' – the abiding, heavenly treasure. It is an alien thing; the only treasure that followers of Christ can call their own is the treasure of heaven. But faithfulness to our trust in the lower things is the condition of our being entrusted with the higher. Verse 13 is another independent logion, which Matthew has introduced in the Sermon on the Mount (Matt. vi. 24; § 34); it is not concerned with the right use of wealth, but with wealth as displacing God in our loyalty and affections; 'mammon' serves as a link-word. The *Gospel of Thomas* (Logion 47) gives an expanded form of the saying: 'It is impossible for a man to mount two horses and to stretch two bows, and it is impossible for a servant to serve two masters, otherwise he will honour the one and offend the other.' Here it has no application to God and mammon; and this application may indeed be secondary.

175. *The Hypocrisy of the Pharisees*

LUKE xvi. 14-15

The theme of the choice that must be made between God and mammon leads Luke to attach this episode at this point, and to make the saying of *v.* 15 a reproach to the Pharisees for their avarice, their service of mammon. But the saying in itself has no reference to avarice, and the Pharisees were not admired and did not seek admiration for their wealth, but for their piety, their righteousness. There is some difficulty, accordingly, in taking *v.* 14 as the proper introduction to the saying. T. W. Manson suggested that the Sadducees would be more likely candidates for this rebuke. 'The people who would be likely to scoff at such teaching were certainly not the Pharisees but the Sadducees who did not believe in any future life worthy of the name. To the Sadducees, and probably to them alone in Judaism, the words "treasure in heaven" meant nothing at all' (*Sayings*, p. 295; since he later abandoned the association of Sadducee with the root *tsdq* ('be righteous'), his further point of a play on the name would not hold). But there is in any case no reason to hold that there was any original connection between this passage and the preceding sayings – the association is of Luke's making.

176. *About the Law and about Divorce*

LUKE xvi. 16-18

The three sayings which Luke has brought together, with no apparent connection either with what precedes or with what follows, are found in Matthew in strikingly different versions and in three different contexts. They seem to be mutually contradictory. The first asserts that a new order has been inaugurated with the work of John the Baptist – before him, the law and the prophets; after him, the proclamation of the kingdom of God. The second asserts that none the less not the slightest detail of the law can be disregarded. The third then introduces a radical revision of the Jewish law of re-marriage after divorce. Luke presumably saw some connection between these pronouncements and was able to reconcile them in his own mind.

In all three the Lucan version seems to be more faithful to the original than that of Matthew. But the problems of interpretation are manifold, and there is little agreement among commentators. It is probably a mistake to seek to interpret the three sayings in relation to one another; each should be considered in isolation. The meaning of *v.* 18 is clear enough – it is an unequivocal declaration of the indissolubility of marriage; *v.* 17 is perhaps an ironical comment on the Pharisaic attitude to the law, not a serious statement of the position of Jesus himself. The understanding of *v.* 16 will depend largely upon the sense in which we take the verb *biazetai* ('use force'). This may have the good sense – all sorts and conditions of people are struggling with all their might to enter; or the bad sense – everyone is assailing it violently. The latter seems to be implied in the Matthaean form of the saying (Matt. xi. 12). In any event, I find it impossible to imagine that Jesus ever uttered these three sentences in succession, without elucidation.

177. *Dives and Lazarus*

Luke xvi. 19-31

The parable falls into two parts. The first part (*vv.* 19-26) is a Jewish version — the earliest known to us — of an old Egyptian folk-tale, which may have been carried to Palestine by Jews of Alexandria, as Jeremias suggests (*Parables*, p. 128); however, tales like this travel far and wide, no man knows how (a variant version of the parable of the Prodigal Son appears in the Lotus Sutra, the great scripture of Mahayana Buddhism). There are seven Rabbinical versions, in which the persons have become the rich tax-collector and the poor scholar. The second part (*vv.* 27-31) is an addition of Jesus (perhaps we should say more cautiously, a Christian addition), which leads up to the saying of *v.* 31: 'If they do not hear Moses and the prophets, neither will they be persuaded if one rise from the dead.' This conclusion has no bearing upon the theme of the reversal of fortunes in the after-life; compare John v. 45-57.

The persons in such stories rarely carry names, and this is the only parable of Jesus in which a proper name is given to a character. Here the name of the poor man is probably introduced in preparation for the dialogue of *vv.* 24-25. Later Christian tradition provided names for the rich man also — Ninive (in the Sahidic version); Phinees (in Priscillian). 'Dives' is not a proper name, but simply the Latin word for 'wealthy', which has come into our usage through the Vulgate. The Lazarus of this story is not in fact raised from the dead; but it seems likely that the Johannine story (John xi) owes something to this parable.

The details of conditions in the world of the dead are merely a reflection of current popular notions and ought not to be taken as data of revelation. The Son of God was not manifested that he might make known the geography of the underworld or set his seal upon the doctrine that the damned suffer the tortures of unquenchable thirst; nor should 'the great gulf fixed' be adduced as evidence that men enter upon their final state immediately after death. (It is true enough that 'Jesus knows no doctrine of purgatory', as Jeremias remarks; but this is really quite irrelevant to the parable.) The ideas expressed here — the souls of the righteous transported to Paradise by the angels; the world of the dead as a region where the damned can converse with the righteous but cannot make contact with them; the ordeal of Tantalus — these are not even peculiarly Jewish, but are commonplaces of Greek religious thought; and the cup of cold water is specifically Egyptian, the precious gift of Osiris to the blessed dead.

Wellhausen (*Evangelium Lucae*, p. 90) makes the acute suggestion that the 'dogs' and the crumbs 'that fall from the table' of *v.* 21 may be an echo from the story of the Canaanite woman (Matt. xv. 27), which Luke omits.

As the parable stands, its central theme is no longer that of the reversal of fortunes in the life to come, but the problem of disbelief in a life after death. It is implied that the testimony of the Old Testament scriptures ('Moses and the prophets') is sufficient of itself to bring conviction of the truth of this doctrine; no external 'sign', not even a rising from the dead, will bring conviction where the testimony of the scriptures is rejected. In this form, the parable seems to reflect the feeling of the early Christians that the Jews, in rejecting the Gospel, are refusing to heed the testimony of their own holy scriptures. The notion that 'Moses and the prophets' in themselves teach a doctrine of personal immortality, with rewards and punishments after death, is not grounded in the facts; a Christian interpretation of the Old Testament is here presupposed. We are inclined to hold, therefore, that the whole pericope is the construction of some early Christian teacher; there is little to confirm its attribution to Jesus himself. At most there is a possibility that it has been developed out of some tradition of controversy between Jesus and the Sadducees. There is, however, no trace of the Sadducees in the parable as it stands. It is very doubtful that 'the hearers ... would have recognized in the story the description of a typical Sadducee' (Manson, *Sayings*, p. 297).

On §§ 178 and 179, see the remarks on the Matthaean parallels in §§ 131, 134 and 135.

180. *On Faith*

Luke xvii. 5-6

Variant versions of this saying on faith are found in Mark and in Matthew (twice, with significant differences of wording; §§ 126, 201).

Verse 5 is probably an editorial introduction supplied by Luke, not to make a connection with the preceding paragraph but simply to provide a transition to the new theme. In the Lucan form the saying uses the figure of transplanting a 'sycamine tree'; in the other versions it is that of the moving of a mountain. T. W. Manson remarks: 'Here again we have a complicated and confused tradition' (*Sayings*, p. 140). In Luke a tree is commanded to uproot itself and be planted in the sea — a strange place for a tree! In Mark, and in the Matthaean parallel to Mark, it is a mountain that is to leave its place and be cast into the sea; in Matthew, indeed, it is 'this mountain' — the Temple Mount itself. As this is placed by Mark and Matthew in the context of the Cursing of the Fig Tree, which Luke omits, it has been suggested by some commentators that Luke's 'sycamine' (*sukaminos*) has come into the saying as a transference of the fig tree (*sukē*) of the Marcan story. In the other Matthaean version, it is a mountain that is moved from one place to another, but not cast into the sea; this appears to be the form of the saying that is reflected in St. Paul's words about the faith that moves mountains (1 Cor. xiii. 2). To quote again from Manson: 'It should be noted that the idea of *planting* a tree in the sea is frankly absurd. It is a plain warning against taking the saying in a sense that was never intended. ... By faith men can do things that seem to be as absurd and impossible as transplanting trees and making them grow in the sea' (*Sayings*, p. 141).

181. *The Servant's Wages*

Luke xvii. 7-10

The title given to this section is misleading (in the English rendering). It is not a matter of a 'servant', but of a *slave* (*doulos*), and the parable presupposes conditions of servitude which were drawn accurately from the life of the times, but have no resemblance to the relations between a workman and his employer in a free society. This undoubtedly adds to our difficulty in appreciating its significance for us. Jesus thinks of the relations between God and those who serve him primarily in terms of the relationship between a father and his sons, not of that between a master and his slaves. But it must be observed that the point of the parable is in the attitude of the slave, whose time and toil belong entirely to his master, without limit; the detail ought not to be pressed, as if it were an allegory, to make the inconsiderate demands of the master a type of the attitude of God. The parable is a warning against self-righteousness — against the proud notion that a man can establish a claim upon God by service beyond the line of duty. There are no works of supererogation in the service of God. Basically the thought is that which St. Paul expresses in another way in his warnings against 'boasting' (Rom. iii. 27; iv. 1-4; etc.); it is exemplified in his own attitude to his accomplishments (1 Cor. ix. 16ff.). The rewards of God are always of grace, not of debt; and they far exceed our deserving; but the parable does not go into this aspect of the matter. It confines itself to the warning against presuming that our merits, our distinguished services, can establish a claim upon God as of right.

182. *The Healing of Ten Lepers*

LUKE xvii. 11-19

The story is found only in Luke, but it has certain points of resemblance to the story of the healing of the one leper (Mark i. 40-45 and parallels). The command to show themselves to the priests, however, precedes the cleansing, which takes place as they are on their way. More significant is the fact that the point of interest is here not in the miracle, but in the response of the healed, and especially in the gratitude shown by the one Samaritan in contrast with the carelessness of the nine, who are presumably Israelites.

There are certain difficulties in detail. The geographical note is obscure. We are reminded that Jesus is on his way to Jerusalem, but it is hard to give a meaning to the phrase 'through the midst of Samaria and Galilee.' Perhaps it means 'along the border of Samaria and Galilee' (Creed), but this would hardly carry him towards Jerusalem. More likely Luke is simply preparing a setting for a situation in which a Samaritan might be found in the company of Jews, who normally 'had no dealings with the Samaritans' (John iv. 9). Luke's map of Palestine is pretty vague, and it is evident that his sources did not furnish details of the itinerary. There is a further difficulty in the instruction to a Samaritan to show himself to 'the priests', since the priests of Jerusalem are indicated. Creed is probably right in his suggestion (*St. Luke*, pp. 216-17) that this is 'an ideal scene, founded upon the story in Mark, which has taken shape in a Gentile Church: Jesus is shown as the beneficent healer who lavishes his goodness upon all who need, and receives thankful homage from the alien.' The final saying of Jesus: 'Arise and go on your way; your faith has saved you', raises the further question — are the nine who did not return also saved? Is the expression of gratitude equated with 'faith'? And why are the nine reproached with failing to return to 'give glory to God', when they are simply carrying out their instructions to go and show themselves to the priests? The fact that such questions really admit of no answer confirms the conjecture that the scene is 'ideal' — that is, an artificial construction.

183. *On the Kingdom of God*

LUKE xvii. 20-21

There are few sayings of Jesus which have been so much debated over the centuries as this: 'Lo, the kingdom of God is in the midst of you (or, within you)'. The question cannot be settled on linguistic grounds; it involves fundamental problems of the theology of Jesus. There can be no doubt that the preposition *entos* in Greek usage means 'within', not 'among' or 'in the midst of'. But if the saying is authentic, *entos* will have been used to render an Aramaic preposition, and all the Aramaic prepositions which could underlie it are ambiguous (Manson, *Sayings*, pp. 303f.).

No attempt will be made here to offer a history of the debate or even to indicate the main lines of argument; for this, the reader is referred to the monograph of B. Noack, *Das Gottesreich bei Lukas* (Uppsala, 1948). To the writer, the meaning 'within' seems utterly incompatible with everything else that Jesus has to say about the kingdom of God; he never speaks of it as an inward disposition, but as a sphere of rule — a social order in which the will of God is done on earth as it is done in heaven. It is given to men by God; and men are called to enter it. 'It is a fact of history, not of psychology' (Manson, loc. cit.). Moreover, the thought is not present, but future; and the point is that it will appear suddenly. There can be no *paratērēsis* ('observation') — no scanning of the heavens (as in the divinations of astrologers) for indications of its approach. The question of the Pharisees cannot be answered, no one can predict 'when' it will appear. Its coming will be instantaneous and total.

This saying occurs in an altered form in the *Gospel according to Thomas* (Logion 113). Here it is the disciples who put the question, and Jesus answers: 'It will not come when it is expected; men will not say, Lo, here! or Lo, there! But the kingdom of the Father is spread over the earth and men do not see it.' A similar idea (and probably a reflection of the same text) is found in Logion 51, where Jesus says to his disciples: 'What you expect has come, but you do not know it.'

184. *The Day of the Son of Man*

LUKE xvii. 22-37

The reply of Jesus to the Pharisees is made the starting-point of a discourse to the disciples on the shape of things to come. The association is Luke's; in his editorial arrangement the question and answer of the preceding section are certainly intended to be the introduction to this eschatological discourse, with the lightning-like appearance of the Son of Man taking the place of the sudden and unexpected manifestation of the kingdom of God. But the connection is not primitive, and the passage itself is composite. Much of it is 'Q' material, which Matthew has conflated with the Marcan apocalypse (Mark xiii; Matt. xxiv; §§ 218, 224); the rest is peculiar to Luke. As we have noted before, Luke conflates 'L' and 'Q', but does not conflate either with Marcan material.

The sayings of Jesus about the future have been transmitted in a certain confusion, which can be traced to several causes. First, predictions of the fall of Jerusalem and the destruction of the Temple were intermingled with prophecies of the end of the old world-order and the inauguration of the kingdom of God. Secondly, predictions of the coming of the Son of Man as the minister of God in the Last Judgment were interpreted as predictions of a second coming of Jesus in heavenly glory, to execute judgment and to inaugurate the rule of God on earth; the language that Jesus had used in speaking of the coming of the Son of Man was transferred to himself — he was identified with the Son of Man of whom he had spoken. Finally, the title 'Son of Man' was applied to him in the activities of his earthly life, becoming a surrogate for the title 'Messiah'. This was probably facilitated by the fact that Jesus spoke of himself at times as 'son of man', by an Aramaic idiom in which the phrase is not a title, but merely a surrogate for the personal pronoun 'I' or 'me'. This usage has been reflected in our Gospels, in the occasional variation between 'the Son of Man' and the personal pronoun in parallel versions of the same saying (see notes on § 123).

It should be said that the above paragraph does not represent a consensus of opinion among scholars. There is no consensus; and it will be found that most scholars of the English-speaking world entertain very different views from those expressed above. See especially V. Taylor, *The Names of Jesus*, chap. vii; and G. S. Duncan, *Jesus, Son of Man*, pp. 147-153. A survey of recent discussion is given by A. J. B. Higgins in his article 'Son of Man-*Forschung* since "The Teaching of Jesus"' (*New Testament Essays: Studies in memory of T. W. Manson*, 1959).

Verse 22 offers a difficulty of its own in the use of the plural 'days'. Everywhere else, including the remainder of this very passage, the expression is 'the Day of the Son of Man', and it marks a point of time, not an epoch. It has much the same sense as 'the Day of the Lord' in O. T. usage. A longing for 'one of the days of the Son of Man' is intelligible only in the sense of a longing to have Jesus back on earth again, a wistful desire to relive the days of companionship on the roads of Palestine. Such a meaning would be wholly out of place in this context, and unexampled anywhere else in the New Testament. A solution of the difficulty has been offered by C. C. Torrey (*The Four Gospels*, p. 312), who postulates a mistranslation from Aramaic due to the error of taking the adverb *lachda* ('very much') as the numeral 'one' with the sign of the accusative. The correct rendering would then be 'you will greatly long to see the day of the Son of Man', with the meaning that they will pass through a period of distress, seemingly endless, before the day of light dawns for them. Compare Mark xiii. 19-20, § 216.

Verses 23 and 24, with their Matthaean parallels, speak of the coming of the

Son of Man in terms that closely resemble those concerning the coming of the kingdom of God in *v.* 21; but in *v.* 25 we have a sentence which rests upon the conception that Jesus in his Passion and Rejection is already the Son of Man or the Son-of-Man designate. This verse is not represented in the Matthaean parallels at any point, and must be regarded as a secondary, theological formation. Verses 26 to 30 are cast in a rhythmic structure in two strophes, one built round the example of Noah, the other round Lot; in the Matthaean parallel, the rhythmic structure is abandoned, and the second strophe is dropped. The thought here is not of the wickedness of the generation of the Flood, or of Sodom, but wholly of their bland unconcern with the impending crisis; similarly the present generation goes about its everyday affairs, taking no thought for the disaster that is about to strike – the impending judgment of God which will make their preoccupation with social, business, and agricultural pursuits utterly pointless. Verses 31 and 32 are drawn from a different context of thought, and probably owe their place here to a purely verbal association — the example of Lot leads on to the reference to Lot's wife. But the warning to flee belongs to a temporal crisis, when flight is still possible provided there is no delay; in the Day of the Son of Man, flight is impossible, with or without possessions. This saying is more intelligible in the context of a prophecy of the fall of Jerusalem, as in the Marcan parallel (Mark xiii. 15f., and parallels; § 216); and it is more likely to reflect a prophetic oracle of the time of the Jewish War than a saying of Jesus himself. Verse 33 introduces a saying which we have already encountered in the context of the summons of Jesus to all his followers to bear the Cross (Mark viii. 35 and parallels, § 123). Here it can only mean that while the Christian may flee in the face of danger — and may find himself in a situation which compels him to flee without waiting to get his possessions – he must not seek to save his life at the cost of denying Christ. Verses 34-35 [36] return to the theme of *vv.* 26-30 – the judgment will come upon people in the midst of their daily occupations; it will separate husband from wife, workman from comrade, maid from maid. Verse 37 is an isolated logion, which Matthew has placed differently. It probably bears upon the suddenness of the judgment, comparing it to the swiftness with which the vultures gather around a carcass. It is a grim picture, which emphasizes the ghastliness of the catastrophe which is to strike. But both the question and the answer seem artificial in relation to the theme; and we may conjecture that a popular proverb has found its way into the tradition of the sayings of Jesus.

185. *The Parable of the Unjust Judge*

Luke xviii. 1-8

This parable has something in common with the parable of the Unjust Steward (§ 174), in that the lesson is drawn from the behaviour of a person who is far from admirable in himself. The central thought here is that if the most hardened judge, who cares for neither God nor man, can be moved to take the appropriate action by the importunate pleas of a widow – the very type of those without either wealth or influence to assist them – how much more will God, who is altogether just and merciful, give effect to the unceasing prayers of his elect, and see that their wrongs are righted, and that those who now oppress them are punished.

In its present form, the parable seems to reflect a situation of acute and prolonged persecution, like that of the martyrdoms of the Apocalypse (Rev. vi. 9-11). It is implied that the burden of the prayer is: 'How long, O Lord holy and true, dost thou not judge and avenge our blood upon the inhabitants of the earth?' But this is not the situation of the lifetime of Jesus. It is not sufficient, with Bultmann (*History*, p. 175), to set aside the comment of *vv.* 6 to 8 as secondary, for the importunity of the widow requires its counterpart in the cry that rises day and night from the elect. Probably the whole construction is a prophetic message of assurance from a time of trouble for the Church; or else we must hold that a parable of Jesus which spoke much more generally of the certainty that God will answer the prayers of his people has been radically transformed to meet the despairing mood of the long persecution. (W. L. Knox thinks that 'the amount of alteration required to adapt a promise of answer to persistent prayer into a promise that the end of the persecution and the day of vengeance were at hand was trifling' — *Sources*, II, p. 113). The fact that Jesus is called 'the Lord' would rather favour the conjecture that the parable is in its entirety the creation of a teacher of later times.

In any case, Luke's introduction conveys a mistaken idea of the purpose of the parable; it is not an exhortation to importunity in prayer. It assumes that 'the elect' are in fact praying unceasingly — 'crying to God night and day' — and its central point is the assurance that their prayers will certainly be answered by God, though he seems slow to act. The closing phrase of *v.* 7 describes God's attitude towards the persecutors, not towards the petitioners. It is not that he is slow to heed their prayers, but that he is longsuffering with the evil men, in the hope that they may yet repent. Compare 2 Peter iii. 9, where the same verb is used; and Romans ii. 4. Verse 8b is an isolated logion. Luke must have found it attached to the parable in his source, and the verbal association ('Son of Man') has led him to place the paragraph here, following the catena of sayings on 'the Day of the Son of Man'. Its meaning is obscure. Perhaps it is to be interpreted as a warning that those who so earnestly implore the intervention of God on their behalf may not themselves be found blameless when the great Day dawns. The emissary of God will come, but 'who may abide the day of his coming, and who shall stand when he appears?' (Mal. iii. 2; the suggestion is Wellhausen's).

186. *The Parable of the Pharisee and the Publican*

Luke xviii. 9-14

This parable seems to be coupled with the one before it in Luke's arrangement by the adventitious fact that both of them are concerned with prayer. The theme here reverts to that of chapter xv — God's acceptance of the sinful man who comes to him in humble penitence; but the main emphasis is where Luke's introductory sentence lays it — on the warning to the self-righteous. It contains in itself the essence of St. Paul's whole doctrine of Justification (without, however, his theology of the Cross), in its repudiation of the righteousness which rests upon the confidence that it has fulfilled all God's requirements and has no need of his mercy and grace. It is not suggested that the Publican is a more upright character than the Pharisee; on the contrary, the significant thing about him is that he has no merits at all. God 'justifies' the ungodly, the undeserving, the sinful. This is a fitting climax to 'the Gospel of the Outcast', as T. W. Manson has styled the long block of 'L' material which began in chapter xv (*Sayings*, pp. 282, 312). Luke now picks up again the Marcan framework, and holds to it, with some additions and minor changes of order, till it comes to its conclusion with the story of the Empty Tomb.

The last sentence (*v.* 14b) is a generalizing conclusion which is not directly relevant to the parable; it really bears upon the reversal of fortunes in the age to come.

On this parable, the comments of Jeremias are particularly worthy of attention (*Parables*, pp. 111ff.).

III. THE JUDAEAN PERIOD
§§ 187-253

MATTHEW xix. 1-xxviii. 10 MARK x. i-xvi. 8

LUKE xviii. 15-xxiv. 12

According to the Marcan construction, Jesus now leaves Capernaum (ix. 33 – the last indication of place) and passes by way of Peraea (the region east of the Jordan, still in the territories governed by Herod Antipas), where only five incidents are laid, to enter Judaea by way of Jericho, and so to proceed to Jerusalem. All the remaining scenes of his Gospel are laid in the Holy City itself, and are represented as enacted within a period of eight days, from the Sunday of his entry amid the acclamations of the crowds to the Sunday of his resurrection, when the women come to his tomb and find it empty. Matthew keeps to the same framework, with minor rearrangements, and some notable additions, nearly all of them peculiar to his Gospel. These include a number of parables of major importance (xx. 1-16; xxi. 28-32; xxiv. 37-xxv. 46), and some legendary surcharges in the Passion Story (xxvii. 3-10, 19, 24-25, 51b-53, 62-66), and in the story of the Empty Tomb (xxviii. 2-4, 9-10, 11-15). Besides this, he has expanded the Discourse against the Pharisees (Mark xii. 37b-40) with masses of additional material, some of it from 'Q', much from 'M'; on the other hand he has shortened the Marcan apocalypse (Mark xiii. 5-37), by transferring a considerable section of it to his Mission Charge (x. 17-21) and distributing its closing verses (§ 222) among three separate parables.

Luke does not take notice of the movement into Judaea. He began his account of the journey from Galilee to Jerusalem in ix. 51, and he depicts a steady and unbroken continuance until the city is reached. But from this point on, he holds very closely to the Marcan framework. There are only a few additions of any consequence — the story of Zacchaeus, the Parable of the Pounds, the Lament over Jerusalem, the story of Jesus before Herod (§§ 194, 195, 197, 245); there are also a few omissions — the Cursing of the Fig Tree, the Anointing at Bethany, the Mocking of Jesus (§§ 199, 201, 232, 247); and there are some transpositions of material. The variations in the Passion Story are nevertheless sufficient to have led some scholars to hold that Luke had an independent version; but even so the degree of resemblance between the Lucan account and that of Mark is far more striking than the differences in detail. The most notable change in Luke's treatment comes in the story of the Empty Tomb, where the suggestion of a return to Galilee is explicitly removed, and all the Appearances of the risen Lord are localized in Jerusalem and its environs.

1. *The Journey to Jerusalem*
§§ 187-195

MATTHEW xix, xx MARK x LUKE xviii. 15-xix. 27

Matthew has introduced his parable of the Labourers in the Vineyard into this sequence; otherwise he follows Mark, section by section. Luke does not take note of any change of scene; he omits the whole of § 187, limiting his report of Jesus' teaching about Marriage and Divorce to the single saying which he has given already (xvi. 18). He also omits the story of Jesus and the Sons of Zebedee (§ 192), for he will be using a variant version of it in his account of the Last Supper (xxii. 24-27; § 237). Otherwise he follows the Marcan narrative faithfully. At its end he adds a story drawn from his own store, which is laid in Jericho; and the Parable of the Pounds, which he will present, in an independently transmitted version, as part of a sequence of parables which follows his version of the Synoptic Apocalypse, two days before the Passover (cf. Matt. xxvi. 1-2).

187. *Marriage and Divorce*

MATTHEW xix. 1-12 MARK x. 1-12

Matthew has revised the Marcan introduction by adding his closing formula (to signalize the completion of the discourse of ch. xviii), and speaking of the healing activity of Jesus instead of his teaching. The geographical note is vague, and there is a textual problem in Mark which adds to the obscurity. (See the notes of McNeile and especially of Taylor.) It is fairly clear that Mark had no definite information about the route which Jesus followed on his journey from the north to Jerusalem, and that neither of the other Evangelists could supply the lack. There is really no evidence in the Synoptics that Jesus ever went into Peraea, but the Fourth Gospel places his meeting with John the Baptist in 'Bethany (Bethabara?) beyond the Jordan', and brings him back there for a time towards the end (John i. 28; x. 40-42). On the strength of these indications, M. Goguel has argued that Jesus taught for some time in Jerusalem in the autumn, until the Feast of the Dedication (December), and then retired into

Peraea and remained there until just before the Passover at which he was to be crucified (*Life of Jesus*, pp. 238-50, 401-28); but this whole ingenious argument throws no light upon the account of the Synoptics. Vincent Taylor gives the salutary warning that 'we feel the lack of chronological information in our primary authorities at this stage in the journey, due to their lack of a biographical interest, and the temptation to imagine situations for sayings and parables must in consequence be resisted' (*Life and Ministry*, p. 156). Until we come to the story of Bartimaeus, the tradition as it was available to Mark contained no indications of time or place, and he has arranged his material topically — geography and chronology do not enter into it.

In the Pronouncement-story which follows, Matthew seems to be responsible for turning the unnamed questioners of Mark into Pharisees (although the evidence for the omission in Mark is confined to Codex Bezae, the Sinaitic Syriac, and some Old Latin witnesses). Apart from his rearrangement of the dialogue, we must note that he adds the clause 'except for fornication' to the saying about divorce (so also in *v.* 32; § 24); it is generally agreed by commentators that the excepting clause is not attributable to Jesus. He omits the second clause of the Marcan saying, probably because the provision for a wife divorcing her husband had no relevance in Jewish law, in which divorce was open to the husband alone. The remarkable supplement (Matthew xix. 10-12) is quite unparalleled elsewhere in the Gospels, and the interpretation is difficult. The interpretations of the Fathers uniformly take the phrase about those who 'become eunuchs for the sake of the kingdom of heaven' as a reference to voluntary celibacy, commended not for everyone, but for those who are 'able to receive it'.

Additional Note. On the Sayings concerning Divorce.

The Rev. Charles R. Feilding (Dean of Divinity and Professor of Moral Theology in Trinity College, Toronto) has made some notes for me on the divorce-sayings, to the following effect.

In Mark, x. 12, there are several variant readings, and it is not clear which has been followed in RSV (*Gospel Parallels*). The three most important variants may be represented as follows:

i. The reading generally adopted by modern editors: 'If she (or, if a woman) when she has divorced her husband, marries another, she commits adultery.'

ii. Some MSS. put the first verb in the 3rd singular and the second verb in the passive: 'If a woman divorces her husband and is married to another, she commits adultery.'

iii. An important group of authorities gives a reading which is preferred by C. G. Montefiore, V. Taylor, and others: 'If a woman leaves her husband and marries another', etc.

Dr. Feilding draws attention also to the fact that 'the so-called exceptive clauses in Matt. v. 32 and Matt. xix. 9 are different. Matt. v. 32 may better be translated 'apart from a charge of unchastity' (*parektos logou porneias*). Matt. xix. 9 reads 'except for unchastity' (*mē epi porneias*)'.

He then compares Mark x. 2-12 with 1 Cor. vii. 10-11. The verb *apoluō* ('divorce') of Mark is not used in the Pauline passage; in its place we have *aphiēmi* (literally, 'send away').

'In the epistle the wife is bidden not to *separate* from her husband; in the first two readings of Mark x. 12 given above, the hypothesis is that she *divorces* him; in the third, that she *leaves* him. The last may be compared with the reading of the epistle, though the verb is different.

'There are four phrases of admonition in the epistle: (i) the wife should not separate from her husband; (ii) if she does, let her remain unmarried; (iii) or else, let her be reconciled to her husband; and (iv) the husband should not "send away", i.e. divorce, his wife. None of these expressions is found in Mark; the only similarities are the common reference to a man divorcing his wife and to a wife leaving her husband (using the third Marcan variant).'

He goes on to remark on the different legal assumptions of the first two Marcan readings, against the epistle and the third variant. 'Under Jewish law a husband could divorce his wife, but a wife could at best leave her husband, without right of divorcing him; for convenience we shall call this situation Palestinian. Under Roman law either husband or wife could divorce the other; again for convenience this may be called the Roman situation ... There is another difference, partly of a legal character. The admonitions of the epistle contain no mention whatever of *adultery*, but are confined to forbidding the *separation* of spouses, and to requiring either reconciliation or no further marriage if separation should occur. While the same opposition to divorce occurs in different language in Mark x. 2-9, without mention of adultery, the remainder of the Marcan passage (*vv.* 10-12) is exclusively devoted to defining two hitherto unknown offences against the seventh commandment.'

'Thus while a case can be made for a link between 1 Cor. vii. 10-11 and Mark x. 2-9, there is no parallelism between the epistle and Mark x. 11-12 (apart from the Palestinian legal assumption noted above).'

In Luke xvi. 18 (§ 176), there are no variants of importance. The legal assumption is Palestinian. It is sometimes claimed that there is a common source for this verse and Matt. v. 32, but in fact the first clause deals with a different legal question.

Dean Feilding also says 'When we come to Matt. v. 31-32, it is important to compare this pericope with those which precede and follow it in the Sermon on the Mount. Here the contrast is one between a law concerned with a legal detail (a divorced woman must be given the proper document) and the teaching of Jesus, which opposes divorce altogether on the ground that it *makes* a divorced woman become *an adulteress*. In Greek the expression is even stronger, for the verb "makes" is reinforced by a passive infinitive of the verb *moicheuō* ("to commit adultery"), as if exculpating the wife and emphasizing the guilt of the husband. This general line of thought appears in no other passage; this fact should caution us against regarding it as parallel with any of the other sayings.' This consideration leads Dean Feilding to look upon the phrase 'apart from a charge of unchastity', not as an exception to the prohibition of divorce, but as simply the matter-of-fact recognition that if the wife has already committed adultery, her husband cannot be held guilty of driving her into it by divorcing her. Apart from such a charge (duly proved against her), he must be held responsible for her subsequent behaviour. 'If the exceptive clause had been omitted it would not have altered the meaning, for it only states the obvious.'

Returning now to § 187, Dean Feilding notes that in Mark x. 10 the scene changes, and the saying of Jesus in vv. 11 and 12 is not addressed to the Pharisees, but communicated privately to the disciples; but the parallel saying in Matthew (the second clause, that of Mark x. 12, is omitted) is added to the retort to the Pharisees, and the private discussion which follows is upon a different subject. After drawing attention to the way in which Matthew has changed the Marcan report of the dialogue between Jesus and the Pharisees, he goes on:

'The effect in Matthew thus far agrees well with *vv.* 31-32 and redoubles the Marcan form of the attack on the contemporary practice in the matter of divorce. However, having done this, Matthew adds to this fourth speech of the dialogue his own peculiar construction in v. 9, an entirely new element.

'Matt. xix. 9 presents the following difficulties: (i) it contradicts what has just preceded it; this is a far more serious difficulty than its contradiction of the other New Testament evidence; (ii) it expresses an already familiar rabbinical view, and therefore seems hardly sufficient to provoke the surprised exclamation of *v.* 10; (iii) so many hands have attempted to remedy the text that uncertainty must have been felt about it from an early date.

'I consider the most likely solution to be that in opposition to Pharisees of his own day, Matthew attempted to bring together the attack on divorce which he found in Mark and the perfectly compatible doctrine of *v.* 32, and that in so doing he produced the awkward construction represented by xix. 9. At all events, the verse is his own literary construction, as his treatment of the whole passage shows. It would be an anachronism to suppose that his intention was in any way related to later legal developments in Eastern Orthodoxy or in the Reformation; similarly, anachronisms derived from Western canon law must not be read into the other evidence. The New Testament material was conceived in a totally different legal and cultural milieu.'

188. '*Suffer little Children*'

MATTHEW xix. 13-15 MARK x. 13-16 LUKE xviii. 15-17

The passage has no more connection with the preceding one in Mark and Matthew than with the parable of the Pharisee and the Publican, which it follows in Luke. Commentators are reduced to suggesting that a saying about children is placed after a discussion about marriage. Two points may be noted. First, Mark x. 15 should probably be regarded as a separate saying, which distorts the primary meaning of *v.* 14. The child is prized for his own sake, not as an example of the disposition required for entrance into the kingdom of God. Matthew has felt free to transfer it to a different context. Secondly, both Matthew and Luke have removed the tokens of human emotion from the Marcan story; nothing is said of the displeasure of Jesus, or of his putting his arms round the child. Matthew even introduces the more or less formal rite of the laying on of hands.

189. *The Rich Young Man*

MATTHEW xix. 16-30 MARK x. 17-31 LUKE xviii. 18-30

The theme of conditions of entrance into the kingdom of God is continued, though without any reference to the condition of childlikeness, and we are never told just what quality it is in the child that is the prerequisite for entrance into the kingdom. The condition now stressed is renunciation, and we have the contrast between the rich man who refuses to make the act of renunciation which Jesus requires, and goes away in sadness, and the disciples who have left everything to follow the Lord and are assured of a hundredfold compensation in this life, and in the age to come eternal life.

It is improbable, however, that the whole concatenation of dialogue is primary, though Mark may have found it in substantially this form in his own source. We have again a composite structure, made up of three main elements: (i) the dialogue with the rich man (*vv.* 17-22); (ii) the comment of Jesus, with the astonished reaction of the disciples (*vv.* 23-27); and (iii) Peter's question and the answer of Jesus (*vv.* 28-30). Verse 31 is a floating saying, doubtless authentic, which Luke has used in another context, more appropriate than this (xiii. 30; § 165).

It seems likely that the second part is itself composite, in that the question and answer of *vv.* 26-27 are a secondary supplement to the pronouncement of *v.* 25, which may always have been coupled with that of *v.* 23 (as in Luke). There is certainly something artificial about the question: 'Who then can be saved?' The disciples have not been trained to imagine that if a rich man can hardly enter the kingdom, it will be impossible for others; on the contrary, the kingdom has been promised to the poor from the very beginning of the Gospel. We would conclude that the saying: 'With men it is impossible, but not with God; for all things are possible with God' was transmitted without context, and that a way was found to introduce it here as a supplement to the story of the rich man.

I see no reason to hold (with V. Taylor) that 'Mark has information which enables him to weave x. 17-22, 23-27 and 28-31 into a whole' (*St. Mark*, p. 424). If the weaving was not already done in a pre-Marcan tract (so W. L. Knox, *Sources* I, pp. 69f.), as the triple structure would suggest, there is nothing here which indicates a personal knowledge so detailed; and Mark himself is quite capable of putting together a series of sayings which all bear upon the one theme — the call for the renunciation of earthly possessions for the sake of the kingdom.

Matthew has introduced two major changes in the Marcan story, along with a few verbal alterations and some abridgment. Most striking is his change in the wording of the opening dialogue (*vv.* 16-17). He cannot abide the implications of the reply of Jesus: 'Why do you call me good? There is no one "good" but One — God' (Mark x. 18). He therefore prepares his way by changing the form of the rich man's question; he no longer addresses Jesus as 'Good Teacher', but asks, 'Teacher, what good thing shall I do?' Jesus then replies with the quite inappropriate answer, 'Why do you question me about the good?', as if the man were inviting a debate upon the *summum bonum*. Yet he follows this with a form of the Marcan continuation which has lost its relevance: 'One (masculine) is the good.' This is akin to his recasting of the story of the Baptism to avoid the implication that Jesus, like the others, comes to John for a 'baptism of repentance for the remission of sins' (§ 6). Luke does not fear to retain the troubling words, though it is not to be supposed that either he or Mark doubted that Jesus could be called 'good' as God is good. Taylor's note should be read; after surveying the varying interpretations that have been offered (most of them representing an intolerable apologetic), he insists, correctly and courageously, that 'the question along with the statement that God alone is good implies a contrast of some kind between Jesus and God', and proceeds to the (theological) explanation that Jesus' 'question implies a tacit contrast between the absolute goodness of God and His own goodness as subject to growth and trial in the circumstances of the Incarnation' (*St. Mark*, ad loc.). This is undoubtedly too subtle for either Mark or Luke; but however they may have understood it, it is certain that neither of them saw in it any kind of acknowledgment of a consciousness of sin on the part of Jesus. It is harder to be certain of the mind of Jesus himself in the matter, but it is undeniable that our records never represent him as labouring under any sense of guilt.

The second of Matthew's major changes is the introduction of the saying of *v.* 28, which has a partial parallel in Luke xxii. 28-30 (attached to a catena of sayings on 'Greatness in the Kingdom of God'; § 237b). It bears upon the high destiny of the Twelve Apostles, who are to share with 'the Son of Man' (here certainly identified with Jesus, and depicted as the supreme Ruler of the kingdom of God) in his rule over the kingdom. *Palingenesia* ('regeneration') is not found elsewhere in this sense in the New Testament. It has no connection with the 'Hellenistic' conception of the religious experience of the Christian believer (as in John iii. 3ff.; 1 Pet. i. 3; Titus iii. 5), but denotes the transformation of the whole creation in the age to come (Rom. viii. 21; Acts iii. 21; etc.).

We may also note that it is Matthew who describes the questioner as a 'young' man; this is probably a mistaken inference from the words 'from my youth' (Mark x. 20), which Matthew omits. The words imply rather that he is no longer young. In Luke he becomes a 'ruler'. Both Matthew and Luke omit the statement that 'Jesus looking upon him loved him'. This is in keeping with their general reluctance to attribute human emotions to Jesus.

Professor Cadbury comments (conflating the descriptions): 'How often, like the rich young ruler in the Gospels, a young man comes across our path aware of the advantages that he has received of economic security and good health, of breeding and education, of family and friendships, and aware also that something more is required of him? Here is a burden he cannot today unload by getting rid of what he possesses. He can only be satisfied by a character and service to others proportionate to the advantages he has enjoyed. Nothing less will meet the moral demands he makes upon himself than a kind of voluntary overtime' (*Jesus: What Manner of Man*, pp. 27f.).

The version of this story which appears in the *Gospel according to the Hebrews* is of extraordinary interest. See especially the discussion of Wellhausen (*Einleitung in die drei ersten Evangelien*, pp. 114f.); and compare the very different estimate of Jeremias (*Unknown Sayings of Jesus*, pp. 33-6).

190. *The Parable of the Labourers in the Vineyard*

Matthew xx. 1-16

This parable is found only in Matthew. It has no connection with the thought of the preceding section, and appears to owe its place here to the purely verbal link of the concluding saying (*v.* 16; cf. xix. 30), which must therefore have been in the source. It cannot, however, have been attached to the parable originally, for it does not point out the lesson that is being taught. The parable has nothing to say about a reversal of fortunes in the judgment; it speaks of the equality of reward — the first and the last share and share alike.

The centre of interest here is not so much the labourers as the owner; it might better be called 'the Parable of the Eccentric Employer'. This employer does not deal with men on a strict basis of *quid pro quo*. The first labourers take offence at his generosity. Their complaint is not that he has cheated them by giving them less than he promised, for they have in fact been paid the agreed wage; their complaint is that he has paid their tardy comrades more than was their due, and has given them no bonus for their long toil. 'Is your eye evil?' here is equivalent to our 'Is your nose put out of joint' (because I am generous to the others)?

This parable is not a sketch of the history of salvation, nor yet a lesson in the principle of payment according to need regardless of the service rendered, any more than it is a defence of unregulated capitalism ('Am I not permitted to do what I will with my own?'). It is not an allegory, and the detail cannot be pressed. Basically it is a rebuke to those who protest against the opening of the kingdom of God to the undeserving. Those who have spent their whole lives in the service of God must not be annoyed when they find him bestowing his goodness freely upon the sinners who are entering his service at the eleventh hour. God is like the Eccentric Employer; he does not bestow his rewards in strict proportion to our deserving.

In its present context this parable seems to contradict the promise of xix. 28, that a special honour will be reserved for the Twelve. Here, as Wellhausen has pointed out, 'the moral is akin to that in the story of the sons of Zebedee (*v.* 23, below), where it is said that the martyrs, even the earliest and the most distinguished, cannot look forward to the highest rank in the Messianic kingdom without more ado' (*Evangelium Matthaei*, p. 96). But he follows Jülicher in treating the parable as an allegory from start to finish (and consequently not authentic).

191. *The Third Prediction of the Passion*

MATTHEW xx. 17-19 MARK x. 32-34 LUKE xviii. 31-34

The strange and puzzling words of Mark's introduction (*v.* 32) are probably due to a conflation of sources at this point. This is the first time, in Mark, that Jerusalem is mentioned as the goal of the journey, and the passage conveys the impression that Jesus now makes his final resolve to bring things to their issue in the Holy City; all his followers are affected with his manifest perturbation of spirit. Luke has spoken much earlier of Jesus' fixed intention to go to Jerusalem (ix. 51), and now he omits mention of it; Matthew follows Mark but omits his description of the amazement and fear of his followers. Luke's final verse appears to be introduced as a substitute for Mark's introduction. As before, both Matthew and Luke replace Mark's 'after three days' by the equivalent phrase 'on the third day'. Otherwise they follow Mark very closely, except for Luke's phrases about the fulfilment of prophecy (*v.* 31).

It is apparent that the three prophecies of the Passion are not different pronouncements spoken on three distinct occasions, but three versions of the one saying. As Bishop Rawlinson remarks: 'Each of the three predictions ... taken by itself, would give the impression that the subject had not been mentioned before; and the disciples are represented as showing the same lack of understanding on each occasion' (*Gospel according to St. Mark*, ad loc.). This points clearly to the fact that they have been drawn from three different sources; W. L. Knox takes this version as that of the 'Twelve-source' which he (following Eduard Meyer) believes can be isolated as one of the major written sources of Mark (*Sources* I, pp. 25f.). At all events, the multitude of detail, as compared with the greater generality of the other two predictions, indicates that in this form the prediction has been recast in the light of the Passion-narrative; to that extent it is a *vaticinium ex eventu*; and an examination of the vocabulary supports this view (so Taylor, *St. Mark*, pp. 436f.). Even here it will be noticed that Matthew alone introduces the mention of crucifixion — in itself a sufficient indication that such a prophecy could be amplified beyond the text, as late as the writing of this Gospel — how much more readily in the period of oral transmission.

192. *Christ and the Sons of Zebedee*

MATTHEW xx. 20-28 MARK x. 35-45

The section is composite, and the elements of the composition are extraordinarily hard to unravel. It falls readily enough into two main divisions, *vv.* 35-40 and 41-45 (Mark), but each of these is itself composite and it is in the analysis of the subordinate elements that the great difficulty lies.

The first main division bears upon precedence in the future kingdom of God; the second, upon the present attitudes of the followers of Jesus, in words which naturally establish principles for the leadership of the Church, but are perfectly intelligible without this further application. There is, accordingly, no natural connection between the two divisions; and the conclusion that they were originally separate fragments of tradition is confirmed by the observation that Luke has preserved an independent version of the second part, and has set it in a context (the Last Supper), where the ambitious request of the sons of Zebedee would be utterly incongruous (Luke xxii. 24-27).

If we now examine the first part, we note that it assumes that the disciples (or at least the two petitioners) have come to grasp that the path of suffering of which Jesus speaks is the way to glory, and they are concerned to obtain for themselves the highest possible distinction in the glory that is to follow the sufferings. Matthew has sought to relieve the apostles of the unworthiness of such a request by introducing their mother to voice it on their behalf; but the reply of Jesus is directed to the brothers, not to her, and she is not mentioned again – the artificiality of her appearance is manifest. He also excises the baptism-figure, perhaps for no reason beyond the desire to abbreviate (according to his custom). The addition 'by my Father' (*v.* 23) merely makes explicit the meaning of Mark's impersonal phrase.

These minor alterations do not affect the general character of the paragraph as it stands in Mark. Even taken by itself it cannot be regarded as a unity. The first answer of Jesus (*v.* 38) asserts that the request is based upon the most profound misunderstanding; the second (*v.* 40) implies that he accepts the general conception of the coming kingdom which underlies the request of James and John – that he is to reign in the fashion of an earthly king, surrounded by a court with degrees of precedence; and only denies that the assignment of places is in his hands. That is to say, the petition is first rejected on the ground that it is ill-advised, and then on the ground that it does not lie within the power of Jesus to grant it. The two answers are profoundly incompatible, and the second is in flagrant contradiction of the teaching (itself wholly characteristic of Jesus) which is to be found in the second division – that the followers of Jesus are not to strive for precedence over others, but to devote themselves to the service of others. The significance of this teaching is largely dissipated, if the spirit of service to others on earth is to find its motive in the hope of precedence over others in heaven (or in the age to come – in this respect, the precise form of the future hope makes little difference). Self-seeking ambition is hardly even refined by being transferred to a transcendental realm.

In the view of R. Bultmann, *vv.* 38 and 39 are a secondary element – a *vaticinium ex eventu* interpolated into the unified structure constituted by *vv.* 35 to 37, and *v.* 40 (James and John ask for the highest places, and get the simple answer that they are not at the disposal of Jesus). The primary structure itself he regards as a product of the Christian community; certainly it would be hard to look upon it as a genuine fragment of tradition. Yet it must be said that as a community-product it is strangely thin. It seems better to take the original unit as consisting of *vv.* 35 to 39, with *v.* 40 as a supplement, or a drastic recasting of a saying to the effect that martyrdom does not confer a title to precedence. There is a great deal to be said for the view that *vv.* 38 and 39 are a *vaticinium ex eventu* (Wellhausen, Dibelius, R. H. Lightfoot and many others), though the case has been weakened by the tendency to support it with invalid evidence; it is ridiculous to say that this view 'involves a quite monumental preference for the inferior evidence' (Knox, *Sources* I, pp. 72f.; see also his note, pp. 73-6). It cannot be demonstrated that John died along with his brother James (as this view requires us to conclude), but neither is there a particle of evidence to indicate that John survived James.

McNeile remarks that 'the request of the two, and the indignation of the others, follow the prediction of suffering in *vv.* 18f. [Matthew], as the dispute in xviii. 1 (Mark ix. 33) follows the similar prediction in xvii. 22f. (Mark ix. 31f.), and in both cases the scene is "on the road" (Mark). The possibility must be recognized that they are doublets of the same account' (*St. Matthew*, ad loc.). This 'possibility' seems to me to be close to a certainty, once we have granted that the three predictions of the Passion are variant versions of a single saying. In the doublet, a general dispute over precedence has been particularized into an ambitious request by the two brothers, with consequent indignation on the part of the ten, when they hear about it (taking *v.* 41 as the end of the first part — 'The story ... may simply have ended abruptly with the saying that the Ten were angry with James and John' — Knox, *Sources* I, p. 72). If this general view of the pericope be admitted, it will be hard to deny that the reconstruction of this doublet was built round *vv.* 38 and 39 as a *vaticinium ex eventu*.

In the second division Matthew again follows Mark almost word for word, but the Lucan parallel appears to have been derived from a different source. In both versions the introductory words are little more than a frame for the sayings. In both, Jesus first contrasts the self-assertive temper and conduct of the rulers of earthly kingdoms with the spirit of service to others which is to prevail in the community of his followers, and then offers himself as a pattern. It will be noted that the self-designation 'the Son of Man', of Matthew and Mark, is replaced in Luke's version by the personal pronoun 'I'; once again we are given cause for hesitation in taking 'Son of Man' as a significant *title* of Jesus here. But the most striking difference is the complete lack in the Lucan version of anything corresponding to Mark's concluding phrase: 'to give his life a ransom for many'. The authenticity of this phrase has been much debated, and is still in dispute. This may at least be said, that it does not belong in this context; the shift in the thought from that of service as the whole spirit and purpose of a life of leadership to that of a death — the offering of the same life — which becomes a 'ransom' — this is unquestionably, as Wellhausen remarked long since, a *metabasis eis allo genos*, a transition to a different category (*Evangelium Marci*, pp. 84f.). I should be inclined to regard it as a theological comment, added to the original saying ('the Son of Man came not to be served but to serve') in the feeling that this did not of itself adequately express the purpose of the Incarnation. The idea of the death of Christ as a ransom is not peculiarly Pauline, but a part of the general doctrinal teaching of early Christianity; but apart from this verse it does not appear in the teaching of Jesus as recorded in the Synoptics. It might be added that while Jesus offers himself as a pattern in that he came not to be served but to serve, the same cannot be said of his giving his life as a ransom. His followers lay down their lives for him and for the Gospel, even for the sake of the Church which is his body; but the death of a martyr is not 'a ransom for many'.

We may take occasion here to draw attention to a characteristic feature of these reports. Nothing is ever said of the response of the other parties — whether friends or foes — to the pronouncements of Jesus. Does the teaching on service strike home to the hearts of the disciples? Are the Pharisees satisfied with his defence of his conduct in eating with tax-collectors and sinners? The tradition shows not the slightest interest in such questions. *Ipse dixit* — the Master has spoken; the question is closed.

193. *The Healing of Bartimaeus*

MATTHEW xx. 29-34 MARK x. 46-52 LUKE xviii. 35-43

The story has a number of peculiar features. First, the blind man is named in Mark, but his name is omitted in Matthew and Luke. In no other miracle-story of the Synoptic tradition is the patient given a name; a partial parallel is found in the mention of Jairus (Mark v. 22), which is kept in Luke but omitted in Matthew. In that instance there is the possibility that the name has come into Mark through assimilation to the text of Luke, but no such explanation could be advanced here. As a rule the attachment of names to the characters in these stories is a secondary feature. Secondly, Jesus is hailed as 'Son of David' — the only instance of this appellation in Mark or Luke; it is abandoned in the continuation, where the blind man calls Jesus 'Rabbuni' ('Kyrie' in Matthew and Luke). This may reflect an association between this story and the description of the Entry into Jerusalem in pre-Marcan tradition; the title 'Son of David' prepares us for the acclamation of the crowds.

Both Matthew and Luke hold very closely to the language of Mark, but both remove much of his vivid detail (the encouragement of the crowd, after they have tried to silence him; the picture of the blind man casting aside his cloak and leaping up to come to Jesus). Luke transfers the scene from the departure from Jericho to the approach to the town, and at the end he adds a stock phrase (*v.* 43b). More surprising changes are found in Matthew. As in the story of the Gadarene Demoniac, he turns the one patient into two (on this feature, see the remarks of R. Bultmann on the thematic use of pairs in literature and in art; *History,* pp. 314-17). And in the account of the cure, he adds the phrase: 'Jesus took pity on them and touched their eyes' (*v.* 34). We have seen how frequently Matthew removes from Mark's narrative indications of human emotion in Jesus; here he introduces one which does not come from Mark. The touching of the eyes may be a reminiscence of the Marcan story of the Blind Man of Bethsaida (Mark viii. 22-26; § 121), which Matthew omits.

194. *Zacchaeus*

LUKE xix. 1-10

This Lucan anecdote appears to be a secondary and greatly amplified version of the Marcan story of the hospitality of Levi (Mark ii. 13-17; § 53; note that in the Lucan parallel it is Levi who gives the banquet). See Creed's introduction to the section (*St. Luke*, pp. 228-9); and his general discussion of the presence in the 'L' materials of 'a group of narratives more or less parallel to narratives in Mark' (p. lxviii). The detail of the little man climbing into the sycamore tree is attractive, but improbable; the narrow alleys of an ancient walled town would have no place for trees; Wellhausen takes this as an indication that the incident was originally located outside the town (*Evangelium Lucae*, p. 103).

It is not suggested that there is any *literary* dependence upon the Levi-story; the comparison opens our eyes to the extent of change which could come over a story in oral transmission.

195. *The Parable of the Pounds*

LUKE xix. 11-27

It is obvious that this is a variant version of Matthew's parable of the Talents; both are embraced under Professor Dodd's title, 'The Parable of Money in Trust'. We shall consider the two versions together.

We note, to begin with, that the general framework of the two stories is the same: a man going on a journey puts certain sums of money into the hands of his slaves, with instructions to make profitable use of them during his absence; and on his return he inspects their accounts, and deals with them according to the results which they are able to show. To those who have invested their funds profitably he commits larger responsibilities; to the one who has made no use of his capital but has concentrated on keeping it intact he administers a severe rebuke, deprives him of the sum with which he had been entrusted, and transfers it to the most successful of his fellow-slaves. It is apparent that in both versions the story revolves round the fortunes of three slaves, and the centre of interest is the last of the three, the one who has kept his capital safely guarded, but has not ventured to put it to work, to gainful use.

Now we may take note of the differences. Both versions have undergone a number of the transformations to which so many of the parables were subject in the course of transmission. Both have been embellished in various ways; both have been given an allegorical slant; both have had added to them, as a closing comment, an independent saying of Jesus which mistakes the purport of the parable; and both have been affected by a change of audience. Each of these types of modification may be considered in turn.

(*a*) Embellishment. In Matthew the amounts entrusted are greatly increased, and vary according to the ability of the slaves; in each case they are from fifty to one hundred and fifty times as great as the one mina ('pound') which each of the Lucan slaves receives. In Luke there are ten slaves, though only three are mentioned in the accounting. It is probable that in both cases the lesser number is the original — there were three slaves, and they received one mina each. The words 'You have been faithful over little things' (Matt. xxv. 21) have an odd ring as addressed to a slave who has been entrusted with such a sum as five talents — enough to pay the wages of a centurion and his whole company for four months.

Again, Luke's version introduces elements which seem quite alien to the parable proper. The master has here become a nobleman, and the purpose of his journey is to secure title to a kingdom; for a nobleman with hopes of a kingdom, the investment of ten minas would seem to be hardly worth noticing. Then we learn that the subjects over whom he hopes to rule hate him, and send a delegation to protest against his elevation to the kingship; and on his return he orders these opponents to be brought before him and slaughtered. These features are extraneous to the story of his dealing with his slaves, and it has often been suggested that they reflect a bit of Jewish history — the journey of Archelaus, the eldest son of Herod the Great, to Rome, to secure Roman consent to his accession at the death of his father, when fifty delegates of the Jewish community appeared before Augustus to oppose his petition. This has further influenced the parable, in that the reward given to the two 'good' slaves is the rule over a number of towns.

(*b*) Allegory. In Matthew the parable has been transformed into an allegory of the Last Judgment; indirectly, by its placing in the eschatological discourse of chapters xxiv and xxv; and directly, by the addition of the clauses, 'Enter into the joy of your Lord' (*vv.* 21b, 23b) and 'Throw the useless slave into outer darkness; there shall be wailing and gnashing of teeth' (*v.* 30).

In Luke it has become an allegory of the Parousia. The 'nobleman' represents the Lord Jesus, who has departed from this world 'to receive his kingdom and to return'. His 'citizens', who reject him for their ruler, are the Jews. His accounting with his slaves is the judgment which Christ will exercise upon his followers when he comes (1 Cor. iv. 3-5; 2 Cor. v. 10; etc.); his slaughter of his enemies is partly a reference to the fall of Jerusalem, with the accompanying deaths, viewed as an eschatological event, and partly Christ's execution of the Wrath of God upon 'those who do not know God and do not obey the gospel of our Lord Jesus' (2 Thess. i. 7b-9).

(*c*) The closing comment. In both versions the parable carries the closing comment: 'To him that has shall be given ("and he shall have abundance" — Matthew); and from him that has not shall be taken away even that which he has.' This saying is in all probability authentic; it is preserved independently in Mark iv. 25 and parallels (transferred in Matthew); but it certainly did not belong to the parable originally. The central thought of the parable is not to be found in this sentence. The good slaves are not rewarded because of what they had, but because they made good use of it; the useless slave is not condemned because he had nothing (in the Lucan version, and probably in the original parable, he had as much as the others to start with), but for his failure to make good use of it. This is one of those 'secondary generalizing conclusions' which have been attached to a number of the parables, sometimes by one or other of the Evangelists, sometimes (as here) at an early stage of oral transmission. They represent an early application of the parable in the teaching of the Church, and are not a clue to the sense intended by Jesus. 'The recognition of the fact that these generalizing conclusions occupy a secondary place in their context, is of the greatest importance for the understanding of the parables concerned, since their emphasis, as the result of the new conclusion, has in nearly every case been shifted, often fundamentally' (Jeremias, *Parables*, p. 87; cf. Dodd, *Parables*, pp. 147-9).

(*d*) The change of audience. In Luke the parable is represented as addressed to the company of Jesus' followers, as they are nearing Jerusalem amid feverish expectation of the immediate manifestation of the kingdom of God; and Luke's introduction explicitly states that it was intended to warn that there would be an interval between the coming appearance of Jesus in Jerusalem and his coming in power; that is to say, Luke uses the parable to explain that the expectation of an early Parousia of the Lord was an error from the beginning. Jesus himself had taught that there would be a relatively long interval, which would serve to test the capacity of his followers to exercise responsibility. In Matthew it is apparently addressed to the disciples, privately, upon the Mount of Olives (there is no suggestion of a change of scene after xxiv. 3).

But if the parable be considered in itself, without concern for the elements which have been shown to be secondary, it will appear much more likely that it was originally spoken to the representatives of official Judaism, and that it represents Jesus' condemnation of the longstanding policy of safeguarding the purity of the Jewish religion at the cost of failure to fulfil the mission of Judaism to the world. 'The Judaism of that time had no other aim than to save the tiny nation, the guardian of great ideals, from sinking into the broad sea of heathen culture' (J. Klausner, *Jesus of Nazareth*, cited by Dodd, *Parables*, p. 152). But for the nation, as for the individual, he whose concern is to save his own soul will surely lose it. The discipline of exclusion, of separateness, of 'building a fence about the Law' had all the appearance of deep piety and concern for the truth; but in the last analysis, it was like the burying of treasure in the earth.

The Church risks the danger of the same condemnation whenever she becomes more concerned to preserve her own purity, and to guard the deposit of her traditional faith, than to risk her treasure in the dust and turmoil of missionary enterprise.

2. *The Days in Jerusalem*
§§ 196-230

MATTHEW xxi-xxv MARK xi-xiii LUKE xix. 28-xxi

The Passion Narrative proper will begin with Mark xiv, and with the time-note that 'it was now two days before the Passover and the Feast of Unleavened Bread'. In the Marcan framework all the incidents and sayings of the Jerusalem ministry that precede it are compressed into three days. On the first day Jesus enters the city, visits the Temple, and returns to Bethany for the night. On the next day, he curses a barren fig tree, cleanses the Temple, and again leaves the city in the evening. On the third day the fig tree is seen to have withered away; Jesus enters the Temple again, is asked by what authority he is acting, and refuses to answer; he follows up his refusal by a parable which constitutes an attack on the existing leadership of the Jewish people. In a series of controversies he discomfits the Pharisees and their allies, then the Sadducees, and finally the scribes, putting all his opponents to silence, and warning the people against the scribes. At this point the little story of the Widow's Mites is inserted. Jesus now leaves the Temple, after prophesying that it will be razed to the ground, and withdraws to the Mount of Olives, where he delivers an apocalyptic discourse to four of his disciples privately.

This time-scheme is manifestly arbitrary, and it is probable that some of the incidents belong to an earlier stage of the ministry of Jesus. The tradition available to Mark had a relatively full and fixed account of the Passion, but provided him with little information about the ministry in Jerusalem. See V. Taylor's introductory note to this part of the Gospel (*St. Mark*, p. 450).

In Matthew, only two days are mentioned. On the first day Jesus goes to the Temple and cleanses it forthwith, answers a remonstrance of the chief priests and the scribes, and leaves the city, to spend the night at Bethany. On the second day he curses the fig tree and it withers before their eyes. With no other note of time (apart from 'on the same day' — xxii. 23) all the rest of Mark's material, except the story of the Widow's Mites, follows on the same day, with substantial additions of 'Q' and 'M' materials.

In Luke the time-indications are abandoned entirely; the impression is given that the ministry in Jerusalem continued for some time. Luke notes that 'he was teaching daily in the temple' (xix. 47), and ends this part of his Gospel with the short summary of § 230: 'He spent the days teaching in the temple, but for the nights he went out and camped on the mount called the Mount of Olives; and the whole population came to him in the temple early in the morning, to hear him' (xxi. 37-38). He omits part of the Marcan material (§§ 199, 201, and 222), adds a few verses (§§ 187, 223, and 230), and transfers his version of § 208 to his Travel Narrative (§ 143).

196. *The Entry into Jerusalem*

MATTHEW xxi. 1-9 MARK xi. 1-10 LUKE xix. 28-38

In this incident, both Matthew and Luke follow Mark very closely. The changes made by Luke are mainly verbal, of the nature of stylistic improvements, until we come to the account of the procession (*vv.* 37-38), which may be drawn from a different source ('L'). Matthew takes occasion to cite the prophecy of Zechariah ix. 9, as the prediction which is now being fulfilled. The opening words are actually from Isaiah lxii. 11, replacing the 'Rejoice greatly, daughter of Zion' of the Zechariah passage. The parallel Hebrew phrases: 'an ass, and a colt, the foal of an ass', have led to the strange doubling of the single animal of the Marcan story, and even to the still stranger description of Jesus as riding 'upon them' (*v.* 7). How Matthew pictured to himself a rider mounted upon two animals at once it is hard to say. In the cries of acclamation (*v.* 9), he adds to the first Hosanna the phrase 'to the son of David', thus indicating that the crowds are hailing Jesus as the Messiah. Probably he takes this to be implicit in the Marcan story. It will be noted that the familiar 'palm branches' are not mentioned by any of the Synoptic Evangelists; for them, we must wait for St. John.

If the incident is historical it must have been deliberately staged by Jesus as an object-lesson in his conception of himself as the lowly Messiah pictured by Zechariah. It is possible, however, that the simple circumstance that Jesus rode into the city on an ass, as did hundreds of others every day, has been elaborated in the tradition into this stage-managed demonstration. That he was the centre of a momentary wave of Messianic enthusiasm there is no reason to doubt; it is much less certain that he thought of himself in Messianic categories at all. See the excellent discussion of the incident by G. S. Duncan, in *Jesus, Son of Man*, pp. 126-31. He goes too far, however, in claiming that 'there is no escaping the conclusion that this act on Jesus' part was self-conscious and deliberate, and that it had a symbolical significance' (p. 130).

Attention must be given to the use of *ho kyrios* ('the Lord') in Mark xi. 3, in that this is the first and only instance of the use of this title for Jesus in Mark (and in Matthew). The difficulties raised by this are so great that W. C. Allen suggested that God is meant (*Gospel according to St. Mark* [London, 1915], p. 142), and Taylor thinks it is a reference to the owner of the colt — 'the owner needs him and will send him back here at once.' Equally unprecedented is the expression 'our father David' — there appears to be no instance of this phrase in Jewish literature, and only one elsewhere in N.T. — Acts iv. 25.

The cry 'Hosanna' and the carrying of branches belong to the ceremonies of the Feast of Sukkoth ('Tabernacles'), and these details have led some scholars to suggest that the scene was originally enacted at that festival, in the autumn preceding the Passover of the Passion; or at the Feast of the Dedication (in December). It is more likely that the story has been elaborated with the aid of elements from the ritual practices of one of these feasts.

197. *Prediction of the Destruction of Jerusalem*

Luke xix. 39-44

The section is composite. The first part (*vv.* 39-40) appears to be a parallel, with the place and the persons changed, to the incident which Matthew will incorporate into his account of the Cleansing of the Temple (xxi. 15f.). It attaches much more closely to the acclamations of the Entry (*vv.* 37-38) than to the prophecy which follows. Indeed, the passage (*vv.* 37-40) forms a unity, and may well be an independent version of the approach of Jesus to Jerusalem which Luke has conflated with the Marcan story. The Lucan setting is decidedly preferable to the Matthaean. On the second part, T. W. Manson remarks: 'The lamentation over Jerusalem comes with tremendous dramatic effect in the midst of the jubilant enthusiasm of the crowd' (*Sayings*, p. 319). If Jesus has not undertaken any ministry in Jerusalem before this, it seems strange that he should be convinced before he enters the city that his mission will end in rejection. In its present form, with all the particulars of the siege (*v.* 43), the saying has been modified in the light of the event; but there is every reason to hold that Jesus foresaw and predicted the fall of Jerusalem and the destruction of the Temple as clearly as Jeremiah had done more than six hundred years earlier (Jer. vii. 1-15; etc.).

198 to 201. *The Cleansing of the Temple*

MATTHEW xxi. 10-22 MARK xi. 11-25 (26) LUKE xix. 45-48

These four sections may be considered together. The narrative of the Cleansing of the Temple is the main matter (§ 200), and it alone is used by Luke; the rest consists of subsidiary material. Mark tells of a preliminary tour of inspection of the Temple (xi. 11) on the day before the Cleansing; this is omitted by the other two Evangelists. Matthew has introduced the story of the Cleansing with a brief account of the excitement caused in Jerusalem by the arrival of Jesus (*vv.* 10-11); we may notice that the crowds do not now proclaim him 'Son of David', but describe him only as 'the prophet Jesus'. This would confirm the hypothesis that the Entry was not interpreted as Messianic in the earliest tradition. Matthew adds his independent version of the remonstrance of the authorities, with the reply of Jesus (*vv.* 14-16). The critics are now 'the chief priests and the scribes' (in place of 'some of the Pharisees' of the Lucan version above); but they pass over the violent actions of Jesus (driving out buyers and sellers, overturning tables and benches) and confine their complaints to the shouts of the children. Clearly the incident is better placed in the story of the procession, where Luke has it.

The strange episode of the Cursing of the Fig Tree is the only cursing-miracle of the Gospels. Its symbolic significance leaps to the eye: it is a symbol of Israel, which has failed to bring forth the fruits for which God planted it, and is therefore condemned to perish. The same symbolism lies behind the parable of the Barren Fig Tree (Luke xiii. 6-9; § 162), and it is not unlikely that the miracle-story is a secondary form of the parable (Knox, *Sources* I, p. 82). Luke may have omitted the Marcan story because he recognized it to be a doublet of his parable. In Mark the withering of the tree is not observed until the following day; in Matthew it withers at once. The sayings which Mark has attached to the story (§ 201) are independent *logia* on faith and prayer. Matthew has transferred the last of them to the section of the Sermon on the Mount which deals with prayer (Matt. vi. 14; § 30). Mark xi. 26 is rightly omitted from the printed text; it is an assimilation to the text of Matthew, and is omitted in some of our most important witnesses.

The story of the Cleansing itself requires little comment. Matthew and Luke have abbreviated the Marcan story, without affecting its main lines or even its vocabulary in any significant way. Both have omitted the phrase 'for all the nations' (Mark xi. 11) from the citation, perhaps to throw into high relief the contrast 'house of prayer' — 'den of thieves'. Matthew omits the story of the plot to put Jesus to death (Mark xi. 18-19), which treats the Cleansing as the act which set in train the procedures that were to bring Jesus to the Cross so swiftly.

202. *The Question about Authority*

MATTHEW xxi. 23-27 MARK xi. 27-33 LUKE xx. 1-8

Matthew here follows Mark with only minor changes, none of them noteworthy. Apart from the introductory sentence, the same may be said of Luke; he alters a few phrases to improve the style, and he puts the priests' fears of the mob into articulate form: 'the whole population will stone us to death' (*v.* 6). But the only striking change comes at the very beginning, when he sets the incident not on the day after the Cleansing, as in Mark and Matthew, but much more loosely 'on one of the days that he was teaching the people in the temple, and preaching the Gospel'. The challenge of the authorities is thus made to bear upon the whole ministry of Jesus in teaching and preaching in the Temple, not upon his action in cleansing it.

'The authority' of which the priests speak in their challenge is presumably *legal* authority — has anyone in a responsible position authorized Jesus to act as he has done? The reply of Jesus implicitly transfers the question to a higher realm: the real question is whether his authority comes from heaven (that is, from God) or not. The explanation of the equivocation of the priests (Mark xi. 31-32) is of course secondary, and may be of Mark's own composing; the closing verse is probably secondary as well, for the answer to the challenge is really given in the counter question of Jesus concerning the baptism of John, which carries the implication: 'My authority, like that of John, is given by God.' It is hard to see in this 'a veiled claim that Jesus Himself is the Messiah' (Taylor, *St Mark*, ad loc., and many other commentators). Jesus is making the same claim for himself as he makes for John — that his authority comes from God, nothing more.

203. *The Parable of the Two Sons*

MATTHEW xxi. 28-32

McNeile notes that 'the parable is the first of a trilogy, all teaching that the leaders of the nation being unworthy, those whom they despise will take their places' (*St. Matthew*, ad loc.). This parable is peculiar to Matthew; the second of the trilogy is the Marcan parable of the Wicked Husbandmen; the third is an independently-transmitted parallel to Luke's parable of the Great Supper. We see in this another example of Matthew's fondness for groups of three.

There are extraordinary textual variations in these verses, and the original text is hardly to be constituted with certainty. See the analysis of T. W. Manson, *Sayings*, p. 222. In some witnesses, the order in which the two sons are mentioned is reversed, and the answer to the question of Jesus becomes, 'The last'. The point is unchanged; it is still agreed that the son who first said 'No', but afterwards repented and went, is the one who did his father's will. But in an important group of witnesses, headed by D (Codex Bezae), we have the sons introduced in the order of the text before us, but in *v.* 31 the surprising (defiant?) answer is given, 'The last'. That is, it is claimed that the son who said 'I will', but did not go, is the one who did his father's will.

In any case the point of the parable remains the same, whether the opponents of Jesus pronounce their own condemnation or not. The leaders of Judaism have given a nominal obedience to the will of God, but for all their good words, they have not obeyed him in practice. The tax-collectors and harlots began with open refusal of the commands of God, but since they have repented in response to the call of his prophet John, they are in better case than the religious leaders.

There is no substantial reason for regarding *v.* 32 as secondary, even though it occurs independently in Luke vii. 29-30 (in a very different form). I should be more inclined to feel that the mention of John is integral to the parable, and is an indication that it belongs to an earlier stage of the ministry.

204. *The Parable of the Wicked Husbandmen* (*Tenant-Farmers*)

MATTHEW xxi. 33-46 MARK xii. 1-12 LUKE xx. 9-19

After the discussions of Dodd (*Parables*, pp. 124-32) and Jeremias (*Parables*, pp. 55-60), it is no longer necessary to show that this is a genuine parable of Jesus, and not an allegory constructed by the early Church with the death of Jesus in retrospect. The process of allegorization has indeed set in; its first stages are visible in Mark, and it is carried through to completion in Matthew (not in Luke), but the basic story is a true-to-life vignette of relations between tenants and landlords in first-century Galilee. Even the murder of the owner's son, in the expectation that with his death the tenants themselves will gain permanent possession of the vineyard, is true to the situation. The tenants 'evidently have in mind the law that the estate of a proselyte who dies intestate may be regarded as ownerless property, which may be claimed by anyone, with the proviso that a prior right belongs to a claimant who is already in occupation. The arrival of the son allows them to assume that the owner is dead, and that the son has come to take up his inheritance. If they kill him, the vineyard becomes ownerless property which they can claim as being already in possession' (Jeremias, loc. cit., p. 59). But it is not necessary to suppose that the tenants have weighed the possibilities of the legal situation so closely. Egyptian fellahin would be quite capable of acting with equal brutality and of reasoning in the same way, in our own times, without a chance of finding their claim recognized in law. Indeed, wherever we find absentee landlords and an ignorant and poverty-stricken peasantry, violent outbreaks like this occur sporadically.

The details of the parable, accordingly, must not be pressed. The owner of the vineyard is an absentee landlord, but Jesus certainly does not think of the God of Israel as an absentee God. In its broad lines, however, the parable warns us that as the landlord will take measures to punish the tenants who have abused his representatives and refused to give him his due, so God will punish those to whom he committed the care of his 'vineyard' Israel (the figure goes back to the Song of Isaiah v. 1-7), and who have been unfaithful to their trust. This is about as far as we can go without allegorizing. With much less confidence we may accept the suggestion that the parable also conveys the thought that the affairs of Israel have come to a climax of rebellion; the age-long perversity that has turned a deaf ear to the prophets has come to a head in the execution of John the Baptist; and the blood of all the prophets that have suffered is to be required of this generation. But even John the Baptist would hardly be the 'son' in distinction from the 'slaves' who had been sent before him. Only Jesus himself will fit the picture, and if the detail is to be pressed at all, we shall see in the parable a veiled prediction of the death of Jesus himself. But I suspect that all this reads too much into the parable, however it may be justified by its fidelity to the thought of Jesus as given elsewhere.

The primary motif of the parable, then, is the warning that the leaders of Israel, who have abused their trust, will be called to a terrible accounting. Allied to this is the secondary theme, that the owner 'will give the vineyard to others'. This should probably be interpreted in the first instance in line with the prophecies of Ezekiel xxxiv, where a different figure is used but the same theme is expounded. The 'shepherds' of Israel have been using the flock of God for their own profit; therefore God will call them to account, and will himself be their shepherd, and will set a new David over them. There is no suggestion here of the transference of the privileges of Israel to the Gentiles, nor is it even suggested that the poor and the outcast to whom the Gospel is now preached will be given the responsibilities which the priests and scribes have misused.

The citation of Psalm cxvii. 22-23 (Mark xii. 10-11 and parallels) is a supplement to the parable, which can only have been added in Christian circles, after the Resurrection. The parable itself has nothing to say of 'the son' of the landlord, beyond the report of his shameful death; the citation presupposes the allegorical interpretation of the parable, the identification of 'the son' with Jesus, and the doctrine that he has been 'declared to be the Son of God with power by the resurrection from the dead'. It is probable that the details of the owners' care for his vineyard, drawn from Isaiah v. 2, are secondary; in Isaiah's poem, they are evidence of God's loving care for his people; in the parable, they are irrelevant, and would hardly be introduced until the parable as a whole had come to be viewed as an allegory. We may also look upon Mark's phrase 'many others, beating some and murdering some' (xii. 5b) as secondary, since it distorts the pattern of three, and may be taken to indicate that Mark is thinking of the long succession of prophets who suffered for their testimony. Luke has returned to the original pattern of three slaves; Matthew has multiplied them indefinitely, though this detracts from the realism of the story — for him it has become wholly an allegory of the history of salvation from the covenant of God with Israel, through the coming and rejection of Christ, to the transference of the kingdom to the Gentiles. The closing verse in the Lucan version is a detached saying, which owes its place here to the link-word 'stone'. But the stone is no longer the 'head of the corner' of the preceding quotation; it seems to combine the 'stone cut out of the mountain without hands' of Daniel ii, which smites and smashes the image of Nebuchadnezzar's dream (Luke's verb *likmēsei* is used in Theodotion's rendering of the passage), with the 'stone of offence' of Isaiah viii. 14-15. Matthew xxi. 44 (omitted in our text) is a gloss, inserted by assimilation to the text of Luke.

205. *The Parable of the Marriage Feast*

MATTHEW xxii. 1-14 LUKE xiv. 16-24

On the very different Lucan setting of the parable, see the remarks on § 170.

Here again we have a parable which has been transformed into an allegory in the course of transmission. Luke's version is the simpler, and stands closer to the original; allegorization does not affect the form until we come to the last three verses. The parable proper is complete with *v.* 21; the guests who were first invited have all begged off with flimsy excuses at the last moment, and the offended host has sent his slave to invite the beggars of the city streets in their place. The point is unmistakable. God's invitation to his great feast – a well-known symbol of the joys of the kingdom – is being rejected by the respectable, the 'righteous who need no repentance'; and the outcasts, the 'tax-collectors and sinners', are being invited in their place. Verses 22-23 are secondary; there is nothing corresponding to them in the Matthaean version or in that of the *Gospel of Thomas*, which appears to have been transmitted independently (see below). They represent an elaboration in the use of the parable by the Church; after the outcasts of Israel, the Gentiles receive the gospel invitation. This supplement is probably pre-Lucan, for the evidence indicates that Luke carries over allegorical material from his sources, but does not introduce it on his own account (Jeremias, *Parables*, p. 68). It reflects the missionary interest of the early Church. The closing verse is a further supplement, which hardly makes sense; since the invited guests have refused the invitation, the host does not need to say that none of them will taste of his supper. It is comprehensible only when the story as such is forgotten, and only the allegorical sense remembered; then the words of the host become the sentence of God, pronouncing judgment on the impenitent leaders of Israel.

In Matthew's version, the process of allegorization is far more advanced, and in addition to that, we have a conflation of two or possibly three parables. The ordinary citizen of the Lucan parable, with his one slave, has been transformed into a king with numerous slaves to carry his invitations, and armies to send against those who have insulted him; and the 'great feast' has become a wedding-banquet for the king's son. In Luke the invited guests are content to beg off with excuses; in Matthew they have refused the first invitation (*v.* 3), and now repeat their refusal at the last moment (*v.* 5), and 'the others' (whoever they may be) insult his slaves and put them to death. Verse 7 is an intrusion which makes nonsense of the parable; the king musters his armies, kills the murderers and burns their city (which is presumably his own city), and then sends out his slaves to invite others to the banquet which has apparently been waiting all through the campaign! The slaves are then bidden to go into the cross-roads of the city (which has been burned!) and invite everyone that they find to come to the wedding. Surely this is the strangest wedding-feast imaginable. But there is an equally incongruous supplement in *vv.* 11-13. The slaves have been instructed to invite everyone that they find at the cross-roads; there is no suggestion that they are to go home to dress; but now the king finds that one of them is not properly attired and orders him to be bound hand and foot and thrown into 'outer darkness'. The way for this supplement has been prepared by the addition of the words 'both bad and good' in *v.* 10; but with it the central point of the parable has been quite forgotten — it is no longer remembered that the Gospel is precisely for the outcast. Almost certainly, this is not an allegorical elaboration of the original parable, but a fragment of a different parable altogether, in which the point was the need to be always ready, always properly attired for the wedding, since the summons may come at any moment. There is a rabbinical parable which in its conclusion bears a remarkable resemblance to this Matthaean fragment (Manson, *Sayings*, p. 226). To Matthew, however, the point will be that the Church itself must undergo judgment. It is not a community of the predestined, but a *corpus permixtum*, containing 'both bad and good' (*v.* 10). The separation will take place at the Judgment Day. This is a recurring theme in Matthew; compare his interpretation of the parables of the Wheat and the Tares, and the Drag-net (ch. xiii. §§ 100, 102).

It is possible that *vv.* 6b and 7 should be regarded as a fragment of yet a third parable, which would be a companion-piece to the parable of the Wicked Husbandmen (Manson, *Sayings*, p. 225). But it is more likely that we should see in it nothing more than an elaboration of the allegory, introducing a reference to the fall of Jerusalem, viewed as the punishment inflicted by God for the rejection of Jesus and the deaths of the Christian martyrs.

See further my article, 'The Parable of the Guests at the Banquet', in *The Joy of Study: Papers ... to honor F. C. Grant* [New York, Macmillan & Co., 1951], pp. 1-14).

The version of the parable found in the newly-discovered *Gospel of Thomas* (Logion 64) is of the greatest interest. It lacks all the elements that we have distinguished as secondary in Matthew and Luke; its own modifications amount only to the introduction of a fourth refusal (the conventional pattern of three found in Luke must be regarded as original), and a closing sentence which appears to be a Gnostic contribution: 'Tradesmen and merchants shall not enter the places of my Father.' Apart from these additions, it seems to represent a more primitive form of the parable than either of the canonical versions, and the possibility must be entertained that 'Thomas' has drawn it either from an independent stream of oral tradition or from a very early documentary source.

206. *The Question concerning Tribute to Caesar*

MATTHEW xxii. 15-22 MARK xii. 13-17 LUKE xx. 20-26

Professor David Daube has shown that this and the three sections which follow have been arranged to correspond formally to a fourfold rabbinical pattern of question and answer; he points out particularly striking coincidences with the pattern of questions used in the 'Haggadah of the Seder', the service on Passover eve. Here the first question concerns a point of law; the second introduces the note of scoffing; the third is put by 'the *tam*, the son of plain piety' (corresponding to the scribe of the Marcan version, who is 'not far from the kingdom of God'); and the fourth is put by the father of the family, who now takes the initiative ('Four Types of Question', in *The New Testament and*

Rabbinic Judaism [London: Univ. of London, 1956], pp. 158-69). As the author of Mark is not trained in the literary methods of the makers of rabbinical literature, we must suppose that he found the four sections already thus arranged in his source, and that the source was edited by a Christian scribe at a very early period. The friendliness of the scribe who puts the third question would lend some support to this conjecture; the more so that in Matthew and Luke this question also is put in a more or less hostile spirit, 'testing him'.

The versions of Matthew and Luke are wholly derived from Mark. The strange alliance of Pharisees and Herodians appears again, as in Mark iii. 6; this is retained in Matthew, but in Luke the question is put by secret agents in the employ of the scribes and the chief priests, and this first question is made a pendant to the Parable of the Wicked Husbandmen. He has not been aware of the fourfold rabbinical pattern followed by his source (Mark); or at any rate, he has abandoned it. Luke also makes explicit the purpose of the trap that is being set for Jesus: 'to hand him over to the government, and to the jurisdiction of the procurator'. In keeping with this, Luke will include the charge of forbidding payment of the tribute to Caesar among the accusations laid against Jesus at his trial (Luke xxiii. 2). Other changes in the two later versions are no more than verbal and stylistic.

207. *The Question concerning the Resurrection*

MATTHEW xxii. 23-33 MARK xii. 18-27 LUKE xx. 27-40

After the Pharisees, the Sadducees take up the attack. This is the first time that we have encountered them in Mark; Matthew has introduced them early as objects of the denunciations of John the Baptist (along with the Pharisees), and again as joining the Pharisees in the demand for a sign (iii. 7; xvi. 1, 6). They were the party of the priestly aristocracy, very conservative, and they looked upon the doctrine of the resurrection of the dead as a Pharisaic innovation which found no support in the Torah. It has generally been supposed that their name is derived from Zadok, the high priest of King Solomon; but T. W. Manson made the suggestion that it is a transliteration of the Greek *syndikos* (our 'syndic'), and that 'Pharisee' is a transliteration of *Parsi* ('Persian'), which may have been used at first sneeringly of those who were advancing the Zoroastrian doctrines of resurrection and of angels and spirits into Judaism (*The Servant-Messiah*, pp. 15f., 19f.). At all events, the Evangelists are interested in them only in the matter of their denial of the resurrection.

Matthew's version is in the main a transcript of the Marcan story, with no significant changes. In Luke, however, though he follows Mark closely in the introduction and the putting of the question, with only occasional stylistic improvements, the answer of Jesus is cast in very different language in its first part (*vv.* 34 to 36); and his concluding verses (39-40) appear to be an echo of the Marcan conclusion to the following section (Mark xii. 32-34), which Luke omits at this point because he has used another version of the scribe's question as his introduction to the parable of the Good Samaritan (§§ 143, 144), in his Travel Narrative.

Luke's version of the reply of Jesus can hardly be regarded as his own free composition; there is no reason why he should make such remarkable changes in the words of Jesus at this point when he tends rather (except in the parables) to reproduce his source very faithfully, so far as the utterances of Jesus are concerned. It is almost certain that Luke has drawn upon another source for these three verses (34-36). See on this the remarks of V. Taylor, *Behind the Third Gospel*, p. 100. But if this be granted, we must suppose that the second part of the reply, in which Luke returns to the Marcan wording (37, 38a), was lacking in his other source; and this in turn would lend support to the view of R. Bultmann (*History*, p. 26) that Mark xii. 26-27 is a supplement to the basic reply. Bultmann regards the whole discussion as merely a reflection of 'the theological labour of the Church', and it must be admitted that it has an artificial atmosphere about it.

It is not generally noted that the reply of Jesus supports a doctrine of personal immortality, based upon the imperishable nature of a communion with the immortal God, but tells rather against physical or material notions of resurrection. Abraham, Isaac and Jacob have not 'risen from the dead' in any physical sense; what is claimed is that they continue to live with God.

208. *The Great Commandment*

MATTHEW xx. 34-40 MARK xii. 28-34 LUKE x. 25-28

For the general discussion of the passage, see the notes on § 143. The Marcan supplement (*vv.* 32-34) presents this one questioner in a favourable light; he gives hearty approval to the reply of Jesus and receives in return the assurance that he is 'not far from the kingdom of God'. This is in striking contrast to the generally hostile attitude attributed to the scribes in the Gospels, even in the section which immediately follows.

209. *About David's Son*

MATTHEW xx. 41-46 MARK xii. 35-37a LUKE xx. 41-44

In accordance with the rabbinical fourfold pattern, it is now the turn of Jesus to become the questioner, and to put a question that cannot be answered. Here Matthew has constructed a new introduction (*vv.* 41-42), and Luke has omitted the somewhat incongruous Marcan phrases: 'Jesus answering said, as he was teaching in the temple.' Both omit mention of the scribes as the interpreters who assert that the Messiah is the son of David, probably because of the fact that every Christian known to them would say the same. If this is an authentic saying of Jesus, which is very doubtful, it could only imply that he is challenging the scribal assertion — the Messiah cannot be the son of David, for David himself calls him 'my Lord'. But taken as a later formulation, it is not at all necessary to interpret it in this sense, though most of those who deny its authenticity do so. There is no indication whatever that the Davidic descent of Jesus was ever questioned in Christian circles at any time. It is perfectly possible, however, that the passage was constructed as a conundrum, which could never be answered by an unbelieving Jew, but only by one who had learned that Jesus was 'born of the seed of David according to the flesh, but declared to be the Son of God with power by the resurrection from the dead'.

Professor Daube, in the article mentioned above (§ 206), offers another explanation, based upon his general view of the question-sequence. One of the 'four types of questions' which he discusses concerns apparent contradictions between different verses from Scripture. With some hesitation about relying too much upon his Talmudic parallels, he remarks: 'If the New Testament question of *haggadha*, concerning the contradictory notions of the Messiah contained in Scripture, is closely analogous' (to the Talmudic examples) ... 'then the answer implied is not that one notion is right and the other wrong, but that both are right in different contexts' (op. cit., p. 163).

The Matthaean Discourse on the Approaching Judgment §§ 210-229

MATTHEW xxiii-xxv

These three chapters constitute the fifth of the great discourses into which Matthew has gathered most of the teaching of Jesus. In some ways it might be better to think of the discourse as commencing with chapter xxiv; but on the other hand this chapter of denunciations is placed here as a kind of preface to the apocalyptic sayings and parables of the two following chapters, and it is on the whole better to think of them all together, so far as Matthew's structure is concerned. This is the view of McNeile: 'Thus chs. xxiii-xxv form virtually one collection of sayings, the last of the five principal collections in Matthew' (*St. Matthew*, p. 329). The discourse will then fall into three main parts: (i) the Woes against the Pharisees (ch. xxiii), culminating in the prediction that the blood of all the prophets will be required of this generation, and the lament over the failure of Jerusalem to respond to her last hope of salvation; (ii) the Synoptic Apocalypse, introduced by the prediction of the destruction of the Temple, and ending with a group of parables which stress the need for watchfulness and faithfulness (ch. xxiv); and (iii) three parables of the Last Judgment, presented under different figures — the arrival of the Bridegroom, the Day of Reckoning, and the gathering of all the nations before the Son of Man (ch. xxv).

210. *Woes against the Pharisees*

MATTHEW xxiii. 1-36 MARK xii. 37b-40 LUKE xx. 45-47

It would seem that Mark xii. 37b should be taken as the conclusion of the preceding section. Note that in Mark (followed almost word for word by Luke, except in the introduction), we have a single sentence of warning against the scribes; there is no mention of the Pharisees. In Matthew scribes and Pharisees are grouped together as the recognized leaders of Judaism, sitting 'in Moses' seat' (a conception hardly possible while the Temple was still standing and the powers of the priesthood and of the Great Sanhedrin were still unimpaired); and the single sentence of Mark has been used as the nucleus of a long series of denunciations, under the repeated malediction: 'Woe unto you, scribes and Pharisees, hypocrites!' Part of the additional material is from 'Q', and has been used by Luke in his Travel Narrative (Luke xi. 39ff., § 154), where scribes and Pharisees are denounced separately. The remainder of the chapter is 'M' material, and reflects the intensity of the feeling against the leaders of Judaism in the period after the fall of Jerusalem, when the Christian Jews, as dissenters, felt the full weight of the pressure to close the ranks of Judaism and to impose the pattern of Pharisaic conformity on the whole nation in the effort to recover from the catastrophe. These 'M' verses all reflect a Palestinian environment, and forms of controversy which involve questions of Jewish Halakah of which the Gentile Churches would not even be aware.

On § 211, see the discussion under § 167, the Lucan parallel.

212. *The Widow's Mites*

MARK xii. 41-44 LUKE xxi. 1-4

This passage owes its place in Mark (and Luke) to the link-word 'widow' of the preceding section. Matthew omits it, probably because it has no bearing upon the theme of the coming Judgment, with which he is now concerned. The Lucan changes are again purely verbal and stylistic. The story is 'an isolated fragment as to the source of which there is no clue' (Knox, *Sources* I, p. 91). There are similar stories in Buddhist and in Greek literature, but there is no need to postulate borrowing in one direction or another.

213. *Prediction of the Destruction of the Temple*

MATTHEW xxiv. 1-3 MARK xiii. 1-4 LUKE xxi. 5-7

The section is composite. The first two verses are a self-contained narrative, centred in the prediction; the introduction is merely a frame for the saying. The scene is then abruptly transferred to the Mount of Olives (this change of scene is omitted in Luke); and the request of the disciples, clearly an artificial formulation, is simply the introduction to the apocalyptic discourse which follows. In Mark the apocalypse is delivered to a chosen group of four disciples; in Matthew it is 'the disciples' who come to Jesus; and in Luke there is no indication of the composition of the group. Matthew alone uses the word 'Parousia' – 'the sign when all these things are to be consummated' becomes 'the sign of your Parousia and of the end of the Age'. Needless to say, this is secondary; Matthew and Luke are here revising Mark, not drawing upon other sources. The close association of the apocalypse with the destruction of the Temple reflects the fact that the fall of Jerusalem was regarded in Christian circles as an eschatological event, a token that the end of the age was near.

The Synoptic Apocalypse
§§ 214-223

MATTHEW xxiv. 4-36 MARK xiii. 5-37 LUKE xxi. 8-36

The Marcan apocalypse is the heart of the Matthaean, and is almost wholly incorporated in the Lucan version. Matthew has, however, transferred three verses (Mark xiii. 11-13) to his Mission Charge (x. 19-21), and has not used the Marcan ending (§ 222), because he still has much to add. He has conflated with the Marcan sayings a substantial amount of 'Q' material which Luke has used in his Travel Narrative (§ 218; Matt. xxiv. 26-28 = Luke xvii. 23-24, 37; § 184), and has added a few sayings which are not found in the other Gospels (*vv.* 10-12). In Luke the departures from Mark are trifling, except for § 216. Apart from minor variations in the wording, he omits a few Marcan verses (*vv.* 21-23, 27, 32), substitutes an ending of his own for that of Mark (§ 223), and adds two verses from his own sources (*vv.* 18, 28). In § 216, however, his alterations are significant. He has changed the veiled oracle about the 'Abomination of Desolation' which is to be seen 'standing where it ought not' ('within, in a holy place' — Matthew), into a description of the siege of Jerusalem; the Marcan word 'desolation' remains, but only in the phrase 'her desolation is at hand'. It is really impossible to doubt that this is a recasting of the Marcan oracle, even if, as V. Taylor holds, the verse comes from a non-Marcan source (*St. Mark*, on xiii. 14). It is more probable that Luke himself has seen that the following verses are appropriate to the terrors of war, and not to an apocalyptic catastrophe from which, by its very cosmic nature, there can be no place of escape; and has therefore ventured to interpret Mark's words, which the 'reader' is charged to 'understand' (explain to the congregation?) as an explicit reference to the events of A.D. 66-70. But in its origin it is probable that the Marcan passage is a fragment of a Christian apocalypse which was issued in the time of Caligula, when the mad emperor threatened to profane the Temple by erecting a statue of himself in the Holy of Holies. The phrase 'Abomination of Desolation' in the book of Daniel, from which (as Matthew notes) it is taken, is a play on the name of the Greek god Zeus Ouranios, in Aramaic; and is a reference to the action of Antiochus Epiphanes in setting up an altar and sacrificing swine to Zeus over the altar of burnt offering, in 168 B.C. It is impossible to agree with Taylor's view that the Marcan version may 'have replaced an original reference to armies surrounding Jerusalem and menacing the Temple' (loc. cit.). Luke's word *erēmōsis* ('desolation') betrays its origin.

The Marcan apocalypse is itself a compilation of the most diverse materials. Not all of it, by any means, can be ascribed to Jesus himself; the passage we have just been considering (*vv.* 14-20) preserves 'a form of early Christian apocalyptic which goes back to a period anterior to the assassination of Caligula in A.D. 41' (Knox, *Sources* I, p. 104); much of the remainder consists of conventional commonplaces of Jewish apocalyptic literature, which can certainly not be ascribed to the creative mind of Jesus; and such genuine sayings as are embedded in the discourse are distorted by their context, so that they leave a totally wrong impression. The chapter is carefully analysed by

W. L. Knox (*Sources* I, ch. xiii, 'The "Little Apocalypse"'), and it seems unnecessary to discuss it further here. Modern theories of its composition are passed in review by G. R. Beasley-Murray, and a fresh interpretation offered, in his two recent books, *Jesus and the Future* (1954) and *A Commentary on Mark XIII* (1957). See also W. G. Kümmel, *Promise and Fulfilment*, trans. D. M. Barton (1957), pp. 91-104.

The little parable of the fig tree (§ 220) is probably authentic, but in this context it has been given an application very different from that intended by Jesus. In Mark and Matthew, as the appearance of leaves on the fig tree is a sign that summer is near, the terrible disturbances in society and in nature will be the sign that the Son of Man is about to appear in judgment; in Luke, that the kingdom of God is near. Luke has in a measure recaptured the original sense of the parable: the coming of the predicted disasters is a time for the followers of Christ to lift up their heads, for their redemption is near at hand (*v.* 28; § 219). But in its origin this parable was in all probability not set in the context of a forecast of the future, but was an invitation to men to see in the new spiritual life burgeoning through the ministry of Jesus a sign of the day of salvation. 'It is the day of salvation because the Saviour is already here' (Jeremias, *Parables*, p. 96; cf. Dodd, *Parables*, p. 137, n. 1).

The Marcan Ending to the Discourse (§ 222) seems to contain echoes of two parables which are told in fuller form in Luke and Matthew, namely the parable of the Money in Trust (Talents, Pounds) and the parable of the Doorkeeper (Luke xii. 35f., § 158).

The Lucan Ending (§ 223) is independent of Mark, and serves to close the discourse on a note which reflects the Church's experience of the dangers of succumbing to the lures of the world. Bultmann feels that the terminology is so closely related to that of St. Paul as to justify the conjecture that Luke has used a fragment of a lost letter of Paul (*History*, p. 119). This hazardous conjecture is hardly necessary. Luke might well hesitate to use the Marcan ending, in view of its echoes of parables which he has preserved in full, and so be moved to compose a suitable closing exhortation in his own words.

On §§ 224, 225 and 226, see the comments on the parallel passages in Luke (§§ 184, 158). This is 'Q' material, which Luke has worked into his Travel Narrative; clearly, its insertion at this point is due to the editorial arranging of Matthew.

227. *The Parable of the Ten Virgins*

MATTHEW XXV. 1-13

This parable as it stands is a full-blown allegory of the second coming of Christ as the heavenly Bridegroom. The ten virgins represent the waiting Church, some of its members prepared, and some unprepared; the delayed arrival of the bridegroom reflects the postponement of the awaited Parousia; and the exclusion of the unready members of the waiting party, the judgment of the Church (again viewed as a *corpus permixtum*) by Christ at his coming. In this form it cannot be regarded as authentic. It seems likely that it is an allegorizing recasting of the parable of the Doorkeeper (Mark xiii. 33-36; see comment on Luke xii. 35-46, § 158), which speaks of the return of the master of the house from a journey (Mark) or from a wedding (Luke), but does not make him himself the bridegroom. The notion of a bridegroom delaying his arrival so long that the wedding attendants fall asleep is utterly incongruous; and the refusal of admission to the tardy five, with the assertion of the bridegroom that he does not know them, is equally out of touch with reality, and far removed from the accuracy of observation which characterizes the genuine parables.

Verse 13 is clearly secondary, whatever view we take of the parable as a whole. The lesson is certainly not, in this case, 'Be awake, for you do not know the day or the hour'. It is 'one of those hortatory additions which people were so inclined to add to the parables' (Jeremias, *Parables*, p. 41), often *mal à propos*. Both the wise and the foolish virgins fell asleep, and no blame is attached to them for that; the fault is that the foolish five were not prepared to carry out their duties when they awoke.

The authenticity of the parable is defended by both Dodd and Jeremias, not in its present allegorical form, but as a story which had originally no reference to the Parousia. The point is then seen in the suddenness of the arrival of the bridegroom (*v.* 6), which represents the moment of crisis, and 'has its parallels in the sudden downpour of the Flood, in the unexpected entry of the thief, or in the unlooked-for return of the master of the house from the feast or the journey' (Jeremias, op. cit., p. 42). But the parallels are not really very satisfactory. The arrival of the bridegroom is certainly not unexpected, since the party of ten virgins has been formed precisely to meet him; and it is not sudden, but long delayed! I cannot see how this defence can stand. See also the remarks of Gunther Bornkamm, in his article 'Die Verzögerung der Parusie' (*In Memoriam Ernst Lohmeyer*, pp. 119-26). The delay of the bridegroom was not 'originally quite unstressed' (Jeremias); it is the hinge of the whole story, and its interpretation as representing the delay of the Parousia is not secondary, but precisely what the framer of the allegory intended. It is therefore not conceivable that our Lord himself is the author, for though he may have spoken of his Parousia (and not merely of the Parousia of the Son of Man), no one will claim that he predicted that it would be *delayed*.

On § 228, the Parable of the Talents, see the discussion under § 195, the Parable of the Pounds.

229. *The Last Judgment*

Matthew xxv. 31-46

This is not a true parable, but a prophetic vision; there is nothing comparable to it elsewhere in our tradition of the teaching of Jesus. Its authenticity is doubtful. There can be no doubt that for Matthew, the Son of Man who sits on his glorious throne to judge all the nations is Jesus himself, and the context makes it clear that the Judgment is to take place at his Parousia. It will be observed that here again, as in all the explicitly eschatological passages where the title occurs, it is far from clear that Jesus is thinking of himself as the Judge who is to come. It is not unlikely, then, that Jesus himself spoke of the coming of the Son of Man in substantially these terms; that is, that there is an authentic utterance of Jesus at the basis of this passage. It has, however, like most of the parables, undergone some retouching and modification in the usage of the Church. Thus the surprising shift from 'the Son of Man' to 'the King' at *v.* 34 is a reflection of the dual function of Jesus as Judge of all the world and as ruler over the kingdom of God; and his reference to God as 'my Father' (*v.* 34) reflects the doctrine that Jesus is the Son of God: the Son of Man, the Judge and Deliverer of apocalyptic expectation, is not elsewhere designated as God's son. (This is not to call in question the filial consciousness of Jesus himself.)

It must be admitted, however, that the passage contains virtually nothing that is distinctive of the teaching of Jesus, and the possibility remains open that, like other elements of the 'M' material, it has been borrowed from Jewish apocalyptic sources (Bultmann, *History*, pp. 123-4; C. H. Dodd also appears to suspect it — *Parables*, pp. 85-8, with the concluding remark: 'that the Son of Man Himself is judge is not stated in our earliest sources, nor is the form the judgment will take made plain'). Professor Kilpatrick suggests that: 'It seems to have been a sermon which has passed into the evangelical content' (*Origins*, p. 97). The case for authenticity is best put by Jeremias (*Parables*, pp. 142-5), though he too distinguishes a number of secondary elements; he concludes, with T. W. Manson (*Sayings*, p. 249) that: 'Our pericope, although it may not be authentic in every detail, contains, in fact, "features of such striking originality that it is difficult to credit them to anyone but the Master himself".'

§ 230 is Luke's conclusion to his account of the Jerusalem ministry; as mentioned above, it implies that Jesus taught daily in the Temple for a considerable period before his arrest.

3. *The Passion Narrative*
§§ 231-253

MATTHEW xxvi. 1-xxviii. 10 MARK xiv. 1-xvi. 8 LUKE xxii. 1-xxiv. 12

The Passion Narrative has been transmitted to us, apparently from the beginning, not as a number of self-contained incidents, but as a coherent whole. It is the essential nucleus of the entire Gospel story; it is scarcely too much to say that all the rest is introductory to this. 'Jews ask for a sign and Greeks are in quest of wisdom', writes St. Paul, 'but we preach Christ crucified, an offence to Jews and folly to Gentiles, but to those that are called, both Jews and Greeks, Christ — God's power and God's wisdom' (1 Cor. i. 22-24). The basic framework of the story thus became fixed in the form of its transmission relatively early. It was still capable of receiving occasional accretions, as we can see when we compare Matthew's version with that of Mark, partly by way of legendary growth, still more by details drawn from Old Testament passages which were interpreted as predictions of the Passion. Both these tendencies are illustrated by Matthew's elaboration of the story of Judas; first he introduces 'thirty pieces of silver' as the price of betrayal, from Zech. xi. 12; and later he gives us an obviously legendary account of the remorse and suicide of Judas and of the use of the bribe-money to purchase a burial-ground for foreigners, which is built up out of a peculiar combination of passages from Zechariah and Jeremiah (xxvii. 3-10; § 243). Even in Mark there are a few additions, notably the story of the Anointing at Bethany, which cannot be regarded as integral parts of the primary Passion Narrative; and it is probable that details were preserved, which might otherwise have fallen into oblivion, because it was felt that they were clear fulfilments of prophecies.[1] But the basic structure of the early narrative remains unmodified in its main features — the plot of the Sanhedrin, the treason of Judas, the Last Supper, Peter's denial, the agony in the Garden, the arrest, the questioning before the Sanhedrin, the trial before Pilate, the sentence, the mocking (and scourging — omitted in Luke), the impressing of Simon of Cyrene to carry the cross, the crucifixion, death and burial. The story of the Resurrection was of course inseparable from the Passion Narrative at all times, but the form of its telling was not so firmly fixed; for the essential matter here was not the story, but the apostolic testimony that Jesus was risen. In fact there is no part of the Gospel story that shows less fixity than the accounts of the appearances of the risen Jesus, strange as that may seem; and the appearance that is acknowledged to be the first of all — the appearance to Peter — is never described at all, but only reported at second hand (e.g. Luke xxiv. 34).

In the Marcan story, which stands closest of all to the primitive Passion Narrative, it is striking to see how little is contained in the way of sayings of Jesus. After he has been arrested and haled into the presence of the High Priest (Mark xiv. 53), he speaks only three times, namely, his reply to the High Priest (xiv. 62), his reply to Pilate (xv. 2 — two words), and his cry from the cross (xv. 34 — four words cited). Both Luke and Matthew make considerable additions to this small store, but without greatly weakening the impression of majestic silence. This is the story of a salvation which is accomplished not through words, but through acts, through the endurance of suffering and death in compliance with the will of the Father; and our attention is not diverted from the contemplation of the Victim who offers himself in sacrifice. Yet there is no attempt to evoke our emotions, whether of pity for the Sufferer or of admiration for the Hero. The emphasis is on the accomplishing of the will of God, as it has been revealed in the prophetic oracles; and the intention is to evoke faith in Jesus as the Saviour, not to stir our human feelings of sympathy or indignation. The story is all the more moving for the objectivity with which it is set down.

In this part of the Gospels, accordingly, we are in close touch with the earliest traditions of the Church. There are of course surcharges, but the story as a whole is faithful to the facts. 'What we have in the primitive Passion Narrative is the stark recital of facts, with only a minimum of the current

[1] Two distinct effects are to be observed here. In the earliest stage, particular details, in themselves of minor significance, were preserved in the tradition because men observed how closely they corresponded to passages of the Old Testament which spoke of the sufferings of the upright. In the later stages there is an increasing tendency to add fresh particulars, not because they are found in an existing tradition, but because they can readily be drawn from a passage which has already been interpreted as a prophetic vision of the Crucifixion. Psalm 22 affords instances of both, and it is not always possible to determine whether a given detail belongs to the original tradition conveyed by witnesses of the Crucifixion or is the product of reflection upon the Psalm.

interpretation — the story of Jesus' death as it was recited in the early Christian communities for almost forty years before Mark took pen in hand to write out the full story of Jesus as he had heard it and as he understood it' (F. C. Grant, *The Earliest Gospel*, p. 186).

There are indications that Mark has made use of two versions of the story in documentary form (to which he may have added some elements derived from oral tradition). See the analyses of V. Taylor (*St. Mark*, Additional Note J, 'The Construction of the Passion and Resurrection Narrative', pp. 653-64), and W. L. Knox (*Sources* I, chap. xiv, 'The Passion Story', pp. 115-47).

231. *The Conspiracy of the Jews*

MATTHEW xxvi. 1-5 MARK xiv. 1-2 LUKE xxii. 1-2

233. *The Betrayal by Judas*

MATTHEW xxvi. 14-16 MARK xiv. 10-11 LUKE xxii. 3-6

The original unity of these two sections has been broken by the interpolation of the story of the Anointing in Mark and Matthew; Luke has restored the connection by omitting the interpolated story. Luke otherwise follows Mark closely, with many coincidences of wording. He makes two significant changes. In *v.* 2 he omits the phrase of the priests, 'Not during the feast', because he realizes that it implies that Jesus was arrested before the Passover began and consequently that the Last Supper was not a Passover meal, as he understood it to be from his other sources. And in *v.* 3 he ascribes the treachery of Judas to the prompting of Satan, who thus reappears for the first time since the Temptation, when he 'went away from Jesus until the appointed hour' (iv. 13 — *achri kairou*; Luke has omitted Mark's addition to the story of the Messianic Confession, where Peter is rebuked as Satan's mouthpiece — Mark viii. 32-33). Here (*v.* 4) and again in *v.* 52, Luke introduces the commanders of the Temple police ('captains'), perhaps from the sources which he will use for the book of Acts (Acts iv. 1, etc.); they are not mentioned by Mark or Matthew.

Matthew has rewritten the introduction to incorporate the formula which marks the end of a major discourse (*v.* 1), and has worked Mark's note of time into a forecast of the Crucifixion (*v.* 2). He depicts the plot of 'the high priests and the scribes' (Mark, Luke) as a formal meeting of the Sanhedrin (*v.* 3), and he gives the amount of the bribe to be paid to the traitor as 'thirty pieces of silver' (*v.* 15), and indeed tells us that the money was paid down (in Mark and Luke it is promised him). But this is not to be taken as a fresh piece of information; the significant words are all drawn from Zechariah xi. 12 (LXX): 'They paid down my wages, thirty pieces of silver.' There is no reason to suppose that Matthew found these details in any other source; this is typical of his use of prophetic phrases, without concern for the original context, as predictions of Christ.

The most important feature of this introduction to the Passion Narrative is precisely the matter that Luke omits — that the authorities were anxious to get Jesus into their hands *before* the Passover (Mark xiv. 2). It follows that the indications which describe the Last Supper as a Passover meal must be drawn from a different source. According to the analysis of W. L. Knox (*Sources* I, pp. 16ff.), these two sections formed the introduction to the Passion Narrative in the 'Twelve-source', which continued with the account of the Supper (Mark xiv. 17-21), after a sentence of preparation which has been replaced by the circumstantial narrative of *vv.* 12-16, taken from the 'Disciples-source'. He holds that 'the knowledge that the arrest and crucifixion took place before the Passover is a striking testimony to the value of the Twelve-source, as against the other tradition which Mark combines with it, and the statement may rest on good authority. The later identification of the Last Supper and Eucharist with the new Passover meal has led to the assumption in the other source that the Last Supper must have been the Paschal Supper, in spite of the impossibility of a crucifixion on the day of the feast itself'. Thus the Johannine dating of the Crucifixion is seen to be in keeping with the more reliable of the two Marcan sources.

The modern reader is apt to be astonished at the discrepancy which Mark has allowed to remain in his account of these critical events; but as Knox points out, 'in fact it is characteristic of all but a few of the ancient historians to fail to reconcile their chronology; they are concerned with personalities, and often with propagandist distortions, and indifferent to such details as actual dating' (op. cit., p. 119).

232. *The Anointing at Bethany*

MATTHEW xxvi. 6-13 MARK xiv. 3-9

Luke has incorporated a story of the anointing of Jesus by a woman in the house of a man named Simon into an earlier narrative (vii. 36-50), and evidently regarded it as a doublet of this Marcan story, though it may be quite independent in origin and owe its resemblances to the influence of the Marcan story on Luke (so McNeile, *St. Matthew*, in an Additional Note on the pericope, p. 376). In any case, as we have mentioned above, it is a self-contained anecdote which breaks the unified story of the conspiracy and the suborning of Judas, and must therefore be regarded as an interpolation, perhaps introduced by Mark himself. Nothing is said of the woman's character or purpose. The action itself suggests the anointing of a King, and it is possible that the woman intended her deed as an act of prophetic symbolism, like the anointing of Jehu by the servant of Elisha (2 Kings ix. 1-13). But this King will ascend his throne not by drenching the land with the blood of his enemies, but by offering his own life in sacrifice for others. To anoint him for his kingship is to anoint him for his burial. As Taylor remarks: 'Anointing for burial is not the woman's purpose, but the interpretation Jesus puts upon her action' (*St. Mark*, ad loc.). The final verse, which presupposes the Gentile mission, is clearly secondary (see McNeile's note, ad loc.).

The tendencies of the tradition to develop definition are reflected in the three forms of this story that have come down to us (disregarding the Lucan parallel, which is differently orientated). In Mark the complaint of waste is made by 'some';

in Matthew, by 'the disciples'; in John (xii. 4-6), by Judas Iscariot, who is also said to be a thief, who carried the purse for the group and stole from it. In John, too, we have the further elaboration that the woman who anointed him was Mary; her sister Martha waited at table; and their brother Lazarus was one of the guests; but the host, 'Simon the leper', has disappeared, and the appended saying of Mark xiv. 9 has been dropped. Further, John follows Luke in picturing the woman as anointing the *feet* of Jesus with the ointment, and wiping them with her hair; his version looks like a conflation of the Marcan story with the Lucan. We may note also that John has detached the story of the anointing from the Passion Narrative, setting it 'six days before the Passover', and a day before the entry into Jerusalem.

234. *Preparation for the Passover*

MATTHEW xxvi. 17-19 MARK xiv. 12-16 LUKE xxii. 7-13

The time-note is inexact, in that the day on which they sacrificed the Paschal lamb was not the first day of the Feast of Unleavened Bread, but the day preceding. Matthew has omitted the Marcan phrase 'when they sacrificed the Paschal lamb', probably because he found the juxtaposition of the two phrases intolerable; but he still retains the notion that a Passover supper was being prepared. This involves a conflict in chronology with that which is presupposed in Mark xiv. 2 (Matt. xxvi. 5), and reflects the transition to a different source at this point; it will be noted that in place of 'the Twelve' of the preceding passage, we now have 'the Disciples'. This is one of the clues that have led W. L. Knox (after E. Meyer) to distinguish the 'Disciples-source' from the 'Twelve-source'. But the story itself is legendary. It has many points of resemblance to the story of the preparation for the entry into Jerusalem (Mark xi. 1-6 and parallels; § 196), even to numerous coincidences of vocabulary; and it recalls the instructions given by Samuel to Saul after his anointing (1 Sam. x. 3f.). There is no more reason to think of some prearrangement in the one place than in the other; Jesus has no more arranged in advance to have a man stationed with a water-jar on his head to guide the two disciples than Samuel had arranged to have three men meet Saul with kids, bread, and wine, at the oak of Tabor. In both cases it is a tale of the miraculous gift of second sight exercised by the man of God. Luke has incorporated the Marcan narrative with little change, apart from some stylistic improvement and a measure of abbreviation; the 'two disciples' receive the names of Peter and John, in keeping with the tendency to greater definition in the later form of the tradition. Matthew, however, has not only abbreviated very greatly, but has removed the whole adventure of the man with the pitcher of water; the two disciples are sent directly to the householder, and the story is interpreted as the carrying out of a prearrangement.

Apart from this one section, nothing in Mark or Matthew would lead us to think that the Last Supper was a Passover meal; and in the Fourth Gospel it is explicitly laid on the evening before the Passover. Luke alone among the Evangelists has consistently eliminated all that would be inconsistent with the Passover rite.

The Last Supper
§§ 235-237

MATTHEW xxvi. 20-25 MARK xiv. 17-25 LUKE xxii. 14-38

The much greater length of the passage in Luke is due to the fact that none of § 237 is used by Mark or Matthew at this point; part of it is peculiar to Luke, and part has been used by the other Evangelists in another context.

The narratives of the Last Supper and of the Institution of the Eucharist give rise to an endless number of literary, historical and liturgical problems, and it would be far beyond the scope of this book to offer anything like a general analysis and discussion. We must confine our attention to the comparison of the three versions before us, together with a brief examination of the relationship of the Synoptic narratives with the version given to us by St. Paul in a letter written some fifteen years before Mark.

235. *The Traitor*

MATTHEW xxvi. 20-25 MARK xiv. 17-21 LUKE xxii. 14 (21-23)

If it be granted that the account of the preparation for the Passover given in § 234 is drawn from a different (and inferior) source, it will follow that Mark's primary source must have contained some indication of the preparations for the Supper, to pave the way for that which follows. It will be noted that at this point we again encounter 'the Twelve', not 'the Disciples' (as in *v.* 12); Luke substitutes 'the apostles', perhaps because he is thinking of them in their destined role as representing in their own persons the Church that is to be. The opening verse was probably followed in the primary source by the narrative of the Institution; the repetition of the participial phrase 'while they were eating' (Mark xiv. 18, 22) is in any case an indication that two separate units have been combined. The prophecy of the betrayal would, however, follow appropriately enough upon the story of the bribing of Judas, and it may well be (as Knox takes it) that this was the continuation in the Twelve-source, and that the narrative of the Institution is drawn from elsewhere. In Luke, it will be noticed, an independent narrative of the Institution follows directly upon *v.* 14, and the prediction of the betrayal is postponed until afterwards (*vv.* 21f.). Matthew, on the other hand, follows Mark very closely. He omits the phrase 'he who eats with me', perhaps failing to recognize that it is a quotation from Psalm xli. 10; and he adds *v.* 25; this is a movement towards a more extensive legendary development, which is seen full-blown in the Fourth Gospel (John xiii. 23-30). But the historical character of the entire scene is open to question.

236. *The Institution of the Lord's Supper*

MATTHEW xxvi. 26-29 MARK xiv. 22-25 LUKE xxii. 15-20

Although some account of this solemn action of Jesus at the Last Supper must have been included in the Passion Narrative from the beginning, it is no longer possible to determine exactly what was done and said, or what was the intention of Jesus. The texts themselves are far from uniform, and their form has been affected by the current sacramental practice of the Church. In the earliest version that has come down to us, that of St. Paul (1 Cor. xi. 23-25), it is firmly anchored in the Passion Narrative by the opening words: 'The Lord Jesus, in the night in which he was betrayed.' Though he cites it by itself for its bearing upon the matter with which he is dealing, he does not know it as a separate unit of tradition, but as part of a larger whole. The Marcan version stands close to that of St. Paul — the Benediction, the Fraction, the words: 'This is my body'; it adds the phrase: 'He gave to them', and the command: 'Take'; and omits the phrase: 'which is for you' (following, 'My body'), and the charge to repeat the action as a rite: 'Do this in remembrance of me.' In the second part, it follows the Pauline version in linking 'the cup', 'my blood', and 'the covenant', though with a significant difference of phrasing; it omits the Pauline time-note: 'after they had supped' — leaving the entire action under the phrase 'while they were eating'; it adds the phrase 'which is shed for many' and again it omits the rubric: 'This do ... in remembrance of me.' The changes in the phrasing of the words that accompany the giving of the cup are significant in that they shift the centre of emphasis from 'the covenant' to 'my blood'. Dom Gregory Dix was undoubtedly right in seeing in this the beginnings of a Hellenizing modification (*Jew and Greek*, p. 108), which led to the surprising ultimate result that the ideas of sacrifice virtually displaced all covenant-ideas from the Canon of the Mass, in East and West alike. The later history points to the priority of the Pauline form. The eschatological saying of *v.* 23 is not represented in the words of the Pauline narrative, but is reflected in the Apostle's own comment: 'As often as you eat this bread and drink the cup, you proclaim the death of the Lord, until he comes' (1 Cor. xi. 26).

The Matthaean version follows the Marcan closely. The principal changes are these: the addition of the command, 'Eat' (*v.* 26); the transference into a command: 'Drink of it, all of you' (*v.* 27), of Mark's statement: 'They all drank of it' (not represented in the Pauline narrative, but indicated as the practice in his churches — 1 Cor. x. 3, 16ff.); and the addition of the phrase 'for the remission of sins' (*v.* 28), which may be regarded as theological exegesis of the words: 'for many'.

The Lucan narrative, however, is radically different from the other three. Verses 19 and 20, indeed, follow very closely the Pauline form, with the addition of the Marcan phrase, 'and gave to them', in *v.* 19. But it will be observed that *vv.* 19b and 20 are bracketed in our editions, as an indication that they are regarded as additions to the original text. Verses 15 to 18, on the other hand, have all the appearance of an independent unit of tradition, self-contained and internally consistent. Here we have two sayings, constructed in parallelism. In the first, Jesus speaks of eating the Paschal lamb with his disciples, as he had earnestly desired to do, and tells them that he will never eat of it again 'until it be fulfilled in the kingdom of God'. In the second, he gives thanks over the cup, bids them take it and divide it among themselves, and tells them that he will never again drink of the fruit of the vine 'until the kingdom of God come'. The thought here is wholly eschatological, and in so far as the action represents a sacrament at all, it is a sacrament of communion with a strong eschatological reference — it is simply the Passover interpreted as a symbol of the fellowship of the people of God in the kingdom whose coming is anticipated. There is no mention of the bread, and the words of *v.* 19a stand outside the completed pattern; there is no thought of any representation of the body and blood of Christ, no thought of covenant, no thought of sacrifice, apart from the traditional sacrifice of the Passover lamb itself.

The unity of this passage is obviously disturbed by the addition of *v.* 19a; but we must reckon with the fact that there is not a particle of textual evidence to suggest that it was ever lacking in this Gospel. Verses 19b and 20 are attested almost equally strongly. The bracketed words are found in every one of our Greek manuscripts except the bilingual Codex Bezae (D), in which the Greek text is often subordinated to the Latin; they are omitted in a number of Old Latin witnesses, but are included in all the other ancient versions. Nevertheless, they are rejected by almost all modern editors for two reasons: first, that their inclusion leaves us with a second giving of the cup, which has already been described in *v.* 17; and secondly, that the wording is all but identical with that of the Pauline narrative (1 Cor. xi. 24b, 25), up to the second rubric ('This do, as often as you drink it, in remembrance of me'), which is not included. It is hard to suppose that the tradition was ever transmitted in a form which mentioned the giving of the cup twice.

The evidence seems to suggest, then, that Luke has added the Pauline-Marcan formula about the bread (*v.* 19a) to his own twofold eschatologically orientated form, which mentioned the lamb and the cup. But given the extraordinary weight of textual evidence for the longer form, it must be regarded as distinctly possible that Luke included the whole of the Pauline formula in his conflation, in spite of the awkwardness caused by the second giving of the cup. It is difficult to account for the introduction of the addition into the text of Luke so early and so decisively as to affect every Greek manuscript but one. Compare the remark of W. L. Knox that 'the preference for the shorter text of the Lucan narrative of the institution may not be so well assured as is generally held', with its footnote (*Sources* I, pp. 120-1).

For extended discussions of the passage, see especially W. Manson, *Jesus the Messiah* (London, 1943), ch. vii, 'The Passion and Death of the Messiah', pp. 134-46; J. Jeremias, *The Eucharistic Words of Jesus*, trans. A. Ehrhardt (Oxford: Blackwell, 1955), with comprehensive bibliography; and V. Taylor, *Jesus and his Sacrifice* (London: Macmillan & Co., 1939), pp. 114-42; 175-86; 201-17.

237. *Last Words*

(*a*) The Betrayal Prophesied; (*b*) Greatness in the Kingdom of God; (*c*) Peter's Denial Prophesied; (*d*) The Two Swords

LUKE xxii. 21-38

Luke has transferred the prophecy of the betrayal from its Marcan placing, before the Institution (§ 235), and has recast it in his own words. This is followed by a variant version of the supplement to the Marcan story of the request of the sons of Zebedee (Mark x. 41-45; § 192). James and John are not mentioned, and the reference to a dispute among the disciples (almost grotesque in its incongruity with this context) serves only as an introduction to the sayings of Jesus. The sayings themselves are a compilation of three originally independent units. Verses 25 and 26 are a variant version of Mark x. 42b-44, recast by Luke (rather than drawn from a different source). The term 'kings' (in place of the Marcan 'those who are regarded as rulers') anticipates the 'thrones' of *v.* 30; in this form, the saying implies a conception of the apostles as destined to occupy a position in the Church which will be analogous to that of kings — that is to say, an hierarchical organization of the Church is presupposed; but the whole spirit of the rule which is to be exercised is utterly different from that which prevails in pagan societies. The apostles are not to 'lord it over their charges' (1 Pet. v. 2), but to seek to serve them. The term *euergetai* ('benefactors') introduces a title which was assumed by several Hellenistic monarchs, beginning with Ptolemy III. Probably Luke felt it necessary to avoid the implication of the Marcan saying, that the apostles were not to 'exercise authority' at all ('their great men exercise authority over them, but it is not so among you' — Mark x. 42b, 43a). Verse 27 can hardly be regarded as a modified form of Mark x. 45; rather, Luke has substituted here a quite different saying from a different source. In this form, indeed, the saying is hardly intelligible except as a comment upon an action like that of the washing of the disciples' feet (John xiii). At the Supper as described in Luke (as in all the Synoptics), Jesus does nothing which belongs particularly to the task of a servant; he sits at table like the others, and indeed presides. It is much easier to understand this Lucan saying as the vestige of a story akin to the Johannine narrative than to suppose that John has manufactured his story out of this saying. Verses 28 to 30 form the third unit of the group. Its closing words ('you shall sit on thrones, judging the twelve tribes of Israel' — 30b) are obviously a variant version of the saying of Matthew xix. 28; Luke omits the 'twelve' before 'thrones', because he remembers the presence of Judas. The passage offers all manner of difficulties. Verse 28 puts forward the steadfast loyalty of the Twelve as the ground of their promised exaltation. But what is meant by 'the trials' (or 'temptations' — *peirasmoi*) of Jesus? If the suggestion is that the whole ministry of Jesus has been a succession of 'trials', it must be said that such an idea is not found elsewhere in the Gospels. And in the supreme 'trial' which is about to come, the disciples will not in fact abide steadfast — Judas has already arranged to betray Jesus; at his arrest, they will all forsake him and flee; and Peter will deny that he ever knew him. The whole sentiment suggests rather the later veneration for the apostles than the more realistic representation of their actual character and conduct that is given generally in the Gospel tradition. Verse 29 may reflect the manifold senses of the verb 'appoint' or 'assign' (*diatithēmi*). It is cognate with the noun *diathēkē* — 'covenant', which Luke has not used in his account of the Institution (unless we credit him with the longer text), and may be an echo of the Marcan-Pauline phrasing there. But the proper meaning of *diathēkē* is not 'covenant', but 'testament', and the verb may here have an overtone of the thought that the share in the kingdom is Christ's testamentary disposition, as if to say 'I bequeath' (cf. the play on the double sense of *diathēkē* in Gal. iii. 15f. and Heb. ix. 16f.). The figure of the kingdom as a banquet is well established in Jewish usage, and accounts readily enough for the eating and drinking of *v.* 30; but we are taken aback by the expressions 'My table', and 'My kingdom', for our Lord regularly speaks of the kingdom as 'the kingdom of God'. The thought of the kingdom as Christ's (or as Christ's and God's together) belongs to the developments of a later generation (Eph. vi. 5; Rev. xi. 15; etc.). Accordingly, these verses can hardly be regarded as a fragment of authentic tradition of the sayings of Jesus; they are a theological construction of a subsequent age.

The prophecy of Peter's denial, which Mark places on the way to the Mount of Olives, is here brought forward to form part of the farewell discourse at the Supper. It appears to be an independently transmitted version. Unlike the Marcan narrative, it incorporates the thought that Peter's faith will survive the ordeal, and that in fulfilment of Christ's prayer, he will return to his allegiance and reconstitute the apostolic fellowship. It is possible, however, that we have here again an instance of conflation — that Luke has taken *vv.* 33 and 34 from Mark xiv. 29-31 (entirely recasting them); and that *vv.* 31 and 32 should be considered by themselves, without allowing their meaning to be affected by the prophecy of the denial. In that case we should interpret them as signifying that all the disciples were assailed by Satan, to tempt them to renounce their Lord; and that Peter alone held firm, that his faith did not fail, and that he converted and strengthened his brethren. We shall note that the participle *epistrepsas* is active, and apart from the context of the denial would not be taken to mean 'when you are converted', but as sharing the imperative force of the governing verb — 'convert and strengthen'. It would not be surprising if the story of Peter's temporary lapse had been eliminated from one line of the tradition. The fact that the name 'Simon' of *v.* 31 is changed for 'Peter' in *v.* 34 indicates the use of two sources. Luke's rewriting has probably been affected in its wording by the LXX of 2 Sam. xv. 20-21 (see Creed's note).

Part (*d*) corresponds to the Lucan Mission Charge to the Seventy (x. 4); there is no mention of purse (*ballantion*) or sandals in the Charge to the Twelve. Jesus warns his disciples that they can no longer count on the goodwill of the villagers; they must be prepared for hostility and even violence. But is it conceivable that Jesus now advises his followers to meet force with force? T. W. Manson explains the words of *v.* 36 as 'grim irony ... the utterance of a broken heart' (*Sayings*, p. 341); but the irony is lost on his disciples, who think that he means to fight his way out, and they produce two swords to show that they are ready to fight beside him. The reply of Jesus: 'It is enough', can certainly not be taken as meaning that two swords will suffice; neither can we be satisfied with Manson's suggestion that it represents an abrupt 'No more of this!' The passage is in fact the despair of commentators. This of itself would not be sufficient grounds for denying its authenticity; but its ostensible meaning — that Jesus now advises a resort to violence — would involve the conclusion that he is renouncing all that he has ever taught about trust in God and nonresistance to evil. On the whole, there is much to be said for the suggestion that some stray Zealot phrases have somehow intruded their way into the Gospel record.

The citation of *v.* 37: 'He was numbered with lawless men' (Isa. liii. 12) is 'the only clear reference in the Gospels to Isa. liii' (Creed, ad loc.). In the face of this observation it is astonishing that so many able and learned commentators persist in the view that Jesus looked upon himself as the Suffering Servant of Deutero-Isaiah, and that this is the key to his whole conception of his mission on earth, in combination with the notion of the Danielic Son of Man. If I have not dealt with this hypothesis, it is because I have not found anything in the records that we have been examining to call for raising it. See the dissertation of Miss Morna Hooker, *Jesus and the Servant* (London, 1959), chap. iv, 'The Servant in the Synoptic Gospels', pp. 62-102.

238. *The Way to Gethsemane: Peter's Denial Prophesied*

MATTHEW xxvi. 30-35 MARK xiv. 26-31 LUKE xxii. 39

As Luke has introduced the prophecy of Peter's denial into his catena of sayings at the Supper, he has nothing to report here except the customary evening return to the Mount of Olives. Matthew follows Mark with no more than verbal changes, except that he omits the peculiar Marcan detail of the cock crowing twice — perhaps because it does not fit the pattern of three denials. The citation (Zech. xiii. 7) does not conform to either the Greek or the Hebrew text, which both read the imperative, 'Smite'. The promise of Mark xiv. 28, 'After I have been raised, I will go before you into Galilee' undoubtedly prepares the way for an account of appearances of the risen Christ in Galilee, which Mark has not included in his Gospel; the angel in the tomb will repeat the promise to the women (xvi. 7), but Mark evidently felt that the story of the Resurrection lay outside the scope of his work (there is no real justification for supposing a 'lost ending'). But the words appear to be a secondary element in the pericope. They pass unnoticed by the disciples, who are concerned only to repudiate the thought that they will fall away. The centre of interest is in Peter and his destiny; his experience was a continual reminder to the Church in the days of the persecutions to resist both undue self-confidence and undue pessimism over the lapsed. If the Prince of the Apostles could deny his Lord, every man must fear for his own ability to stand fast; and if one who had denied his Lord could yet become the Prince of the Apostles, there was no need to despair of the restoration of any who renounced their faith under trial, and no justification for unforgiving severity towards the lapsed.

239. *Christ in Gethsemane*

MATTHEW xxvi. 36-46 MARK xiv. 32-42 LUKE xxii. 40-46

The Marcan story is clearly enough the source of the Matthaean and Lucan versions. Matthew's changes are hardly noticeable except for *v.* 40, where he offers a slightly different version of the prayer of Jesus, in place of Mark's phrase, 'saying the same sentence'; and *v.* 44, which supplies the lack in Mark of any mention of his leaving them for the third time. Luke has greatly abbreviated the story, omitting the detail of Jesus' taking Peter, James and John apart from the rest (Mark xiv. 32-34), and reducing the threefold prayer and return of Jesus to a single instance; he also omits the closing sentences of the Marcan story, with their mention of the approach of the traitor. The one addition, *vv.* 43 and 44, is not found in a number of our most important witnesses, and may be an early interpolation in the text of Luke; but its authenticity is defended by many capable critics, and its omission may have been occasioned by the feeling that the agony portrayed in them went beyond what could be admitted of Jesus in the way of human weakness.

There seems to be no good reason to doubt that the substance of the story rests upon apostolic recollections of the night of the Arrest; but it is hardly possible to doubt that most of the details have been supplied by the imagination of Christian narrators. Since Jesus has moved away from his followers, and they have fallen asleep, there was no one to hear what Jesus said in his prayers, and the words, magnificent as they are, can only have been framed by others. The threefold going and return, which Luke has not reproduced, may be simply an instance of formal triplication; the second and third instances do not add anything substantial. The words of the closing verses (Mark xiv. 41-42) offer several difficulties. How can Jesus bid them in one moment to sleep and take their rest, and in the next urge them to rise and go? This incongruity may be removed by taking the first words as a reproachful question: 'Are you sleeping, now at the moment of danger?' But the greater difficulty of the words, 'Arise, let us go away; see, my betrayer is near', still faces us. The most natural sense of these words is that Jesus bids his followers flee with him to another place, where the traitor will not be able to find them; but such a thought is certainly not in the mind of any of the Evangelists and is quite out of keeping with the whole spirit of the narrative. The verb *apechei* ('it is enough'—Mark xiv. 41, AV, RSV) has never been satisfactorily explained; we must postulate an error in translation from the Aramaic or else a corruption in the Greek text.

It is held by some scholars that Luke's version is not to be understood as a rewriting of Mark, but as drawn from a different source; but apart from the doubtful addition of *vv.* 43-44, there is nothing that is not most naturally explained as a Lucan abbreviation of Mark, with the usual modifications of phrasing here and there.

240. *Christ taken Captive*

MATTHEW xxvi. 47-56 MARK xiv. 43-52 LUKE xxii. 47-53

The Marcan account of the Arrest has been followed closely by Matthew and much more freely by Luke. Both of them have omitted the little incident of the young man who was seized at the same time, but slipped out of the linen wrapper (*sindōn*) which he had thrown around him, and escaped naked. It is held by many modern commentators that the author of the Gospel is recounting an experience of his own; ancient writers suggested that the young man of the story was John. There is, of course, no means of identifying him; and there is perhaps more to be said for the suggestion of John Knox, that we have here a piece of symbolism, prefiguring the Resurrection. Jesus too is wrapped in a *sindōn* (Mark xv. 46), and he too escapes from his enemies, leaving only the *sindōn* behind. ('A Note on Mark 14: 51-52', in *The Joy of Study: Papers ... to honor F. C. Grant*, pp. 27-30). Matthew adds a group of sayings of Jesus (*vv.* 52-54); *v.* 52a can never have stood apart from its present context, but 52b may be an independent logion, and 52a may have been framed by the Evangelist himself (or his source) to link the more general saying with the incident of the slave's ear. Verse 53 is almost certainly a later construction, expressing the Church's conviction that Jesus went willingly to his cross, not under the compulsion of superior forces; in place of twelve disciples, he could have summoned to his aid twelve legions of angels. Verse 54 then gives the explanation; the fulfilment of the scriptures, here as throughout the Passion Narrative, is viewed as necessary ('It *must* so come to pass'), because the scriptures reveal the predetermined 'counsel and foreknowledge of God' (Acts ii. 23). Matthew has also added the reproach to Judas (*v.* 50a); otherwise, his changes are merely verbal and stylistic. Luke has again greatly abbreviated the Marcan story, omitting the graphic description of the mob that comes with Judas. Some of his modifications are legendary, and may be derived from another source which he has conflated with Mark. Thus he seems to suggest that Judas attempted to kiss Jesus, but was stopped by a rebuke (*v.* 48); before the sudden blow of the Marcan story, he tells us that the companions of Jesus ask him if they are to make armed resistance (*v.* 49); the slave's ear is said to be the 'right' ear; and Jesus heals the mutilation by a touch (*v.* 51). His changes in *vv.* 52-53, however, appear to be his own modifications of Mark. He cannot suppose that the Arrest was carried out by a mob, as the Marcan version indicates; and he sees that the words of Jesus must be addressed to responsible persons of some kind and therefore speaks of the presence of 'chief priests and commanders of the Temple and elders'. It is most unlikely that the Arrest would be effected by a gang of hired thugs, guided by Judas, though this is the impression left by the Marcan story; but it is equally unlikely that chief priests and elders would come out in person. Almost certainly the task would be the work of the Temple police (cf. John xviii. 3 – 'a band of soldiers and some officers'). But the Christians who transmitted the tradition were not interested in such particulars. For them the spotlight was on Jesus, and the other figures were vague and shadowy. Note that Luke omits the flight of the disciples, just as he has omitted the prediction which corresponds to it (Mark xiv. 27).

The Marcan story is itself a compilation. Verse 44, with its surprising change from 'Judas, one of the Twelve' to 'the Betrayer' is a kind of footnote; W. L. Knox takes it to be an insertion from the 'Disciples-source' into a passage from the 'Twelve-source' (*Sources* I, pp. 126, 129-30). The incident of the slave's ear (*v.* 47) is quite loosely connected with the preceding verses; the sayings of *vv.* 48-49 are a further supplement; and *vv.* 51-52 are an appended fragment. With the removal of these materials, we are left with a unified, straightforward account of the Arrest, consisting of *vv.* 43, 45-46, and 50. It is doubtful, however, if the construction can be attributed to the conflation of *written* sources; more probably the older Passion Narrative alone was before Mark in writing, and gave him the basic story, and he himself has added the other elements from floating bits of oral tradition. It will be noted that the saying of *v.* 49: 'I was with you daily in the temple, teaching' gives an incidental Marcan confirmation to the Lucan picture of a ministry in Jerusalem of a considerable period — far more than the three days of Mark's formal arrangement.

241. *Christ before the Sanhedrin. Peter's Denial*

MATTHEW xxvi. 57-75 MARK xiv. 53-72 LUKE xxii. 54-71

In this section, Matthew again follows Mark with some abbreviation, but scarcely any changes that are worth noticing. In Luke, on the other hand, we have major rearrangements of the materials and differences of substance which raise the problem of sources in a peculiar way. The Marcan narrative consists of four parts, namely, (i) the setting — the twofold scene of Christ before the Sanhedrin and Peter in the courtyard outside (*vv.* 53-54); (ii) the night session of the Sanhedrin (*vv.* 55-64), recounting (*a*) failure to find grounds of action against Jesus in the conflicting testimony of witnesses, who are seen to be lying (*vv.* 55-61a), (*b*) the direct question put by the High Priest, and the answer of Jesus (*vv.* 61b-62), and (*c*) the judgment delivered by the Sanhedrin (*vv.* 63-64); (iii) the maltreatment of Jesus by the attendants (*v.* 65); and (iv) the story of Peter's denial (*vv.* 66-72). Luke modifies the introduction — Jesus is brought to the High Priest's house, but there is no gathering of the Sanhedrin, nor does the High Priest himself appear. The story of Peter's denial follows immediately, in a form very close to that of Mark, with the additional touch (*v.* 61) that a glance from Jesus reminds Peter of the prediction of the denial. The night session of the Sanhedrin, with the testimony of the false witnesses, is omitted entirely; the Sanhedrin assembles in the morning (*v.* 66), and demands that Jesus state frankly whether he claims to be the Messiah. He does not give the unequivocal reply of the Marcan story ('I am'), but answers: 'If I tell you, you will not believe; and if I ask, you will not answer' (*vv.* 67-68), and the prophecy of the coming of the Son of Man is modified into a proclamation of his approaching exaltation: 'The Son of Man shall be seated at the right hand of the power of God' (*v.* 69). The question of the Sanhedrin is repeated, and Jesus again refuses to give a direct answer (*v.* 70); here it is assumed that 'Messiah' and 'the Son of God' are equivalent terms, but this is a Christian, not a Jewish equation. The conclusion of this scene (the judgment delivered) gives the substance of Mark in slightly different words (*v.* 71). Strangely, the last part of the Marcan story, the maltreatment of Jesus by the attendants, is transferred by Luke to a point immediately before the gathering of the Sanhedrin, where it follows upon the story of Peter's Denial and could actually be taken as referring to maltreatment of Peter and not of Jesus. This scene is misplaced, but Luke is certainly right in taking it as an account of rough play to which Jesus was subjected when he was brought to the residence of the

High Priest, not when he was in the presence of the Sanhedrin after the examination.

The Lucan version is a great improvement on the Marcan, in that the night session of the Sanhedrin is highly improbable, and the picture of a more or less formal trial of Jesus, with the hearing of witnesses, is almost equally inconceivable under the circumstances. It will be seen, moreover, that Mark proceeds in the next section to record a meeting of the Sanhedrin in the morning (Mark xv. 1), which makes no reference to the night session of the preceding chapter, but simply puts Jesus in bonds and delivers him to Pilate. It is possible – indeed highly probable – that this is all that was made of the meeting of the Sanhedrin in the earliest tradition, which knew only that the authorities had got Jesus into their power with the assistance of a traitor among his disciples, and had handed him over to the Roman governor as a Messianic pretender who was likely to cause trouble if he were not put out of the way. We should then regard the story of the night session as a Marcan, or possibly a pre-Marcan construction, which did not rest upon any real information, but was designed to show that Jesus had not (as was alleged) said anything to the effect that he would destroy the Temple and in three days raise another (Mark xiv. 58); and that he was not put to death on this charge, but simply and solely because he claimed to be the Messiah. The story thus constructed does not stand up to criticism;[1] this 'trial' contravenes all the rules of Jewish legal procedure, apart from the intrinsic improbability of such a session in the middle of the night. Luke has perceived that the meeting of the Sanhedrin could be held only for the purpose of formulating the charges against Jesus which would be laid before Pilate. There is nothing in his version which requires us to suppose that he has had another and more reliable source available; it is all readily enough understood as a reconstruction of Mark, based upon his sense of the historical possibilities. As Dibelius remarks: 'Everything which serves the purpose of *historization* holds good as the work of the evangelist in the Passion story as elsewhere, i.e. the presentation of a graphic and comprehensible historical connection' (*From Tradition to Gospel*, trans. B. L. Woolf [London: 1934], pp. 199f.).

242. *Christ delivered to Pilate*

MATTHEW xxvii. 1-2 MARK xv. 1 LUKE xxiii. 1

Mark's first clause has been used by Luke, with slight adaptations, to introduce his account of the morning session, to which he has attached such parts of the Marcan story of the 'trial' as he wished to use. As the words stand in Mark, they convey the strange impression of a second trial, for there is nothing to indicate an adjournment, or any reason for a second conference after the decision of xiv. 64 that Jesus is liable to the death penalty. Matthew has borrowed two phrases (1b) from his own introduction to the trial-scene above (xxvi. 59), seeking to re-emphasize the purpose of the Sanhedrin to put Jesus to death.

[1] For the fullest critical discussion, see Paul Winter's book *On the Trial of Jesus* (Berlin: De Gruyter, 1961)

243. *The Death of Judas*

MATTHEW xxvii. 3-10

Another legend of the death of Judas is given in Acts i. 18-19. The only thing common to the two is the mention of the 'field of blood' (this strange name for the cemetery in which foreigners were buried is perhaps due to a popular corruption of its name in Aramaic). On the elements that have contributed to the formation of the Matthaean passage, see McNeile's Additional Note (*St. Matthew*, pp. 408f.). The citation which the Evangelist ascribes to Jeremiah is in fact taken from Zechariah xi. 12-13; the story of Jeremiah's visit to the potter's house (Jer. xviii. 2) may have led to the error; the words 'as the Lord appointed for me' do not occur in the Zechariah passage.

244. *The Trial before Pilate*

MATTHEW xxvii. 11-14 MARK xv. 2-5 LUKE xxiii. 2-5

Both Matthew and Luke have felt the awkwardness of Pilate's question introduced in Mark without any kind of preparation, and each has provided a brief introduction. Luke has transposed the accusations of the Sanhedrin to precede the procurator's question instead of following it as in Mark and Matthew, and has made them into specific charges of incitement to refuse payment of taxes and of claiming to be Messiah, a king. There is some literary relationship between Mark xv. 4-5 (= Matt. xxvii. 13-14) and the similar passage in the Marcan story of the appearance of Jesus before the High Priest (xiv. 60-61b = Matt. xxvi. 62, 63a), which is probably a doublet of this passage. It is possible, however, that the whole picture of Jesus maintaining silence before his accusers is based upon the imagery of Isaiah liii. 7.

The Lucan addition (*vv.* 4-5) is probably a construction of this Evangelist. He has built up Marcan suggestions that Pilate suspected that the charges against Jesus were not brought in good faith (Mark xv. 10, 14) into the direct assertion, repeated three times, that the procurator found him not guilty and pronounced this verdict openly (see also *vv.* 14f., 22). Luke thus tells his readers that Jesus was formally acquitted of any offence against the Roman law, and that his execution was brought about against the declared judgment of the procurator, by the demands of the mob, inflamed by the Jewish priests. It is really impossible to see in this anything but Luke's apologetic for Christianity. It was common knowledge that Jesus had been crucified, and commonly supposed that he had been executed as a dangerous agitator; and Roman governors who knew nothing of Christianity would assume that all who professed and called themselves Christians were adherents of a seditious movement. Luke is concerned to show that this is all a misapprehension. All through Acts, he represents the Roman authorities as exercising their powers for the protection of Paul and his associates against mob violence, and here he depicts Pilate as convinced of the innocence of Jesus and making repeated efforts to release him, which were rendered vain only by the savage insistence of the Jews. The upshot was that he released a known malefactor and insurrectionist, and sent to the cross a man whom he knew to be innocent.

The further development of the charges in *v.* 5 is introduced primarily to pave the way for the scene which follows, by the mention of Galilee.

245. *Christ before Herod*

LUKE xxiii. 6-16

This story may have been provided by one of Luke's sources, but it is more probable that he has constructed it himself out of the implications which seemed to him to be manifest in the second Psalm. In Acts iv. 25-27, he gives a kind of midrash on this Psalm, embodied in a Christian prayer, which specifically applies the words about 'the kings of the earth' and 'the rulers' to Herod and Pontius Pilate 'in this city'. If he found this prayer in his sources, he may very well have supplied the lack of any mention of Herod in the Passion Narrative by composing this story. It must in any case be regarded as fictitious. Apart from the intrinsic improbability that the Roman procurator, within the area of his own jurisdiction, would send a prisoner to the non-Roman puppet ruler of a neighbouring territory, we have to note the absolute impossibility of fitting this trip to Herod into the morning of the Crucifixion. According to the old tradition preserved by Mark (xv. 25), it was 'the third hour' — that is, nine o'clock in the morning — when the Crucifixion began. Jesus has already appeared before the Sanhedrin, has been transferred to the tribunal of Pilate, has been tried and condemned, scourged and mocked, and has made the journey afoot outside the city to Golgotha. The few hours since dawn barely allow time for all this, and certainly leave no time for the removal of Jesus to Herod's residence, the further accusations, the mocking by Herod and his soldiers, and the return to Pilate.

246. *The Sentence of Death*

MATTHEW xxvii. 15-26 MARK xv. 6-15 LUKE xxiii. 17-25

Matthew here introduces two legendary additions to the Marcan story, namely, the Dream of Pilate's Wife (*v.* 19) and Pilate's Washing of his Hands (*vv.* 24-25). Apart from this he follows Mark very closely, even to the Latinism *phragellōsas* (from *flagellum*, 'whip') of the closing verse. He makes some slight abbreviations (*vv.* 16, 26) and rewrites the demand for Barabbas (*vv.* 20-21). Luke has made rather drastic changes, but there is nothing to suggest the use of another source. He omits the whole of Mark's introduction to the demand for Barabbas (Mark xv. 6-10), and says nothing of the practice of an act of amnesty at the festival. Pilate has proposed to have Jesus flogged (as a sop to the demand for action against him?), and to release him, not by way of an act of amnesty, but because he has found him not guilty (*v.* 16, above); and the cry for the release of Barabbas appears to rise spontaneously from the crowd (*v.* 18). It is possible, however, that *v.* 17, which has quite strong manuscript testimony to support it, should be given a place in the text; it is more in accord with Luke's practice to supply a needed link than to omit completely one which was provided in his source. The effect of his rewriting is to emphasize much more strongly the Jewish responsibility for the Crucifixion, with renewed insistence that the Roman procurator had 'found nothing worthy of death in him' (*v.* 22), and had sentenced to death one whom he knew to be innocent, in response to the clamour of the mob. Matthew accomplishes the same end even more conclusively by representing the whole people as accepting the responsibility for themselves and for their children (*v.* 25), when Pilate seeks to absolve himself. Even in the simpler Marcan story there are indications of a desire to dull the edge of the conflict with Rome by making the Jews bear the chief guilt for the death of Christ; and this tendency has evidently increased in the later development of the tradition. We can scarcely doubt that all the Evangelists have treated Pilate far too considerately, in the interests of Christian apologetic. The Creed has kept more faithfully to the central fact, that Jesus 'suffered under Pontius Pilate'. Whatever the pressure from the Jewish side, Jesus was sentenced in a Roman court and executed by Roman soldiers in the Roman mode – not for blasphemy, but for sedition.

247. *The Mocking by the Soldiers*

MATTHEW xxvii. 27-31 MARK xv. 16-20

As Luke has already described the mocking of Jesus by Herod and his soldiery, including the detail of clothing Jesus with royal robes, he omits this passage entirely. Matthew makes few changes in the Marcan narrative; contrary to his custom, he adds details to the picture – the 'purple' of Mark becomes 'a scarlet chlamys', and the soldiers put a reed, as a mock sceptre, in the right hand of Jesus; and he transfers the kneeling of the soldiers to a more appropriate place.

248. *The Road to Calvary*

MATTHEW xxvii. 32 MARK xv. 21 LUKE xxiii. 26-32

The way in which the name of Simon is introduced, together with the mention of his two sons as if they were well known to the readers, would suggest that Alexander and Rufus are members of the Church (probably Rome) for which Mark is writing; and this little detail was perhaps contributed by them directly to the Evangelist, and not a part of the basic Passion Narrative. Matthew and Luke omit the names of the sons, for there would not be the same personal interest in them in other Churches. Luke alone adds the description of the crowd that follows, and of the weeping women, and gives the mournful warning of Jesus (*vv.* 27-31). The two thieves who are to be crucified along with Jesus are not mentioned in Mark until later (xv. 27); Luke introduces them here (*v.* 32) to give a more coherent development to the story. The saying of *v.* 31 is difficult, and may be a kind of proverb which would not necessarily be applied to the execution of Christ; it does not appear to be integrally connected with the remainder of the oracle. The contrast of green and dry wood does not seem appropriate to a comparison of the Crucifixion with the national disaster of A.D. 70; in itself, it suggests rather a contrast between the brutality with which some minor uprising was suppressed and the unbridled savagery that must be expected when the authorities have to deal with a serious outbreak. Even more, it suggests that if a new regime shows itself merciless when it is barely in the saddle, much worse must be expected once it is firmly established.

249. *The Crucifixion*

MATTHEW xxvii. 33-44 MARK xv. 22-32 LUKE xxiii. 33-43

The Marcan story is followed closely in Matthew, with changes that are chiefly verbal and stylistic, not affecting the substance. Matthew adds a detail concerning the soldiers (*v.* 36), and supplements the taunts of the Marcan story with a verse taken directly from Psalm xxii. 19 — a clear instance of the tendency to fill in the story with the aid of this Psalm. The basic story (Mark xv. 24) has preserved the detail, insignificant in itself, of the division of Christ's garments among the soldiers, because this was regarded as a fulfilment of Psalm xxii. 18; in this case, there is no reason to suppose that the words of the psalm led to the invention of the incident — it is rather that this was one of the incidents of the scene which led Christians to view the whole psalm as a prophecy of the Crucifixion and consequently to quarry additional details out of it. The further development of the incident in the Fourth Gospel (the 'seamless robe' for which they cast lots instead of dividing it) represents an attempt to do justice to every word in the passage (the psalm itself does not envisage two methods of sharing the garments). Neither Matthew nor Luke mentions the third hour (Mark xv. 25) for the beginning of the Crucifixion; perhaps they both felt that this was too early to allow for all that had happened since the Arrest; however, both of them retain the sixth hour (noon) for the onset of the darkness (Mark xv. 33 and parallels). It must be admitted that the time-intervals in Mark (the third, the sixth, the ninth hour) have all the appearance of a formal construction.

The Lucan changes are much more substantial. The transposition of the mention of the two malefactors to the beginning of the scene is merely a stylistic improvement; but following this we have the great saying of *v.* 34. Though this verse is omitted by some of our principal witnesses, it has sufficient early support to justify us in regarding it as an integral part of the text; it may have been omitted in some manuscripts because of a feeling that this prayer for forgiveness was out of place. The wording of the taunts is somewhat changed, and in part omitted (*v.* 35), and to the mockery of the rulers, Luke adds mockery by the soldiery (*vv.* 36-37), and attributes to them the offer of the vinegar (the change from Mark's 'wine mingled with myrrh' to 'vinegar' — cf. Mark xv. 36 — is probably an echo of Psalm lxix. 21). In Mark and Matthew the givers are not specified, but there is no suggestion that it is offered in mockery and we are told that by Jewish custom it was given in mercy, as a mild narcotic (cf. Prov. xxxi. 6; and see Strack and Billerbeck, *Kommentar zum N.T. aus Talmud und Midrasch*, vol. I, pp. 1037f.). But the most striking variation in Luke is the (legendary) development of the narrative in respect of the two thieves. In the old tradition, as given in Mark and retained in Matthew, the two thieves join in the reviling of Jesus; but in Luke one of them turns to Jesus in penitence and is rewarded by the promise: 'Today you will be with me in Paradise' (*vv.* 39-43).

250. *The Death on the Cross*

MATTHEW xxvii. 45-56 MARK xv. 33-41 LUKE xxiii. 44-49

Here again Matthew makes a substantial addition of legendary matter to the Marcan version. The rending of the veil of the Temple is itself mythical (rather than legendary) in character, signifying that through the death of Jesus the way into the Holy of Holies is opened once and for all (cf. Heb. ix. 8ff.; vi. 19f.). The curtain of the sanctuary would of course not be visible from the courts of the Temple itself, let alone from the hill of the Crucifixion; there is no question of the testimony of witnesses in such a matter. The earthquake, the splitting of the rocks, and the walking of the dead of the Matthaean addition (*vv.* 51b-53) are typical of the popular legends that grow around the death of a great man; similar stories were told of stupendous events accompanying the death of Caesar — the veiling of the sun, the statue of Pompey running blood, the dead walking the streets of Rome, etc. — and the passing of the Buddha into Nirvana. The Lucan alterations are of a different character, but equally substantial. Luke explains the darkness at noon by an eclipse of the sun — an impossibility at the time of the full moon of the Passover season; and he transfers the rending of the veil to the sixth hour, when the darkness began, from its Marcan placing at the moment of the death of Jesus. He omits the whole episode of the 'cry of dereliction' with its misunderstanding by the spectators, and the second proffer of 'vinegar' (Mark xv. 34-36). In place of this he gives as the last cry of Jesus a totally different saying from Psalm xxx. 6 (*v.* 46). There is no reason for regarding this as an independently preserved fragment of ancient tradition; it is probable that Luke found intolerable the tradition that the last words of Jesus were a cry of dereliction, and therefore substituted for them a calm profession of faith. He has also changed the words attributed to the centurion (*v.* 47). Finally, he has almost completely rewritten the Marcan conclusion (Mark xv. 40-41), which mentions only the women who had been devoted to Jesus during his ministry and now watch over his last moments. Part of this Luke has already used, in a more elaborate form, in a note attached to an episode of the Galilean Ministry (viii. 2-3; § 84); part of it he retains, giving it a briefer expression (*v.* 49 = *v.* 40, Mark); and part of it (*v.* 48) is material peculiar to this Gospel, telling of the dismay of the watching throngs. Traditions preserved in Syrian documents add to this a saying (with some variation in its form) which voices this dismay: 'Woe to us! What a thing has come to pass! Woe to us for our sins!' This is reminiscent of the story of the dismay of the English soldiery at the death of Joan of Arc.

The so-called 'cry of dereliction' (Mark xv. 34 = Matt. xxvii. 46; Ps. xxii. 1) is not to be understood as a cry of despair. Certainly it had no such sense for Mark or for the circles which transmitted the tradition to him. In its Marcan form, the words are a curious combination of Aramaic and Hebrew; in Matthew, the Hebrew form of the first two words is restored, but the third is altered to Aramaic. Many critics feel certain that the incident is based on the solidest tradition, on the ground that such a saying would never have been attributed to Jesus in the tradition if he had not in fact spoken it. But this conclusion rests upon the erroneous assumption that the Church which transmitted the tradition interpreted the words in isolation, apart from the general purport of the psalm. Whether the report be authentic or not, we must insist that the saying was not taken in the early Church, and ought not to be taken by us, as an indication that Jesus even momentarily thought of himself as forsaken by God. 'In this view one assumes a chronicler who, concerned only with history, faithfully hands on to the next age also what is painful and, to Christendom, intolerable. There never was such a chronicler, for the whole Passion story was written for the edification and not the bewilderment of Christians' (Dibelius, *From Tradition to Gospel*, p. 193; cf. his remarks about the Gethsemane story, which are applicable here also: 'The scene ... does not bear witness to a disillusionment — for then it would not have been accepted into the Gospel at all — but to a certain understanding of a revelation. Like the entire Marcan Passion it is orientated not psychologically but soteriologically'; ibid. p. 211). It is impossible for us to go behind the work of the Evangelist in order to read between the lines a reflection of a mood of despair of which the writer himself was unconscious. But there are good grounds for calling the whole story into question. Once it has been accepted as common Christian understanding that Psalm xxii is a prophetic picture of the Crucifixion, its words can only be taken as words that will be uttered by Christ (and certainly it would never occur to Mark and his readers to suppose that he would stop with the first four words). There is, accordingly, no difficulty at all about understanding how the words would come to be incorporated into the narrative of the Crucifixion. But it is quite impossible to suppose that an Aramaic-speaking group in Jerusalem would ever have taken these familiar words from their own scriptures as an appeal to Elijah. Again, the offer of the vinegar appears to be a doublet (probably from another source) of the offer of the wine mixed with myrrh of Mark xv. 23, which was not offered in mockery but in kindness; here it has been accommodated to the hostile sense of Psalm lxix. 22 — 'They gave me poison for food; and ... vinegar to drink.' The whole section (Mark xv. 34-36) thus appears to be a secondary formation from start to finish — an elaboration of the simple statement of *v.* 37. The 'loud cry' of this verse is certainly not to be interpreted as a gasp of despair; almost certainly, it is intended by Mark as a cry of victory. The suggestion that there is something miraculous about the manner of Christ's passing, whereby the centurion is convinced that 'this man was a son of God' (*v.* 39) is enhanced in Matthew by the significant change of Mark's wording. The participle of Mark's phrase — 'having sent forth a loud cry' — becomes the main verb in Matthew, with a change of object — 'having made a loud cry, Jesus sent forth his spirit' (the noun *pneuma* echoing the Marcan verb *exepneusen*). Jesus lays down his life of his own accord; his executioners do not take it from him (cf. John x. 17f.). According to Mark, this is sign enough for the centurion; Matthew has attributed the recognition of the divinity of

Jesus rather to the effects of the earthquake. For all the Evangelists, the centurion is the first-fruits of the Gentiles who will look upon the Cross of Christ and believe in him as the Son of God. If Luke changes the wording, it is not to diminish the force of the confession of faith, but to conform to his design of showing that the Romans who were concerned with the execution of Jesus were at one in acknowledging his innocence.

251. *The Burial of Christ*

MATTHEW xxvii. 57-61 MARK xv. 42-47 LUKE xxiii. 50-56

Apart from a measure of abbreviation, and the omission of the whole of *v.* 44 (and in Luke, *v.* 45 as well) the changes made by Matthew and Luke are mainly interpretative. Mark's word *euschēmōn* — 'respected' or even 'distinguished' — is interpreted by Matthew as 'wealthy' and by Luke as 'good and righteous'. Matthew interprets Joseph's expectation of the kingdom of God to mean that he was actually a disciple of Jesus; Luke thinks it necessary to remark that he had had no part in the machinations of the Sanhedrin. The rock tomb is said by Matthew to be a new tomb belonging to Joseph himself; and Luke tells us that no one had ever been buried in it; no doubt this seemed the appropriate thing, just as it was felt that for his entry into Jerusalem the Lord must be provided with an ass 'on which no man had ever sat' (Mark xi. 2 = Luke xix. 30). Luke's addition (*vv.* 55-56) is drawn partly from Mark xv. 41 and partly from Mark xvi. 1. According to Mark the spices for embalming were not purchased by the women until the sabbath was over; in Luke's revision, they were made ready immediately after the Crucifixion. In all this there is nothing to suggest that the other two Evangelists have used any source but Mark.

§ 252, 'The Guard at the Tomb' (Matt. xxvii. 62-66), is another of Matthew's legendary supplements to the Passion Narrative; it is continued with two supplements to the story of the Empty Tomb (Matt. xxviii. 2-4, 11-15), and is obviously a bit of apologetic fiction devised to refute the absurd Jewish claim that the disciples had stolen the body of Jesus during the night.

253. *The Resurrection*

MATTHEW xxviii. 1-10 MARK xvi. 1-8 LUKE xxiv. 1-11 [12]

The Marcan narrative ends at this point, with the discovery of the empty tomb, and there is abundant evidence that the supplements found in manuscripts of the fifth century and later are not part of the original text of the Gospel. Scholars still disagree on the question whether this is the way in which Mark brought his work to an end, or whether his original ending was lost. It must be emphasized that there is no basis for postulating a 'lost ending', except in the feeling of some scholars that this is no way to end a gospel; it is far from certain that Mark shared this feeling. If the ending was lost, the loss must have occurred before a copy of the manuscript came into the hands of Matthew or Luke, for they make use of no common source from this point on. This really involves the assumption that the original manuscript was mutilated before it could be copied; that the author was dead and could not restore the lacuna; and that no one else in the Church, until the third century or later, ventured to complete the gap. All this I find totally inconceivable. We must assume that Mark was acquainted with stories of the appearances of Jesus after his resurrection; the words of the angel in this very pericope presuppose some tradition of appearances to Peter and the other disciples in Galilee; but it was no part of Mark's purpose to tell of them in this book. Quite possibly the stories of the appearances were regarded as belonging to the arcana of Christian teaching, not to be set down in writing for general publication. But his motives for stopping at this point must remain a matter for speculation.

The story ends on the strange note that the women, although they have been given a message for the disciples, with special mention of Peter, fled from the tomb terror-stricken, and 'said nothing to anyone, for they were afraid'. There is not the shadow of a suggestion that this silence was broken, and the words may reasonably be taken as an indication that the story of the empty tomb did not form part of the earliest tradition of the Resurrection; they explain why the story was not generally known. There are, in fact, several indications that what we have here is a legend of relatively late growth, which reflects a material notion of resurrection and leads on to still further emphasis on tangible, physical evidences of the presence of the risen Jesus. For St. Paul, the Resurrection of Christ is the first-fruits of the resurrection of all believers (1 Cor. xv. 20-24), and is not conceived in terms of the re-animation of the corpse. Flesh and blood cannot inherit the kingdom of God. 'It is sown in corruption; it is raised in incorruption; it is sown in dishonour; it is raised in glory; it is sown in weakness; it is raised in power; it is sown a natural body; it is raised a spiritual body' (1 Cor. xv. 42-44). In all that the apostle teaches about the Resurrection, there is not a word to suggest that he has ever heard the story of the empty tomb, or that such a story would be relevant to his doctrine. Spiritual things, for him, must be spiritually discerned, and faith is not established by sight.

In fact the story is of no significance as evidence for the Resurrection, apart from the message of the angel. The discovery that a tomb is empty does not of itself point to the conclusion that the body which once lay in it has been re-animated; the natural assumption would be that it had been taken away (cf. John xx. 2 — 'They have taken the Lord out of the tomb, and we do not know where they have laid him'). As there is no reason to suppose that the story ever existed without the angel and his message, our opinion of its historicity will depend entirely upon the historical value that we are prepared to attach to any stories of the intervention of angels in human form and with human speech. If we do not share the early Christian belief in angels who thus take part in incidents of human life, there is no reason for us to attach any historical value whatsoever to the story, even to the minimum element that women came to the tomb and found it empty. We may apply to the whole story the words of Dr. McNeile about the rolling away of the stone. 'Like the appearance of the angel, or angels, and the earthquake, it is in no way necessary for a full belief in the Resurrection, the truth of which does not depend upon the form which the narratives took in the growth of Christian tradition' (*St. Matthew*, p. 430).

Both Matthew and Luke have made changes of substance as well as of form in the Marcan story. Matthew advances the time from 'very early on the first day of the week' to 'late on the sabbath', and reduces the number of the women from three to two, omitting Salome. He adds a long fragment belonging to his legend of the guard at the tomb (*vv.* 2-4), and omits the perplexity of the women over the removal of the stone (Mark xvi. 3-4). In Mark the angel (described only as 'a youth clad in a white robe') is seated within the tomb and is not seen by the women until they have entered; in Matthew he is seated outside, upon the stone, which he himself has rolled away (*v.* 2), and his description is amplified (*v.* 3). His message remains substantially the same, with the exception that no special mention is made of Peter. But the greatest change comes in the sequel. Matthew, like many modern commentators, cannot believe that the women said nothing to anyone; their fear is mingled with joy, and they run to bring the word to the disciples (*v.* 8). Even more, they are met by Jesus himself, and permitted to embrace him; and he repeats the message of the angel, that his disciples must return to Galilee and will see him there (*vv.* 9-10). This is in the most flagrant contradiction, not only with the Marcan story, but with the established tradition that the first appearance of the risen Jesus was granted to Peter. Apart from this surprising revision of Mark's story, Matthew holds to the old tradition that the resurrection-appearances took place not in Jerusalem, but in Galilee (cf. *vv.* 16f.). Clearly, these Matthaean changes do not reflect an independent tradition, but a secondary development of the Marcan legend of the discovery of the empty tomb.

Luke's changes are still more radical. He is convinced that the appearances of the risen Christ took place in Jerusalem, not in Galilee, and therefore he feels free to excise every suggestion that the disciples must return to Galilee and that they will see Jesus there. The single angel of the Marcan story becomes two, and they do not appear until the women have discovered that the body of Jesus is missing (*vv.* 3-4). The words of the message are radically recast, and Galilee is mentioned only in retrospect, as the place in which Jesus had foretold his Resurrection, not as the place in which he will be seen again, alive from the dead (*vv.* 6-7). Luke, like Matthew, will have none of the silence of the women; they fulfil their instructions and report all these things 'to the Eleven and to all the rest' (*v.* 9); Luke probably thinks of the group as consisting of a larger body of Galilean followers of Jesus — the company of about a hundred and twenty, of whom he will speak in the beginning of Acts (i. 15). It is only now that he mentions the names and the number of the women. Mark's three are mentioned in the first place, with the substitution of Joanna for Salome, but they are accompanied by a number of others, described vaguely as 'the others along with them' (*vv.* 9-10). But their testimony does not inspire faith in the disciples, who take it all for a pack of rubbish (*v.* 11). Luke seems thus to indicate that he does not regard the story of the empty tomb as an integral part of the apostolic testimony to the resurrection of Jesus. Verse 12, relegated to the margin in both our texts, is found in all Greek manuscripts except Codex Bezae, and in all ancient versions except the Old Latin. It seems to be required as an anticipation of *v.* 24, and we must hesitate to accept the view that it is an interpolation based upon the Johannine story (John xx. 3-10).

THE POST-RESURRECTION NARRATIVES

A. The Matthaean Post-Resurrection Narrative

Matthew xxviii. 11-20

The story of the Bribing of the Soldiers (*vv.* 11-15) rounds off the legend of the measures taken to guard the tomb (§ 252). There is no reason for doubting the truth of the last statement, that the Jews of Matthew's time attempted to counter the Christian testimony to the resurrection of Jesus by alleging that his body was stolen from the tomb by his disciples. This whole legend must have grown as a naive bit of Christian counter-propaganda.

The closing verses (16-20) constitute the only account in the Synoptic Gospels of an appearance of the risen Jesus in Galilee; it is the complement to the message of the angel to the women at the tomb (*v.* 7). 'The mountain' (*v.* 16) cannot be identified; probably, like the mount of the Sermon and the mount of the Transfiguration, it is a symbol of the place of revelation. The remark that 'some doubted' can hardly be attributed to anything but a solidly based tradition that the appearances of Jesus were not of a kind to *compel* belief in his resurrection even on the part of his closest disciples. Matthew makes no attempt to describe the nature of this appearance. His interest is wholly directed to the content of the message given to his disciples by the Risen Lord. The form of this message reflects the liturgical practice of Matthew's own time. The earliest Christian baptism was 'in the name of Jesus Christ' (Acts ii. 38; cf. 1 Cor. i. 13ff.; Rom. vi. 3; etc.); the use of the trinitarian formula is undoubtedly a later development. It is probable, indeed, that the Fourth Gospel is right in its information that the disciples of Jesus baptized his adherents during his lifetime (John iv. 1-2). In any case, the chief significance of the passage for Matthew is not that the rite of baptism is here instituted, but that it is extended in application to all the nations. During his earthly ministry, Jesus bade his disciples go to 'the lost sheep of the house of Israel' (Matt. x. 5-6); and the great apostle of the Gentiles recognizes that 'Christ was made a minister of the circumcision for the sake of the truth of God, to confirm the promises made to the fathers' (Rom. xv. 8). With the Resurrection, all limitations are removed. 'All authority in heaven and on earth' is given to him; and the mission of his disciples must now become a mission not to Israel alone, but to all the world.

Words of the risen Jesus do not belong to that order of reality which is open to historical investigation, and the question of 'authenticity' does not arise in any intelligible sense. But it may be remarked that Matthew is faithful to historical fact in representing the transformation of the Christian movement into a world faith as consequent upon the death and resurrection of Jesus Christ. The words which he here attributes to Jesus give expression to fundamental convictions by which the Church continues to live: the faith that all power in heaven and on earth is given to the crucified and risen Lord, the knowledge that she bears an apostolic commission to carry his Gospel of salvation to all the nations, and the confidence that he is with her and will continue to be with her to the end of time.

B. The Lucan Post-Resurrection Narrative

1. *The Road to Emmaus*

Luke xxiv. 13-35

The two appearances of the Matthaean narrative (*vv.* 9-10 and 16-20) are told in the concise, unadorned manner characteristic of communal tradition, without names and other details which are not absolutely essential to the central point. Jesus appears, is recognized, and gives his command. This Lucan story belongs to a different category. Here we have names and places and all manner of circumstantial detail; the story is full of movement and colour; it is not a deposit of popular tradition, but 'a highly finished literary composition' with traits 'characteristic of the practised story-teller, who knows just how to "put his story across" ... a carefully composed statement which, in the framework of a narrative of intense dramatic interest, includes most of what needs (from this Evangelist's point of view) to be said about the resurrection of Christ.'[1]

It is, of course, conceivable that some nucleus of early Christian tradition may lie beneath the developed story that Luke has given us; but against this is the fact that the earliest statement of the resurrection-appearances which has come down to us, and which has an almost official air (1 Cor. xv. 5-8), makes no mention of anything like this story and has no place for it. It seems best, accordingly, to treat it in its entirety as the work of an artist in religious symbolism, perhaps of the Evangelist himself. Certainly it is charged with his theology and couched in his characteristic language. There are two main elements of interest. First, there is the doctrine that the Passion of Christ is the central theme of the Old Testament, which is regarded in all its parts as the work of prophets who foretold the events of the Gospel story (*vv.* 25-27); the risen Christ explains how even the books of the Law ('Moses') are filled with 'the things concerning himself'. Secondly, there is the linking of the Resurrection with the Eucharist — 'he was known of them in the breaking of bread' (*vv.* 30-31). In a sense, the presence of Christ with his people in the celebration of the Eucharist is a fresh manifestation to them that he is alive for evermore.

It is only at the end of this narrative, and almost as an afterthought, that we are told of an appearance of the risen Jesus to Simon Peter (*v.* 34), and then nothing is reported beyond the bare fact. We are reminded most forcibly that the post-resurrection narratives of the Gospels are quite independent of the primary tradition of the appearances which is set down for us by St. Paul, and which he claims was common ground: 'Whether it were I or they, so we preached and so you believed' (1 Cor. xv. 11). 'It appears, then, that the narratives in the Gospels were not produced as expansion, by way of commentary or "midrash", of the list of appearances in the primitive tradition; while it is quite certain that the list was not compiled out of the Gospels. We must conclude that the list of successive appearances on the one hand, as we have it in 1 Cor. 15, and as it is implied in Luke 24. 33-34, and on the other hand the different types of

[1] C. H. Dodd, 'The Appearances of the Risen Christ: An Essay in Form-Criticism of the Gospels', in *Studies in the Gospels: Essays in Memory of R. H. Lightfoot*, ed. D. E. Nineham (Oxford: Blackwell, 1955), pp. 13-14.

narrative in the Gospels, are independent of one another, and represent alternative methods of supplementing the simple statements of the *kerygma* in its baldest form, that Christ rose from the dead and that the apostles were witnesses to the fact, since He appeared to them after His Passion' (Dodd, ibid., p. 29).

2. *The Appearance of the Risen Christ in Jerusalem*

LUKE xxiv. 36-49

The early list of appearances given by St. Paul tells us that Christ 'appeared to Cephas, then to the twelve'. The Marcan narrative, as we have seen, presupposes that these appearances took place in Galilee; and in Matthew we have read a story of an appearance to the disciples (the number is not mentioned) in Galilee. Here, in keeping with Luke's consistent excision of every mention of a return to Galilee, the appearance to the apostolic group is transferred to Jerusalem. The group itself is enlarged; it includes, apparently, 'the Eleven and those with them' and the two who have already received the revelation on the road to Emmaus (*v.* 33). But apart from these details, it is clear that the whole story has been given a strong apologetic tone, and that the theological notions of the Emmaus narrative are taken up again and developed. The physical nature of the resurrection-body is strongly stressed, to counter allegations that those who professed to have seen the risen Jesus had seen only a ghost; we are told that this was indeed the first impression of the apostles themselves, but that they were invited to handle the Visitant and to assure themselves that he had flesh and bones; and to cap it all, he even eats a piece of broiled fish before their eyes. It scarcely needs to be said that all this is legendary embroidery of the crudest type.

In the second part of this narrative the risen Christ speaks as Revealer of the purposes of God. As in the Emmaus story, the central emphasis is laid upon the testimony of the Old Testament scriptures in all their parts — the Law of Moses and the prophets and the psalms. For those whose minds are opened to understand, the whole story of salvation is set forth in the ancient writings — that the Messiah must suffer, and on the third day rise again, and that in his name the gospel of repentance for the remission of sins must be preached to all nations, 'beginning from Jerusalem' (*v.* 47b). This phrase indicates that Luke's transference of the appearances to Jerusalem, and the elimination of Galilee from the tradition, is based upon his reading of the Old Testament. Had it not been decreed that 'out of Zion shall go forth the law, and the word of the Lord from Jerusalem' (Isa. ii. 3; Mic. iv. 2)? The closing verse looks forward to the opening of Luke's second volume, and the story of Pentecost (Acts i. 4, 8; ii).

3. *The Ascension*

LUKE xxiv. 50-53

In the book of Acts, Luke will tell us that the risen Jesus continued to show himself to his disciples, and to instruct them in the things of the kingdom of God, over a period of forty days, and that his final departure from earth took place only at that time. The Ascension is here conceived as taking place at the close of the first Easter day. It may be that Luke has made use of two independent versions of the Ascension-story, and has not concerned himself with the contradiction. The story here given is much the more restrained; the departure of Christ is not even described in terms of an 'ascension' – though it will be noted that there is very strong attestation for the additional words, 'and was carried up into heaven'. It is not clear why the scene is transferred to Bethany; perhaps this is a belated echo of Mark. xi. 11.

This is the *analēmpsis* towards which the whole story has been moving ever since Jesus 'set his face steadfastly to go to Jerusalem' (ix. 51; § 137). Here it is the consummation of the earthly ministry of Jesus. In Luke's second volume, it will be told as the introduction to the history of the Church. Here the apostles are reminded that they are 'witnesses of these things' (*v.* 48); in Acts, they enter upon their task of being witnesses for Jesus 'in Jerusalem and in all Judaea and Samaria and unto the end of the earth' (Acts i. 8).

C. The Longer Ending of Mark

Mark xvi. 9-20

These verses are printed in the Received Text, and are therefore found in the Authorized Version and used in part (*vv.* 14-20) as the Gospel for the Ascension Day in the Book of Common Prayer. But there can be no doubt that the passage did not form part of the original text of this Gospel. It is lacking in the great fourth-century manuscripts, and though it is known to Eusebius (early fourth century) and to St. Jerome (late fourth century), both of them tell us that it was missing in nearly all the Greek manuscripts known to them. No serious critic would attempt to defend the passage. It is a scribal construction, probably put together late in the third century, consisting in the main of short digests of resurrection-narratives from the other Gospels, with some new sayings (*vv.* 16-18) of late coinage (V. Taylor, on *vv.* 17-18: 'Here, without doubt, is the atmosphere of A.D. 100-140'). In one manuscript, the great Washington Codex of the Gospels (W), this ending is enlarged by a few sentences which were formerly known only through a partial citation in the writings of St. Jerome; this 'Freer Logion' follows *v.* 14. The Shorter Ending, found in only a half-dozen Greek manuscripts and occasionally in manuscripts of the Egyptian and Ethiopic versions, is an independent attempt to supply a more conventional ending to Mark.

These 'post-resurrection' narratives are all relatively late constructions, which tell us little of the experiences of the days following the Crucifixion. Historically they are of interest only as reflections of Christian ideas of a later age. The evidences of the Resurrection of our Lord are not to be found in these stories; they are given massively in the life of his Church.

'From what has been said, it follows that we are to understand the Easter stories too as evidence of the faith, and not as records and chronicles, and that it is the *message* of Easter that we must seek in the Easter *stories*. That is not to say by any means that the message of Jesus' resurrection is only a product of the believing community. Certainly the form in which it comes down to us is stamped with this faith. But it is just as certain that the appearances of the risen Christ and the word of his witnesses have in the first place given rise to this faith' (G. Bornkamm, *Jesus of Nazareth*, p. 183).

I. Index of Scripture References

OLD TESTAMENT

NEW TESTAMENT

(*omitting cross-references to* MATTHEW, MARK AND LUKE)

II. Index of Other Ancient Writings

III. Index of Greek, Latin, Aramaic and Hebrew Words (*in Transliteration*)

IV. Index of Names, Places and Subjects

DATE DUE